CERTIFICATE ATLAS FOR THE CARIBBEAN 4th edition

CONTENTS

Note: Each section is colour-coded on this contents page and on the heading of each page for ease of reference.

Published in Great Britain in 2000
by George Philip Limited,
a division of Octopus Publishing Group Limited,
2–4 Heron Quays, London E14 4JP

Cartography by Philip's

Fourth edition
© 2000 George Philip Limited

ISBN 0-540-07785-2
Printed in China

CARIBBEAN MAPS

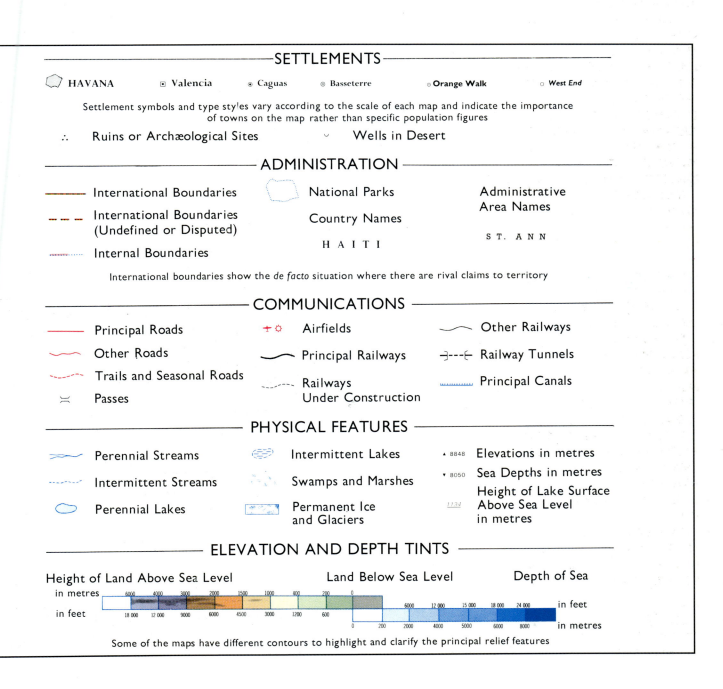

SETTLEMENTS

HAVANA ▢ Valencia ◉ Caguas ◎ Basseterre ○ Orange Walk ○ West End

Settlement symbols and type styles vary according to the scale of each map and indicate the importance of towns on the map rather than specific population figures

∴ Ruins or Archæological Sites ⌄ Wells in Desert

ADMINISTRATION

——— International Boundaries

– – – International Boundaries (Undefined or Disputed)

······· Internal Boundaries

National Parks

Country Names

HAITI

Administrative Area Names

ST. ANN

International boundaries show the de facto situation where there are rival claims to territory

COMMUNICATIONS

——— Principal Roads

⌁ Other Roads

····· Trails and Seasonal Roads

⌤ Passes

+ ☼ Airfields

⌁ Principal Railways

-⌁- Railways Under Construction

⌁ Other Railways

⌿-⌿ Railway Tunnels

⌗ Principal Canals

PHYSICAL FEATURES

⌁ Perennial Streams

····· Intermittent Streams

�ⁿ Perennial Lakes

Intermittent Lakes

Swamps and Marshes

Permanent Ice and Glaciers

▲ 8848 Elevations in metres

▼ 8050 Sea Depths in metres

1134 Height of Lake Surface Above Sea Level in metres

ELEVATION AND DEPTH TINTS

Height of Land Above Sea Level

in metres 6000 4000 3000 2000 1500 1000 400 200 0

in feet 18 000 12 000 9000 6000 4500 3000 1200 600

Land Below Sea Level

6000 12 000 15 000 18 000 24 000 in feet

0 200 2000 4000 5000 6000 8000 in metres

Depth of Sea

Some of the maps have different contours to highlight and clarify the principal relief features

WORLD STATISTICS: *countries*

This alphabetical list includes all the countries and territories of the world. If a territory is not completely independent, then the country it is associated with is named. The area figures give the total area of land, inland water and ice.

Units for areas and populations are thousands. The population figures are 1998 estimates. The annual income is the Gross National Product per capita in US dollars. The figures are the latest available, usually 1997.

Country/Territory	Area km² Thousands	Area miles² Thousands	Population Thousands	Capital	Annual Income US $
Adélie Land (France)	432	167	0.03	–	–
Afghanistan	652	252	24,792	Kabul	600
Albania	28.8	11.1	3,331	Tirana	750
Algeria	2,382	920	30,481	Algiers	1,490
American Samoa (US)	0.20	0.08	62	Pago Pago	2,600
Andorra	0.45	0.17	75	Andorra La Vella	16,200
Angola	1,247	481	11,200	Luanda	340
Anguilla (UK)	0.1	0.04	11	The Valley	6,800
Antigua & Barbuda	0.44	0.17	64	St John's	7,330
Argentina	2,767	1,068	36,265	Buenos Aires	8,750
Armenia	29.8	11.5	3,422	Yerevan	530
Aruba (Netherlands)	0.19	0.07	69	Oranjestad	15,890
Ascension Is. (UK)	0.09	0.03	1.5	Georgetown	–
Australia	7,687	2,968	18,613	Canberra	20,540
Austria	83.9	32.4	8,134	Vienna	27,980
Azerbaijan	86.6	33.4	7,856	Baku	510
Azores (Portugal)	2.2	0.87	238	Ponta Delgada	–
Bahamas	13.9	5.4	280	Nassau	11,940
Bahrain	0.68	0.26	616	Manama	7,840
Bangladesh	144	56	125,000	Dhaka	270
Barbados	0.43	0.17	259	Bridgetown	6,560
Belarus	207.6	80.1	10,409	Minsk	2,150
Belgium	30.5	11.8	10,175	Brussels	26,420
Belize	23	8.9	230	Belmopan	2,700
Benin	113	43	6,101	Porto-Novo	380
Bermuda (UK)	0.05	0.02	62	Hamilton	31,870
Bhutan	47	18.1	1,908	Thimphu	390
Bolivia	1,099	424	7,826	La Paz/Sucre	950
Bosnia-Herzegovina	51	20	3,366	Sarajevo	300
Botswana	582	225	1,448	Gaborone	4,381
Brazil	8,512	3,286	170,000	Brasília	4,720
British Antarctic Terr. (UK)	1,709	660	0.3	–	–
Brunei	5.8	2.2	315	Bandar Seri Begawan	15,800
Bulgaria	111	43	8,240	Sofia	1,140
Burkina Faso	274	106	11,266	Ouagadougou	240
Burma (= Myanmar)	677	261	47,305	Rangoon	1,790
Burundi	27.8	10.7	5,531	Bujumbura	180
Cambodia	181	70	11,340	Phnom Penh	300
Cameroon	475	184	15,029	Yaoundé	650
Canada	9,976	3,852	30,675	Ottawa	19,290
Canary Is. (Spain)	7.3	2.8	1,494	Las Palmas/Santa Cruz	–
Cape Verde Is.	4	1.6	399	Praia	1,010
Cayman Is. (UK)	0.26	0.10	35	George Town	20,000
Central African Republic	623	241	3,376	Bangui	320
Chad	1,284	496	7,360	Ndjaména	240
Chatham Is. (NZ)	0.96	0.37	0.05	Waitangi	–
Chile	757	292	14,788	Santiago	5,020
China	9,597	3,705	1,236,915	Beijing	860
Christmas Is. (Australia)	0.14	0.05	2	The Settlement	–
Cocos (Keeling) Is. (Australia)	0.01	0.005	1	West Island	–
Colombia	1,139	440	38,581	Bogotá	2,280
Comoros	2.2	0.86	545	Moroni	450
Congo	342	132	2,658	Brazzaville	660
Congo (= Zaïre)	2,345	905	49,001	Kinshasa	110
Cook Is. (NZ)	0.24	0.09	20	Avarua	900
Costa Rica	51.1	19.7	3,605	San José	2,640
Croatia	56.5	21.8	4,672	Zagreb	4,610
Cuba	111	43	11,051	Havana	1,300
Cyprus	9.3	3.6	749	Nicosia	13,420
Czech Republic	78.9	30.4	10,286	Prague	5,200
Denmark	43.1	16.6	5,334	Copenhagen	32,500
Djibouti	23.2	9	650	Djibouti	850
Dominica	0.75	0.29	78	Roseau	3,090
Dominican Republic	48.7	18.8	7,999	Santo Domingo	1,670
Ecuador	284	109	12,337	Quito	1,590
Egypt	1,001	387	66,050	Cairo	1,180
El Salvador	21	8.1	5,752	San Salvador	1,810
Equatorial Guinea	28.1	10.8	454	Malabo	530
Eritrea	94	36	3,842	Asmara	570
Estonia	44.7	17.3	1,421	Tallinn	3,330
Ethiopia	1,128	436	58,390	Addis Ababa	110
Falkland Is. (UK)	12.2	4.7	2	Stanley	–
Faroe Is. (Denmark)	1.4	0.54	41	Tórshavn	23,660
Fiji	18.3	7.1	802	Suva	2,470
Finland	338	131	5,149	Helsinki	24,080
France	552	213	58,805	Paris	26,050
French Guiana (France)	90	34.7	162	Cayenne	10,580
French Polynesia (France)	4	1.5	237	Papeete	7,500
Gabon	268	103	1,208	Libreville	4,230
Gambia, The	11.3	4.4	1,292	Banjul	320
Georgia	69.7	26.9	5,109	Tbilisi	840
Germany	357	138	82,079	Berlin/Bonn	28,260
Ghana	239	92	18,497	Accra	370
Gibraltar (UK)	0.007	0.003	29	Gibraltar Town	5,000
Greece	132	51	10,662	Athens	12,010
Greenland (Denmark)	2,176	840	59	Nuuk (Godthåb)	15,500
Grenada	0.34	0.13	96	St George's	2,880
Guadeloupe (France)	1.7	0.66	416	Basse-Terre	9,200
Guam (US)	0.55	0.21	149	Agana	6,000
Guatemala	109	42	12,008	Guatemala City	1,500
Guinea	246	95	7,477	Conakry	570
Guinea-Bissau	36.1	13.9	1,206	Bissau	240
Guyana	215	83	820	Georgetown	690
Haiti	27.8	10.7	6,781	Port-au-Prince	330
Honduras	112	43	5,862	Tegucigalpa	700
Hong Kong (China)	1.1	0.40	6,707	–	22,990
Hungary	93	35.9	10,208	Budapest	4,430
Iceland	103	40	271	Reykjavik	26,580
India	3,288	1,269	984,000	New Delhi	390
Indonesia	1,905	735	212,942	Jakarta	1,110
Iran	1,648	636	64,411	Tehran	4,700
Iraq	438	169	21,722	Baghdad	2,000
Ireland	70.3	27.1	3,619	Dublin	18,280
Israel	27	10.3	5,644	Jerusalem	15,810
Italy	301	116	56,783	Rome	20,120
Ivory Coast (Côte d'Ivoire)	322	125	15,446	Yamoussoukro	690
Jamaica	11	4.2	2,635	Kingston	1,560
Japan	378	146	125,932	Tokyo	37,850
Jordan	89.2	34.4	4,435	Amman	1,570
Kazakstan	2,717	1,049	16,847	Astana	1,340
Kenya	580	224	28,337	Nairobi	330
Kerguelen Is. (France)	7.2	2.8	0.7	–	–
Kermadec Is. (NZ)	0.03	0.01	0.1	–	–
Kiribati	0.72	0.28	85	Tarawa	920
Korea, North	121	47	21,234	Pyŏngyang	1,000
Korea, South	99	38.2	46,417	Seoul	10,550
Kuwait	17.8	6.9	1,913	Kuwait City	17,390
Kyrgyzstan	198.5	76.6	4,522	Bishkek	440
Laos	237	91	5,261	Vientiane	400
Latvia	65	25	2,385	Riga	2,430
Lebanon	10.4	4	3,506	Beirut	3,350
Lesotho	30.4	11.7	2,090	Maseru	670

Country/Territory	Area km² Thousands	Area miles² Thousands	Population Thousands	Capital	Annual Income US $
Liberia	111	43	2,772	Monrovia	770
Libya	1,760	679	4,875	Tripoli	6,510
Liechtenstein	0.16	0.06	32	Vaduz	33,000
Lithuania	65.2	25.2	3,600	Vilnius	2,230
Luxembourg	2.6	1	425	Luxembourg	45,360
Macau (China)	0.02	0.006	429	Macau	7,500
Macedonia	25.7	9.9	2,009	Skopje	1,090
Madagascar	587	227	14,463	Antananarivo	250
Madeira (Portugal)	0.81	0.31	253	Funchal	–
Malawi	118	46	9,840	Lilongwe	220
Malaysia	330	127	20,993	Kuala Lumpur	4,680
Maldives	0.30	0.12	290	Malé	1,080
Mali	1,240	479	10,109	Bamako	260
Malta	0.32	0.12	379	Valletta	12,000
Marshall Is.	0.18	0.07	63	Dalap-Uliga-Darrit	1,890
Martinique (France)	1.1	0.42	407	Fort-de-France	10,000
Mauritania	1,030	412	2,511	Nouakchott	450
Mauritius	2.0	0.72	1,168	Port Louis	3,800
Mayotte (France)	0.37	0.14	141	Mamoundzou	1,430
Mexico	1,958	756	98,553	Mexico City	3,680
Micronesia, Fed. States of	0.70	0.27	127	Palikir	2,070
Midway Is. (US)	0.005	0.002	2	–	–
Moldova	33.7	13	4,458	Chişinău	540
Monaco	0.002	0.0001	32	Monaco	25,000
Mongolia	1,567	605	2,579	Ulan Bator	390
Montserrat (UK)	0.10	0.04	12	Plymouth	4,500
Morocco	447	172	29,114	Rabat	1,250
Mozambique	802	309	18,641	Maputo	90
Namibia	825	318	1,622	Windhoek	2,220
Nauru	0.02	0.008	12	Yaren District	10,000
Nepal	141	54	23,698	Katmandu	210
Netherlands	41.5	16	15,731	Amsterdam/The Hague	25,820
Netherlands Antilles (Neths)	0.99	0.38	210	Willemstad	10,400
New Caledonia (France)	18.6	7.2	192	Nouméa	8,000
New Zealand	269	104	3,625	Wellington	16,480
Nicaragua	130	50	4,583	Managua	410
Niger	1,267	489	9,672	Niamey	200
Nigeria	924	357	110,532	Abuja	260
Niue (NZ)	0.26	0.10	2	Alofi	–
Norfolk Is. (Australia)	0.03	0.01	2	Kingston	–
Northern Mariana Is. (US)	0.48	0.18	50	Saipan	11,500
Norway	324	125	4,420	Oslo	36,090
Oman	212	82	2,364	Muscat	4,950
Pakistan	796	307	135,135	Islamabad	490
Palau	0.46	0.18	18	Koror	5,000
Panama	77.1	29.8	2,736	Panama City	3,080
Papua New Guinea	463	179	4,600	Port Moresby	940
Paraguay	407	157	5,291	Asunción	2,010
Peru	1,285	496	26,111	Lima	2,460
Peter 1st Is. (Norway)	0.18	0.07	0	–	–
Philippines	300	116	77,736	Manila	1,220
Pitcairn Is. (UK)	0.03	0.01	0.05	Adamstown	–
Poland	313	121	38,607	Warsaw	3,590
Portugal	92.4	35.7	9,928	Lisbon	10,450
Puerto Rico (US)	9	3.5	3,860	San Juan	7,800
Qatar	11	4.2	697	Doha	11,600
Réunion (France)	2.5	0.97	705	Saint-Denis	4,500
Romania	238	92	22,396	Bucharest	1,420
Russia	17,075	6,592	146,861	Moscow	2,740
Rwanda	26.3	10.2	7,956	Kigali	210
St Helena (UK)	0.12	0.05	7	Jamestown	–
St Kitts & Nevis	0.36	0.14	42	Basseterre	5,870
St Lucia	0.62	0.24	150	Castries	3,500
St Pierre & Miquelon (France)	0.24	0.09	7	Saint Pierre	–
St Vincent & Grenadines	0.39	0.15	120	Kingstown	2,370
San Marino	0.06	0.02	25	San Marino	20,000
São Tomé & Príncipe	0.96	0.37	150	São Tomé	330
Saudi Arabia	2,150	830	20,786	Riyadh	6,790
Senegal	197	76	9,723	Dakar	550
Seychelles	0.46	0.18	79	Victoria	6,850
Sierra Leone	71.7	27.7	5,080	Freetown	200
Singapore	0.62	0.24	3,490	Singapore	32,940
Slovak Republic	49	18.9	5,393	Bratislava	3,700
Slovenia	20.3	7.8	1,972	Ljubljana	9,680
Solomon Is.	28.9	11.2	441	Honiara	900
Somalia	638	246	6,842	Mogadishu	500
South Africa	1,220	471	42,835	C. Town/Pretoria/Bloem.	3,400
South Georgia (UK)	3.8	1.4	0.05	–	–
Spain	505	195	39,134	Madrid	14,510
Sri Lanka	65.6	25.3	18,934	Colombo	800
Sudan	2,506	967	33,551	Khartoum	800
Surinam	163	63	427	Paramaribo	1,000
Svalbard (Norway)	62.9	24.3	4	Longyearbyen	–
Swaziland	17.4	6.7	966	Mbabane	1,210
Sweden	450	174	8,887	Stockholm	26,220
Switzerland	41.3	15.9	7,260	Bern	44,220
Syria	185	71	16,673	Damascus	1,150
Taiwan	36	13.9	21,908	Taipei	12,400
Tajikistan	143.1	55.2	6,020	Dushanbe	330
Tanzania	945	365	30,609	Dodoma	210
Thailand	513	198	60,037	Bangkok	2,800
Togo	56.8	21.9	4,906	Lomé	330
Tokelau (NZ)	0.01	0.005	2	Nukunonu	–
Tonga	0.75	0.29	107	Nuku'alofa	1,790
Trinidad & Tobago	5.1	2	1,117	Port of Spain	4,230
Tristan da Cunha (UK)	0.11	0.04	0.33	Edinburgh	–
Tunisia	164	63	9,380	Tunis	2,090
Turkey	779	301	64,568	Ankara	3,130
Turkmenistan	488.1	188.5	4,298	Ashkhabad	630
Turks & Caicos Is. (UK)	0.43	0.17	16	Cockburn Town	5,000
Tuvalu	0.03	0.01	10	Fongafale	600
Uganda	236	91	22,167	Kampala	320
Ukraine	603.7	233.1	50,125	Kiev	1,040
United Arab Emirates	83.6	32.3	2,303	Abu Dhabi	17,360
United Kingdom	243.3	94	58,970	London	20,710
United States of America	9,373	3,619	270,290	Washington, DC	28,740
Uruguay	177	68	3,285	Montevideo	6,020
Uzbekistan	447.4	172.7	23,784	Tashkent	1,010
Vanuatu	12.2	4.7	185	Port-Vila	1,290
Vatican City	0.0004	0.0002	1	–	–
Venezuela	912	352	22,803	Caracas	3,450
Vietnam	332	127	76,236	Hanoi	320
Virgin Is. (UK)	0.15	0.06	13	Road Town	–
Virgin Is. (US)	0.34	0.13	118	Charlotte Amalie	12,000
Wake Is.	0.008	0.003	0.3	–	–
Wallis & Futuna Is. (France)	0.20	0.08	15	Mata-Utu	–
Western Sahara	266	103	280	El Aaiún	300
Western Samoa	2.8	1.1	224	Apia	1,170
Yemen	528	204	16,388	Sana	270
Yugoslavia	102.3	39.5	10,500	Belgrade	2,000
Zambia	753	291	9,461	Lusaka	380
Zimbabwe	391	151	11,044	Harare	750

Each topic list is divided into continents and within a continent the items are listed in order of size. The bottom part of many of the lists is selective in order to give examples from as many different countries as possible. The figures are rounded as appropriate.

World, Continents, Oceans

	km²	miles²	%
The World	509,450,000	196,672,000	–
Land	149,450,000	57,688,000	29.3
Water	360,000,000	138,984,000	70.7
Asia	44,500,000	17,177,000	29.8
Africa	30,302,000	11,697,000	20.3
North America	24,241,000	9,357,000	16.2
South America	17,793,000	6,868,000	11.9
Antarctica	14,100,000	5,443,000	9.4
Europe	9,957,000	3,843,000	6.7
Australia & Oceania	8,557,000	3,303,000	5.7
Pacific Ocean	179,679,000	69,356,000	49.9
Atlantic Ocean	92,373,000	35,657,000	25.7
Indian Ocean	73,917,000	28,532,000	20.5
Arctic Ocean	14,090,000	5,439,000	3.9

Ocean Depths

Atlantic Ocean	m	ft
Puerto Rico (Milwaukee) Deep	9,220	30,249
Cayman Trench	7,680	25,197
Gulf of Mexico	5,203	17,070
Mediterranean Sea	5,121	16,801
Black Sea	2,211	7,254
North Sea	660	2,165

Indian Ocean	m	ft
Java Trench	7,450	24,442
Red Sea	2,635	8,454

Pacific Ocean	m	ft
Mariana Trench	11,022	36,161
Tonga Trench	10,882	35,702
Japan Trench	10,554	34,626
Kuril Trench	10,542	34,587

Arctic Ocean	m	ft
Molloy Deep	5,608	18,399

Mountains

Europe		m	ft
Elbrus	*Russia*	5,642	18,510
Mont Blanc	*France/Italy*	4,807	15,771
Monte Rosa	*Italy/Switzerland*	4,634	15,203
Dom	*Switzerland*	4,545	14,911
Liskamm	*Switzerland*	4,527	14,852
Weisshorn	*Switzerland*	4,505	14,780
Taschorn	*Switzerland*	4,490	14,730
Matterhorn/Cervino	*Italy/Switzerland*	4,478	14,691
Mont Maudit	*France/Italy*	4,465	14,649
Dent Blanche	*Switzerland*	4,356	14,291
Nadelhorn	*Switzerland*	4,327	14,196
Grandes Jorasses	*France/Italy*	4,208	13,806
Jungfrau	*Switzerland*	4,158	13,642
Grossglockner	*Austria*	3,797	12,457
Mulhacen	*Spain*	3,478	11,411
Zugspitze	*Germany*	2,962	9,718
Olympus	*Greece*	2,917	9,570
Triglav	*Slovenia*	2,863	9,393
Gerlachovka	*Slovak Republic*	2,655	8,711
Galdhöpiggen	*Norway*	2,468	8,100
Kebnekaise	*Sweden*	2,117	6,946
Ben Nevis	*UK*	1,343	4,406

Asia		m	ft
Everest	*China/Nepal*	8,848	29,029
K2 (Godwin Austen)	*China/Kashmir*	8,611	28,251
Kanchenjunga	*India/Nepal*	8,598	28,208
Lhotse	*China/Nepal*	8,516	27,939
Makalu	*China/Nepal*	8,481	27,824
Cho Oyu	*China/Nepal*	8,201	26,906
Dhaulagiri	*Nepal*	8,172	26,811
Manaslu	*Nepal*	8,156	26,758
Nanga Parbat	*Kashmir*	8,126	26,660
Annapurna	*Nepal*	8,078	26,502
Gasherbrum	*China/Kashmir*	8,068	26,469
Broad Peak	*China/Kashmir*	8,051	26,414
Xixabangma	*China*	8,012	26,286
Kangbachen	*India/Nepal*	7,902	25,925
Trivor	*Pakistan*	7,720	25,328
Pik Kommunizma	*Tajikistan*	7,495	24,590
Demavend	*Iran*	5,604	18,386
Ararat	*Turkey*	5,165	16,945
Gunong Kinabalu	*Malaysia (Borneo)*	4,101	13,455
Fuji-San	*Japan*	3,776	12,388

Africa		m	ft
Kilimanjaro	*Tanzania*	5,895	19,340
Mt Kenya	*Kenya*	5,199	17,057
Ruwenzori	*Uganda/Congo (Zaïre)*	5,109	16,762
Ras Dashan	*Ethiopia*	4,620	15,157
Meru	*Tanzania*	4,565	14,977
Karisimbi	*Rwanda/Congo (Zaïre)*	4,507	14,787
Mt Elgon	*Kenya/Uganda*	4,321	14,176
Batu	*Ethiopia*	4,307	14,130
Toubkal	*Morocco*	4,165	13,665
Mt Cameroon	*Cameroon*	4,070	13,353

Oceania		m	ft
Puncak Jaya	*Indonesia*	5,029	16 499
Puncak Trikora	*Indonesia*	4,750	15,584
Puncak Mandala	*Indonesia*	4,702	15,427
Mt Wilhelm	*Papua New Guinea*	4,508	14,790
Mauna Kea	*USA (Hawaii)*	4,205	13,796
Mauna Loa	*USA (Hawaii)*	4,170	13,681
Mt Cook (Aoraki)	*New Zealand*	3,753	12,313
Mt Kosciuszko	*Australia*	2,237	7,339

North America		m	ft
Mt McKinley (Denali)	*USA (Alaska)*	6,194	20,321
Mt Logan	*Canada*	5,959	19,551
Citlaltepetl	*Mexico*	5,700	18,701
Mt St Elias	*USA/Canada*	5,489	18,008
Popocatepetl	*Mexico*	5,452	17,887
Mt Foraker	*USA (Alaska)*	5,304	17,401
Ixtaccihuatl	*Mexico*	5,286	17,342
Lucania	*Canada*	5,227	17,149
Mt Steele	*Canada*	5,073	16,644
Mt Bona	*USA (Alaska)*	5,005	16,420
Mt Whitney	*USA*	4,418	14,495
Tajumulco	*Guatemala*	4,220	13,845
Chirripó Grande	*Costa Rica*	3,837	12,589
Pico Duarte	*Dominican Rep.*	3,175	10,417

South America		m	ft
Aconcagua	*Argentina*	6,960	22,834
Bonete	*Argentina*	6,872	22,546
Ojos del Salado	*Argentina/Chile*	6,863	22,516
Pissis	*Argentina*	6,779	22,241
Mercedario	*Argentina/Chile*	6,770	22,211
Huascaran	*Peru*	6,768	22,204
Llullaillaco	*Argentina/Chile*	6,723	22,057
Nudo de Cachi	*Argentina*	6,720	22,047
Yerupaja	*Peru*	6,632	21,758
Sajama	*Bolivia*	6,542	21,463
Chimborazo	*Ecuador*	6,267	20,561
Pico Colon	*Colombia*	5,800	19,029
Pico Bolivar	*Venezuela*	5,007	16,427

Antarctica		m	ft
Vinson Massif		4,897	16,066
Mt Kirkpatrick		4,528	14,855

Rivers

Europe		km	miles
Volga	*Caspian Sea*	3,700	2,300
Danube	*Black Sea*	2,850	1,770
Ural	*Caspian Sea*	2,535	1,575
Dnepr (Dnipro)	*Black Sea*	2,285	1,420
Kama	*Volga*	2,030	1,260
Don	*Volga*	1,990	1,240
Petchora	*Arctic Ocean*	1,790	1,110
Oka	*Volga*	1,480	920
Dnister (Dniester)	*Black Sea*	1,400	870
Vyatka	*Kama*	1,370	850
Rhine	*North Sea*	1,320	820
N. Dvina	*Arctic Ocean*	1,290	800
Elbe	*North Sea*	1,145	710

Asia		km	miles
Yangtze	*Pacific Ocean*	6,380	3,960
Yenisey–Angara	*Arctic Ocean*	5,550	3,445
Huang He	*Pacific Ocean*	5,464	3,395
Ob–Irtysh	*Arctic Ocean*	5,410	3,360
Mekong	*Pacific Ocean*	4,500	2,795
Amur	*Pacific Ocean*	4,400	2,730
Lena	*Arctic Ocean*	4,400	2,730
Irtysh	*Ob*	4,250	2,640
Yenisey	*Arctic Ocean*	4,090	2,540
Ob	*Arctic Ocean*	3,680	2,285
Indus	*Indian Ocean*	3,100	1,925
Brahmaputra	*Indian Ocean*	2,900	1,800
Syrdarya	*Aral Sea*	2,860	1,775
Salween	*Indian Ocean*	2,800	1,740
Euphrates	*Indian Ocean*	2,700	1,675
Amudarya	*Aral Sea*	2,540	1,575

Africa		km	miles
Nile	*Mediterranean*	6,670	4,140
Congo	*Atlantic Ocean*	4,670	2,900
Niger	*Atlantic Ocean*	4,180	2,595
Zambezi	*Indian Ocean*	3,540	2,200
Oubangi/Uele	*Congo (Zaïre)*	2,250	1,400
Kasai	*Congo (Zaïre)*	1,950	1,210
Shaballe	*Indian Ocean*	1,930	1,200
Orange	*Atlantic Ocean*	1,860	1,155
Cubango	*Okavango Swamps*	1,800	1,120
Limpopo	*Indian Ocean*	1,600	995
Senegal	*Atlantic Ocean*	1,600	995

Australia		km	miles
Murray–Darling	*Indian Ocean*	3,750	2,330
Darling	*Murray*	3,070	1,905
Murray	*Indian Ocean*	2,575	1,600
Murrumbidgee	*Murray*	1,690	1,050

North America		km	miles
Mississippi–Missouri	*Gulf of Mexico*	6,020	3,740
Mackenzie	*Arctic Ocean*	4,240	2,630
Mississippi	*Gulf of Mexico*	3,780	2,350
Missouri	*Mississippi*	3,780	2,350
Yukon	*Pacific Ocean*	3,185	1,980
Rio Grande	*Gulf of Mexico*	3,030	1,880
Arkansas	*Mississippi*	2,340	1,450
Colorado	*Pacific Ocean*	2,330	1,445
Red	*Mississippi*	2,040	1,270
Columbia	*Pacific Ocean*	1,950	1,210
Saskatchewan	*Lake Winnipeg*	1,940	1,205

South America		km	miles
Amazon	*Atlantic Ocean*	6,450	4,010
Paraná–Plate	*Atlantic Ocean*	4,500	2,800
Purus	*Amazon*	3,350	2,080
Madeira	*Amazon*	3,200	1,990
São Francisco	*Atlantic Ocean*	2,900	1,800
Paraná	*Plate*	2,800	1,740
Tocantins	*Atlantic Ocean*	2,750	1,710
Paraguay	*Paraná*	2,550	1,580
Orinoco	*Atlantic Ocean*	2,500	1,550
Pilcomayo	*Paraná*	2,500	1,550
Araguaia	*Tocantins*	2,250	1,400

Lakes

Europe		km²	miles²
Lake Ladoga	*Russia*	17,700	6,800
Lake Onega	*Russia*	9,700	3,700
Saimaa system	*Finland*	8,000	3,100
Vänern	*Sweden*	5,500	2,100

Asia		km²	miles²
Caspian Sea	*Asia*	371,800	143,550
Lake Baykal	*Russia*	30,500	11,780
Aral Sea	*Kazakstan/Uzbekistan*	28,687	11,086
Tonlé Sap	*Cambodia*	20,000	7,700
Lake Balqash	*Kazakstan*	18,500	7,100

Africa		km²	miles²
Lake Victoria	*East Africa*	68,000	26,000
Lake Tanganyika	*Central Africa*	33,000	13,000
Lake Malawi/Nyasa	*East Africa*	29,600	11,430
Lake Chad	*Central Africa*	25,000	9,700
Lake Turkana	*Ethiopia/Kenya*	8,500	3,300
Lake Volta	*Ghana*	8,500	3,300

Australia		km²	miles²
Lake Eyre	*Australia*	8,900	3,400
Lake Torrens	*Australia*	5,800	2,200
Lake Gairdner	*Australia*	4,800	1,900

North America		km²	miles²
Lake Superior	*Canada/USA*	82,350	31,800
Lake Huron	*Canada/USA*	59,600	23,010
Lake Michigan	*USA*	58,000	22,400
Great Bear Lake	*Canada*	31,800	12,280
Great Slave Lake	*Canada*	28,500	11,000
Lake Erie	*Canada/USA*	25,700	9,900
Lake Winnipeg	*Canada*	24,400	9,400
Lake Ontario	*Canada/USA*	19,500	7,500
Lake Nicaragua	*Nicaragua*	8,200	3,200

South America		km²	miles²
Lake Titicaca	*Bolivia/Peru*	8,300	3,200
Lake Poopo	*Peru*	2,800	1,100

Islands

Europe		km²	miles²
Great Britain	*UK*	229,880	88,700
Iceland	*Atlantic Ocean*	103,000	39,800
Ireland	*Ireland/UK*	84,400	32,600
Novaya Zemlya (N.)	*Russia*	48,200	18,600
Sicily	*Italy*	25,500	9,800
Corsica	*France*	8,700	3,400

Asia		km²	miles²
Borneo	*South-east Asia*	744,360	287,400
Sumatra	*Indonesia*	473,600	182,860
Honshu	*Japan*	230,500	88,980
Celebes	*Indonesia*	189,000	73,000
Java	*Indonesia*	126,700	48,900
Luzon	*Philippines*	104,700	40,400
Hokkaido	*Japan*	78,400	30,300

Africa		km²	miles²
Madagascar	*Indian Ocean*	587,040	226,660
Socotra	*Indian Ocean*	3,600	1,400
Réunion	*Indian Ocean*	2,500	965

Oceania		km²	miles²
New Guinea	*Indonesia/Papua NG*	821,030	317,000
New Zealand (S.)	*Pacific Ocean*	150,500	58,100
New Zealand (N.)	*Pacific Ocean*	114,700	44,300
Tasmania	*Australia*	67,800	26,200
Hawaii	*Pacific Ocean*	10,450	4,000

North America		km²	miles²
Greenland	*Atlantic Ocean*	2,175,600	839,800
Baffin Is.	*Canada*	508,000	196,100
Victoria Is.	*Canada*	212,200	81,900
Ellesmere Is.	*Canada*	212,000	81,800
Cuba	*Caribbean Sea*	110,860	42,800
Hispaniola	*Dominican Rep./Haiti*	76,200	29,400
Jamaica	*Caribbean Sea*	11,400	4,400
Puerto Rico	*Atlantic Ocean*	8,900	3,400

South America		km²	miles²
Tierra del Fuego	*Argentina/Chile*	47,000	18,100
Falkland Is. (E.)	*Atlantic Ocean*	6,800	2,600

SCALE

The plan below shows the top of a desk. It is drawn to **scale**. Its real size is 1 m long and 0.4 m wide. 1 mm on the plan represents 20 mm on the desk.

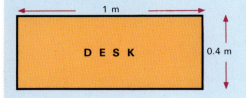

1 m

DESK 0.4 m

Scale 1 : 20

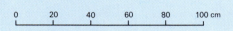

0   20   40   60   80   100 cm

In this atlas the scale of the maps is shown in 2 ways:

◄ 1. This gives the scale as a ratio or representative fraction.

◄ 2. This shows the scale as a line or bar

SCALE AND DISTANCE

Maps represent rooms, buildings, towns, countries, continents or even the world on one piece of paper. For example, Barbados appears on page 9, page 32 and on page 36.

The page size is the same but the maps show different areas and distances because they are drawn to different scales. The table shows how far apart some places are on these maps, in centimetres. It also gives the real **distances** between these places in kilometres.

	A Ground distance kilometres	B Map distance centimetres	C Scale
Bridgetown - Whitehaven	16	13.3	120 000
Bridgetown - Fort-de-France	227.5	6.5	3 500 000
Bridgetown - Kingston	1920	12.8	15 000 000

Check this out on the maps.
Example of calculation. *Bridgetown - Kingston*
1920 x 100 000 ÷ 12.8 = 15 000 000 or 1:15 000 000

	B Map distance centimetres	C Scale	B × C = Ground distance kilometres
Belleplane - Jackson	8.2	120 000	9.8
Castries - Kingstown	2.8	3 500 000	98
Havana - San Juan	11.8	15 000 000	1770

Check this out on the maps.
Example of calculation.
Havana - San Juan 11.8 x 15 000 000 ÷ 100 000 = 1770km.

Column C in the table shows the scale of the maps. It tells you how many centimetres on the Earth are represented by 1 cm on the map. So, 120 000 means 1 cm on the map is equal to 120 000 cm on the earth. On the maps this is written as a proportion: 1 : 120 000

Distances between places can therefore be read off a map as long as the scale is known. They can either be measured using a ruler and then read directly off the scale bar in kilometres, or they can be calculated by multiplying the map distance in centimetres by the scale, giving the ground distance in centimetres, which can be converted to kilometres.

DIRECTION

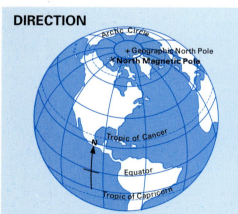

THE MAGNETIC NORTH POLE

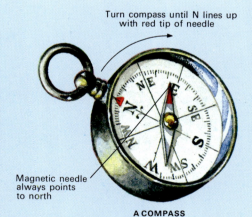

Turn compass until N lines up with red tip of needle

Magnetic needle always points to north

A COMPASS

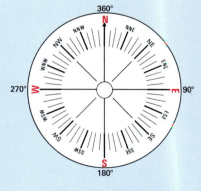

POINTS OF THE COMPASS

If you want to find your way from one place to another you can use a compass. A compass shows **directions**. Compasses have a needle with a magnetic tip. The tip is attracted towards the North Magnetic Pole which is close to the North Pole, so the compass tells you where North is. You can see the North Magnetic Pole on the map above. It is also shown on the larger scale maps in the atlas.

On some maps direction is shown by a North arrow. On most of the maps in this atlas North is at the top. The vertical blue lines go from North to South and the lines across the map go from East on the right to West on the left.

Look at the drawing of the points of the compass. The directions North, South, East and West are called **cardinal points**. Direction is sometimes given in degrees. This is measured going clockwise from North. East is 90°, South is 180° and West 270°.

Between the cardinal points of the compass are some other directions. For example, between North and East there is North North East, North East and East North East.

See if you can work out where the cardinal directions are where you live. **Clue**: the Sun rises in the East and sets in the West.

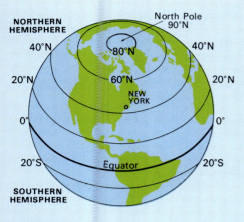

LATITUDE

This map shows the Earth as if it was seen from thousands of kilometres above New York. The lines running around the map are lines of **latitude**. They run from East to West and get shorter as they get nearer to the North and South Poles. The longest latitude line is called the **Equator**. It runs around the centre of the Earth midway between the Poles.

Latitude lines are measured in **degrees**. The Equator is at latitude 0°. The North and South Poles are at latitude 90°.

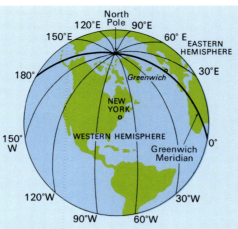

LONGITUDE

The map above shows lines of **longitude**. These run from North to South. Longitude lines are all the same length. Longitude 0° goes through Greenwich. It is called the **Greenwich meridian**. There are 180° East and West from Greenwich. Longitude line 180° runs through the Pacific Ocean.

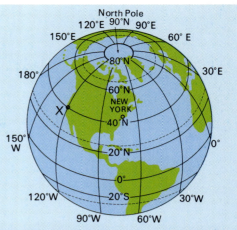

USING LATITUDE AND LONGITUDE

Latitude and longitude lines make a **grid**. You can find a place if you know its latitude and longitude number. The latitude number is either North or South of the Equator. The longitude number is either East or West of the Greenwich meridian. For example X is located at 40°N latitude and 120°W longitude. At the Equator a degree measures about 110 km. To be more accurate each degree is divided into 60 **minutes** ('). Each minute is made up of 60 **seconds** ("). At the Equator a second measures about 30 m.

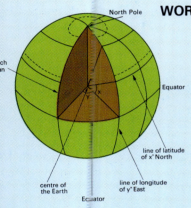

WORKING OUT LATITUDE AND LONGITUDE

◄ The diagram shows how latitude and longitude are worked out.

Latitude line numbers are worked out by measuring the angle they make with the Equator. Angle x on the diagram shows one example.

Longitude line numbers are worked out by measuring the angle they make with the Greenwich meridian. This is shown by angle y.

GREENWICH MERIDIAN

◄ This is an aerial photograph of Greenwich Observatory. The red line goes through the telescope that fixed the Greenwich meridian at 0° longitude.

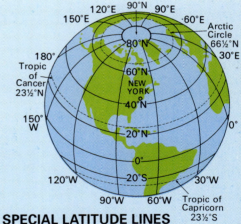

SPECIAL LATITUDE LINES

Some special latitude lines are shown on maps. The diagrams on page 50 show that the Sun is only overhead vertically in the tropical regions. These regions are between 23°30' North and South of the Equator. On maps these are shown as blue dotted lines. The **Tropic of Cancer** is at 23°30' North and the **Tropic of Capricorn** is at 23°30' South.

In the North and South polar regions there are places where the Sun does not rise or set above or below the horizon at certain times of the year. These places are also shown by a blue dotted line. The **Arctic Circle** is at 66°30' North and the **Antarctic Circle** is at 66°30' South.

GULF OF MEXICO

UNITED STATES

PACIFIC OCEAN

MEXICO

BELIZE

GUATEMALA

HONDURAS

EL SALVADOR

NICARAGUA

COSTA RICA

PANAMA

CUBA

GREATER

CARIB...

JAMAICA

BA...

Yucatan Strait

Straits of Florida

Florida Keys

Great Bahama Bank

Cayman Trench

Gulf of Honduras

Gulf of Darien

Gulf of Panama

Gulf of Chiriqui

Cities and places (selection):

Miami, West Palm Beach, Fort Lauderdale, Boca Raton, Fort Myers, Hialeah, Key West, Freeport, Grand Bahama I., Great Abaco I., Nassau, New Providence I., Eleuthera I., Nicolls Town, Berry Is., Bimini Is.

HAVANA, Havana, Guanabacoa, Marianao, Guanajay, San Antonio de los Baños, Pinar del Río, Güines, Matanzas, Cárdenas, Colón, Jovellanos, Sagua la Grande, Santa Clara, Caibarién, Cienfuegos, Trinidad, Sancti-Spíritus, Placetas, Morón, Ciego de Ávila, Camagüey, Florida, Nuevitas, Victoria de las Tunas, Holguín, Bayamo, Manzanillo, Palma Soriano, SANTIAGO DE CUBA, Sierra Maestra, Batabanó, Isla de la Juventud, Nueva Gerona

Montego Bay, St. Ann's Bay, Port Antonio, KINGSTON, Spanish Town, Savanna la Mar, May Pen, Pedro Cays (Jamaica)

Progreso, Mérida, Motul, Temax, Tizimín, Izamal, Espita, Valladolid, Ticul, Tekax, Peto, Campeche, Champotón, Ciudad del Carmen, Cancún, Pta. Juárez, Isla Cozumel, Felipe Carrillo Puerto, B. de Chetumal

Belize City, Belmopan, Ambergris Cay, Turneffe Is., Maya Mts., Dangriga

Puerto Barrios, Puerto Cortés, San Pedro Sula, La Ceiba, Tela, Trujillo, Comitán, Cobán, Huehuetenango, San Marcos, Totonicapán, Quezaltenango, Antigua, Mazatenango, Jalapa, Chiquimula, GUATEMALA, Escuintla, San José, Ahuachapán, Santa Ana, SAN SALVADOR, Cojutepeque, Zacatecoluca, Usulután, San Miguel, Golfo de Fonseca, TEGUCIGALPA

Choluteca, Chinandega, León, Corinto, Estelí, Jinotega, Matagalpa, Boaco, Juigalpa, MANAGUA, Masaya, Granada, Diriamba, Rivas, Bluefields, Puerto Cabezas, Cayos Miskitos (Nicaragua), Islas del Maíz (Nicaragua), I. de Providencia (Colombia), I. de San Andrés (Colombia), Cayos Roncador (Colombia), Cayos de Albuquerque (Colombia)

Liberia, Santa Cruz, Puntarenas, Pen. de Nicoya, Alajuela, San José, Cartago, Limón, David, Puerto Armuelles, Colón, Panamá, PANAMA, Panama Canal, Balboa, Sierrania del Darién, Arch. de las Perlas, La Palma, Serrania de Tabasará

Swan Islands (Honduras), Cayman Islands (Br.), Grand Cayman, Cayman Brac, Little Cayman

Projection: Bi-polar oblique Conical Orthomorphic

MAS

A T L A N T I C

O C E A N

Tropic of Cancer

Arthur's Town
Old Bight
Cat I.
San Salvador
(Watling I., Cuanahani)

Rum Cay

Long I.

Crooked I.

Ackins I.

Mayaguana I.

Little Inagua I.

Caicos Islands (Br.)

Turks Islands (Br.)

Matthew Town

Great Inagua I.

anes

ayari

Baracoa

Pta. de Maisi

Î. de la Tortue

Port-de-Paix

Cap-Haïtien

Monte Cristi

Puerto Plata

San Francisco de Macoris

Puerto Rico Trench

Milwaukee Deep ▼9200

Guantánamo

Windward Passage

Cap-à-Foux

Golfe de la Gonâve

Gonaïves

Santiago de los Cabelleros

HISPANIOLA

3175

Bayamón

SAN JUAN

Virgin Is. (Br.)

Road Town

Anguilla (Br.)

Jérémie

Î. de la Gonâve

HAITI

DOMINICAN REP.

San Juan

San Pedro de Macoris

Higüay

Arecibo

C. Engano

Fajardo

Virgin Is. (U.S.A.)

St.-Martin (Fr.)

St.-Barthélemy (Fr.)

Avassa I. (U.S.A.)

PORT-AU-PRINCE

2280

Enriquillo

Barahona

C. Rojo

Les Cayes

Jacmel

Pointe-à-Gravois

Santa de la Compostela

San Cristóbal

SANTO DOMINGOS

Mona Passage

1338

Mayagüez

Isla Mona (U.S.A.)

PUERTO RICO (U.S.A.)

Ponce

Caguas

Guayama

Charlotte Amalie

St. John

St. Croix

Christiansted

St. Maarten (Neth.)

Saba (Neth.)

St. Eustatius (Neth.)

Basseterre

ST. KITTS -NEVIS

St. Johns

Antigua

Barbuda

ANTIGUA & BARBUDA

Montserrat

A N T I L L E S

L E E W A R D   I S L A N D S

Ste-Rose

GUADELOUPE

Basse-Terre

Moule

Pointe-à-Pitre

Marie-Galante (Fr.)

Dominica Passage

L E S S E R

I. de Aves (Bird I.) (Venezuela)

Portsmouth

DOMINICA

Roseau

B E A N   S E A

A N T I L L E S

Mt. Pelée 1397

Fort-de-France

MARTINIQUE (Fr.)

W I N D W A R D

Castries

ST. LUCIA

St. Vincent

I S L A N D S

Kingstown

Bridgetown

BARBADOS

ST. VINCENT & THE GRENADINES

St. George's

GRENADA

L E S S E R   A N T I L L E S

Aruba (Neth.)

Curaçao (Neth.)

Bonaire (Neth.)

Pta. Gallinas

Pen. de Paraguaná

Willemstad

Neth. Antilles

I. de Aves (Ven.)

I. Orchila (Ven.)

I. Los Roques (Ven.)

I. Blanquilla (Ven.)

I. Los Hermanos (Ven.)

I. Los Testigos (Ven.)

Tobago

Scarborough

Pen. de la Guajira

G. of Venezuela

Punto Fijo

Puerto Cumarebo

Coro

I. La Tortuga (Ven.)

I. Margarita

Porlamar

Pen. de Paria

Port of Spain

Arima

Trinidad

Riohacha

Santa Marta

Sierra Nevada de Santa Marta 5800

MARACAIBO

La Concepción

Santa Rita

Cabimas

Carora

San Felipe

Macaray

Maiquetia

CARACAS

Guatire

Los Teques

Cumaná

Carúpano

Río Caribe

Güiria

Golfo de Paria

San Fernando

TRINIDAD & TOBAGO

ARRAN-QUILLA

Baranoa

Soledad

Sabanalarga

Fundación

Calamar

Cienaga

Valledupar

Agustin Codaz

Machiques

Ciudad Ojeda

L. de Maracaibo

La Ceiba

Carora

BARQUISIMETO

Yaritagua de los Morros

El Tocuyo

San Carlos

Acarigua

Los Morros de Orituco

Valencia

Villa de Cura

S. Juan de los Morros

Altagracia de Orituco

Aragua de Barcelona

Puerto La Cruz

Barcelona

Caripito

Caicara

Maturín

jona

Carmen Bolívar

Plato

Magangué

Sincé

Sahagún

El Banco

Ocaña

San Carlos del Zulia

Trujillo

Valera

Guanare

Barinas

Cord. de Mérida

Ciudad Bolívar

Libertad

San Fernando de Apure

Achaguas

Apure

Calabozo

Valle de la Pascua

El Sombrero

Santa Maria de Ipire

Pariaguan

Cantaura

El Tigre

Anaco

Soledad

Tucupita

Ciudad Guayana

Upata

ce-jo

Planeta Rica

Santa Bárbara

Cúcuta

V E N E Z U E L A

Orinoco

Caicara

Ciudad Bolívar

El Callao

Tumeremo

OLOMBIA

West from Greenwich

75 · 70 · 65

COPYRIGHT GEORGE PHILIP & SON. LTD.

1:8 000 000

50 0 50 100 150 200 250 300 km

m
4000
3000
2000
1500
1000
400
200
0
200
2000
4000
6000
8000
m

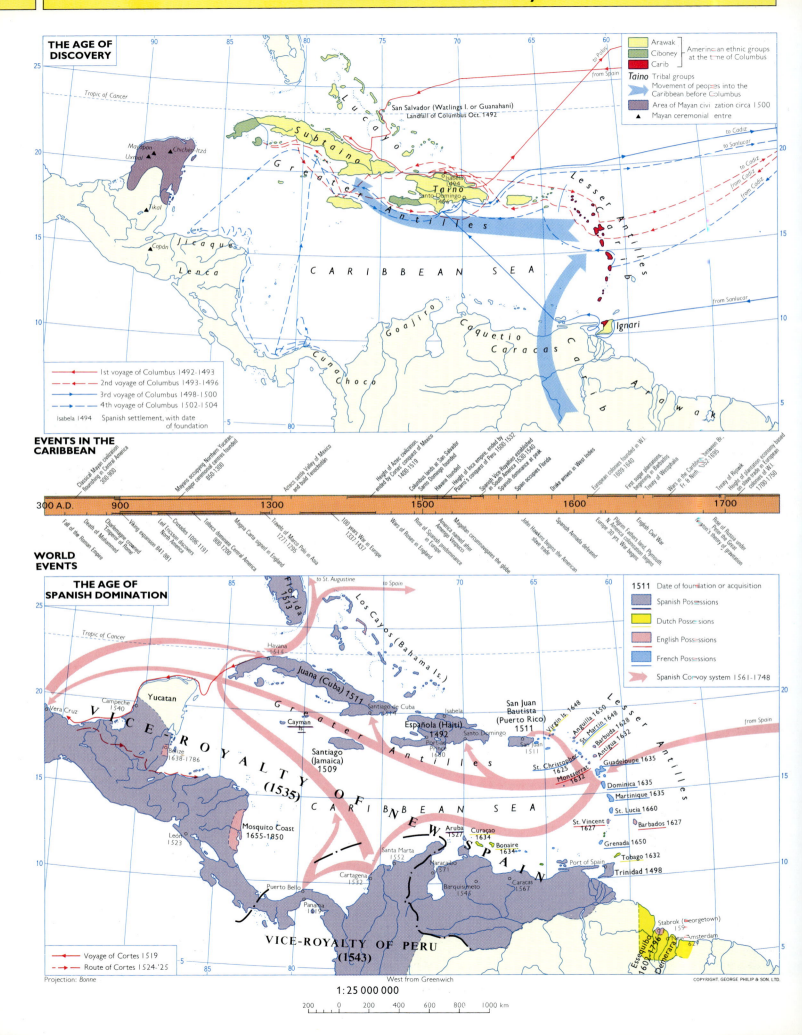

THE AGE OF DISCOVERY

	Arawak	American ethnic groups at the time of Columbus
	Ciboney	
	Carib	

Taino Tribal groups

Movement of peoples into the Caribbean before Columbus

Area of Mayan civilization circa 1500

▲ Mayan ceremonial centre

1st voyage of Columbus 1492-1493
2nd voyage of Columbus 1493-1496
3rd voyage of Columbus 1498-1500
4th voyage of Columbus 1502-1504

Isabela 1494 Spanish settlement, with date of foundation

EVENTS IN THE CARIBBEAN

WORLD EVENTS

300 A.D.   900   1300   1500   1600   1700

THE AGE OF SPANISH DOMINATION

1511 Date of foundation or acquisition

Spanish Possessions
Dutch Possessions
English Possessions
French Possessions

Spanish Convoy system 1561-1748

VICE-ROYALTY OF NEW SPAIN (1535)

VICE-ROYALTY OF PERU (1543)

Voyage of Cortes 1519
Route of Cortes 1524-'25

Projection: Bonne

1:25 000 000

200   0   200   400   600   800   1000 km

West from Greenwich

COPYRIGHT. GEORGE PHILIP & SON, LTD.

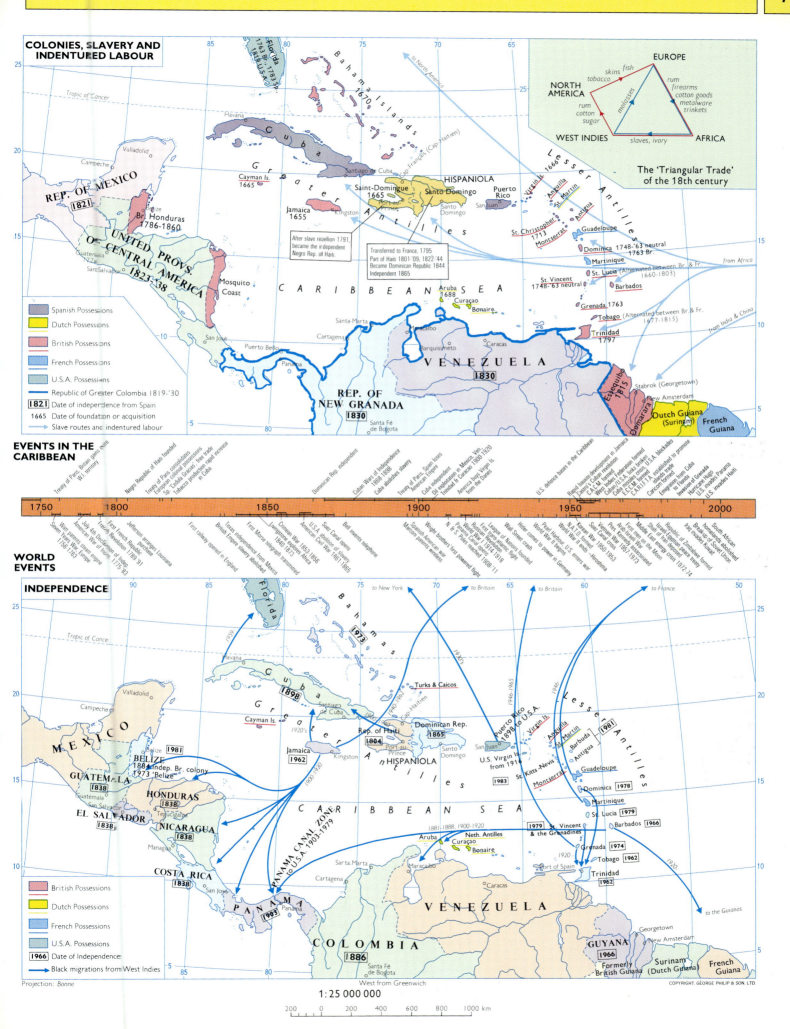

COLONIES, SLAVERY AND INDENTURED LABOUR

The 'Triangular Trade' of the 18th century

EUROPE

NORTH AMERICA — skins, fish, tobacco — rum, firearms, cotton goods, metalware, trinkets

WEST INDIES — rum, cotton, sugar — molasses — slaves, ivory — AFRICA

Legend:
- Spanish Possessions
- Dutch Possessions
- British Possessions
- French Possessions
- U.S.A. Possessions
- Republic of Greater Colombia 1819-'30
- [1821] Date of independence from Spain
- 1665 Date of foundation or acquisition
- Slave routes and indentured labour

REP. OF MEXICO [1821]

UNITED PROVS. OF CENTRAL AMERICA 1823-38

Br. Honduras 1786-1860

Mosquito Coast

CARIBBEAN SEA

REP. OF NEW GRANADA [1830]

VENEZUELA [1830]

Cuba

Greater Antilles

Cayman Is. 1665

Jamaica 1655

HISPANIOLA
Saint-Domingue 1665
Santo Domingo
Puerto Rico

After slave rebellion 1791, became the independent Negro Rep. of Haiti

Transferred to France, 1795
Part of Haiti 1801-'09, 1822-'44
Became Dominican Republic 1844
Independent 1865

Bahama Islands 1670

Florida 1763 Br. 1783 Sp. 1819 U.S.A.

Lesser Antilles

Virgin Is. 1666
Anguilla
St. Martin
St. Christopher 1713
Montserrat
Antigua
Guadeloupe
Dominica 1748-'63 neutral 1763 Br.
Martinique
St. Lucia (Alternated between Br. & Fr. 1660-1803)
St. Vincent 1748-63 neutral
Barbados
Grenada 1763
Tobago (Alternated between Br. & Fr. 1677-1815)
Trinidad 1797

Aruba 1688
Curaçao
Bonaire

Esequibo 1815
Demarara
Stabrok (Georgetown)
New Amsterdam
Dutch Guiana (Surinam)
French Guiana

from Africa
from India & China

EVENTS IN THE CARIBBEAN

Timeline 1750 — 1800 — 1850 — 1900 — 1950 — 2000

WORLD EVENTS

INDEPENDENCE

Legend:
- British Possessions
- Dutch Possessions
- French Possessions
- U.S.A. Possessions
- [1966] Date of Independence
- Black migrations from West Indies

MEXICO

BELIZE [1981]
1884 Indep. Br. colony
1973 'Belize

GUATEMALA [1838]
HONDURAS [1838]
EL SALVADOR [1838]
NICARAGUA [1838]
COSTA RICA [1838]

PANAMA [1903]
PANAMA CANAL ZONE to U.S.A. 1903-1979

COLOMBIA [1886]

VENEZUELA

GUYANA [1966]
Formerly British Guiana
Surinam (Dutch Guiana)
French Guiana

Florida

Bahamas [1973]

Cuba [1898]
Greater Antilles
Cayman Is.
Jamaica [1962]

Turks & Caicos

Rep. of Haiti [1804]
HISPANIOLA
Dominican Rep. [1865]
Santo Domingo

Puerto Rico 1898 to U.S.A.
U.S. Virgin Is. from 1916
Virgin Is.
Anguilla
St. Martin [1981]
Barbuda
Antigua
St. Kitts-Nevis [1983]
Montserrat
Guadeloupe
Dominica [1978]
Martinique
St. Lucia [1979]
Barbados [1966]
St. Vincent & the Grenadines [1979]
Grenada [1974]
Tobago [1962]
Trinidad [1962]

Aruba
Neth. Antilles
Curaçao
Bonaire

to New York
to Britain
to Britain
to France
to the Guianas

CARIBBEAN SEA

Projection: Bonne

West from Greenwich

1:25 000 000

200   0   200   400   600   800   1000 km

COPYRIGHT. GEORGE PHILIP & SON. LTD.

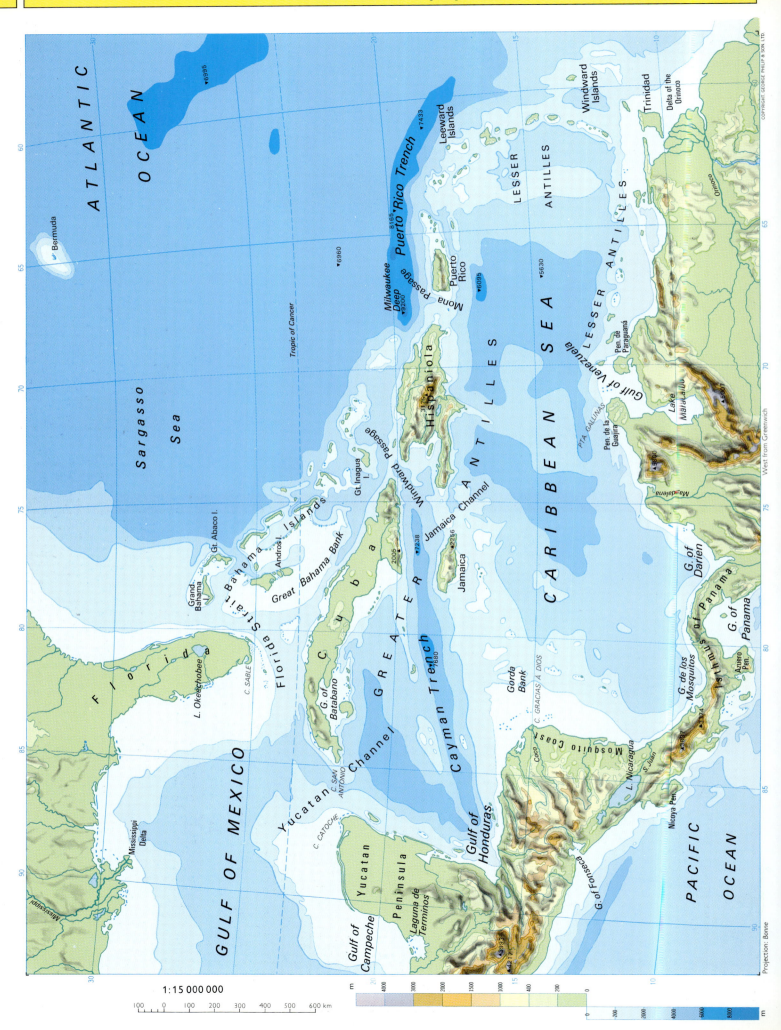

ATLANTIC OCEAN

Bermuda

Sargasso Sea

▼6995

Tropic of Cancer

▼6960

Puerto Rico Trench

▼7433

Leeward Islands

LESSER ANTILLES

Windward Islands

Trinidad

Delta of the Orinoco

Orinoco

Milwaukee Deep
9200 ▼
8165 ▼

Mona Passage

Puerto Rico

▼6095

▼5630

Gulf of Venezuela

LESSER ANTILLES

PTA. GALLINAS

Pen. de Paraguaná

Pen. de la Guajira

Lake Maracaibo

Hispaniola

Magdalena

▲5800

GREATER ANTILLES

Windward Passage

Gt. Inagua

Bahama Islands

Androz I.

Gt. Abaco I.

Grand Bahama

Bahama

Florida Strait

Great Bahama Bank

Cuba

Jamaica Channel

▲2256

Jamaica

▼7238
2005

Cayman Trench
7680 ▼

Gorda Bank

G. of Darien

G. of Panama

Isthmus of Panama

Azuero Pen.

FLORIDA

L. Okeechobee

C. SABLE

C. SAN ANTONIO

G. of Batabano

Yucatan Channel

Gulf of Honduras

C. GRACIAS A DIOS

Coco

Mosquito Coast

G. de los Mosquitos

▲3837

L. Nicaragua

S. Juan

Nicoya Pen.

G. of Fonseca

Mississippi Delta

Mississippi

GULF OF MEXICO

Yucatan Peninsula

Yucatan

C. CATOCHE

Laguna de Terminos

Gulf of Campeche

▲3993
4217

CARIBBEAN SEA

PACIFIC OCEAN

West from Greenwich

COPYRIGHT GEORGE PHILIP & SON, LTD.

Projection: Bonne

1:15 000 000

100   0   100   200   300   400   500   600 km

m								
4000	3000	2000	1500	1000	400	200	0	

| 0 | 200 | 2000 | 4000 | 6000 | 8000 | m |

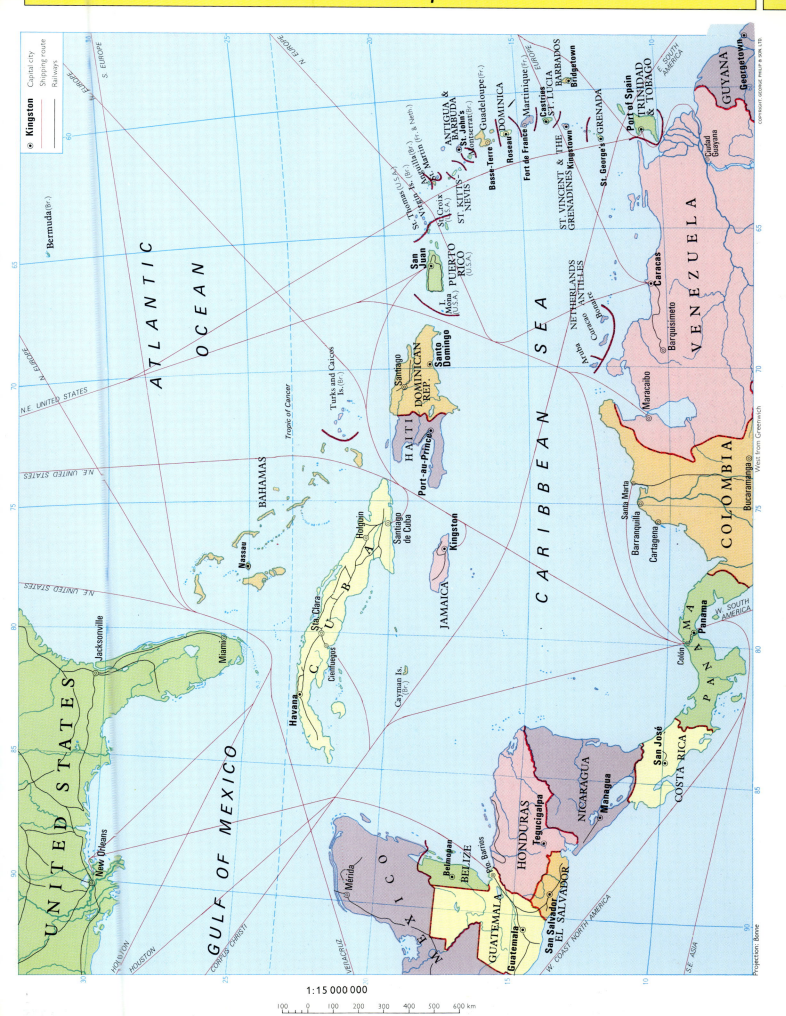

⊚ Kingston   Capital city
——   Shipping route
——   Railways

1:15 000 000

100   0   100   200   300   400   500   600 km

Projection: Bonne

COPYRIGHT. GEORGE PHILIP & SON LTD.

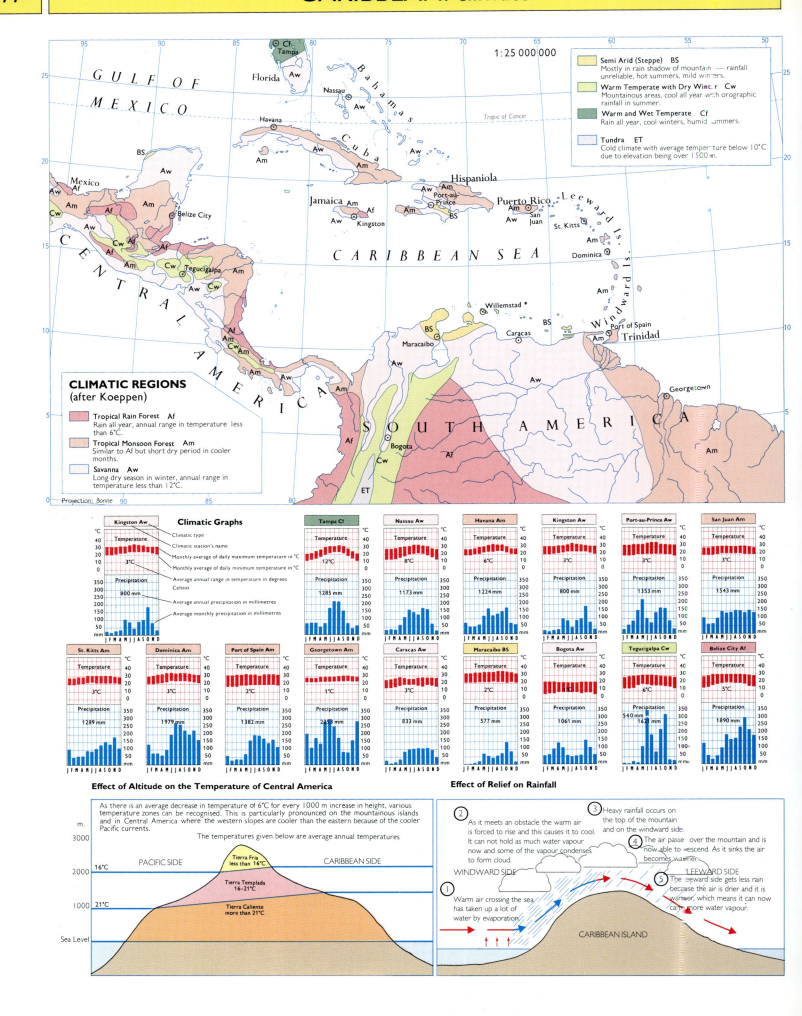

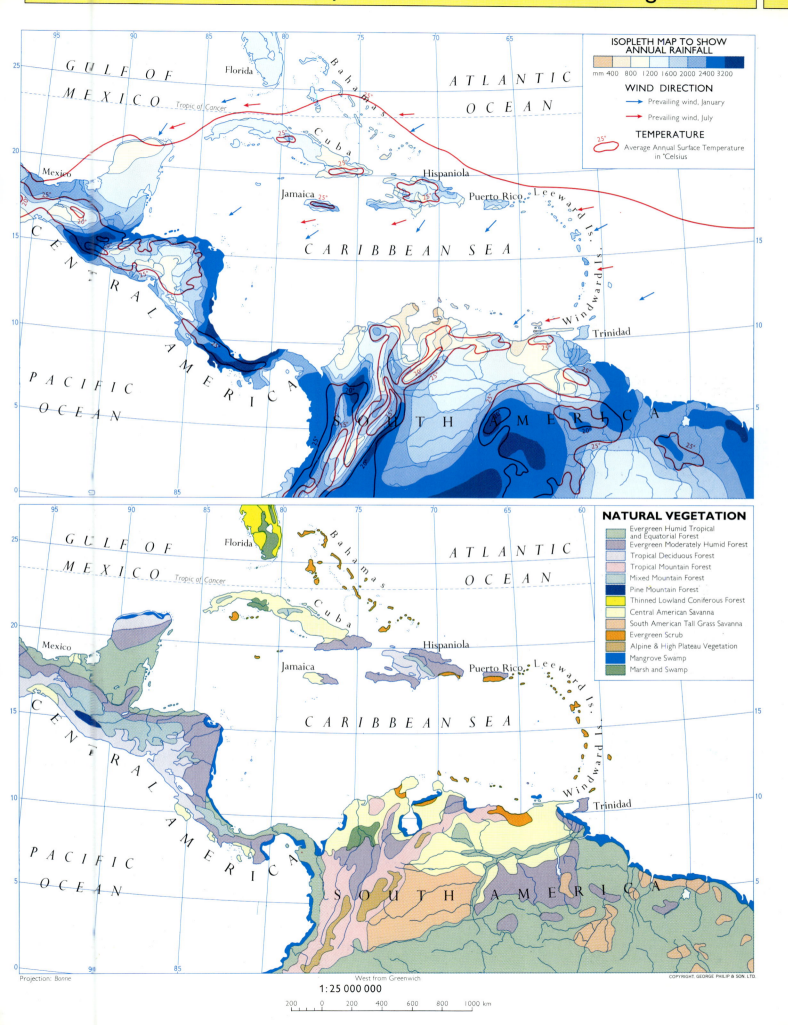

ISOPLETH MAP TO SHOW ANNUAL RAINFALL

mm 400 800 1200 1600 2000 2400 3200

WIND DIRECTION

→ Prevailing wind, January

→ Prevailing wind, July

TEMPERATURE

25° Average Annual Surface Temperature in °Celsius

NATURAL VEGETATION

- Evergreen Humid Tropical and Equatorial Forest
- Evergreen Moderately Humid Forest
- Tropical Deciduous Forest
- Tropical Mountain Forest
- Mixed Mountain Forest
- Pine Mountain Forest
- Thinned Lowland Coniferous Forest
- Central American Savanna
- South American Tall Grass Savanna
- Evergreen Scrub
- Alpine & High Plateau Vegetation
- Mangrove Swamp
- Marsh and Swamp

Projection: *Bonne*

West from Greenwich

COPYRIGHT. GEORGE PHILIP & SON. LTD.

1:25 000 000

200 0 200 400 600 800 1000 km

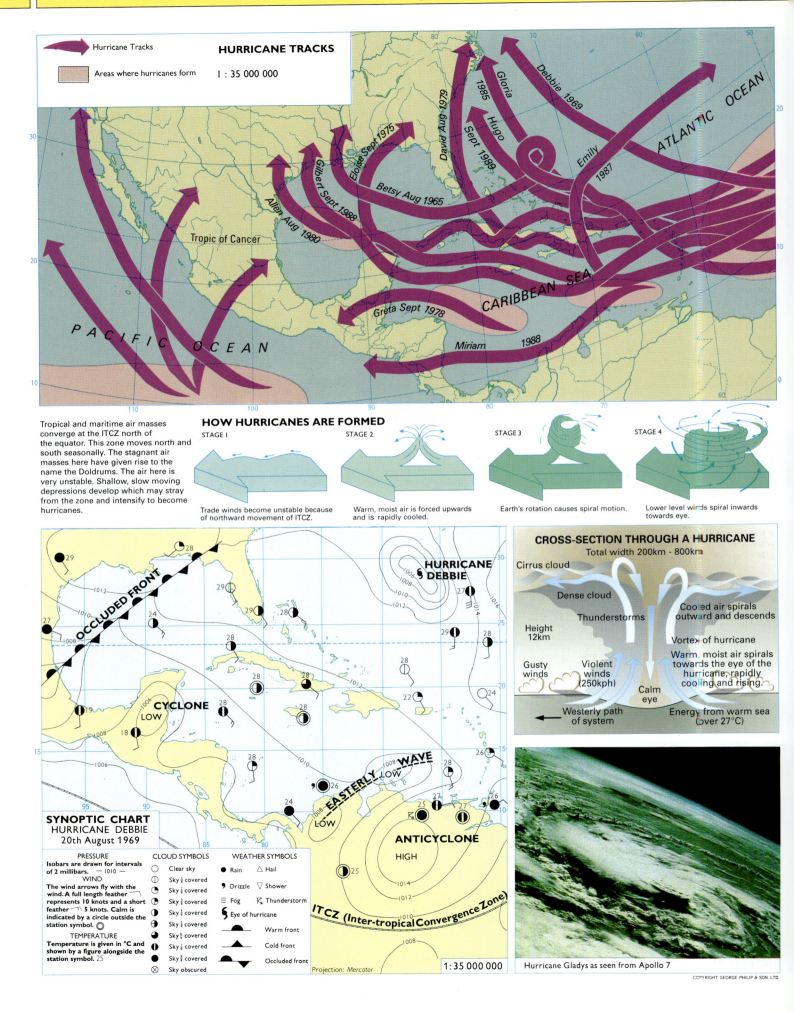

HURRICANE TRACKS

Hurricane Tracks

Areas where hurricanes form

1 : 35 000 000

Hurricane track labels: Debbie 1969, Gloria, 1985, David Aug 1979, Hugo Sept 1989, Emily 1987, Eloise Sept 1975, Gilbert Sept 1988, Betsy Aug 1965, Allen Aug 1980, Greta Sept 1978, Miriam 1988

ATLANTIC OCEAN

CARIBBEAN SEA

PACIFIC OCEAN

Tropic of Cancer

Tropical and maritime air masses converge at the ITCZ north of the equator. This zone moves north and south seasonally. The stagnant air masses here have given rise to the name the Doldrums. The air here is very unstable. Shallow, slow moving depressions develop which may stray from the zone and intensify to become hurricanes.

HOW HURRICANES ARE FORMED

STAGE 1 — Trade winds become unstable because of northward movement of ITCZ.

STAGE 2 — Warm, moist air is forced upwards and is rapidly cooled.

STAGE 3 — Earth's rotation causes spiral motion.

STAGE 4 — Lower level winds spiral inwards towards eye.

CROSS-SECTION THROUGH A HURRICANE
Total width 200km - 800km

Cirrus cloud

Dense cloud

Thunderstorms

Height 12km

Gusty winds

Violent winds (250kph)

Calm eye

Westerly path of system

Cooled air spirals outward and descends

Vortex of hurricane

Warm, moist air spirals towards the eye of the hurricane, rapidly cooling and rising.

Energy from warm sea (over 27°C)

HURRICANE DEBBIE

OCCLUDED FRONT

CYCLONE LOW

EASTERLY LOW WAVE

LOW

ANTICYCLONE HIGH

ITCZ (Inter-tropical Convergence Zone)

SYNOPTIC CHART
HURRICANE DEBBIE
20th August 1969

PRESSURE
Isobars are drawn for intervals of 2 millibars. — 1010 —

WIND
The wind arrows fly with the wind. A full length feather represents 10 knots and a short feather 5 knots. Calm is indicated by a circle outside the station symbol.

TEMPERATURE
Temperature is given in °C and shown by a figure alongside the station symbol. 25

CLOUD SYMBOLS
- Clear sky
- Sky ⅛ covered
- Sky ¼ covered
- Sky ⅜ covered
- Sky ½ covered
- Sky ⅝ covered
- Sky ¾ covered
- Sky ⅞ covered
- Sky ⁸⁄₈ covered
- Sky obscured

WEATHER SYMBOLS
- Rain
- Drizzle
- Fog
- Eye of hurricane
- Hail
- Shower
- Thunderstorm
- Warm front
- Cold front
- Occluded front

Projection: Mercator

1 : 35 000 000

Hurricane Gladys as seen from Apollo 7

STRUCTURE

Plate Tectonics

The Earth's crust is made up of a series of plates which float on a soft layer of the Earth's mantle and are moved about by convection currents within the mantle (see pages 54-55 for more detail).

Plate Tectonics in the Caribbean

(see cross section on the right)

The North American plate is diverging from the mid-Atlantic ridge and is moving towards the Caribbean plate at a rate of 30-40mm a year. The edge of the thinner North American plate is forced downwards under the less dense Caribbean plate at an angle of approximately 45°. As the North American plate descends it buckles and breaks and the rocks become hot enough to melt and are destroyed. This is called a *destructive boundary*. The destructive boundary to the east of the Caribbean is responsible for the Puerto Rico trench and the chain of volcanoes in the Windward Islands such as Mont Pelée and Soufrière (see diagram). The molten rocks along the destructive boundary are forced upwards through cracks at the edge of the Caribbean plate to pour out as lava from volcanoes

In the region of the Greater Antilles the plates move alongside each other. As a result the Cayman and Puerto Rican Trenches have been forced down, the Greater Antilles have been forced upwards and many faults have appeared. The boundary here is called a *conservative boundary*. No volcanic activity is present here, but sudden plate movements cause earthquakes.

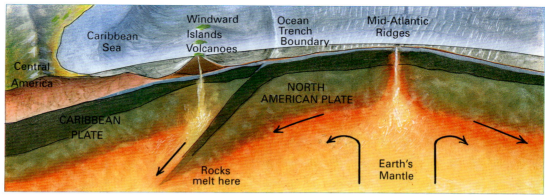

EARTHQUAKES

Earthquakes occur at depths varying from eight to thirty kilometres. Severe earthquakes cause extensive damage if they occur in populated areas, severing communications and destroying buildings. Most loss of life is due to secondary causes, such as falling masonry or fires.

SOUFRIÈRE HILLS, MONTSERRAT

In 1995, after almost 400 years of lying dormant, the Soufrière Hills volcano began a series of eruptions. Further eruptions in 1996 and 1997 left the south of the island uninhabitable and 5 000 people had to be evacuated to the northern zone.

MAJOR ACTIVE VOLCANOES IN THE CARIBBEAN

Name (latest activity)	Location (see map below)		Height (m)
Fuego (1991)	Guatemala	(1)	3836
Irazu (1991)	Costa Rica	(2)	3434
Poas (1991)	Costa Rica	(3)	2724
Pacaya (1991)	Guatemala	(4)	2546
Arenal (1991)	Costa Rica	(5)	1553
La Soufrière (1836)	Guadeloupe	(6)	1467
Mt. Pelée (1902)	Martinique	(7)	1397
Soufrière (1979)	St. Vincent	(8)	1234
Telica (1987)	Nicaragua	(9)	1039
Soufrière Hills (1995)	Montserrat	(10)	914

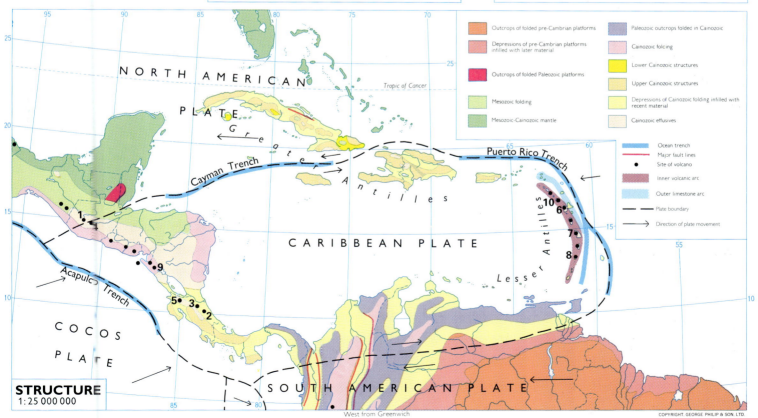

STRUCTURE

1:25 000 000

West from Greenwich

COPYRIGHT. GEORGE PHILIP & SON. LTD.

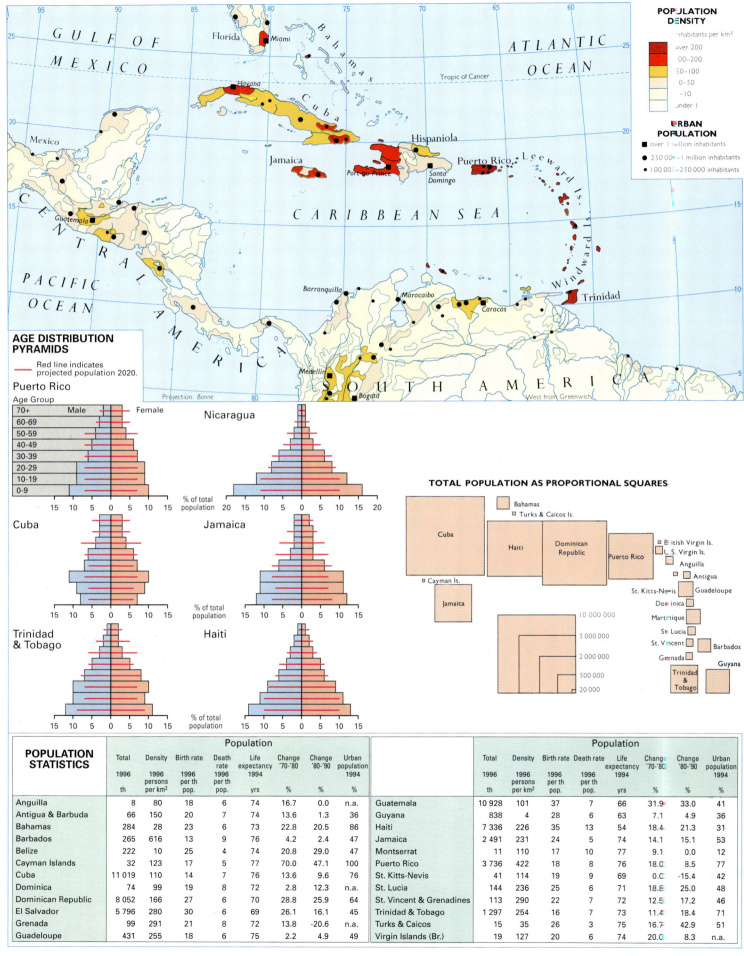

POPULATION DENSITY

inhabitants per km²

- over 200
- 100–200
- 50–100
- 0–50
- 1–10
- under 1

URBAN POPULATION

- over 1 million inhabitants
- 250 000–1 million inhabitants
- 100 000–250 000 inhabitants

AGE DISTRIBUTION PYRAMIDS

Red line indicates projected population 2020.

Puerto Rico

Nicaragua

Cuba

Jamaica

Trinidad & Tobago

Haiti

TOTAL POPULATION AS PROPORTIONAL SQUARES

Projection: Bonne

POPULATION STATISTICS

	Total	Density	Birth rate	Death rate	Life expectancy	Change '70-'80	Change '80-'90	Urban population
	1996	1996	1996	1996	1994			1994
	th	persons per km²	per th pop.	per th pop.	yrs	%	%	%
Anguilla	8	80	18	6	74	16.7	0.0	n.a.
Antigua & Barbuda	66	150	20	7	74	13.6	1.3	36
Bahamas	284	28	23	6	73	22.8	20.5	86
Barbados	265	616	13	9	76	4.2	2.4	47
Belize	222	10	25	4	74	20.8	29.0	47
Cayman Islands	32	123	17	5	77	70.0	47.1	100
Cuba	11 019	110	14	7	76	13.6	9.6	76
Dominica	74	99	19	8	72	2.8	12.3	n.a.
Dominican Republic	8 052	166	27	6	70	28.8	25.9	64
El Salvador	5 796	280	30	6	69	26.1	16.1	45
Grenada	99	291	21	8	72	13.8	-20.6	n.a.
Guadeloupe	431	255	18	6	75	2.2	4.9	49
Guatemala	10 928	101	37	7	66	31.9	33.0	41
Guyana	838	4	28	6	63	7.1	4.9	36
Haiti	7 336	226	35	13	54	18.4	21.3	31
Jamaica	2 491	231	24	5	74	14.1	15.1	53
Montserrat	11	110	17	10	77	9.1	0.0	12
Puerto Rico	3 736	422	18	8	76	18.0	8.5	77
St. Kitts-Nevis	41	114	19	9	69	0.0	-15.4	42
St. Lucia	144	236	25	6	71	18.8	25.0	48
St. Vincent & Grenadines	113	290	22	7	72	12.5	17.2	46
Trinidad & Tobago	1 297	254	16	7	73	11.4	18.4	71
Turks & Caicos	15	35	26	3	75	16.7	42.9	51
Virgin Islands (Br.)	19	127	20	6	74	20.0	8.3	n.a.

1 : 25 000 000

200   0   200   400   600   800   1000 km

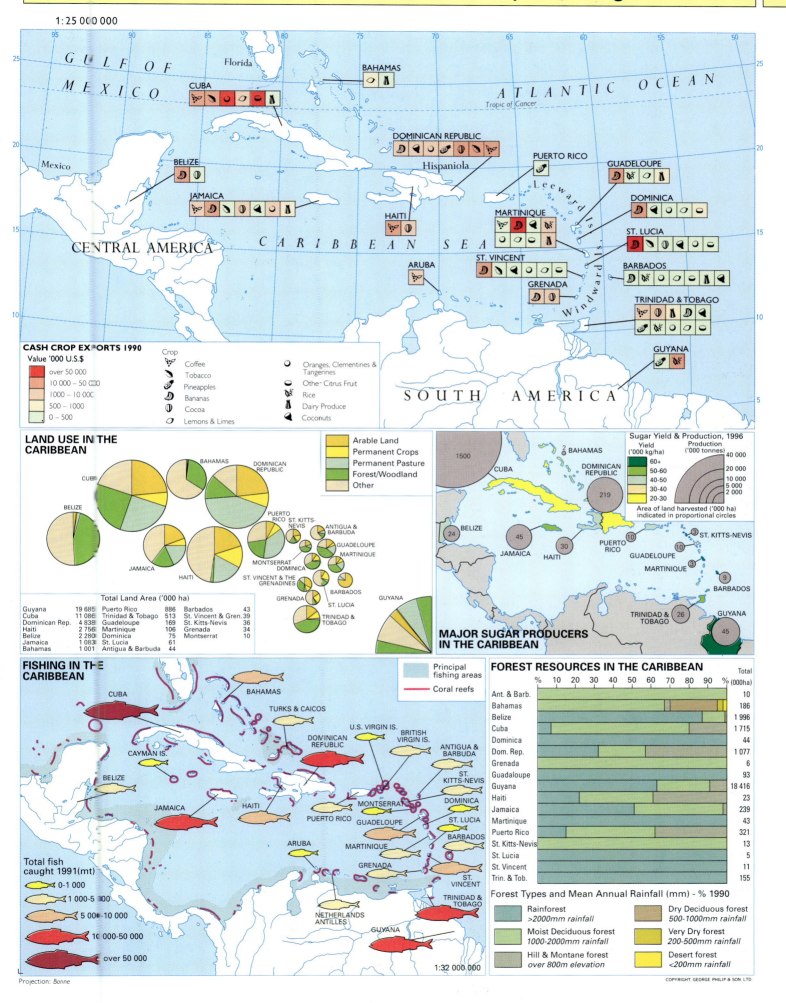

1 : 25 000 000

CASH CROP EXPORTS 1990

Value '000 U.S.$

over 50 000	
10 000 – 50 000	
1000 – 10 000	
500 – 1000	
0 – 500	

Crop

- Coffee
- Tobacco
- Pineapples
- Bananas
- Cocoa
- Lemons & Limes
- Oranges, Clementines & Tangerines
- Other Citrus Fruit
- Rice
- Dairy Produce
- Coconuts

LAND USE IN THE CARIBBEAN

- Arable Land
- Permanent Crops
- Permanent Pasture
- Forest/Woodland
- Other

Total Land Area ('000 ha)

Guyana	19 685	Puerto Rico	886	Barbados	43
Cuba	11 085	Trinidad & Tobago	513	St. Vincent & Gren.	39
Dominican Rep.	4 838	Guadeloupe	169	St. Kitts-Nevis	36
Haiti	2 756	Martinique	106	Grenada	34
Belize	2 280	Dominica	75	Montserrat	10
Jamaica	1 083	St. Lucia	61		
Bahamas	1 001	Antigua & Barbuda	44		

Sugar Yield & Production, 1996

Yield ('000 kg/ha)
- 60+
- 50-60
- 40-50
- 30-40
- 20-30

Production ('000 tonnes)
- 40 000
- 20 000
- 10 000
- 5 000
- 2 000

Area of land harvested ('000 ha) indicated in proportional circles

MAJOR SUGAR PRODUCERS IN THE CARIBBEAN

FISHING IN THE CARIBBEAN

- Principal fishing areas
- Coral reefs

Total fish caught 1991(mt)
- 0-1 000
- 1 000-5 000
- 5 000-10 000
- 10 000-50 000
- over 50 000

1 : 32 000 000

FOREST RESOURCES IN THE CARIBBEAN

	Total %	Total (000ha)
Ant. & Barb.		10
Bahamas		186
Belize		1 996
Cuba		1 715
Dominica		44
Dom. Rep.		1 077
Grenada		6
Guadeloupe		93
Guyana		18 416
Haiti		23
Jamaica		239
Martinique		43
Puerto Rico		321
St. Kitts-Nevis		13
St. Lucia		5
St. Vincent		11
Trin. & Tob.		155

Forest Types and Mean Annual Rainfall (mm) - % 1990

- Rainforest >2000mm rainfall
- Moist Deciduous forest 1000-2000mm rainfall
- Hill & Montane forest over 800m elevation
- Dry Deciduous forest 500-1000mm rainfall
- Very Dry forest 200-500mm rainfall
- Desert forest <200mm rainfall

Projection: Bonne

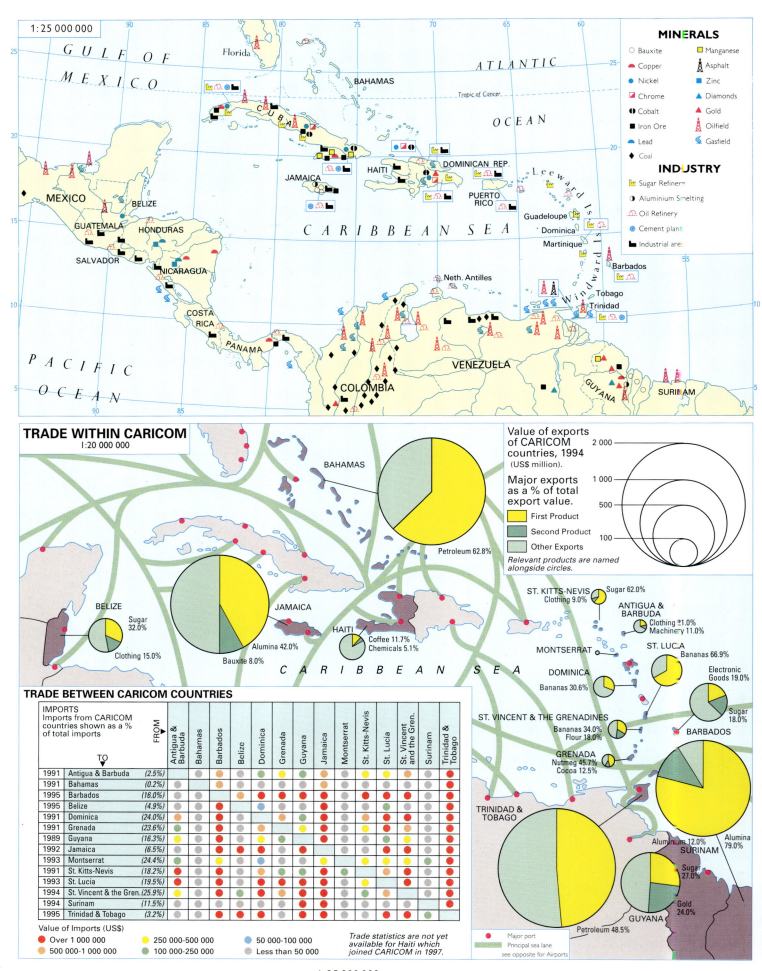

1:25 000 000

MINERALS

- ○ Bauxite
- ◆ Copper
- ● Nickel
- ◰ Chrome
- ◑ Cobalt
- ■ Iron Ore
- ◖ Lead
- ◆ Coal
- ▨ Manganese
- ⟋ Asphalt
- ■ Zinc
- ▲ Diamonds
- ▲ Gold
- ⛏ Oilfield
- ⬳ Gasfield

INDUSTRY

- ▨ Sugar Refinery
- ◖ Aluminium Smelting
- 🏭 Oil Refinery
- ● Cement plant
- ▬ Industrial area

TRADE WITHIN CARICOM

1:20 000 000

Value of exports of CARICOM countries, 1994 (US$ million).

Major exports as a % of total export value.

- First Product
- Second Product
- Other Exports

Relevant products are named alongside circles.

BAHAMAS
Petroleum 62.8%

BELIZE
Sugar 32.0%
Clothing 15.0%

JAMAICA
Alumina 42.0%
Bauxite 8.0%

HAITI
Coffee 11.7%
Chemicals 5.1%

ST. KITTS-NEVIS
Sugar 62.0%
Clothing 9.0%

ANTIGUA & BARBUDA
Clothing 21.0%
Machinery 11.0%

MONTSERRAT

DOMINICA
Bananas 30.6%

ST. LUCIA
Bananas 66.9%
Electronic Goods 19.0%
Sugar 18.0%

ST. VINCENT & THE GRENADINES
Bananas 34.0%
Flour 18.0%

GRENADA
Nutmeg 45.7%
Cocoa 12.5%

BARBADOS

TRINIDAD & TOBAGO
Petroleum 48.5%

SURINAM
Aluminium 12.0%
Alumina 79.0%

GUYANA
Sugar 27.0%
Gold 24.0%

TRADE BETWEEN CARICOM COUNTRIES

IMPORTS Imports from CARICOM countries shown as a % of total imports	FROM ▶ TO ▼	Antigua & Barbuda	Bahamas	Barbados	Belize	Dominica	Grenada	Guyana	Jamaica	Montserrat	St. Kitts-Nevis	St. Lucia	St. Vincent and the Gren.	Surinam	Trinidad & Tobago
1991	Antigua & Barbuda (2.5%)	⬤	⬤	🟠	⬤	⬤	🟢	⬤	🟡	⬤	⬤	⬤	🟡	⬤	🔴
1991	Bahamas (0.2%)	⬤		⬤	⬤	⬤	⬤	⬤	🟢	⬤	⬤	⬤	⬤	⬤	🔴
1995	Barbados (16.0%)	⬤	⬤		🟠	🔴	🔴	🔴	🔴	⬤	🟢	🔴	🔴	🔴	🔴
1995	Belize (4.9%)	⬤	⬤	🔴		⬤	⬤	🟢	🟢	⬤	⬤	🟢	⬤	⬤	🔴
1991	Dominica (24.0%)	🟠	⬤	🔴	⬤		🔴	🔴	🔴	⬤	⬤	🔴	🔴	⬤	🔴
1991	Grenada (23.6%)	⬤	⬤	🔴	⬤	🟡		🔴	🔴	⬤	⬤	🔴	🔴	⬤	🔴
1989	Guyana (16.3%)	⬤	⬤	🔴	⬤	⬤	⬤		🔴	⬤	⬤	⬤	⬤	⬤	🔴
1992	Jamaica (6.5%)	⬤	⬤	🔴	⬤	⬤	⬤	🔴		⬤	⬤	⬤	🟡	🟡	🔴
1993	Montserrat (24.4%)	🟢	⬤	🔴	⬤	🟢	🔴	🟡	🟡		🟡	🟡	🟡	⬤	🔴
1991	St. Kitts-Nevis (18.2%)	🔴	⬤	🔴	⬤	⬤	⬤	🔴	🔴	🟡		🟢	⬤	⬤	🔴
1993	St. Lucia (19.5%)	⬤	⬤	🔴	⬤	🔴	🔴	🔴	🔴	⬤	⬤		🔴	⬤	🔴
1994	St. Vincent & the Gren. (25.9%)	🟡	⬤	🔴	⬤	🔴	🔴	🔴	🔴	🟢	🟢	🔴		⬤	🔴
1994	Surinam (11.5%)	⬤	⬤	🔴	⬤	⬤	⬤	🔴	🟢	⬤	⬤	⬤	⬤		🔴
1995	Trinidad & Tobago (3.2%)	⬤	⬤	🔴	🔴	⬤	🔴	🔴	🔴	⬤	⬤	⬤	⬤	🟢	

Value of Imports (US$)

- 🔴 Over 1 000 000
- 🟠 500 000-1 000 000
- 🟡 250 000-500 000
- 🟢 100 000-250 000
- 🔵 50 000-100 000
- ⬤ Less than 50 000

Trade statistics are not yet available for Haiti which joined CARICOM in 1997.

- 🔴 Major port
- Principal sea lane see opposite for Airports

1:25 000 000

200   0   200   400   600   800   1000 km

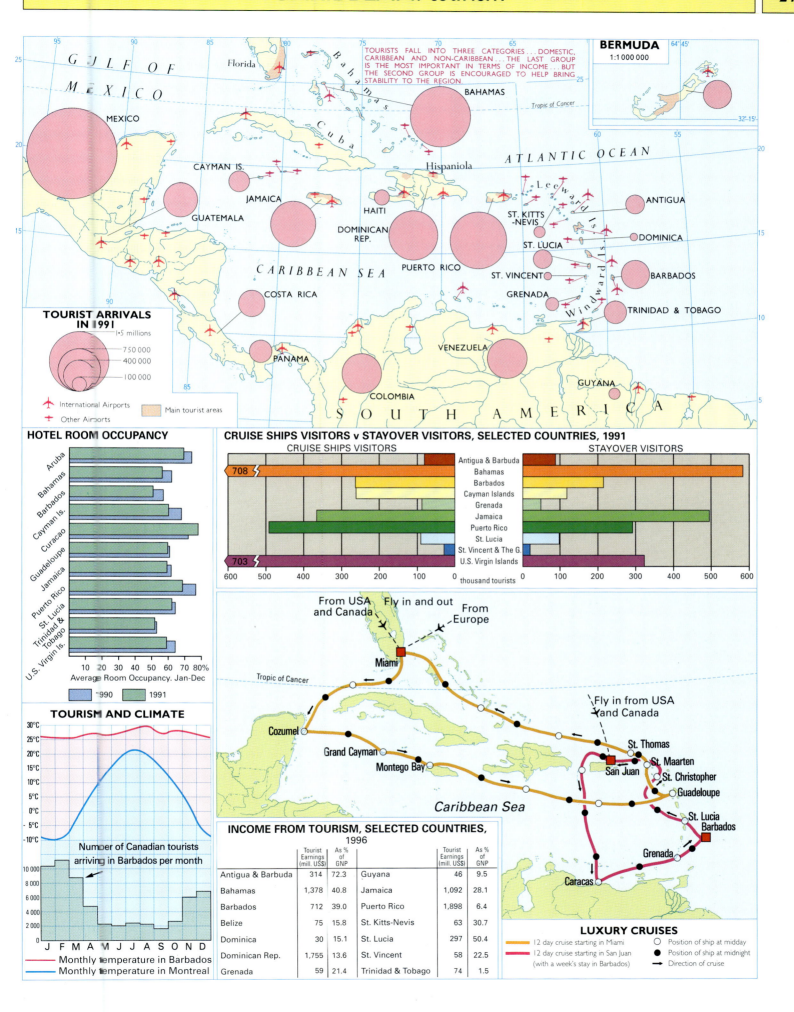

TOURISTS FALL INTO THREE CATEGORIES...DOMESTIC, CARIBBEAN AND NON-CARIBBEAN...THE LAST GROUP IS THE MOST IMPORTANT IN TERMS OF INCOME...BUT THE SECOND GROUP IS ENCOURAGED TO HELP BRING STABILITY TO THE REGION.

BERMUDA 1:1 000 000

TOURIST ARRIVALS IN 1991

- 1·5 millions
- 750 000
- 400 000
- 100 000

✈ International Airports — Main tourist areas
✛ Other Airports

HOTEL ROOM OCCUPANCY

Aruba, Bahamas, Barbados, Cayman Is., Curacao, Guadeloupe, Jamaica, Puerto Rico, St. Lucia, Trinidad & Tobago, U.S. Virgin Is.

10 20 30 40 50 60 70 80%
Average Room Occupancy. Jan-Dec

☐ 1990   ☐ 1991

TOURISM AND CLIMATE

30°C 25°C 20°C 15°C 10°C 5°C 0°C -5°C -10°C

Number of Canadian tourists arriving in Barbados per month

10 000 / 8 000 / 6 000 / 4 000 / 2 000 / 0
J F M A M J J A S O N D

— Monthly temperature in Barbados
— Monthly temperature in Montreal

CRUISE SHIPS VISITORS v STAYOVER VISITORS, SELECTED COUNTRIES, 1991

CRUISE SHIPS VISITORS — STAYOVER VISITORS

Antigua & Barbuda
Bahamas — 708
Barbados
Cayman Islands
Grenada
Jamaica
Puerto Rico
St. Lucia
St. Vincent & The G.
U.S. Virgin Islands — 703

600 500 400 300 200 100 0 | 100 200 300 400 500 600
thousand tourists

From USA and Canada — Fly in and out — From Europe

Miami, Cozumel, Grand Cayman, Montego Bay, Caracas, Grenada, Barbados, St. Lucia, Guadeloupe, St. Christopher, San Juan, St. Maarten, St. Thomas

Tropic of Cancer

Fly in from USA and Canada

Caribbean Sea

LUXURY CRUISES

— 12 day cruise starting in Miami
— 12 day cruise starting in San Juan (with a week's stay in Barbados)

○ Position of ship at midday
● Position of ship at midnight
→ Direction of cruise

INCOME FROM TOURISM, SELECTED COUNTRIES, 1996

	Tourist Earnings (mill. US$)	As % of GNP		Tourist Earnings (mill. US$)	As % of GNP
Antigua & Barbuda	314	72.3	Guyana	46	9.5
Bahamas	1,378	40.8	Jamaica	1,092	28.1
Barbados	712	39.0	Puerto Rico	1,898	6.4
Belize	75	15.8	St. Kitts-Nevis	63	30.7
Dominica	30	15.1	St. Lucia	297	50.4
Dominican Rep.	1,755	13.6	St. Vincent	58	22.5
Grenada	59	21.4	Trinidad & Tobago	74	1.5

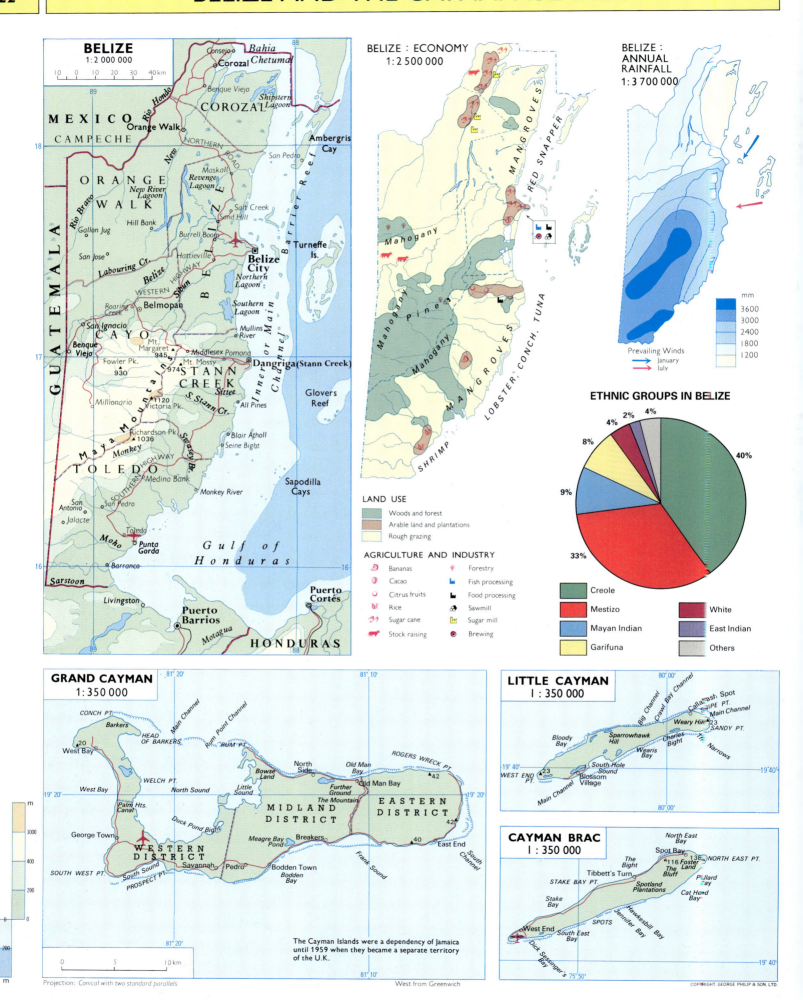

BELIZE
1:2 000 000

10 0 10 20 30 40km

MEXICO
CAMPECHE

Consejo
Corozal
Bahia Chetumal
Benque Viejo
Shipstern Lagoon
COROZAL
Orange Walk
Ambergris Cay
San Pedro
ORANGE WALK
Maskall
Revenge Lagoon
New River Lagoon
Rio Bravo
Gallon Jug
Hill Bank
Salt Creek
Sand Hill
Burrell Boom
Barrier Reef
San Jose
Labouring Cr.
Hattieville
Belize
Turneffe Is.
Belize City
Northern Lagoon
WESTERN HIGHWAY
Roaring Creek
Belmopan
Sibun
Southern Lagoon
San Ignacio
CAYO
Mt. Margaret 945
Middlesex Pomona
Mullins River
Benque Viejo
Fowler Pk. 930
Mt. Mossy 974
STANN CREEK
Dangriga (Stann Creek)
Sittee
1120
Millionario
Victoria Pk.
S. Stann Cr.
All Pines
Glovers Reef
Richardson Pk. 1036
Blair Atholl
Seine Bight
Monkey
TOLEDO
Medina Bank
Sapodilla Cays
San Antonio
San Pedro
Jalacte
Monkey River
Toledo
Moho
Punta Gorda
Gulf of Honduras
Barranco
Sarstoon
Livingston
Puerto Cortés
Puerto Barrios
Motagua
HONDURAS
GUATEMALA
Maya Mountains
Southern Highway
Swasey Br.
Innner or Main Channel

BELIZE : ECONOMY
1:2 500 000

MANGROVES
RED SNAPPER
Mahogany
Mahogany
Pine
Mahogany
MANGROVES
LOBSTER, CONCH, TUNA
SHRIMP

LAND USE
- Woods and forest
- Arable land and plantations
- Rough grazing

AGRICULTURE AND INDUSTRY
- Bananas
- Cacao
- Citrus fruits
- Rice
- Sugar cane
- Stock raising
- Forestry
- Fish processing
- Food processing
- Sawmill
- Sugar mill
- Brewing

BELIZE : ANNUAL RAINFALL
1:3 700 000

mm
3600
3000
2400
1800
1200

Prevailing Winds
→ January
→ July

ETHNIC GROUPS IN BELIZE

40%
33%
9%
8%
4%
2%
4%

- Creole
- Mestizo
- Mayan Indian
- Garifuna
- White
- East Indian
- Others

GRAND CAYMAN
1:350 000

CONCH PT.
Barkers
HEAD OF BARKERS
20
West Bay
West Bay
WELCH PT.
North Sound
Main Channel
Rum Point Channel
RUM PT.
Bowse Land
Little Sound
North Side
Old Man Bay
Further Ground
Old Man Bay
ROGERS WRECK PT.
42
MIDLAND DISTRICT
The Mountain
EASTERN DISTRICT
George Town
Palm Hts. Canal
Duck Pond Bight
42
WESTERN DISTRICT
Meagre Bay Pond
Breakers
40
East End
SOUTH WEST PT.
Savannah
Pedro
Bodden Town
Bodden Bay
Frank Sound
South Channel
PROSPECT PT.
South Sound

0 5 10 km

m
1000
400
200
0
200

LITTLE CAYMAN
1:350 000

Big Channel
Crawl Bay Channel
Calla?ash Spot
?IPE PT.
Main Channel
Bloody Bay
Sparrowhawk Hill
Weary Hill
23
SANDY PT.
Wearis Bay
Charles Bight
Narrows
WEST END PT.
23
South Hole Sound
Blossom Village
Main Channel

CAYMAN BRAC
1:350 000

North East Bay
Spot Bay
The Bight
13E
NORTH EAST PT.
116 Foster Land
Tibbett's Turn
The Bluff
Pollard Bay
STAKE BAY PT.
Spotland Plantations
Cat Head Bay
Stake Bay
Hawkesbill Bay
Jennifer Bay
West End
SPOTS
South East Bay
Dick Sessinger's Bay
75° 50'

The Cayman Islands were a dependency of Jamaica until 1959 when they became a separate territory of the U.K.

Projection: Conical with two standard parallels

West from Greenwich

COPYRIGHT. GEORGE PHILIP & SON. LTD.

GRAND BAHAMA ISLAND
1:1 000 000
10 | 10 | 20 km

BERMUDA
1:375 000
0 | 10 km

NEW PROVIDENCE I.
1:375 000
0 | 4 | 8 km

BAHAMA ISLANDS
1:3 500 000
20 | 0 | 20 | 40 | 60 | 80 | 100 | 120 km

TURKS AND CAICOS ISLAND
1:2 000 000
10 | 0 | 10 | 20 | 30 | 40 | 50 km

Projection: Bonne

West from Greenwich

COPYRIGHT GEORGE PHILIP & SON LTD.

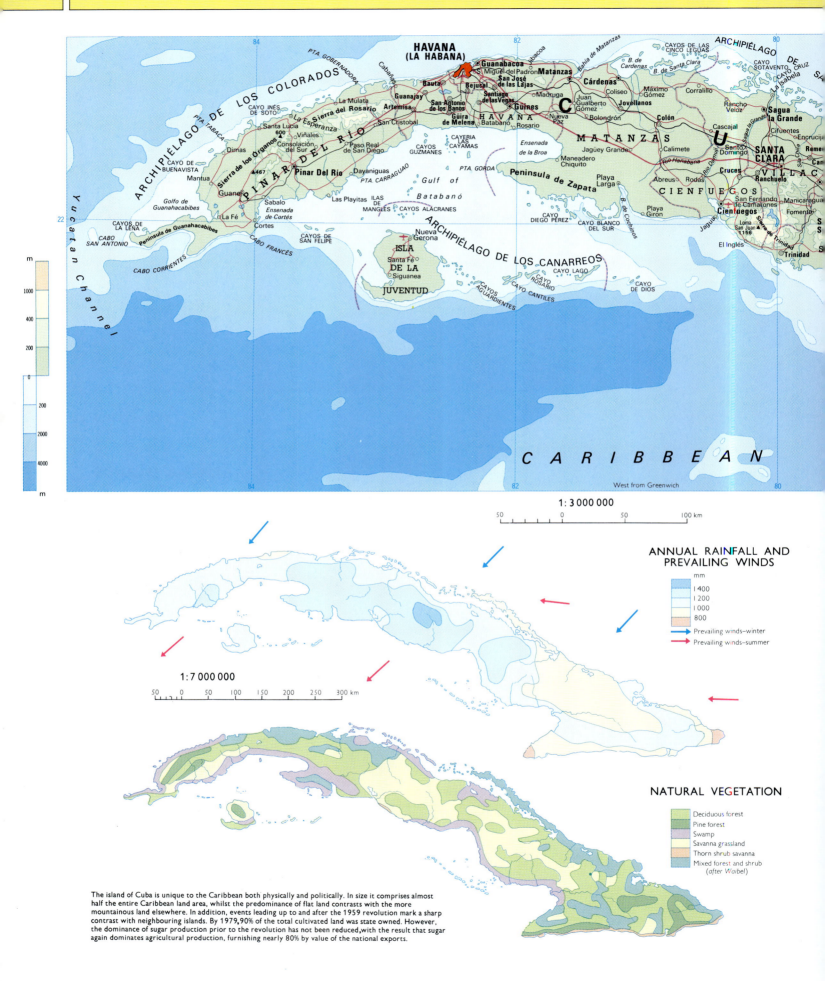

1:3 000 000

50 | 0 | 50 | 100 km

ANNUAL RAINFALL AND PREVAILING WINDS

mm
- 1 400
- 1 200
- 1 000
- 800

→ Prevailing winds–winter
→ Prevailing winds–summer

1:7 000 000

50 | 0 | 50 | 100 | 150 | 200 | 250 | 300 km

NATURAL VEGETATION

- Deciduous forest
- Pine forest
- Swamp
- Savanna grassland
- Thorn shrub savanna
- Mixed forest and shrub
  (after Waibel)

The island of Cuba is unique to the Caribbean both physically and politically. In size it comprises almost half the entire Caribbean land area, whilst the predominance of flat land contrasts with the more mountainous land elsewhere. In addition, events leading up to and after the 1959 revolution mark a sharp contrast with neighbouring islands. By 1979, 90% of the total cultivated land was state owned. However, the dominance of sugar production prior to the revolution has not been reduced, with the result that sugar again dominates agricultural production, furnishing nearly 80% by value of the national exports.

78 76 74

LONG I.

BAHAMAS

CROOKED I.

RAGGED I. RANGE

ACKLINS I.

Great Bahama Bank

CAYO FRAGOSO

Old Bahama Channel

22

CAYOS DE LA HERRADURA

Caibarién

ARCHIPIÉLAGO DE CAMAGÜEY

Yaguajay

Mayalagua

Chambas

CAYO COCO

Central Máximo Gómez

Laguna de Leche

CAYO ROMANO

B

SANCTI

Morón

Marroqui

Piña

Cunagua

CIEGO

Jatibonico

SPIRITUS

Esmeralda

CAYO GUAJABA

DE ÁVILA

A

Ciego de Ávila

Gaspar

Piedrecitas

309

Sola

CAYO SABINAL

PTA. PRÁCTICOS

El Jibaro

Júcaro

Florida

Lugareño

Minas

Nuevitas

Puerto Manati

20

CAYOS ANA MARIA

Gulf of Ana Maria

Playa Florida

R. Saramaguacán

Santa Lucia

CAMAGÜEY

Puerto Padre

CAMAGÜEY

Vertientes

Sibanicú

Chaparra

Gibara

Santa Lucia

CABO LUCRECIA

Banes

PTA. MACURIJES

Marti

LAS

Guáimaro

Victoria de las Tunas

Auras

CAYOS DE LAS DOCE LEGUAS

Río San Pedro

Cuatro Compañeros

TUNAS

Jobabo

San Lorenzo

Omaja

HOLGUÍN

Samá

Antilla

B. de Nipe

PTA. CABAÑAS

LABERINTO DE LAS DOCE LEGUAS

Santa Cruz del Sur

Guayabal

Guamo Embarcadero

Río Cauto

Babiney

Cueto

995

Mayari

Sierra del Cristal

1231

Sagua de Tánamo

Cuchillasda Toa

1139

PTA. GUARICO

JARDINES DE LA REINA

CAYOS PINGUES

CAYOS MORDAZO

Gulf of

Bayamo

Jiguani

Alto Cedro

Sierra de Nipe

Mayari Arriba

Sierra de Sagua Baracoa

Baracoa

SEA

Guacanayabo

Manzanillo

Veguitas

Contramaestre

SANTIAGO

Tiguabos

GUANTÁNAMO

Maisi

PTA. MAISI

GRANMA

Campechuela

Palma Soriano

La Maya

GUANTÁNAMO

1181

Media Luna

Sierra Maestra

El Cristo

Los Caños

Playitas

PTA. CALETA

Niquero

Pico Turquino 2005

San Luis DE CUBA

1125

1250

San Antonio del Sur

20

CABO CRUZ

319

Portillo

Turquino

Aserradero

1250

Caimanera

GUANTANAMO BAY (USA Naval Station)

Windward Passage

SANTIAGO DE CUBA

Juraguá

74

76

LAND USE, MINERALS AND INDUSTRY

Havana

Matanzas

Sagua la Grande

Santa Clara

Cienfuegos

Camagüey

Nuevitas

Guayabal

Santiago de Cuba

Arable	
Plantations	
Wood and forest	
Non productive land	
Permanent pastures	

Coffee	Nickel
Sugar cane	Iron
Rice	Manganese
Tobacco	Cobalt
Cattle	Sugar exporting port
Citrus fruit	Textiles
Fishing	Engineering
Forestry	Tobacco manufacturing
	Oil refinery
	Sugar processing
	Cement
	Food processing
	Chemicals
	Copper
	Chrome
	Gold

POPULATION DENSITY

Havana

Matanzas

Pinar Del Rio

Santa Clara

Cienfuegos

Camagüey

Victoria

Holguin

Bayamo

Guantánamo

Santiago de Cuba

Persons per km²

over 200	
100–200	
50–100	
20–50	
10–20	
under 10	

■ Over 500 000 inhabitants

● 100 000–500 000 inhabitants

• 10 000–100 000 inhabitants

1:7 000 000

0 50 100 150 200 250 300 km

C A R I B B

C A R I B B E A

NEW BANK

BLOSSOM
BANK

KINGSTON
BANK

WALTON
BANK

SUNBURY
BANK

Montego Bay area and towns:

Mahoe Bay
Lucea Harbour
NORTH-WEST PT.
(PEDRO PT.)
Davis' Cove
Green Island Harbour
Orange Bay
N. NEGRIL PT.
Long Bay
S. NEGRIL PT.
The Great Morass
Negril
Sheffield
Little London
SOUTH-WEST PT.
New Broughton
Hopewell
Mosquito Cove
Sandy Bay
Reading
Lucea
Jericho
Maryland
HANOVER
Green Island
Clifton
Cabarita
Frome
Grange Hill
280
CORNWALL
Petersfield
WESTMORELAND
Whithorn
Bethal Town
Darliston
Leamington
Bluefields Bay
BELMONT PT.
Bluefields
New Hope
Crab Pond Bay
Middle Quarters
Scott's Cove
Crawford
LUANA PT.
Malcolm Bay
Black River Bay
PAROTTEE PT.
Williamsfield
Starve Gut Bay
Treasure Beach
GT. PEDRO BLUFF
Pedro Plains
Top Hill
Junction

Montego Bay
MONTEGO BAY
Chatham
Queen of Spain's Valley
Adelphi
Wakefield
Johns Hall
Anchovy
ST. JAMES
Montpelier
Great Valley
Miles Town
545
Cambridge
Catadupa
The Cockpit Country
Quick Step
Elderslie
Jointwood
Aberdeen
Ipswich
Newmarket
699 Blackwood Hill
Maggotty
Siloah
Newton
St. Elizabeth
Lacovia
The Great Morass
Black River
Santa Cruz
Wilton
Braes River
Santa Cruz Mts.
Malvern
723
Malvern
Myersville
Nain
Cross Keys
Bull Savanna
Alligator Pond
Port Kaiser
Alligator Pond Bay
Alligator Reef

Falmouth
Half Moon
MOUNTAIN SPRING PT.
Burwood
Silver Sands
Rio Bueno Harbour
Runaway Bay
Discovery Bay
St. An
Sal
Duncans
Rio Bueno
Jackson Town
Browns Town
Bamboo
Clark's Town
Duanvale
Stewart Town
Gibraltar
St. D'Acre
TRELAWNY
Maroon Town
Spring Garden
Ulster Spring
Albert Town
DRY
Alexandria
Harbour
Warsop
Cockpit
746
Wait-a-Bit
Mountains
Craig Head
Mt. Denham
985
Coleyville
M
Milton
Christiana
Tweedside
Balaclava
St. Pauls
Spaldings
Frankfield
Huntley
960
Walderston
Williamsfield
Rio Minho
Don Figuerero Mts.
Mocho Mts.
Chapelton
Gutters
Mandeville
Porus
Brixton
MANCHESTER
CLARE
Old England
Newport
Osborne Store
Fo
Pat
Blenheim
Woodstock
Pratville
Kemps Hill
Long Ba
Springfield
Race Course
Macarry Bay
Alley
Rocky Point
Carlisle Bay

m
2000
1500
1000
400
200
0
200
2000
4000
m

Projection: Conical with two standard parallels

17° 30'

18°

18° 30'

78°

77° 30'

CARIBBEAN SEA

EAN SEA

N SEA

18°30'

18°

17°30'

77°

76°30'

Ocho Rios
Britonville
remont
Golden Grove
Alderton
Bensonton
Kellits
ofts
ill
Rock River
las Gate
ON
MAY PEN
Old Harbour
Freetown
P. Esquivel
ayes
Lionel Town
Mitchell Town
West Harbour

Alterry
Roxborough
Turtle Beach
ay

Salt Gut
Oracabessa
Gayle
Walkers Wood
Moneague
Guys Hill
ST. MARY
Highgate
Richmond

GALINA PT.
Galina
Port Maria
Salt Bay
Hampstead

DON CHRISTOPHERS POINT
Annotto Bay
PALMETTO PT.
SAVANNA PT.
Orange Bay
Hope Bay
Blue Lagoon
NORTHEAST PT.
Boston Bay

White
Rio Nuevo
Water Water

MIDDLESEX

Mount Diablo
Ewarton
Linstead
Lluidas Vale
Point Hill
ST. CATHERINE
Bartons
Friendship
Spanish Town
Spring Village
Portmore
Naggo Head
Old Harbour Bay
Galleon Hbr
Little Goat I.
Gt. Goat I.
Salt River B.
Salt River

Rio D'Oro
Castleton
Enfield
Buff Bay
Orange Bay
St. Margarets Bay
Chepstow

PORTLAND
Port Antonio
Fellowship
Long Bay
Windsor Forest
Robins Bay
Manchioneal
Williamsfield
Hectors River

Glengoffe
Parks Road
Bog Walk
Rio Cobre
Glengoffe
ST. ANDREW
▲777
Stony Hill
Constant Spring
Half Way Tree
Lower St. Andrew
Ferry
August Town

Wakefield
Newcastle
1540
St. Catherine's Pk.
SURREY
Gordon Town
The Blue Mountains
R2256R
▲Blue Mountain Pk.
1336
Macca Sucker ▲
Moore Town
John Crow Mts.

KINGSTON
Kingston Harbour
Port Royal
The Palisadoes
Fort Clarence
Gt. Salt Pond
South East Cay
South Cay
Grants Pen
Cow Bay
Poor Mans Corner

Cedar Valley
010
Bull Bay
Easington
Heartease
Yallahs
The Salt Ponds
Bailey's Beach

Trinity Ville
Plantam Garden
Seaforth
Bath
ST. THOMAS
Morant Bay
Prospect Retreat
Port Morant
Bowden

Shell Bay
Holland Bay
Golden Grove
The Gt. Morass
MORANT PT.
Folly Bay

NORSEMAN BANK

DINGLE BANK

Hellshire Hills
Long Bay
Coquar Bay
Manatee Bay
POLINK PT.
Wreck Reef

Portland Bight
Portland Cay
PORTLAND PT.

CALIFORNIA BANK

MACKEREL BANK

1:600 000

See page 41 for large scale map of Kingston

5   0   5   10   15   20   25 km

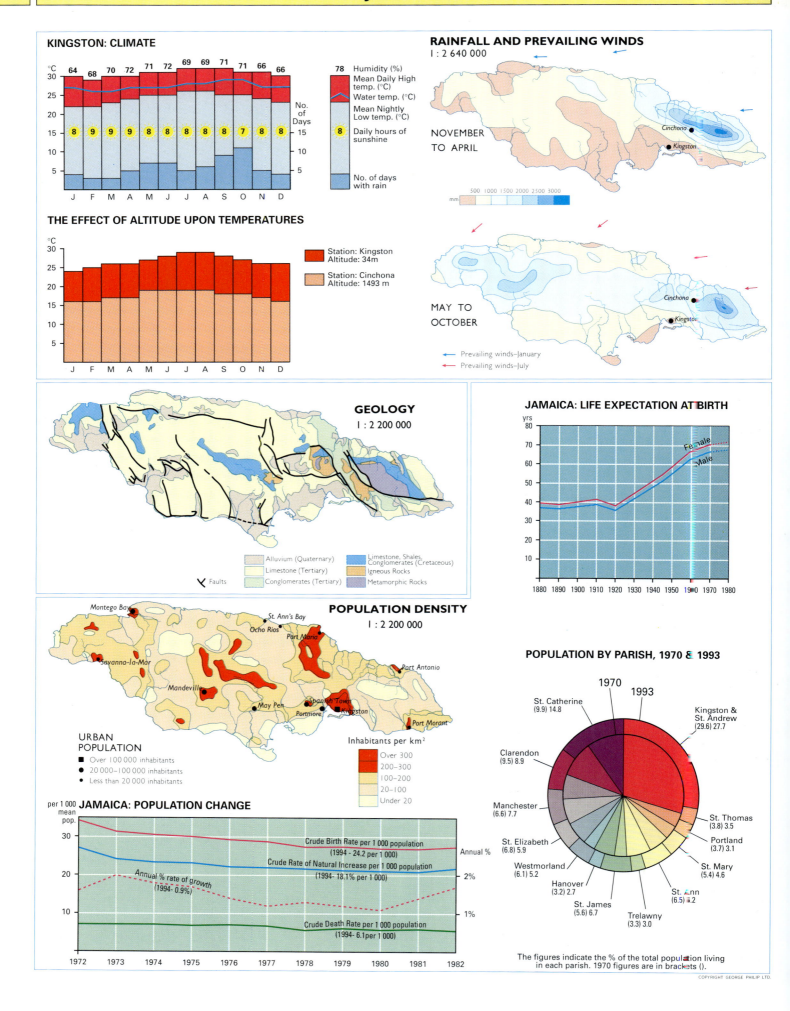

KINGSTON: CLIMATE

°C
30 · 25 · 20 · 15 · 10 · 5

64 68 70 72 71 72 69 69 71 71 66 66

8 9 9 9 8 8 8 8 8 7 8 8

No. of Days
15 · 10 · 5

J F M A M J J A S O N D

78 Humidity (%)
Mean Daily High temp. (°C)
Water temp. (°C)
Mean Nightly Low temp. (°C)
Daily hours of sunshine
No. of days with rain

THE EFFECT OF ALTITUDE UPON TEMPERATURES

°C
30 · 25 · 20 · 15 · 10 · 5

J F M A M J J A S O N D

Station: Kingston
Altitude: 34m

Station: Cinchona
Altitude: 1493 m

RAINFALL AND PREVAILING WINDS
1 : 2 640 000

NOVEMBER TO APRIL

Cinchona
Kingston

mm 500 1000 1500 2000 2500 3000

MAY TO OCTOBER

Cinchona
Kingston

→ Prevailing winds–January
→ Prevailing winds–July

GEOLOGY
1 : 2 200 000

Alluvium (Quaternary)
Limestone (Tertiary)
Conglomerates (Tertiary)
Limestone, Shales, Conglomerates (Cretaceous)
Igneous Rocks
Metamorphic Rocks
✗ Faults

JAMAICA: LIFE EXPECTATION AT BIRTH

yrs
80 · 70 · 60 · 50 · 40 · 30 · 20 · 10

Female
Male

1880 1890 1900 1910 1920 1930 1940 1950 1960 1970 1980

POPULATION DENSITY
1 : 2 200 000

Montego Bay
St. Ann's Bay
Ocho Rios
Port Maria
Savanna-la-Mar
Port Antonio
Mandeville
May Pen
Spanish Town
Portmore
Kingston
Port Morant

URBAN POPULATION
■ Over 100 000 inhabitants
● 20 000–100 000 inhabitants
· Less than 20 000 inhabitants

Inhabitants per km²
Over 300
200–300
100–200
20–100
Under 20

POPULATION BY PARISH, 1970 & 1993

1970
1993

St. Catherine (9.9) 14.8
Clarendon (9.5) 8.9
Manchester (6.6) 7.7
St. Elizabeth (6.8) 5.9
Westmorland (6.1) 5.2
Hanover (3.2) 2.7
St. James (5.6) 6.7
Trelawny (3.3) 3.0
St. Ann (6.5) 6.2
St. Mary (5.4) 4.6
Portland (3.7) 3.1
St. Thomas (3.8) 3.5
Kingston & St. Andrew (29.6) 27.7

The figures indicate the % of the total population living in each parish. 1970 figures are in brackets ().

JAMAICA: POPULATION CHANGE

per 1 000 mean pop.
30 · 20 · 10

Crude Birth Rate per 1 000 population (1994 - 24.2 per 1 000)
Crude Rate of Natural Increase per 1 000 population (1994 - 18.1% per 1 000)
Annual % rate of growth (1994- 0.9%)
Crude Death Rate per 1 000 population (1994 - 6.1per 1 000)

Annual %
2%
1%

1972 1973 1974 1975 1976 1977 1978 1979 1980 1981 1982

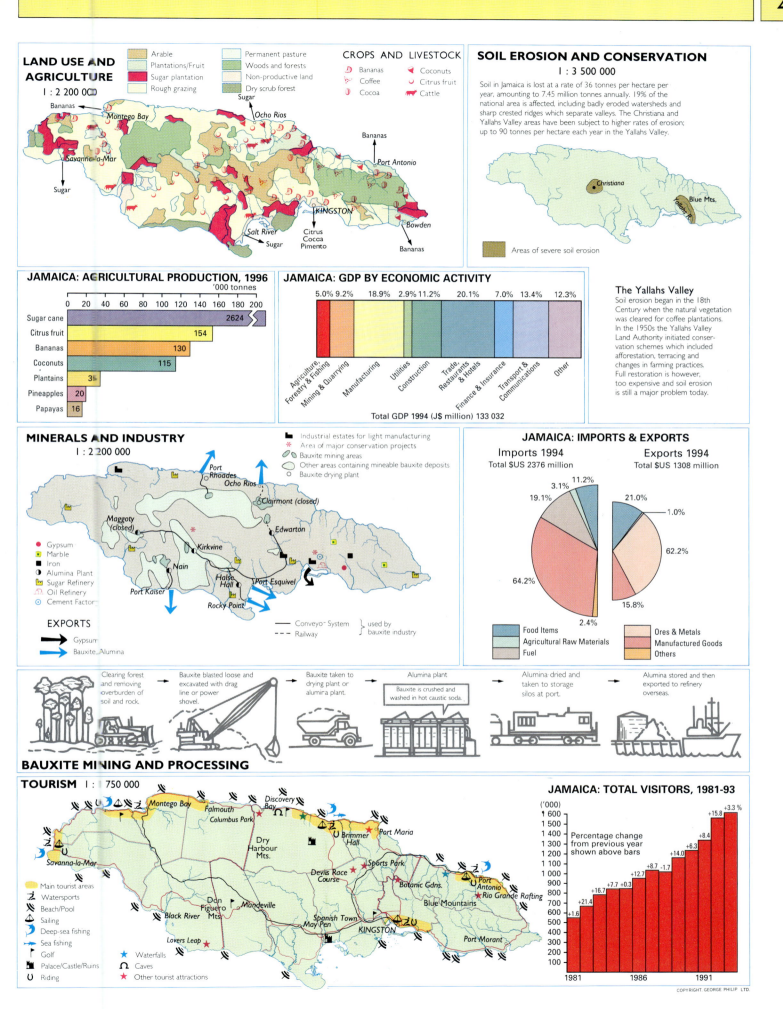

LAND USE AND AGRICULTURE
1 : 2 200 000

Legend:
- Arable
- Plantations/Fruit
- Sugar plantation
- Rough grazing
- Permanent pasture
- Woods and forests
- Non-productive land
- Dry scrub forest

CROPS AND LIVESTOCK
- Bananas
- Coffee
- Cocoa
- Coconuts
- Citrus fruit
- Cattle

Map labels: Bananas, Montego Bay, Savanna-la-Mar, Sugar, Sugar, Ocho Rios, Bananas, Port Antonio, KINGSTON, Salt River, Sugar, Citrus Cocoa Pimento, Bowden, Bananas

SOIL EROSION AND CONSERVATION
1 : 3 500 000

Soil in Jamaica is lost at a rate of 36 tonnes per hectare per year, amounting to 7.45 million tonnes annually. 19% of the national area is affected, including badly eroded watersheds and sharp crested ridges which separate valleys. The Christiana and Yallahs Valley areas have been subject to higher rates of erosion; up to 90 tonnes per hectare each year in the Yallahs Valley.

Map labels: Christiana, Blue Mts., Yallahs R.

- Areas of severe soil erosion

The Yallahs Valley
Soil erosion began in the 18th Century when the natural vegetation was cleared for coffee plantations. In the 1950s the Yallahs Valley Land Authority initiated conservation schemes which included afforestation, terracing and changes in farming practices. Full restoration is however, too expensive and soil erosion is still a major problem today.

JAMAICA: AGRICULTURAL PRODUCTION, 1996
'000 tonnes

Sugar cane	2624
Citrus fruit	154
Bananas	130
Coconuts	115
Plantains	35
Pineapples	20
Papayas	16

JAMAICA: GDP BY ECONOMIC ACTIVITY

Activity	%
Agriculture, Forestry & Fishing	5.0%
Mining & Quarrying	9.2%
Manufacturing	18.9%
Utilities	2.9%
Construction	11.2%
Trade, Restaurants & Hotels	20.1%
Finance & Insurance	7.0%
Transport & Communications	13.4%
Other	12.3%

Total GDP 1994 (J$ million) 133 032

MINERALS AND INDUSTRY
1 : 2 200 000

- Industrial estates for light manufacturing
- Area of major conservation projects
- Bauxite mining areas
- Other areas containing mineable bauxite deposits
- Bauxite drying plant

- Gypsum
- Marble
- Iron
- Alumina Plant
- Sugar Refinery
- Oil Refinery
- Cement Factory

EXPORTS
- Gypsum
- Bauxite, Alumina

- Conveyor System
- Railway
} used by bauxite industry

Map labels: Port Rhoades, Ocho Rios, Clairmont (closed), Maggoty (closed), Edwarton, Kirkvine, Nain, Halse Hall, Port Esquivel, Port Kaiser, Rocky Point

JAMAICA: IMPORTS & EXPORTS

Imports 1994
Total $US 2376 million
- 11.2%
- 3.1%
- 19.1%
- 64.2%
- 2.4%

Exports 1994
Total $US 1308 million
- 21.0%
- 1.0%
- 62.2%
- 15.8%

Legend:
- Food Items
- Agricultural Raw Materials
- Fuel
- Ores & Metals
- Manufactured Goods
- Others

BAUXITE MINING AND PROCESSING

1. Clearing forest and removing overburden of soil and rock.
2. Bauxite blasted loose and excavated with drag line or power shovel.
3. Bauxite taken to drying plant or alumina plant.
4. Alumina plant. Bauxite is crushed and washed in hot caustic soda.
5. Alumina dried and taken to storage silos at port.
6. Alumina stored and then exported to refinery overseas.

TOURISM
1 : 1 750 000

Legend:
- Main tourist areas
- Watersports
- Beach/Pool
- Sailing
- Deep-sea fishing
- Sea fishing
- Golf
- Palace/Castle/Ruins
- Riding
- Waterfalls
- Caves
- Other tourist attractions

Map labels: Montego Bay, Falmouth, Columbus Park, Discovery Bay, Port Maria, Dry Harbour Mts., Brimmer Hall, Sports Park, Devils Race Course, Botanic Gdns., Port Antonio, Rio Grande Rafting, Savanna-la-Mar, Black River, Don Figuero Mts., Mandeville, Blue Mountains, Spanish Town, May Pen, KINGSTON, Lovers Leap, Port Morant

JAMAICA: TOTAL VISITORS, 1981-93
('000)

Percentage change from previous year shown above bars

Percentage labels: +1.6, +21.4, +16.7, +7.7, +0.3, +8.7, +12.7, -1.7, +14.0, +6.3, +8.4, +15.8, +3.3 %

Years: 1981, 1986, 1991

COPYRIGHT GEORGE PHILIP LTD.

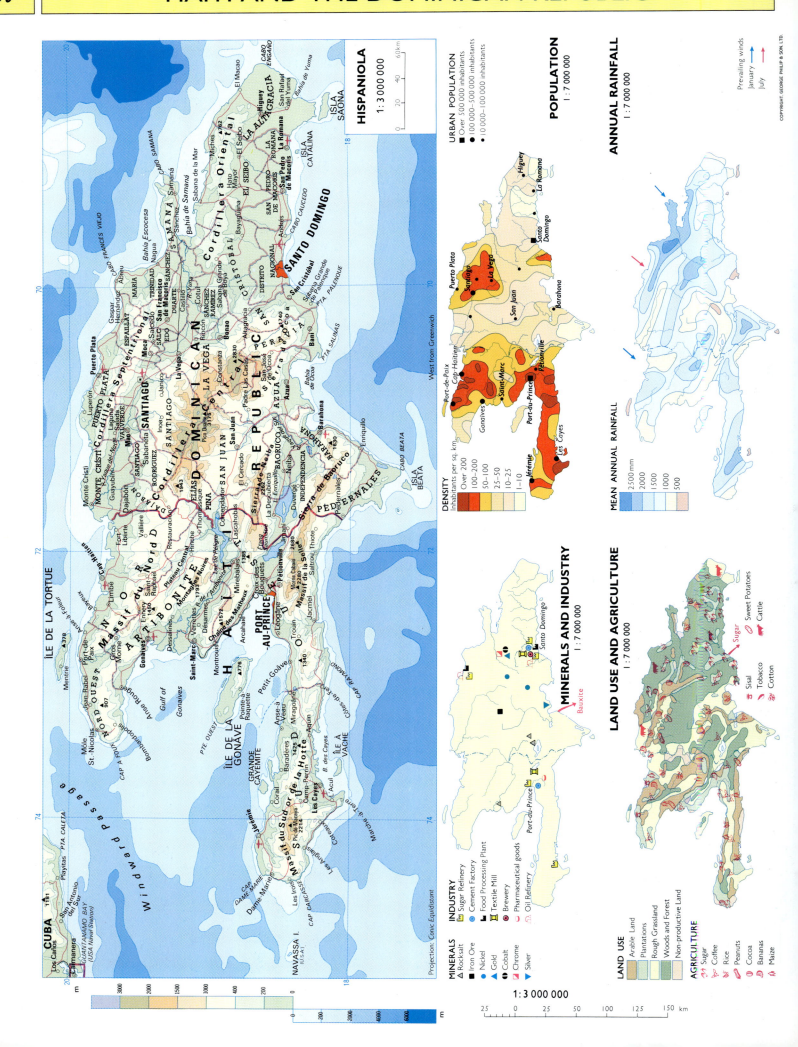

HISPANIOLA
1 : 3 000 000

POPULATION
1 : 7 000 000

URBAN POPULATION
- ■ Over 500 000 inhabitants
- ● 100 000–500 000 inhabitants
- • 10 000–100 000 inhabitants

DENSITY
Inhabitants per sq. km.
- Over 200
- 100–200
- 50–100
- 25–50
- 10–25
- 1–10

ANNUAL RAINFALL
1 : 7 000 000

MEAN ANNUAL RAINFALL
- 2500 mm
- 2000
- 1500
- 1000
- 500

Prevailing winds
- January
- July

MINERALS AND INDUSTRY
1 : 7 000 000

MINERALS
- Rocksalt
- Iron Ore
- Nickel
- Gold
- Cobalt
- Chrome
- Silver

INDUSTRY
- Sugar Refinery
- Cement Factory
- Food Processing Plant
- Textile Mill
- Brewery
- Pharmaceutical goods
- Oil Refinery

Bauxite

LAND USE AND AGRICULTURE
1 : 7 000 000

LAND USE
- Arable Land
- Plantations
- Rough Grassland
- Woods and Forest
- Non-productive Land

AGRICULTURE
- Sugar
- Coffee
- Rice
- Peanuts
- Cocoa
- Bananas
- Maize
- Sisal
- Tobacco
- Cotton
- Sweet Potatoes
- Cattle
- Sugar

Projection: Conic Equidistant

1 : 3 000 000

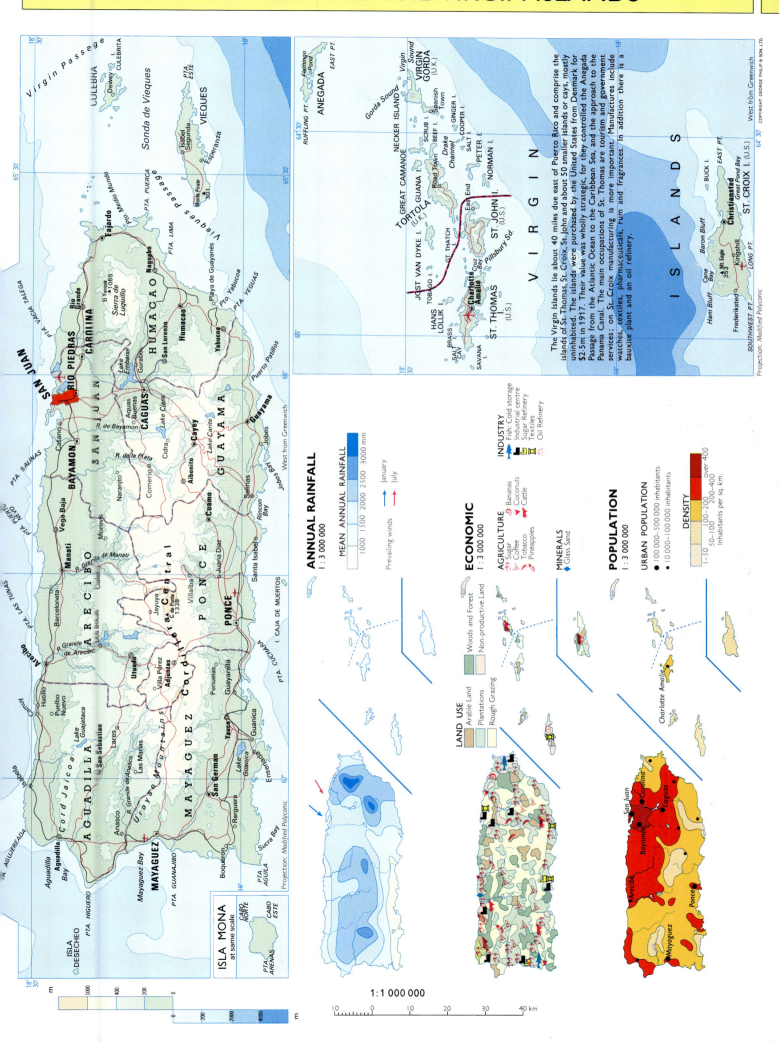

The Virgin Islands lie about 40 miles due east of Puerto Rico and comprise the islands of St. Thomas, St. Croix, St. John and about 50 smaller islands or cays, mostly uninhabited. The islands were purchased by the United States from Denmark for $2.5m in 1917. Their value was wholly strategic, for they controlled the Anegada Passage from the Atlantic Ocean to the Caribbean Sea, and the approach to the Panama Canal. The main occupations of St. Thomas are tourism and government services; on St. Croix manufacturing is more important. Manufactures include watches, textiles, pharmaceuticals, rum and fragrances. In addition there is a bauxite plant and an oil refinery.

Projection: Modified Polyconic

West from Greenwich

COPYRIGHT. GEORGE PHILIP & SON LTD.

ANNUAL RAINFALL
1 : 3 000 000

MEAN ANNUAL RAINFALL
1000 1500 2000 2500 3000 mm

Prevailing winds
January
July

ECONOMIC
1 : 3 000 000

AGRICULTURE
Sugar
Coffee
Tobacco
Pineapples
Bananas
Coconuts
Cattle

MINERALS
Glass Sand

INDUSTRY
Fish: Cold storage
Industrial centre
Sugar Refinery
Textiles
Oil Refinery

POPULATION
1 : 3 000 000

URBAN POPULATION
● 100 000–500 000 inhabitants
• 10 000–100 000 inhabitants

DENSITY
over 400
200–400
100–200
50–100
1–50
Inhabitants per sq. km.

LAND USE
Arable Land
Plantations
Rough Grazing
Woods and Forest
Non-productive Land

ISLA MONA
at same scale

Projection: Modified Polyconic

1 : 1 000 000

10   0   10   20   30   40 km

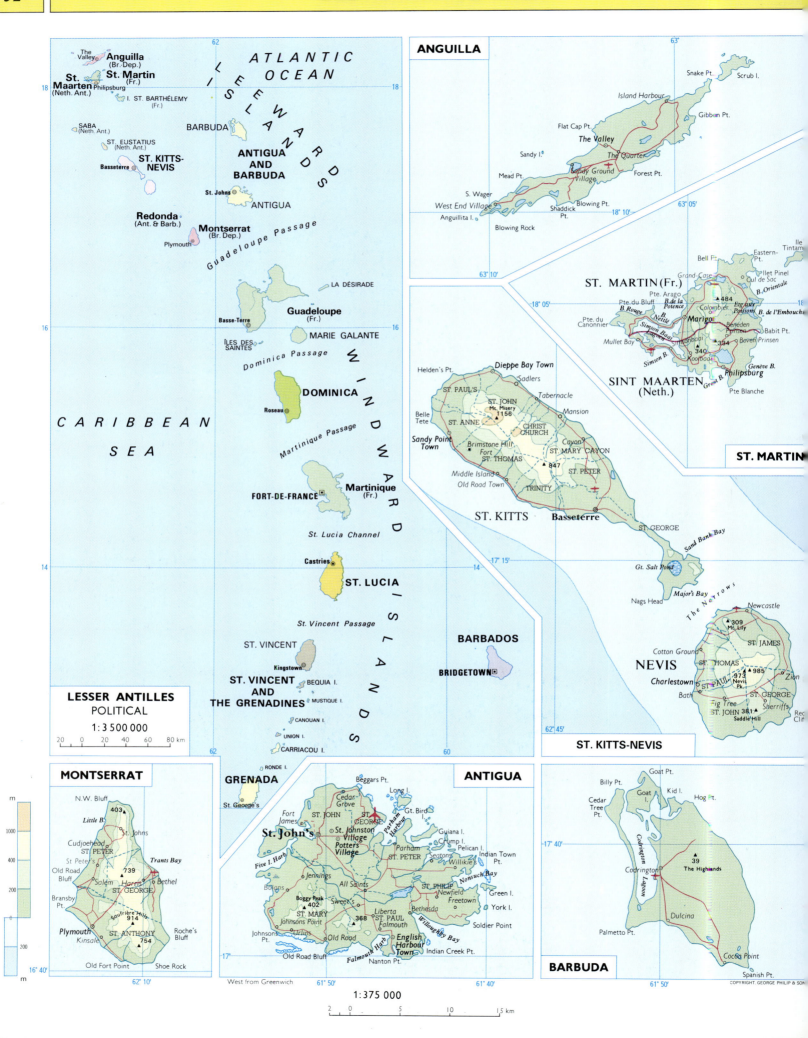

LESSER ANTILLES
POLITICAL
1:3 500 000
20 0 20 40 60 80 km

ANGUILLA

ST. MARTIN (Fr.)

SINT MAARTEN (Neth.)

ST. MARTIN

ST. KITTS

ST. KITTS-NEVIS

NEVIS

BARBADOS

MONTSERRAT

GRENADA

ANTIGUA

BARBUDA

West from Greenwich

1:375 000

2 0 5 10 1·5 km

COPYRIGHT. GEORGE PHILIP & SON

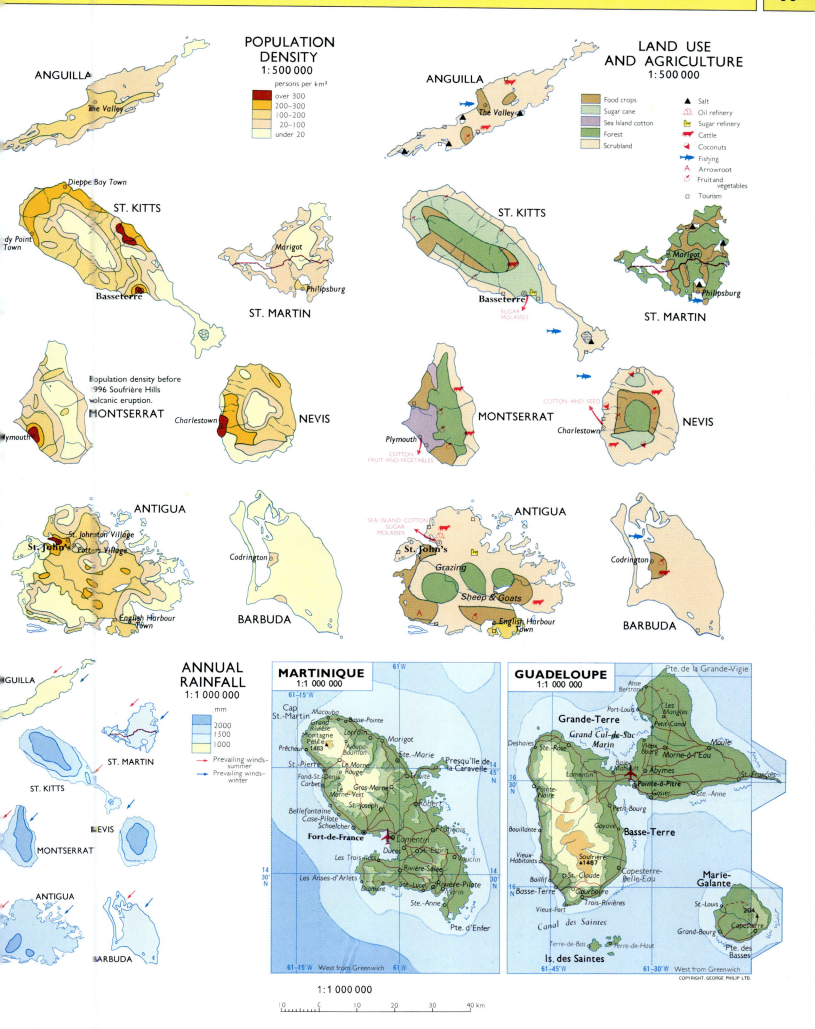

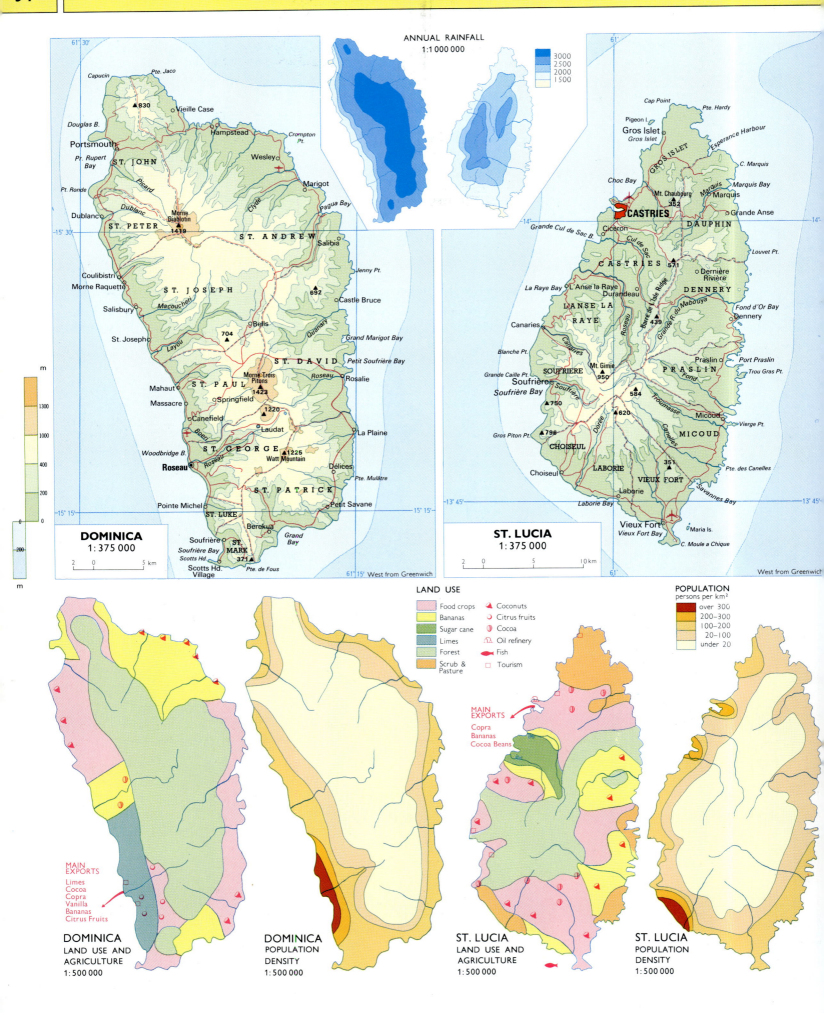

ANNUAL RAINFALL
1 : 1 000 000

	3000
	2500
	2000
	1500

DOMINICA
1 : 375 000
2 0 5 km

ST. LUCIA
1 : 375 000
2 0 5 10 km

West from Greenwich

West from Greenwich

LAND USE

Food crops	Coconuts
Bananas	Citrus fruits
Sugar cane	Cocoa
Limes	Oil refinery
Forest	Fish
Scrub & Pasture	Tourism

POPULATION
persons per km²

over 300	
200–300	
100–200	
20–100	
under 20	

MAIN EXPORTS
Limes
Cocoa
Copra
Vanilla
Bananas
Citrus Fruits

MAIN EXPORTS
Copra
Bananas
Cocoa Beans

DOMINICA
LAND USE AND
AGRICULTURE
1 : 500 000

DOMINICA
POPULATION
DENSITY
1 : 500 000

ST. LUCIA
LAND USE AND
AGRICULTURE
1 : 500 000

ST. LUCIA
POPULATION
DENSITY
1 : 500 000

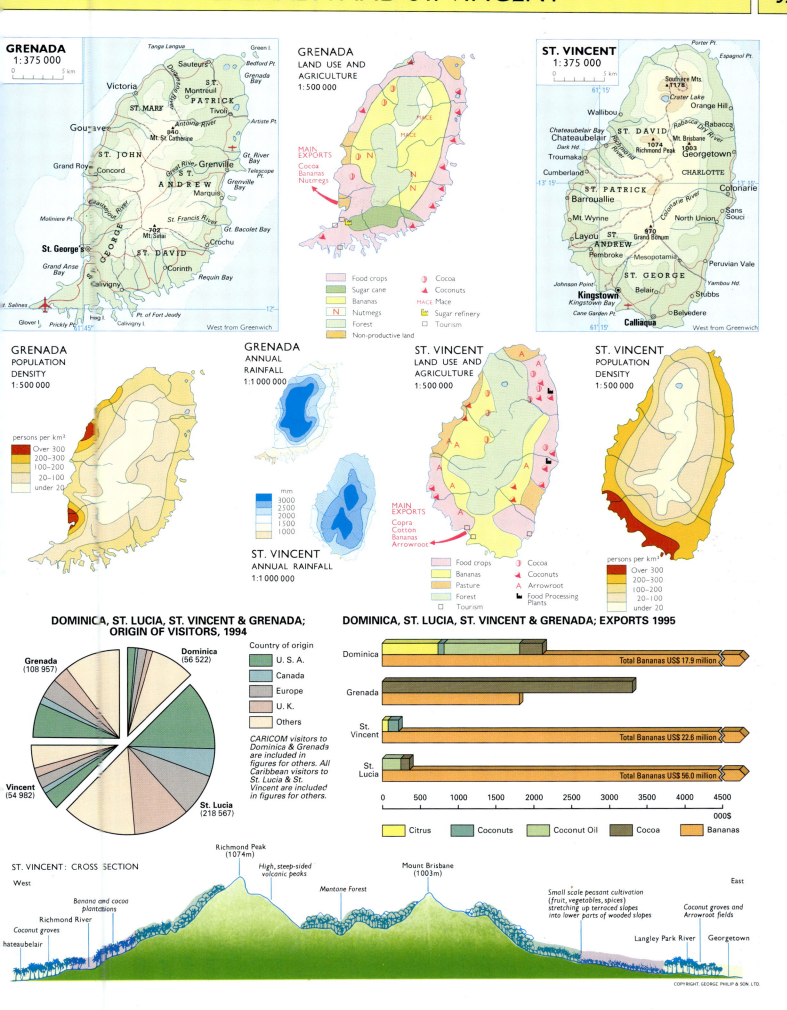

GRENADA
1:375 000

0   5 km

GRENADA LAND USE AND AGRICULTURE
1:500 000

MAIN EXPORTS
Cocoa
Bananas
Nutmegs

ST. VINCENT
1:375 000

0   5 km

Food crops
Sugar cane
Bananas
Forest
Non-productive land

Cocoa
Coconuts
Mace
Sugar refinery
Tourism

GRENADA POPULATION DENSITY
1:500 000

persons per km²
Over 300
200–300
100–200
20–100
under 20

GRENADA ANNUAL RAINFALL
1:1 000 000

mm
3000
2500
2000
1500
1000

ST. VINCENT ANNUAL RAINFALL
1:1 000 000

ST. VINCENT LAND USE AND AGRICULTURE
1:500 000

MAIN EXPORTS
Copra
Cotton
Bananas
Arrowroot

Food crops
Bananas
Pasture
Forest
Tourism

Cocoa
Coconuts
Arrowroot
Food Processing Plants

ST. VINCENT POPULATION DENSITY
1:500 000

persons per km²
Over 300
200–300
100–200
20–100
under 20

DOMINICA, ST. LUCIA, ST. VINCENT & GRENADA; ORIGIN OF VISITORS, 1994

Grenada (108 957)
Dominica (56 522)
Vincent (54 982)
St. Lucia (218 567)

Country of origin
U.S.A.
Canada
Europe
U.K.
Others

CARICOM visitors to Dominica & Grenada are included in figures for others. All Caribbean visitors to St. Lucia & St. Vincent are included in figures for others.

DOMINICA, ST. LUCIA, ST. VINCENT & GRENADA; EXPORTS 1995

Dominica — Total Bananas US$ 17.9 million
Grenada
St. Vincent — Total Bananas US$ 22.6 million
St. Lucia — Total Bananas US$ 56.0 million

0 500 1000 1500 2000 2500 3000 3500 4000 4500
000$

Citrus   Coconuts   Coconut Oil   Cocoa   Bananas

ST. VINCENT: CROSS SECTION

West

Richmond Peak (1074m)
High, steep-sided volcanic peaks
Montane Forest
Mount Brisbane (1003m)
Small scale peasant cultivation (fruit, vegetables, spices) stretching up terraced slopes into lower parts of wooded slopes

East

Banana and cocoa plantations
Richmond River
Coconut groves
Chateaubelair

Coconut groves and Arrowroot fields
Langley Park River
Georgetown

COPYRIGHT. GEORGE PHILIP & SON. LTD.

Projection: Transverse Mercator

West from Greenwich

COPYRIGHT GEORGE PHILIP LTD.

See page 41 for large scale map of Bridgetown

1 : 143 000

0   1   2   3   4   5km

LAND USE AGRICULTURE AND INDUSTRY   1 : 300 000

LAND USE
- Arable
- Plantation/fruit growing
- Woods and forests
- Rough grazing
- Non-productive land

AGRICULTURE
- Sugar cane
- Sugar refinery
- Main exporting port
- Fishing

INDUSTRY
- Oil production
- Oil refinery
- Industrial area
- R Rum refinery

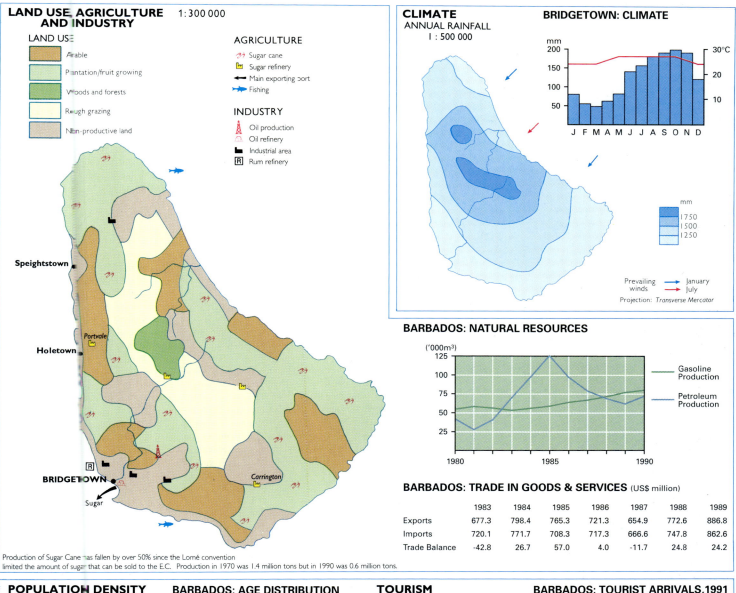

Speightstown
Portvale
Holetown
BRIDGETOWN
Sugar
Carrington

Production of Sugar Cane has fallen by over 50% since the Lomé convention
limited the amount of sugar that can be sold to the E.C. Production in 1970 was 1.4 million tons but in 1990 was 0.6 million tons.

CLIMATE
ANNUAL RAINFALL
1 : 500 000

BRIDGETOWN: CLIMATE

mm

| 1750 |
| 1500 |
| 1250 |

Prevailing winds — January
— July

Projection: Transverse Mercator

BARBADOS: NATURAL RESOURCES

('000m³)

— Gasoline Production
— Petroleum Production

1980   1985   1990

BARBADOS: TRADE IN GOODS & SERVICES (US$ million)

	1983	1984	1985	1986	1987	1988	1989
Exports	677.3	798.4	765.3	721.3	654.9	772.6	886.8
Imports	720.1	771.7	708.3	717.3	666.6	747.8	862.6
Trade Balance	-42.8	26.7	57.0	4.0	-11.7	24.8	24.2

POPULATION DENSITY
1 : 500 000

persons per km²
- over 1900
- 900–1900
- 400–900
- 300–400
- 200–300
- under 200
- over 50000 inhabitants

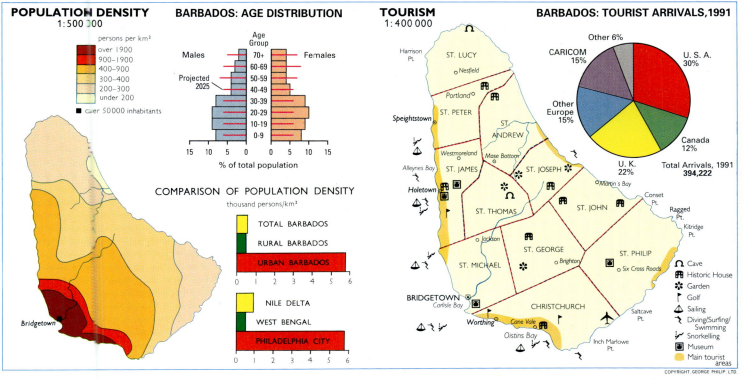

Bridgetown

BARBADOS: AGE DISTRIBUTION

Age Group
Males   Females
70+
60-69
Projected 2025
50-59
40-49
30-39
20-29
10-19
0-9

15 10 5 0 5 10 15
% of total population

COMPARISON OF POPULATION DENSITY
thousand persons/km²

- TOTAL BARBADOS
- RURAL BARBADOS
- URBAN BARBADOS

0 1 2 3 4 5 6

- NILE DELTA
- WEST BENGAL
- PHILADELPHIA CITY

0 1 2 3 4 5 6

TOURISM
1 : 400 000

BARBADOS: TOURIST ARRIVALS, 1991

Other 6%
CARICOM 15%
U. S. A. 30%
Other Europe 15%
Canada 12%
U. K. 22%

Total Arrivals, 1991
394,222

Harrison Pt.
ST. LUCY
Nesfield
Portland
Speightstown
ST. PETER
ST. ANDREW
Westmoreland
Mose Bottom
Alleynes Bay
ST. JAMES
ST. JOSEPH
Martin's Bay
Holetown
Conset Pt.
Ragged Pt.
ST. THOMAS
ST. JOHN
Kitridge Pt.
Jackson
ST. GEORGE
ST. PHILIP
Brighton
Six Cross Roads
ST. MICHAEL
BRIDGETOWN
Carlisle Bay
CHRISTCHURCH
Saltcave Pt.
Worthing
Cane Vale
Oistins Bay
Inch Marlowe Pt.

- Cave
- Historic House
- Garden
- Golf
- Sailing
- Diving/Surfing/ Swimming
- Snorkelling
- Museum
- Main tourist areas

COPYRIGHT. GEORGE PHILIP. LTD.

TRINIDAD AND TOBAGO

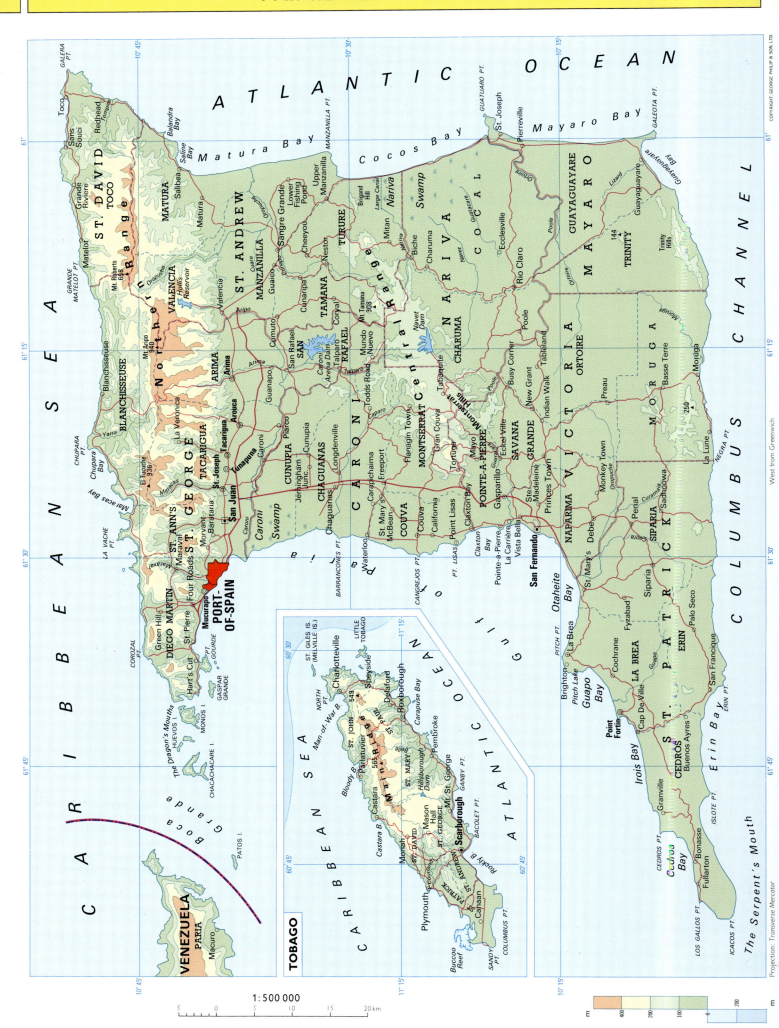

Projection: Transverse Mercator

West from Greenwich

COPYRIGHT GEORGE PHILIP & SON, LTD.

1 : 500 000

5   0   5   10   15   20km

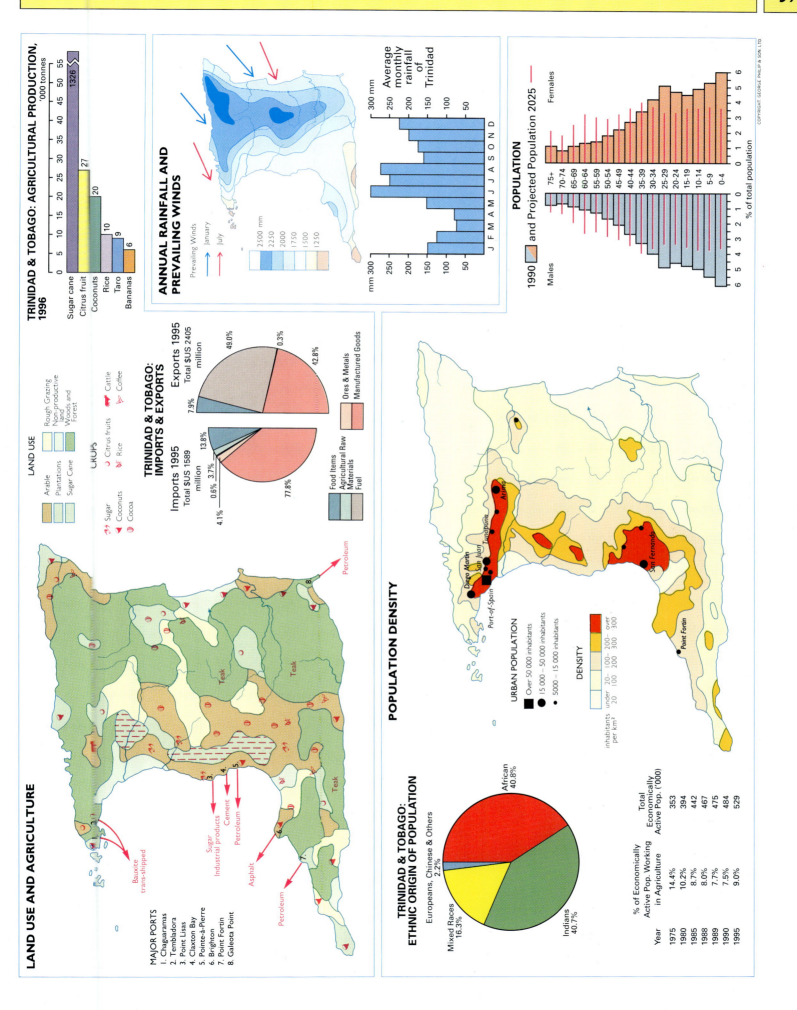

LAND USE AND AGRICULTURE

LAND USE

Arable
Plantations
Sugar Cane
Rough Grazing
Non-productive land
Woods and Forest

CROPS

Sugar
Coconuts
Cocoa
Citrus fruits
Rice
Cattle
Coffee

MAJOR PORTS
1. Chaguaramas
2. Tembladora
3. Point Lisas
4. Claxton Bay
5. Pointe-à-Pierre
6. Brighton
7. Point Fortin
8. Galeota Point

Petroleum
Bauxite trans-shipped
Sugar
Industrial products
Cement
Petroleum
Asphalt
Petroleum
Teak

TRINIDAD & TOBAGO: AGRICULTURAL PRODUCTION, 1996

'000 tonnes

Sugar cane 1326
Citrus fruit 27
Coconuts 20
Rice 10
Taro 9
Bananas 6

ANNUAL RAINFALL AND PREVAILING WINDS

Prevailing Winds
January
July

2500 mm
2250
2000
1750
1500
1250

Average monthly rainfall of Trinidad
300 mm
250
200
150
100
50

J F M A M J J A S O N D

mm 300
250
200
150
100
50

TRINIDAD & TOBAGO: IMPORTS & EXPORTS

Exports 1995
Total $US 2405 million

49.0%
0.3%
42.8%
7.9%

Imports 1995
Total $US 1589 million

13.8%
77.8%
3.7%
0.6%
4.1%

Food Items
Agricultural Raw Materials
Fuel
Ores & Metals
Manufactured Goods

TRINIDAD & TOBAGO: ETHNIC ORIGIN OF POPULATION

African 40.8%
Indians 40.7%
Mixed Races 16.3%
Europeans, Chinese & Others 2.2%

Year	% of Economically Active Pop. Working in Agriculture	Total Economically Active Pop. ('000)
1975	14.4%	353
1980	10.2%	394
1985	8.7%	442
1988	8.0%	467
1989	7.7%	475
1990	7.5%	484
1995	9.0%	529

POPULATION

1990 and Projected Population 2025
Females
Males

75+
70-74
65-69
60-64
55-59
50-54
45-49
40-44
35-39
30-34
25-29
20-24
15-19
10-14
5-9
0-4

% of total population

POPULATION DENSITY

Arima
Tunapuna
San Juan
Diego Martin
Port-of-Spain
San Fernando
Point Fortin

URBAN POPULATION
Over 50 000 inhabitants
15 000 – 50 000 inhabitants
5000 – 15 000 inhabitants

DENSITY
over
300
200 – 300
100 – 200
20 – 100
under 20

inhabitants per km²

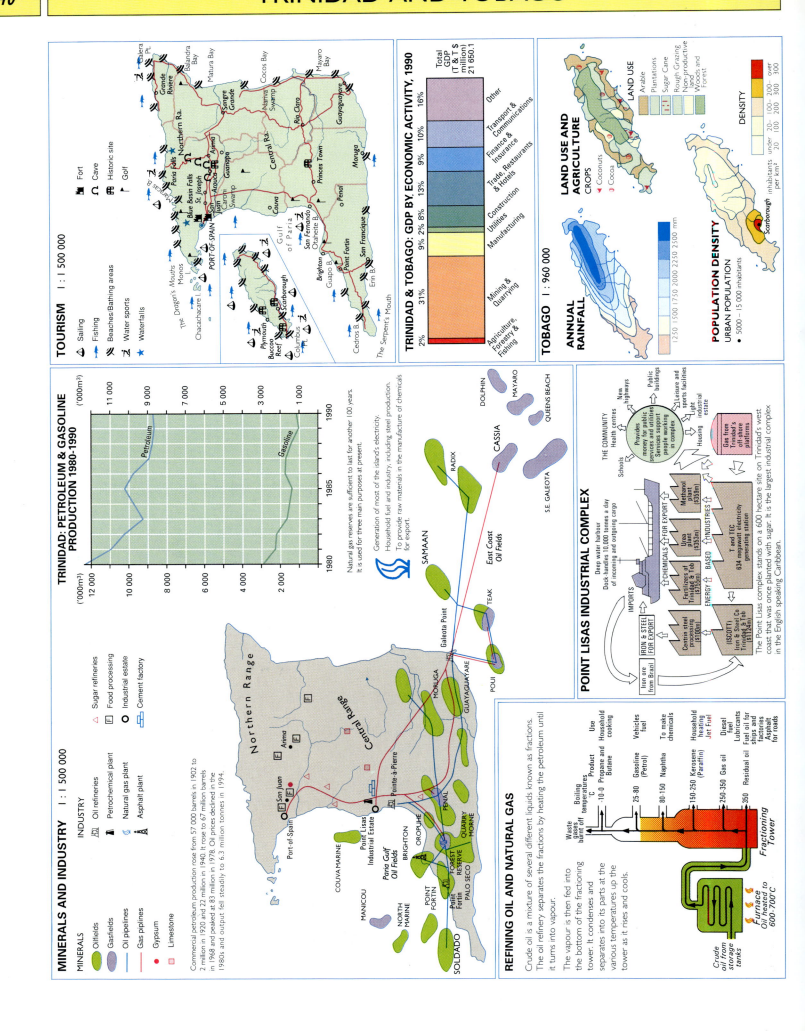

TOURISM 1 : 1 500 000

TOURISM
- ⛵ Sailing
- 🎣 Fishing
- Beaches/Bathing areas
- Water sports
- ⭐ Waterfalls
- ⚔ Fort
- ∩ Cave
- Historic site
- ⛳ Golf

TRINIDAD & TOBAGO: GDP BY ECONOMIC ACTIVITY, 1990

Total GDP (T & T $ million) 21 650.1

- 16% Other
- 10% Transport & Communications
- 9% Finance & Insurance
- 13% Trade, Restaurants & Hotels
- 2% Construction
- 8% Utilities
- 9% Manufacturing
- 31% Mining & Quarrying
- 2% Agriculture, Forestry & Fishing

LAND USE AND AGRICULTURE

LAND USE
- Arable
- Plantations
- Sugar Cane
- Rough Grazing
- Non-productive land
- Woods and Forest

CROPS
- Coconuts
- Cocoa

TOBAGO 1 : 960 000

ANNUAL RAINFALL
1250 1500 1750 2000 2250 2500 mm

POPULATION DENSITY

URBAN POPULATION
- 5000 – 15 000 inhabitants

DENSITY
under 20 — 100 — 200 — over
20 100 200 300
inhabitants per km²

MINERALS AND INDUSTRY 1 : 1 500 000

MINERALS
- Oilfields
- Gasfields
- Oil pipelines
- Gas pipelines
- Gypsum
- Limestone

INDUSTRY
- Oil refineries
- Petrochemical plant
- Natural gas plant
- Asphalt plant
- △ Sugar refineries
- Food processing
- [E] Industrial estate
- ○ Cement factory

Commercial petroleum production rose from 57 000 barrels in 1902 to 2 million in 1920 and 22 million in 1940. It rose to 67 million barrels in 1968 and peaked at 83 million in 1978. Oil prices declined in the 1980s and output fell steadily to 6.3 million tonnes in 1994.

TRINIDAD: PETROLEUM & GASOLINE PRODUCTION 1980-1990

(000m³)
Petroleum
Gasoline

Natural gas reserves are sufficient to last for another 100 years. It is used for three main purposes at present.
- Generation of most of the island's electricity.
- Household fuel and industry, including steel production.
- To provide raw materials in the manufacture of chemicals for export.

East Coast Oil Fields

DOLPHIN
MAYARO
QUEENS BEACH
CASSIA
RADIX
SAMAAN
TEAK
S.E. GALEOTA
POUI
Galeota Point

POINT LISAS INDUSTRIAL COMPLEX

Deep water harbour. Dock-handles 10,000 tonnes a day of incoming and outgoing cargo.

The Point Lisas complex stands on a 600 hectare site on Trinidad's west coast that was once planted with sugar. It is the largest industrial complex in the English speaking Caribbean.

THE COMMUNITY — Health centres, Schools, Housing, New highways, Public buildings, Leisure and sports facilities, Light industrial estate

Provides money for public services and utilities. Services support people working in complex.

Gas from Trinidad's off-shore platforms

IMPORTS — Iron ore from Brazil

CHEMICALS FOR EXPORT — Methanol plant ($359m), Urea plant ($353m), Fertilizers of Trinidad & Tobago ($575m)

IRON & STEEL FOR EXPORT — Centrin steel processing ($100m), (ISCOTT) Iron & Steel Co Trinidad & Tobago ($1.24m)

ENERGY BASED INDUSTRIES — T and TEC 634 megawatt electricity generating station

REFINING OIL AND NATURAL GAS

Crude oil is a mixture of several different liquids known as fractions. The oil refinery separates the fractions by heating the petroleum until it turns into vapour.

The vapour is then fed into the bottom of the fractioning tower. It condenses and separates into its parts at the various temperatures up the tower as it rises and cools.

Boiling temperatures °C	Product	Use
-10-0	Propane and Butane	Household cooking
25-80	Gasoline (Petrol)	Vehicles fuel
80-150	Naphtha	To make chemicals
150-250	Kerosene (Paraffin)	Household heating / Jet fuel
250-350	Gas oil	Diesel fuel / Lubricants
350	Residual oil	Fuel oil for ships and factories / Asphalt for roads

Waste gases burnt off

Fractioning Tower

Crude oil from storage tanks

Furnace Oil heated to 600-700°C

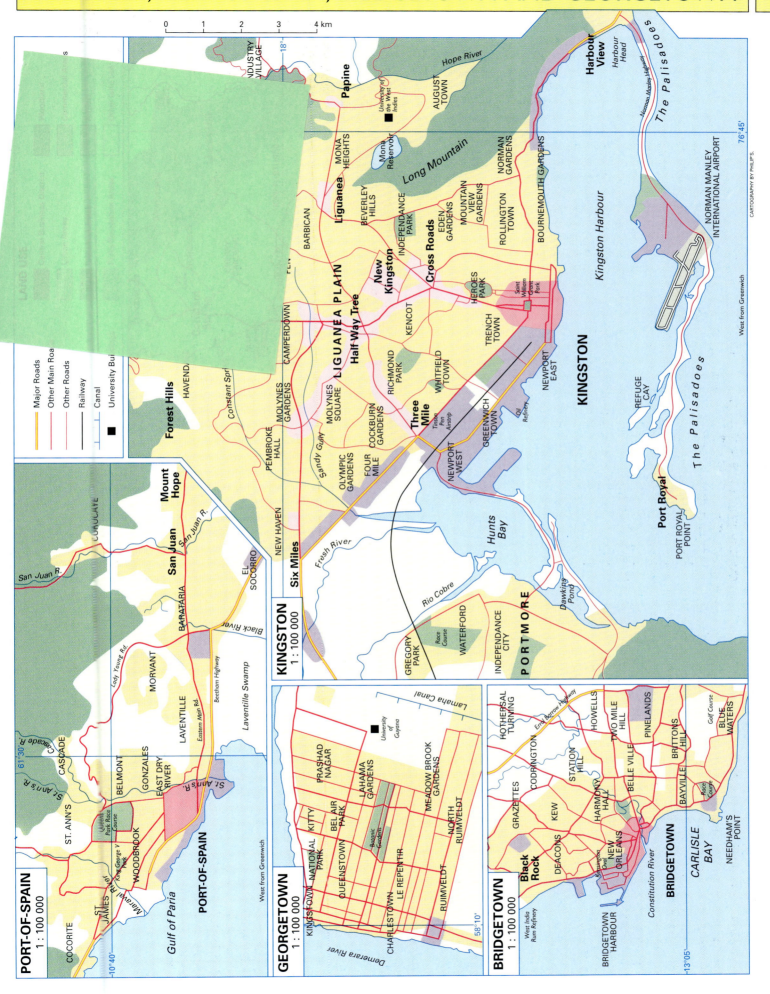

0 1 2 3 4 km

KINGSTON
1 : 100 000

PORT-OF-SPAIN
1 : 100 000

GEORGETOWN
1 : 100 000

BRIDGETOWN
1 : 100 000

Major Roads
Other Main Roads
Other Roads
Railway
Canal
University Buildings

CARTOGRAPHY BY PHILIP'S.

West from Greenwich

Kingston
INDUSTRY VILLAGE
Papine
University of the West Indies
MONA HEIGHTS
Mona Reservoir
Hope River
AUGUST TOWN
Harbour View
Harbour Head
Norman Manley Highway
The Palisadoes
76°45'
18°
NORMAN MANLEY INTERNATIONAL AIRPORT
Long Mountain
Liguanea
BEVERLEY HILLS
BARBICAN
NORMAN GARDENS
MOUNTAIN VIEW GARDENS
EDEN GARDENS
INDEPENDANCE PARK
ROLLINGTON TOWN
BOURNEMOUTH GARDENS
Kingston Harbour
New Kingston
Cross Roads
HEROES PARK
Saint William Grant Park
KENCOT
TRENCH TOWN
NEWPORT EAST
KINGSTON
Half Way Tree
LIGUANEA PLAIN
RICHMOND PARK
WHITFIELD TOWN
CAMPERDOWN
Oil Refinery
REFUGE CAY
HAVEND...
Constant Spr...
MOLYNES GARDENS
MOLYNES SQUARE
COCKBURN GARDENS
Three Mile
Tinson Pen Airstrip
GREENWICH TOWN
NEWPORT WEST
The Palisadoes
Forest Hills
PEMBROKE HALL
Sandy Gully
OLYMPIC GARDENS
FOUR MILE
NEW HAVEN
Fresh River
Hunts Bay
Port Royal
PORT ROYAL POINT
Six Miles
Rio Cobre
Dawkins Pond
GREGORY PARK
Race Course
WATERFORD
INDEPENDANCE CITY
PORTMORE

Port-of-Spain
CUMULAYE
San Juan R.
San Juan R.
Mount Hope
San Juan
EL SOCORRO
BARATARIA
MORVANT
LAVENTILLE
Lady Young Rd.
Eastern Main Rd.
Beetham Highway
Black River
Laventille Swamp
St. Ann's R.
Cascade R.
61°30'
CASCADE
ST. ANN'S
BELMONT
GONZALES
EAST DRY RIVER
WOODBROOK
Maraval R.
St. James R.
ST. JAMES
COCORITE
Gulf of Paria
10°40'
Queen's Park Race Course
King George V Park
PORT-OF-SPAIN
West from Greenwich

Georgetown
Lamaha Canal
University of Guyana
KINGSTOWN
PRASHAD NAGAR
KITTY
BEL AIR PARK
LAHAMA GARDENS
Botanic Gardens
MEADOW BROOK GARDENS
NORTH RUIMVELDT
QUEENSTOWN
LE REPENTIR
RUIMVELDT
CHARLESTOWN
Demerara River
58°10'
West from Greenwich

Bridgetown
HOTHERSAL TURNING
Errol Barrow Highway
HOWELLS
TWO MILE HILL
PINELANDS
Golf Course
BLUE WATERS
CODRINGTON
STATION HILL
BELLE VILLE
BRITTONS HILL
GRAZETTES
KEW
HARMONY HALL
BAYVILLE
Race Course
Kensington Oval
Black Rock
DEACONS
NEW ORLEANS
BRIDGETOWN
West India Rum Refinery
Constitution River
CARLISLE BAY
NEEDHAM'S POINT
BRIDGETOWN HARBOUR
13°05'

ADMINISTRATIVE REGIONS

1 Barima-Waini
2 Pomeroon-Supernaam
3 Essequibo Islands-West
   Demerara
4 Demerara-Mahaica
5 Mahaica-Berbice
6 East Berbice-Corentyne
7 Cuyuni-Mazaruni
8 Potaro-Siparuni
9 Upper Demerara-Berbice
10 Upper Takutu-Upper
    Essequibo

**POPULATION, 1990 &
PROJECTED POPULATION
2025 —**

Males   Females

70+
60-69
50-59
40-49
30-39
20-29
10-19
0-9

15   10   5   0   0   5   10   15
% of total population

Projection: Conical with two standard parallels

1 : 3 500 000

20   0   20   40   60   80   100   120   140 km

COPYRIGHT. GEORGE PHILIP & SON. LTD.

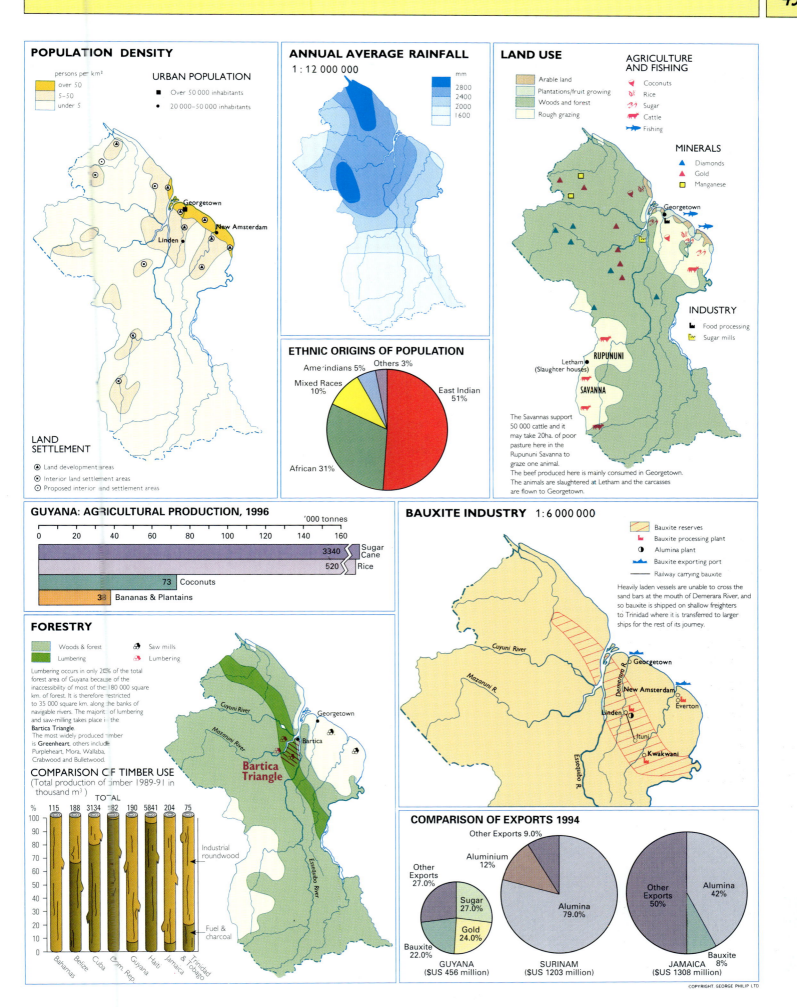

POPULATION DENSITY

persons per km²
over 50
5–50
under 5

URBAN POPULATION
■ Over 50 000 inhabitants
● 20 000–50 000 inhabitants

Georgetown
New Amsterdam
Linden

LAND SETTLEMENT
Ⓐ Land development areas
⊙ Interior land settlement areas
⊙ Proposed interior land settlement areas

ANNUAL AVERAGE RAINFALL
1 : 12 000 000

mm
2800
2400
2000
1600

ETHNIC ORIGINS OF POPULATION

Amerindians 5%   Others 3%
Mixed Races 10%
East Indian 51%
African 31%

LAND USE

AGRICULTURE AND FISHING
Arable land
Plantations/fruit growing
Woods and forest
Rough grazing
Coconuts
Rice
Sugar
Cattle
Fishing

MINERALS
▲ Diamonds
▲ Gold
■ Manganese

Georgetown

INDUSTRY
Food processing
Sugar mills

Letham (Slaughter houses)
RUPUNUNI
SAVANNA

The Savannas support 50 000 cattle and it may take 20ha. of poor pasture here in the Rupununi Savanna to graze one animal. The beef produced here is mainly consumed in Georgetown. The animals are slaughtered at Letham and the carcasses are flown to Georgetown.

GUYANA: AGRICULTURAL PRODUCTION, 1996
'000 tonnes

0 20 40 60 80 100 120 140 160

Sugar Cane 3340
Rice 520
Coconuts 73
Bananas & Plantains 33

FORESTRY

Woods & forest
Lumbering
Saw mills
Lumbering

Lumbering occurs in only 20% of the total forest area of Guyana because of the inaccessibility of most of the 180 000 square km. of forest. It is therefore restricted to 35 000 square km. along the banks of navigable rivers. The majority of lumbering and saw-milling takes place in the Bartica Triangle. The most widely produced timber is Greenheart, others include Purpleheart, Mora, Wallaba, Crabwood and Bulletwood.

Cuyuni River
Mazaruni River
Georgetown
Bartica
Bartica Triangle
Essequibo River

COMPARISON OF TIMBER USE
(Total production of timber 1989–91 in thousand m³)

TOTAL
% 115 188 3134 182 190 5841 204 75
100 ... 0

Industrial roundwood
Fuel & charcoal

Bahamas, Belize, Cuba, Dom. Rep., Guyana, Haiti, Jamaica, Trinidad & Tobago

BAUXITE INDUSTRY   1 : 6 000 000

Bauxite reserves
Bauxite processing plant
Alumina plant
Bauxite exporting port
Railway carrying bauxite

Heavily laden vessels are unable to cross the sand bars at the mouth of Demerara River, and so bauxite is shipped on shallow freighters to Trinidad where it is transferred to larger ships for the rest of its journey.

Cuyuni River
Mazaruni R.
Georgetown
New Amsterdam
Everton
Linden
Ituni
Kwakwani
Demerara R.
Essequibo R.

COMPARISON OF EXPORTS 1994

Other Exports 9.0%
Aluminium 12%
Other Exports 27.0%
Sugar 27.0%
Gold 24.0%
Bauxite 22.0%
GUYANA ($US 456 million)

Alumina 79.0%
SURINAM ($US 1203 million)

Other Exports 50%
Alumina 42%
Bauxite 8%
JAMAICA ($US 1308 million)

COPYRIGHT GEORGE PHILIP LTD

INDEX TO CARIBBEAN MAPS

This index lists the placenames which appear on the large-scale maps of the Caribbean (pages *8-43* with the yellow band). Placenames for the rest of the world can be found in the World Index, with the turquoise band at the back of the atlas.

The first number beside each name in the index gives the map page on which that feature or place will be found. The geographical co-ordinates which follow give the latitude and longitude of each place. The first co-ordinate indicates latitude – the distance north of the Equator. The second co-ordinate indicates longitude – the distance west (or east) of the Greenwich Meridian. Both latitude and longitude are measured in degrees and minutes (there are 60 minutes in a degree). Please refer to pages 6–7 for a more detailed explanation of latitude and longitude.

Thus the entry for Aberdeen, Jamaica, reads:
Aberdeen, *Jamaica*..........................**26** 18 12N 77 42W

This indicates that Aberdeen appears on map page 26 at latitude 18 degrees, 23 minutes north, and at longitude 77 degrees, 42 minutes west. To find Aberdeen look at the edges of the map on page 26. The degrees of latitude are indicated by blue figures on the left-hand edge of the map and the degrees of longitude are marked on the bottom edge of the map. Aberdeen will be found where lines extended from the two points on the map edge would cross on the map.

A solid square ■ follows the name of a country, while an open square □ indicates that the name refers to an administrative unit such as a county or region. Rivers are indicated by an arrow ⤳ and are indexed to the mouths or confluence. Names composed of a proper name (Gonave) and a description (I. de la) are positioned alphabetically by the proper name. Names beginning with Mc are indexed as if they were spelt Mac. Names beginning St. are alphabetized under Saint, but Santa and San are spelt in full and are alphabetized accordingly.

ABBREVIATIONS USED IN THE INDEX

Antigua & B. – Antigua and Barbuda	E. – East	Mt(s). – Mont, Monte, Mount, Mountain(s)	Pta. – Punta	Res. – Reservoir	St. Kitts–N. – St. Kitts-Nevis	Str. – Strait
Arch. – Archipelago	G. – Golfe, Golfo, Gulf	N. – North	Pte. – Pointe	S. – South		Trinidad & T. – Trinidad & Tobago
B. – Baie, Bahia, Bay	I(s). – Ile, Ilha, Isla, Island, Isle(s)	Pk. – Peak	R. – Rio, River	Sa. – Sierra	St. Vincent & G. – St. Vincent & the Grenadines	
C. – Cabo, Cap, Cape	L. – Lagoa, Lake	Pt. – Point	Ra. – Range	Sd. – Sound		W. – West
				Rep. – Republic	St. – Saint	

A

Aberdeen, *Jamaica* ....**26** 18 12 N 77 42 W
Abraham's Bay, *Bahamas*....**23** 22 23 N 72 58 W
Abreu, *Dominican Rep.* ....**30** 19 40 N 69 58 W
Abreus, *Cuba* ....**24** 22 17 N 80 34 W
Abymes, *Guadeloupe* ....**33** 16 16 N 01 31 W
Acarai Mts., *Guyana*..............**42**   1 50 N 57 30 W
Acklins I., *Bahamas*................**23** 22 26 N 73 58 W
Adelaide, *Bahamas*................**23** 25   0 N 77 31 W
Adjuntas, *Puerto Rico*............**31** 18 10 N 66 43 W
Aguadilla, *Puerto Rico*...........**31** 18 27 N 67 10 W
Aguadilla □, *Puerto Rico*........**31** 18 27 N 67 10 W
Aguadilla Bay, *Puerto Rico*.....**31** 18 26 N 67 10 W
Agujereada., Pta, *Puerto Rico*.**31** 18 31 N 67   8 W
Aibonito, *Puerto Rico*.............**31** 18   8 N 66 16 W
Albert Town, *Bahamas*............**23** 22 36 N 74 21 W
Albert Town, *Jamaica*..............**26** 18 17 N 77 33 W
Alderton, *Jamaica*...................**27** 18 18 N 77 13 W
Alexandria, *Jamaica*................**26** 18 18 N 77 21 W
Alice Town, *Bahamas*..............**23** 25 44 N 79 18 W
All Saints, *Antigua & B.* ....**32** 17 10 N 61 48 W
Alley, *Jamaica*.........................**26** 17 48 N 77 17 W
Alleynes Bay, *Barbados* ....**36** 13 13 N 59 39 W
Alligator Pond, *Jamaica*...........**26** 17 52 N 77 34 W
Alligator Pond B., *Jamaica* ......**26** 17 51 N 77 35 W
Ambergris Cay, *Belize*............**22** 18   0 N 88   0 W
Ambergris Cay,
  Turks & Caicos ....**23** 21 20 N 71 40 W
Ana Maria, G. of, *Cuba*...........**25** 21 25 N 78 46 W
Anasco, *Puerto Rico*...............**31** 18 19 N 67 11 W

Anasco, R. Grande de
  Puerto Rico ....**31** 18 16 N 67 11 W
Anchovy, *Jamaica*...................**26** 18 24 N 77 55 W
Andrés, *Dominican Rep.* ....**30** 18 26 N 69 38 W
Andros I., *Bahamas*.................**23** 24 26 N 77 57 W
Anegada, *Virgin Is.*.................**31** 18 46 N 64 24 W
Anguila, Pta, *Puerto Rico*.......**31** 23 34 N 79 33 W
Anguilla ■...............................**32** 18 14 N 63   5 W
Anguillita I., *Anguilla*.............**32** 18   9 N 63 11 W
Anna Regina, *Guyana*.............**42**   7 16 N 58 30 W
Annai, *Guyana*........................**42**   3 47 N 59   6 W
Annotto Bay, *Jamaica* ....**27** 18 16 N 76 47 W
Anse-à-Foleur, *Haiti*................**30** 19 54 N 72 37 W
Anse-à-Veaux, *Haiti*................**30** 18 30 N 73 20 W
Anse Rouge, *Haiti* ....**30** 19 38 N 73   3 W
Antigua & Barbuda ■................**32** 17   3 N 61 48 W
Antilla, *Cuba*..........................**25** 20 53 N 75 46 W
Antoine River ⤳, *Grenada* ......**35** 12 10 N 61 36 W
Apoteri, *Guyana*.....................**42**   4   0 N 58 32 W
Aquas Buenas, *Puerto Rico*....**31** 18 18 N 65 42 W
Arcahaie, *Haiti*.......................**30** 18 46 N 72 31 W
Arecibo, *Puerto Rico* ....**31** 18 29 N 66 44 W
Arecibo □, *Puerto Rico*..........**31** 18 25 N 66 37 W
Arecibo, R. Grande de ⤳,
  Puerto Rico..........................**31** 18 29 N 66 42 W
Arima, *Trinidad & T.* ....**38** 10 38 N 61 17 W
Arimac *Trinidad & T.*...............**38** 10 39 N 61 16 W
Arima ⤳, *Trinidad & T.*............**38** 10 35 N 61 16 W
Arimu Mine, *Guyana*...............**42**   6 28 N 59   9 W
Aripo ⤳, *Trinidad & T.* ....**38** 10 35 N 61 14 W
Aripo, Mt., *Trinidad & T.* ....**38** 10 43 N 61 15 W
Arouca, *Trinidad & T.* ....**38** 10 38 N 61 20 W

Artemisa, *Cuba*......................**24** 22 49 N 82 47 W
Arthur's Town, *Bahamas*.........**23** 24 40 N 75 41 W
Artibonite □, *Haiti*..................**30** 19 15 N 72 25 W
Artibonite, R. de ⤳, *Haiti*........**30** 19 15 N 72 47 W
Artwood Cay =
  Samana Cay, *Bahamas*.........**23** 23   5 N 73 45 W
Aruba ■ ....**9** 12 30N 70   0 W
Aserradero, *Cuba*..................**25** 22   1 N 79 59 W
Attagracia, *Dominican Rep.*.....**30** 18 33 N 70 20 W
Atto Cedro, *Cuba*...................**25** 20 31 N 75 58 W
August Town, *Jamaica*............**27** 17 59 N 76 44 W
Auras, *Cuba*...........................**25** 22   1 N 76 14 W
Azua, *Dominican Rep.*.............**30** 18 29 N 70 44 W

B

Bacolet Pt., *Trinidad & T.* ....**38** 11 10 N 60 43 W
Bahama Beach Marina,
  Bahamas..............................**23** 26 33 N 78 52 W
Bahamas ■ ....**23** 24 15 N 76   0 W
Bailey Town, *Bahamas*............**23** 25 48 N 79 10 W
Balaclava, *Jamaica*..................**26** 18 10 N 77 39 W
Balandra., *Trinidad & T.*..........**38** 26   0 N   7 40 W
Banes, *Cuba*...........................**25** 20 59 N 75 24 W
Bani, *Dominican Rep.*..............**30** 18 19 N 70 21 W
Bannerman Town, *Bahamas*...**23** 24 41 N 76   9 W
Baoruco □, *Dominican Rep.*....**30** 18 30 N 71 21 W
Baoruco, Sierra de,
  Dominican Rep. ....**30** 18 10 N 71 25 W

Baracoa, *Cuba* ....**25** 15 46 N 87 50 W
Baradères, *Haiti*.....................**30** 18 30 N 73 39 W
Barahona, *Dominican Rep* ......**30** 18 13 N 71   7 W
Barataria, *Trinidad & T.* ....**38** 10 39 N 61 28 W
Barbados ■.............................**36** 13 10 N 59 33 W
Barbuda, *Antigua & B.*............**32** 17 41 N 61 48 W
Barceloneta, *Puerto Rico* ....**31** 18 27 N 66 32 W
Barima-Waini □, *Guyana*........**58**   7 55 N 59 30 W
Barrancones Pt., *Trinidad & T.*.**38** 10 31 N 61 28 W
Barre de L'Isle Ridge,
  St. Lucia................................**34** 13 55 N 61 13 W
Barrouallie, *St. Vincent & G.*....**35** 13 14 N 61 17 W
Bartica, *Guyana*......................**42**   6 24 N 58 38 W
Bartons, *Jamaica*....................**27** 18   2 N 77   8 W
Basse-Terre, *Guadeloupe*.......**33** 16   0 N 61 43 W
Basse Terre, *Trinidad & T.* ......**38** 10   8 N 61 18 W
Basseterre, *St. Kitts-N.*...........**32** 17 17 N 62 43 W
Batabanó, G. of, *Cuba* ....**24** 22   0 N 83   0 W
Bath, *Jamaica*.........................**27** 17 57 N 76 22 W
Bath, *St. Kitts-N.*.....................**32** 17   8 N 62 37 W
Bathsheba, *Barbados*.............**36** 13 13 N 59 31 W
Bauta, *Cuba*...........................**24** 22 59 N 82 33 W
Bayaguana, *Dominican Rep.*....**30** 18 45 N 69 38 W
Bayamo, *Cuba*........................**25** 20 23 N 76 39 W
Bayamon, *Puerto Rico* ....**31** 18 24 N 66 10 W
Bayamon, R. de ⤳,
  Puerto Rico..........................**31** 18 28 N 66   8 W
Bayeux, *Haiti* ....**30** 19   1 N 72 32 W
Bayville, *Barbados*..................**41** 13   5 N 59 37 W
Beata, C., *Dominican Rep.*......**30** 17 41 N 71 24 W
Beata, I., *Dominican Rep*........**30** 17 35 N 71 31 W
Beef I., *Virgin Is.*....................**31** 18 26 N 64 30 W

Mastic Pt., *Bahamas* **23** 25 3 N 77 57 W
Matanzas, *Cuba* **24** 23 3 N 81 35 W
Matanzas □, *Cuba* **24** 23 4 N 81 35 W
Matelot, *Trinidad & T.* **38** 10 49 N 61 7 W
Matheux, Chaine des, *Haiti* **30** 18 55 N 72 30 W
Matthew Town, *Bahamas* **23** 20 58 N 73 40 W
Matura, *Trinidad & T.* **38** 10 40 N 61 4 W
Matura □, *Trinidad & T.* **38** 10 42 N 61 4 W
Matura B., *Trinidad & T.* **38** 10 40 N 61 4 W
Maximo Gómez, *Cuba* **24** 22 54 N 81 2 W
May Pen., *Jamaica* **27** 17 58 N 77 15 W
Mayaguana I., *Bahamas* **23** 22 23 N 72 57 W
Mayaguana Passage, *Bahamas* **23** 22 32 N 73 15 W
Mayaguez, *Puerto Rico* **31** 18 12 N 67 9 W
Mayaguez □, *Puerto Rico* **31** 18 13 N 67 9 W
Mayaguez B., *Puerto Rico* **31** 18 12 N 67 10 W
Mayajigua, *Cuba* **25** 22 14 N 79 4 W
Mayari, *Cuba* **25** 20 40 N 75 41 W
Mayari Arriba, *Cuba* **25** 20 25 N 75 32 W
Mayaro □, *Trinidad & T.* **38** 10 10 N 61 5 W
Mayaro B, *Trinidad & T.* **38** 10 15 N 60 58 W
Mayo, *Trinidad & T.* **38** 10 21 N 61 23 W
Mazaruni →, *Guyana* **42** 6 24 N 58 39 W
Mead Pt., *Anguilla* **32** 18 11 N 63 8 W
Meadow Brook Gardens, *Guyana* **41** 6 48 N 58 11 W
Media Luna, *Cuba* **25** 20 8 N 77 27 W
Medio Mundo, Pto., *Puerto Rico* **31** 18 16 N 65 36 W
Mexico, Gulf of **12** 26 0 N 90 0 W
Miches, *Dominican Rep.* **30** 18 59 N 69 3 W
Micoud, *St. Lucia* **34** 13 49 N 60 54 W
Middle Island, *St. Kitts-N.* **32** 17 20 N 62 48 W
Middle Quarters, *Jamaica* **26** 18 5 N 77 50 W
Middlesex □, *Jamaica* **27** 18 10 N 77 5 W
Miles Town, *Jamaica* **26** 18 23 N 78 0 W
Milton, *Jamaica* **26** 18 10 N 77 34 W
Minas, *Cuba* **25** 23 7 N 82 12 W
Minho, Rio →, *Jamaica* **26** 17 47 N 77 17 W
Miragoâne, *Haiti* **30** 18 27 N 73 6 W
Mirebalais, *Haiti* **30** 18 50 N 72 6 W
Misery, Mt., *Barbados* **36** 17 22 N 62 48 W
Mitan, *Trinidad & T.* **38** 10 51 N 61 7 W
Mitchell Town, *Jamaica* **27** 17 48 N 77 13 W
Moca, *Dominican Rep.* **30** 19 26 N 70 33 W
Môle St. Nicholas, *Haiti* **30** 19 48 N 73 23 W
Mona Passage, *Puerto Rico* **12** 18 0 N 67 0 W
Monati, *Puerto Rico* **31** 18 25 N 66 28 W
Moneague, *Jamaica* **27** 18 16 N 77 7 W
Monkey Town, *Trinidad & T.* **38** 10 12 N 61 25 W
Monos I., *Trinidad & T.* **38** 10 42 N 61 42 W
Monte Cristi, *Dominican Rep.* **30** 19 52 N 71 39 W
Montego Bay, *Jamaica* **26** 18 27 N 77 56 W
Montpelier, *Jamaica* **26** 18 22 N 77 56 W
Montreuil, *Grenada* **35** 12 11 N 61 38 W
Montrouis, *Haiti* **30** 18 57 N 72 42 W
Montserrat □, *Trinidad & T.* **38** 10 25 N 61 21 W
Montserrat ■ **32** 16 45 N 62 14 W
Montserrat Hills, *Trinidad & T.* **38** 10 23 N 61 21 W
Moore Town, *Jamaica* **27** 18 5 N 76 26 W
Morant →, *Jamaica* **27** 17 55 N 76 26 W
Morant Bay, *Jamaica* **27** 17 53 N 76 25 W
Morant Pt., *Jamaica* **27** 17 55 N 76 10 W
Morgans Bluff, *Bahamas* **23** 25 11 N 78 2 W
Moriah, *Trinidad & T.* **38** 11 15 N 60 43 W
Morne Cabaio, Mt., *Haiti* **30** 18 21 N 72 16 W
Morne Raquette, *Dominica* **34** 15 27 N 61 27 W
Morón, *Cuba* **25** 22 9 N 78 39 W
Morovis, *Puerto Rico* **31** 18 20 N 66 24 W
Moruga, *Trinidad & T.* **38** 10 6 N 61 17 W
Moruga □, *Trinidad & T.* **38** 10 8 N 61 19 W
Moruga →, *Trinidad & T.* **38** 10 5 N 61 16 W
Morvant, *Trinidad & T.* **41** 10 40 N 61 29 W
Mose Bottom, *Barbados* **36** 13 13 N 59 36 W
Moule, *Guadeloupe* **33** 16 20 N 61 21 W
Moule à Chique, C., *St. Lucia* **34** 13 43 N 60 57 W
Mount St. George, *Trinidad & T.* **38** 11 12 N 60 41 W
Mount Wynne, *St. Vincent & G.* **35** 13 14 N 61 16 W
Mountain Spring Pt., *Jamaica* **26** 18 30 N 77 40 W
Mucurapo, *Trinidad & T.* **38** 10 40 N 61 32 W
Mulatre, Pt., *Dominica* **34** 15 17 N 61 15 W
Mullet Bay, *St. Maarten* **32** 18 4 N 63 7 W
Mundo Nuevo, *Trinidad & T.* **38** 10 28 N 61 15 W
Mustique I., *St. Vincent & G.* **32** 12 52 N 61 11 W
Myersville, *Jamaica* **26** 17 58 N 77 37 W

N

Nags Head, *St. Kitts-N.* **32** 17 13 N 62 38 W
Nagua, *Dominican Rep.* **30** 19 23 N 69 50 W
Naguabo, *Puerto Rico* **31** 18 13 N 65 44 W
Nain, *Jamaica* **26** 17 57 N 77 38 W
Nanton Pt., *Antigua & B.* **32** 17 0 N 61 45 W
Naparima □, *Trinidad & T.* **38** 10 14 N 61 27 W
Naranjito, *Puerto Rico* **31** 18 18 N 66 15 W
Nariva □, *Trinidad & T.* **38** 10 22 N 61 10 W
Nariva →, *Trinidad & T.* **38** 10 24 N 61 14 W
Nariva Swamp, *Trinidad & T.* **38** 10 25 N 61 4 W
Nassau, *Bahamas* **23** 25 5 N 77 21 W
Nassau East, *Bahamas* **23** 25 5 N 77 18 W
Navet →, *Trinidad & T.* **38** 10 24 N 61 5 W
Navet Dam, *Trinidad & T.* **38** 10 26 N 61 14 W
Necker, I., *Virgin Is.* **31** 18 32 N 64 28 W
Needham's Pt., *Barbados* **36** 13 5 N 59 36 W
Negra Pt., *Trinidad & T.* **38** 10 4 N 61 23 W
Negril, *Jamaica* **26** 18 22 N 78 20 W
Neiba, *Dominican Rep.* **30** 18 28 N 71 25 W
Nesfield, *Barbados* **36** 13 13 N 59 32 W
Nestor, *Trinidad & T.* **38** 10 31 N 61 9 W
Netherlands Antilles ■ **9** 12 10 N 69 0 W
Nevis, *St. Kitts-N.* **32** 17 11 N 62 35 W
Nevis Pk., *St. Kitts-N.* **32** 17 9 N 62 34 W
New Amsterdam, *Guyana* **42** 6 18 N 57 30 W
New Broughton, *Jamaica* **26** 18 12 N 78 13 W
New Grant, *Trinidad & T.* **38** 10 17 N 61 19 W
New Kingston, *Jamaica* **41** 18 0 N 76 48 W
New Plymouth, *Bahamas* **23** 26 50 N 77 23 W
New Providence I., *Bahamas* **23** 25 3 N 77 25 W
Newcastle, *Jamaica* **27** 18 5 N 76 42 W
Newcastle, *St. Kitts-N.* **32** 17 14 N 62 42 W
Newfield, *Antigua & B.* **32** 17 2 N 61 44 W
Newmarket, *Jamaica* **26** 18 9 N 77 55 W
Newport, *Jamaica* **26** 17 57 N 77 17 W
Newton, *Jamaica* **26** 18 5 N 77 43 W
Nicolls Town, *Bahamas* **23** 25 8 N 78 0 W
Nipe, Sa. de, *Cuba* **25** 20 28 N 75 49 W
Niquero, *Cuba* **25** 20 3 N 77 34 W
Noires Mts., *Haiti* **30** 18 27 N 72 20 W
Nonsuch B., *Antigua & B.* **32** 17 3 N 61 42 W
Nord □, *Haiti* **30** 19 30 N 72 10 W
Nord, Massif du, *Haiti* **30** 19 40 N 72 10 W
Nord-Ouest □, *Haiti* **30** 19 45 N 73 5 W
Norman I., *Virgin Is.* **31** 18 20 N 64 32 W
Normans Castle, *Bahamas* **23** 26 44 N 77 27 W
North Caicos, *Turks & Caicos* **23** 21 54 N 72 0 W
North Negril Pt., *Jamaica* **26** 18 21 N 78 21 W
North Pt., *Barbados* **36** 13 20 N 59 37 W
North Pt., *Trinidad & T.* **38** 11 17 N 60 33 W
North Ruimveldt, *Guyana* **41** 6 49 N 58 13 W
North Side, *Cayman Is.* **22** 19 21 N 81 13 W
North Union, *St. Vincent & G.* **35** 13 14 N 61 12 W
North West Bluff, *Montserrat* **32** 16 49 N 62 12 W
North West Pt., *Jamaica* **26** 18 27 N 78 13 W
Northeast Providence Channel, *Bahamas* **23** 25 40 N 77 9 W
Northern Range, *Trinidad & T.* **38** 10 44 N 61 15 W
Northernwest Providence Channel, *Bahamas* **23** 26 10 N 78 20 W
Nueva Gerona, *Cuba* **24** 21 53 N 82 49 W
Nueva Paz, *Cuba* **24** 22 46 N 81 45 W
Nuevitas, *Cuba* **25** 21 31 N 77 12 W
Nuevo, Rio →, *Jamaica* **27** 18 25 N 77 1 W

O

Ocho Rios, *Jamaica* **27** 18 24 N 77 6 W
Ohimborazo, *Barbados* **36** 13 12 N 59 33 W
Oistins B., *Barbados* **36** 13 4 N 59 33 W
Old Bahama Channel, *Cuba* **25** 22 30 N 78 50 W
Old England, *Jamaica* **26** 17 58 N 77 29 W
Old Fort Pt., *Montserrat* **32** 17 0 N 61 54 W
Old Harbour, *Jamaica* **27** 17 56 N 77 7 W
Old Harbour B., *Jamaica* **27** 17 54 N 77 6 W
Old Man B., *Cayman Is.* **22** 19 22 N 81 11 W
Old Road, *Antigua & B.* **32** 17 0 N 61 50 W
Old Road Bluff, *Antigua & B.* **32** 16 59 N 61 50 W
Old Road Bluff, *Montserrat* **32** 16 45 N 62 14 W
Old Road Town, *St. Kitts-N.* **32** 17 17 N 62 47 W
Omaja, *Cuba* **25** 20 41 N 76 45 W
Oracabessa, *Jamaica* **27** 18 24 N 76 57 W
Orange B., *Jamaica* **26** 18 22 N 78 19 W
Orange Hill, *St. Vincent & G.* **35** 13 18 N 61 12 W
Orange Walk, □ *Belize* **22** 18 6 N 88 33 W
Organos, Sierra de los, *Cuba* **24** 22 25 N 84 0 W
Oriental, Cordillera, *Dominican Rep.* **30** 18 55 N 69 15 W
Oropuche →, *Trinidad & T.* **38** 10 36 N 61 6 W
Ortoire □, *Trinidad & T.* **38** 16 16 N 61 19 W
Ortoire →, *Trinidad & T.* **38** 10 20 N 61 0 W
Osborne Store, *Jamaica* **26** 17 58 N 77 23 W
Otaheite B., *Trinidad & T.* **38** 10 14 N 61 33 W
Ouest □, *Haiti* **30** 18 35 N 72 10 W

P

Padre Las Cases, *Dominican Rep.* **30** 18 44 N 70 56 W
Pagua Bay, *Dominica* **34** 15 32 N 61 17 W
Pakaraima Mts., *Guyana* **42** 4 5 N 61 30 W
Palma Soriano, *Cuba* **25** 20 15 N 75 59 W
Palo Seco, *Trinidad & T.* **38** 10 5 N 61 35 W
Palmetto Pt., *Antigua & B.* **32** 17 37 N 61 51 W
Palmetto Pt., *Bahamas* **23** 25 5 N 76 5 W
Palmetto Pt., *Jamaica* **27** 18 18 N 76 41 W
Paradise, *Guyana* **42** 5 34 N 57 56 W
Parham, *Antigua & B.* **32** 17 6 N 61 46 W
Parham Harbour, *Antigua & B.* **32** 17 7 N 61 46 W
Paria, Gulf of, *Trinidad & T.* **38** 10 20 N 62 0 W
Parika, *Guyana* **42** 6 51 N 58 25 W
Parks Road, *Jamaica* **27** 18 8 N 76 52 W
Parlatuvier, *Trinidad & T.* **38** 11 18 N 60 39 W
Parottee Pt., *Jamaica* **26** 17 56 N 77 50 W
Paso Real de San Diego, *Cuba* **24** 22 34N 83 18 W
Patillos, Puerto, *Puerto Rico* **31** 17 58 N 66 1 W
Patos I., *Trinidad & T.* **38** 10 38 N 61 52 W
Paul's Pt., *Barbados* **36** 13 17 N 59 34 W
Pelée, Mt., *Martinique* **33** 14 48 N 61 10 W
Pelican Pt., *Bahamas* **23** 26 38 N 78 7 W
Péligre, L. de, *Haiti* **30** 18 52 N 71 56 W
Pembroke, *St. Vincent & G.* **35** 17 7 N 62 35 W
Pembroke, *Trinidad & T.* **38** 11 13 N 60 37 W
Penal, *Trinidad & T.* **38** 10 10 N 61 28 W
Penuelas, *Puerto Rico* **31** 18 3 N 66 43 W
Peravia □, *Dominican Rep.* **30** 18 30 N 70 27 W
Peruvian Vale, *St. Vincent & G.* **35** 13 13 N 61 12 W
Peter I., *Virgin Is.* **31** 18 22 N 64 32 W
Peter's Mine, *Guyana* **42** 6 15 N 59 19 W
Petersfield, *Jamaica* **26** 18 15 N 78 5 W
Pétionville, *Haiti* **30** 18 31 N 72 17 W
Petit-Goâve, *Haiti* **30** 18 27 N 72 51 W
Petit Soufrière B, *Dominica* **34** 15 23 N 61 15 W
Philipsburg, *St. Vincent & G.* **32** 18 3 N 63 5 W
Piarco, *Trinidad & T.* **38** 10 35 N 61 20 W
Picard →, *Dominica* **34** 15 33 N 61 31 W
Piedrecitas, *Cuba* **25** 21 37 N 78 20 W
Pierreville, *Trinidad & T.* **38** 10 17 N 61 2 W
Pigeon I., *St. Lucia* **34** 17 47 N 77 5 W
Pillsbury Sound, *Virgin Is.* **31** 18 20 N 64 49 W
Pina, *Cuba* **25** 22 1 N 78 43 W
Pinar del Rio, *Cuba* **24** 22 24 N 83 42 W
Pinar del Rio □, *Cuba* **24** 22 25 N 83 42 W
Pinder Point, *Bahamas* **23** 26 30 N 78 44 W
Pinelands, *Barbados* **41** 13 6 N 59 35 W
Pirara, *Guyana* **42** 3 30 N 50 45 W
Pitch L., *Trinidad & T.* **38** 10 13 N 61 38 W
Pitch, Pt., *Trinidad & T.* **38** 10 15 N 61 37 W
Pitts Town, *Bahamas* **23** 22 48 N 74 21 W
Placetas, *Cuba* **24** 22 18 N 78 40 W
Plantain Garden →, **27** 17 57 N 76 13 W
Plata, R. de la →, *Puerto Rico* **31** 18 29 N 66 15 W
Playa de Guayanés, *Puerto Rico* **31** 18 4 N 65 49 W
Playa Giron, *Cuba* **24** 22 4 N 81 2 W
Playa Larga, *Cuba* **24** 22 16 N 81 10 W
Playitas, *Cuba* **25** 20 4 N 74 29 W
Plymouth, *Montserrat* **32** 16 41 N 62 12 W
Plymouth, *Trinidad & T.* **38** 11 13 N 60 47 W
Point, Cap, *St. Lucia* **34** 14 7 N 60 57 W
Point Fortin, *Trinidad & T.* **38** 10 21 N 61 41 W
Point Hill, *Jamaica* **27** 18 5 N 77 6 W
Pointe-a-Pierre, *Trinidad & T.* **38** 10 18 N 61 17 W
Pointe-a-Pierre □, *Trinidad & T.* **38** 10 20 N 61 24 W
Pointe-a-Pitre, *Guadeloupe* **33** 16 14 N 61 32 W
Pointe-à-Raquette, *Haiti* **30** 18 47 N 73 4 W
Pointe Noire, *Guadeloupe* **33** 16 14 N 61 47 W
Polink Pt., *Jamaica* **26** 17 50 N 76 57 W
Pomeroon-Supernaam □, *Guyana* **42** 7 0 N 59 0 W
Ponce, *Puerto Rico* **31** 18 1 N 66 37 W
Ponce □, *Puerto Rico* **31** 18 1 N 66 36 W
Poole, *Trinidad & T.* **38** 10 17 N 61 14 W
Poole →, *Trinidad & T.* **38** 10 15 N 61 5 W
Port Antonio, *Jamaica* **27** 18 10 N 76 27 W
Port-au-Prince, *Haiti* **30** 18 33 N 72 20 W
Port-de-Paix, *Haiti* **30** 19 56 N 72 52 W
Port Kaiser, *Jamaica* **26** 17 53 N 77 33 W
Port Kaituma, *Guyana* **42** 7 44 N 59 53 W
Port Maria, *Jamaica* **27** 18 22 N 76 54 W
Port Morant, *Jamaica* **27** 17 53 N 76 20 W
Port Nelson, *Bahamas* **23** 23 41 N 74 51 W
Port-of-Spain, *Trinidad & T.* **41** 10 38 N 61 31 W
Port Praslin, *St. Lucia* **34** 13 52 N 60 51 W
Port Royal, *Jamaica* **41** 17 56 N 76 51 W
Portland, *Barbados* **36** 13 16 N 59 36 W
Portland □, *Jamaica* **27** 18 8 N 76 32 W
Portland Pt., *Jamaica* **27** 17 42 N 77 11 W
Portmore, *Jamaica* **41** 17 53 N 77 33 W
Portsmouth, *Dominica* **34** 15 34 N 61 27 W
Porus, *Jamaica* **26** 18 2 N 77 25 W
Potaro, *Guyana* **42** 5 23 N 59 8 W
Potaro →, *Guyana* **42** 5 22 N 58 54 W
Potaro-Siparuni □,*Guyana* **42** 5 0 N 59 20 W
Potters Village, *Antigua & B.* **32** 17 5 N 61 49 W
Prashad Nagar, *Guyana* **41** 6 50 N 58 8 W
Praslin, *St. Lucia* **34** 13 53 N 60 54 W
Pratville, *Jamaica* **26** 17 54 N 77 25 W
Preau, *Trinidad & T.* **38** 10 12 N 61 19 W
Prince Rupert B., *Dominica* **34** 15 34 N 61 29 W
Princes Town, *Trinidad & T.* **38** 10 16 N 61 23 W
Providenciales I., *Turks & Caicos* **23** 21 48 N 72 48 W
Puelbo Nuevo, *Puerto Rico* **31** 18 11 N 66 58 W
Puerca, Pta., *Puerto Rico* **31** 18 14 N 65 36 W
Puerto Manati, *Cuba* **25** 21 24 N 76 50 W
Puerto Nevo, Pta., *Puerto Rico* **31** 18 30 N 66 24 W
Puerto Padre, *Cuba* **25** 21 13 N 76 35 W
Puerto Plata, *Dominican Rep.* **30** 19 48 N 70 41 W
Puerto Rico ■ **31** 18 0 N 67 0 W
Puerto Rico Trench **12** 18 0 N 65 0 W
Punta Gorda, *Belize* **22** 16 10 N 88 45 W

Q

Quanary →, *Dominica* **34** 15 20 N 61 17 W
Queen of Spain's Valley, *Jamaica* **26** 18 26 N 77 45 W
Queen's Cave, *Bahamas* **23** 26 32 N 78 42 W
Queenstown, *Guyana* **41** 7 12 N 58 30 W

R

Rabacca, *St. Lucia* **35** 13 18 N 61 9 W
Race Course, *Jamaica* **26** 17 51 N 77 20 W
Ragged Island Range, *Bahamas* **23** 22 12 N 75 44 W
Ragged Pt., *Barbados* **36** 13 10 N 59 10 W
Rancho Veloz, *Cuba* **24** 22 53 N 80 23 W
Ranchuelo, *Cuba* **24** 22 20 N 80 10 W
Raymond, C., *Haiti* **30** 18 9 N 72 51 W
Reading, *Jamaica* **26** 18 26 N 77 57 W
Red Bays, *Bahamas* **23** 19 18 N 81 21 W
Redhead, *Trinidad & T.* **38** 10 44 N 60 58 W
Remedios, *Cuba* **24** 22 30 N 79 32 W
Richmond, *Jamaica* **27** 18 14 N 76 54 W
Richmond Peak, *St. Vincent & G.* **35** 13 17 N 61 13 W
Richmond River →, *St. Vincent & G.* **35** 13 18 N 61 15 W
Rincon B., *Puerto Rico* **31** 18 0 N 66 20 W
Rio Bueno, *Jamaica* **26** 18 28 N 77 28 W
Rio Claro, *Trinidad & T.* **38** 10 33 N 61 11 W
Rio Cobre →, *Jamaica* **27** 17 59 N 76 52 W
Rio Grande, *Puerto Rico* **31** 18 23 N 65 50 W
Rio Minho →, *Jamaica* **27** 17 47 N 77 17 W
Rio Piedras, *Puerto Rico* **31** 18 25 N 66 3 W
Riviere-Pilote, *Martinique* **33** 14 29 N 60 54 W
Road Town, *Virgin Is.* **31** 18 28 N 64 39 W
Roberts, Mt., *Trinidad & T.* **38** 10 47 N 61 10 W
Roche's Bluff, *Montserrat* **32** 16 42 N 62 9 W
Rock River, *Jamaica* **27** 18 5 N 77 13 W
Rock Sound, *Bahamas* **23** 24 56 N 76 11 W
Rockly B., *Trinidad & T.* **38** 11 10 N 60 44 W
Rockstone, *Guyana* **42** 6 0 N 58 30 W
Rocky Pt., *Jamaica* **26** 17 49 N 77 9 W
Rodas, *Cuba* **24** 22 20 N 80 33 W
Rolleville, *Bahamas* **23** 23 41 N 76 0 W
Romano, Cayo, *Cuba* **25** 22 4 N 77 50 W
Ronde I., *Grenada* **32** 12 29 N 61 36 W
Rosalie, *Dominica* **34** 15 22 N 61 16 W
Rosario, Sa. del, *Cuba* **24** 22 48 N 83 15 W
Rose Hall, *Guyana* **42** 6 16 N 57 23 W
Roseau , *Dominica* **34** 15 18 N 61 23 W
Roseau→, *Dominica* **34** 15 18 N 61 24 W
Roseau→,*St. Lucia* **34** 13 58 N 61 2 W
Roses, *Bahamas* **23** 22 59 N 74 53 W
Rosignol, *Guyana* **42** 6 18 N 57 34 W
Roxborough, *Trinidad & T.* **38** 11 15 N 60 35 W
Rum Cay, *Bahamas* **23** 23 41 N 74 53 W
Runaway B., *Jamaica* **26** 18 27 N 77 20 W
Rupununi→, *Guyana* **42** 4 3 N 58 34 W

S

Saba, *Neth. Antilles* **32** 17 42 N 63 20 W
Saba Grande de Boya, *Dominican Rep.* **30** 18 57 N 69 48 W
Saba Grande de Palenque, *Dominican Rep.* **30** 18 16 N 70 9 W
Sabana, Arch. de, *Cuba* **24** 23 0 N 80 0 W
Sabinal, Cayo, *Cuba* **25** 21 40 N 77 20 W
Saddle Hill, *St. Kitts-N.* **32** 17 7 N 62 33 W
Sadhoowa, *Trinidad & T.* **38** 10 8 N 61 27 W
Sadlers, *St. Kitts-N.* **32** 17 24 N 62 47 W
Sagua de Tánamo, *Cuba* **25** 20 38 N 75 14 W
Sagua la Grande, *Cuba* **24** 22 48 N 80 6 W
Sagua la Grande →, *Cuba* **24** 22 56 N 80 1 W
St. Andrew □, *Barbados* **36** 13 14 N 59 34 W
St. Andrew □, *Jamaica* **27** 18 5 N 76 50 W
St. Andrew □, *Trinidad & T.* **38** 10 35 N 61 10 W
St. Ann □, *Jamaica* **26** 18 21 N 77 16 W
St. Ann's □, *Trinidad & T.* **38** 10 41 N 61 28 W
St. Ann's Bay, *Jamaica* **27** 18 26 N 77 12 W
St. Barthélemy,I., *St. Martin* **32** 17 55 N 62 50 W
St. Catherine □, *Jamaica* **27** 18 4 N 77 1 W
St. Catherine, Mt., *Grenada* **35** 12 10 N 61 40 W
St. Catherine Pt., *Bermuda* **23** 32 24 N 64 42 W
St. Christopher = St. Kitts, *St. Kitts-N.* **32** 17 25 N 61 45 W
St. Clair, *Trinidad & T.* **41** 10 40 N 61 31 W
St. Croix I., *Puerto Rico* **31** 17 45 N 64 45 W
St. D'Acre, *Jamaica* **26** 18 19 N 77 22 W
St. David □, *Trinidad & T.* **38** 10 47 N 61 3 W
St. David's I., *Bermuda* **23** 32 23 N 64 42 W
St. Elizabeth □, *Jamaica* **26** 18 5 N 77 50 W
St. Eustatius, *Neth. Antilles* **32** 17 41 N 62 48 W
St. George □, *Barbados* **36** 13 7 N 59 33 W
St. George □, *Trinidad & T.* **38** 10 40 N 61 25 W
St. Georges, *Bahamas* **23** 25 33 N 76 46 W
St. George's, *Grenada* **35** 12 4 N 61 44 W
St. George's Harbour, *Bermuda* **23** 32 33 N 64 42 W
St. George's I., *Bermuda* **23** 32 24 N 64 42 W
St. Giles Is., *Trinidad & T.* **38** 11 21 N 60 32 W
St. James, *Trinidad & T.* **41** 10 40 N 61 31 W
St. James □, *Barbados* **36** 12 7 N 61 39 W
St. James □, *Jamaica* **26** 18 23 N 77 53 W
St. John □, *Barbados* **36** 13 10 N 59 30 W
St. John I., *Virgin Is.* **31** 18 21 N 64 48 W
St. John's, *Antigua & B.* **32** 17 7 N 61 51 W
St. Johns, *Montserrat* **32** 16 46 N 62 11 W
St. Joseph, *Dominica* **34** 15 24 N 61 26 W
St. Joseph, *Trinidad & T.* **38** 10 18 N 59 59 W
St. Joseph, *Trinidad & T.* **38** 10 40 N 61 25 W
St. Joseph □, *Barbados* **36** 15 12 N 59 33 W
St. Kitts - Nevis ■ **32** 17 25 N 62 45 W

WORLD MAPS

EUROPE 4-15, ASIA 16-25, AFRICA 26-33, AUSTRALIA AND OCEANIA 34-37,
NORTH AMERICA 38-45, SOUTH AMERICA 46-47

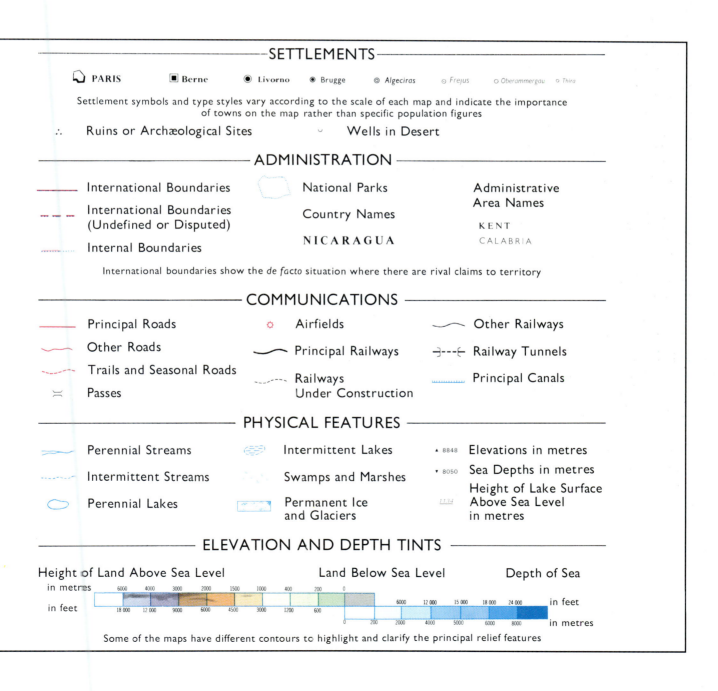

--- SETTLEMENTS ---

⬡ PARIS   ■ Berne   ◉ Livorno   ◉ Brugge   ◎ Algeciras   ⊙ *Frejus*   ○ *Oberammergau*   ○ *Thira*

Settlement symbols and type styles vary according to the scale of each map and indicate the importance
of towns on the map rather than specific population figures

∴ Ruins or Archæological Sites   ᴗ Wells in Desert

--- ADMINISTRATION ---

International Boundaries

International Boundaries
(Undefined or Disputed)

Internal Boundaries

National Parks

Country Names

NICARAGUA

Administrative
Area Names

KENT

CALABRIA

International boundaries show the *de facto* situation where there are rival claims to territory

--- COMMUNICATIONS ---

Principal Roads   ✿ Airfields   ⌣ Other Railways

Other Roads   Principal Railways   ⌐---⌐ Railway Tunnels

Trails and Seasonal Roads   Railways Under Construction   Principal Canals

⌦ Passes

--- PHYSICAL FEATURES ---

Perennial Streams   Intermittent Lakes   ▲ 8848   Elevations in metres

Intermittent Streams   Swamps and Marshes   ▼ 8050   Sea Depths in metres

Perennial Lakes   Permanent Ice and Glaciers   *1134*   Height of Lake Surface Above Sea Level in metres

--- ELEVATION AND DEPTH TINTS ---

Height of Land Above Sea Level   Land Below Sea Level   Depth of Sea

in metres   6000 4000 3000 2000 1500 1000 400 200 0
in feet   18 000 12 000 9000 6000 4500 3000 1200 600

6000 12 000 15 000 18 000 24 000   in feet
0 200 2000 4000 5000 6000 8000   in metres

Some of the maps have different contours to highlight and clarify the principal relief features

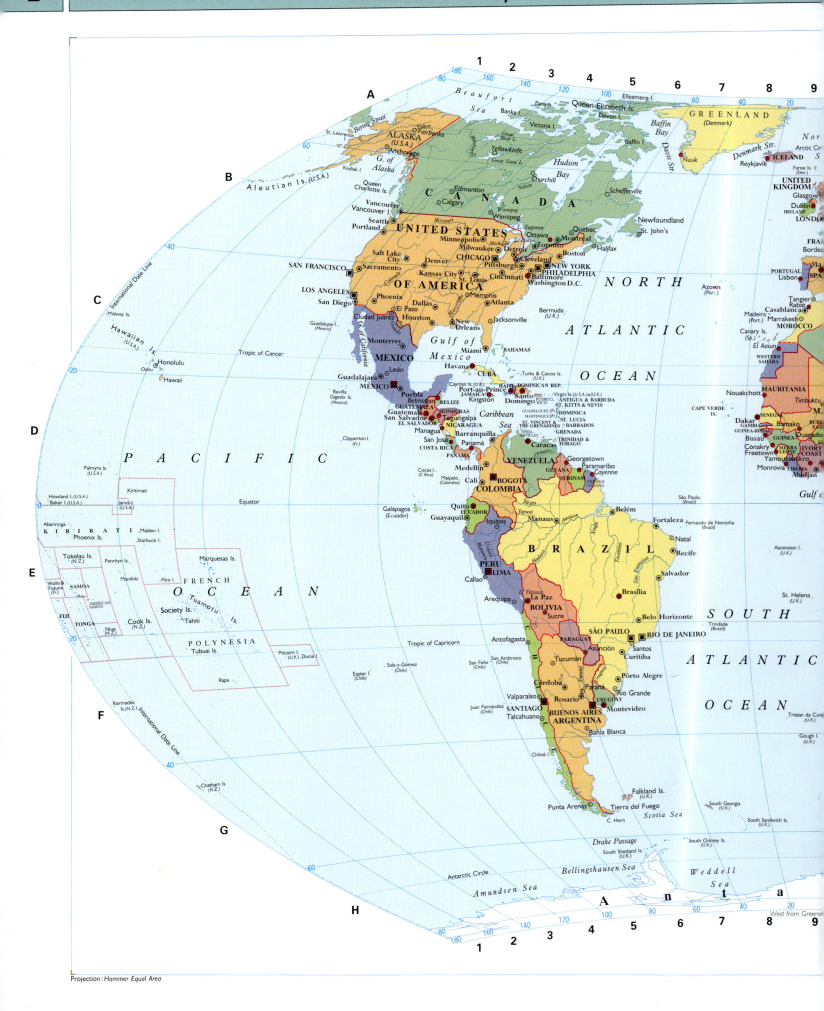

Projection : *Hammer Equal Area*

Hanoi ● Capital Cities

CARTOGRAPHY BY PHILIP'S.

1:20 000 000

Projection: Bonne
CARTOGRAPHY BY PHILIP'S

ICELAND
On the same scale West from Greenwich

Projection : Conical with two standard parallels

East from Greenwich

1 : 10 000 000

COPYRIGHT GEORGE PHILIP & SON, LTD.

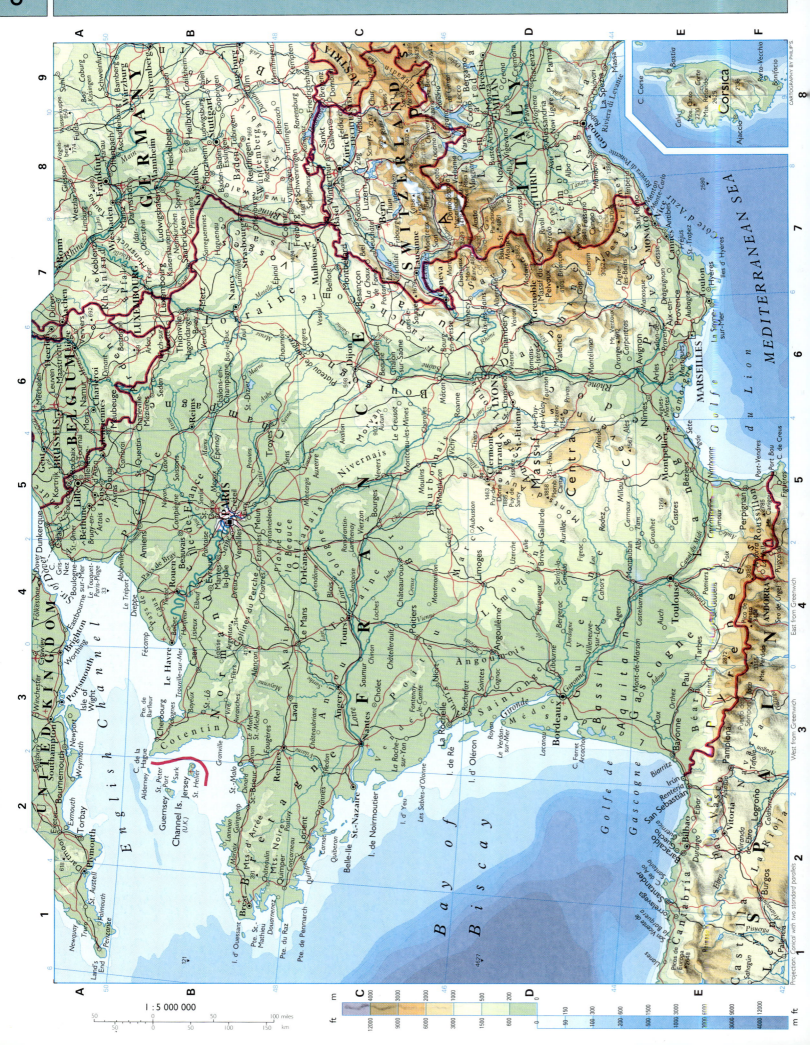

1 : 5 000 000

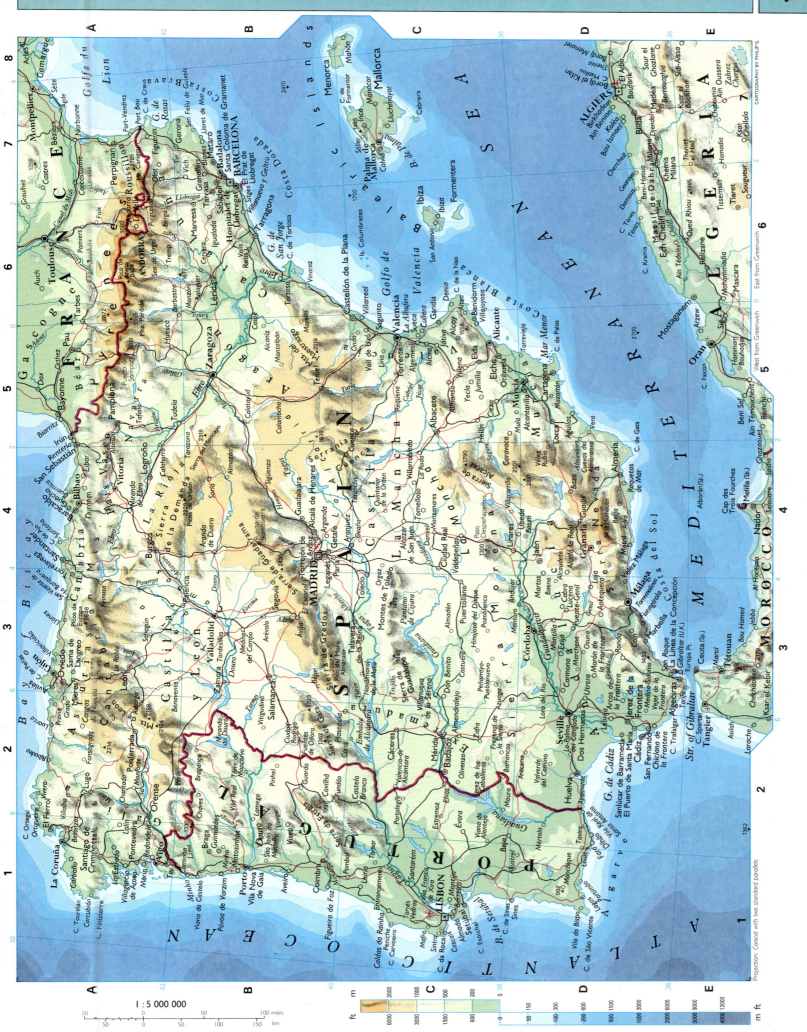

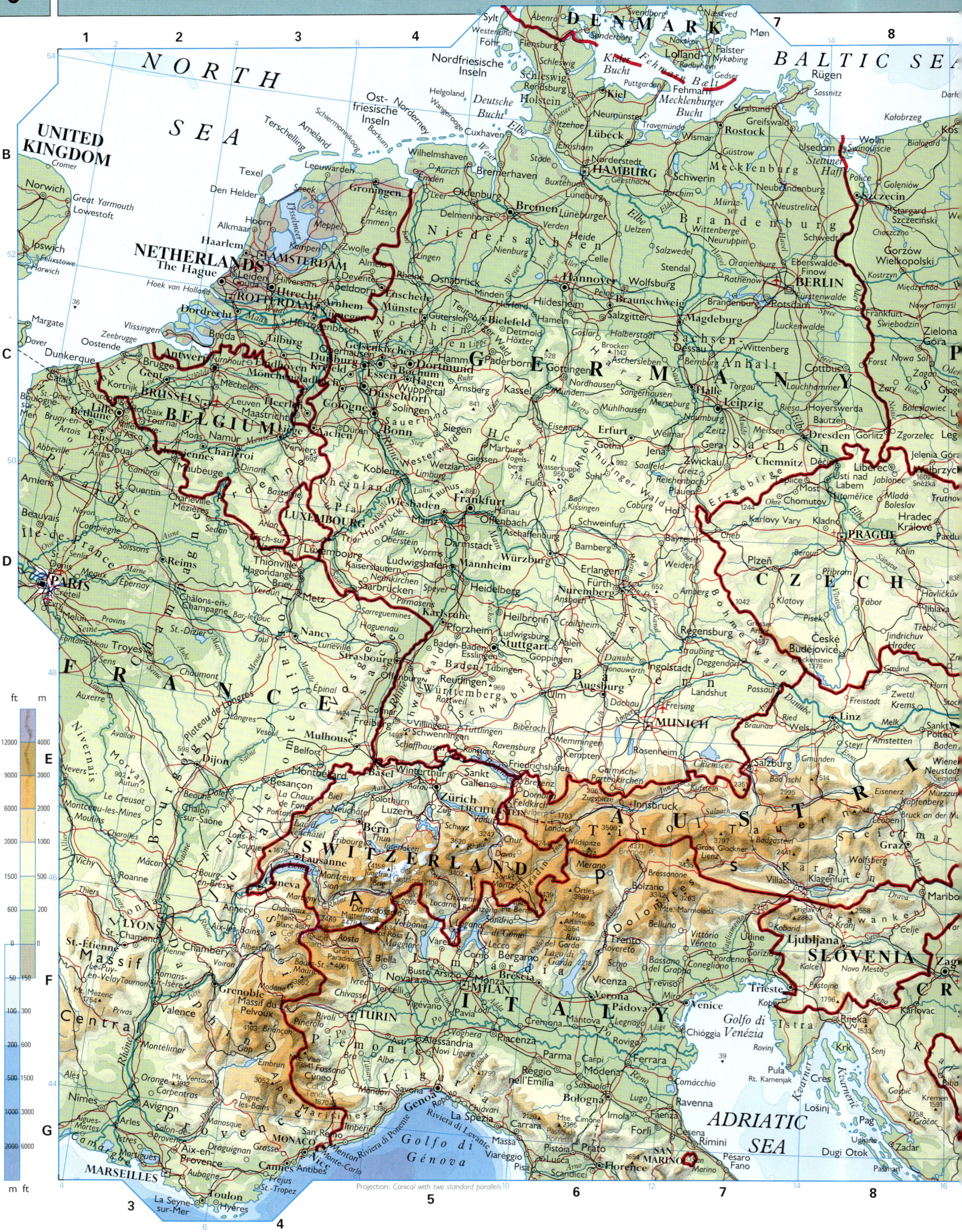
NORTH SEA
BALTIC SEA
ADRIATIC SEA
Golfo di Génova
Golfo di Venézia
UNITED KINGDOM
DENMARK
NETHERLANDS
BELGIUM
LUXEMBOURG
GERMANY
FRANCE
SWITZERLAND
LIECHTENSTEIN
AUSTRIA
ITALY
SLOVENIA
CZECH
MONACO
SAN MARINO
Amsterdam
The Hague
Rotterdam
Brussels
Paris
Berlin
Hamburg
Bremen
Hannover
Frankfurt
Stuttgart
Munich
Cologne
Düsseldorf
Dresden
Leipzig
Prague
Zürich
Bern
Geneva
Lausanne
Basel
Innsbruck
Salzburg
Linz
Graz
Ljubljana
Milan
Turin
Genoa
Venice
Trieste
Bologna
Verona
Florence
Nice
Marseilles
Lyons
Strasbourg
Dijon
Reims
Lille
Niedersachsen
Nordrhein-Westfalen
Hessen
Rheinland-Pfalz
Bayern
Sachsen
Brandenburg
Mecklenburg
Schwarzwald
Alpes
Massif Central
Dolomiti
Projection: Conical with two standard parallels

9 18 **10** 20 22 **11** 24 **12** 26 **13** 28 30 **14** 32 **15** 34 **16**

Wejherowo
Łeborz
Bytów
Starogard
Gdański
Chojnice
Świecie
Grudziądz
Brodnica

Baltijsk
Gdynia
Sopot
Gdańsk 329 Tczew
Elbląg
Braniewo
Malbork
Kwidzyn
Iława
Ostróda
Szczytno

Kaliningrad (Russia)
Gvardeysk
Bagrationovsk
Kętrzyn
Giżycko
Masurian Lakes
Ełk

Polessk
Gusev
Chernyakhovsk
Marijampolė
Suwałki
Augustów
Sokółka

Prienai
Vilnius
Druskininkai
Lida
Grodno

LITHUANIA
Ashmyany Smarhon
Varėna
Navahrudak
Masty
Dzyatlava

Vileyka
Maladzyechna
342
Zhodzina
MINSK
Cherven
Nyasvizh
Stowbtsy
Asipovichy

Borisov
346
Barysaw

Krupki 30
Shklow
Mstsislaw
Mogilev
Krychaw
Cherykaw
Slawharad

B

Bydgoszcz
Inowrocław
Toruń
Rypin

Starogard
Chełmno
Dzialdowo
Mława
Ciechanów

Łomża
Ostrołęka
Ostrów
Mazowiecka
Pułtusk

Białystok
Bielsk
Podlaski
Hajnówka

Svisloch
Pruzhany
Bereza

Slonim
Vawkavysk
Baranovichi
Klyetsk
Ivatsevichy

Lyakhavichy
Slutsk
Salihorsk

Nyasvizh
Hantsavichy

Bobruysk
Zhlobin
Svyetlahorsk
Rechytsa

Berezina
Aktsyabrski
Glusk

Rahachow
Gomel
Dnieper

52

Gniezno
Września
Konin
Wloclawek
Płock
Kutno
Lowicz

WARSAW
Legionowo
Pruszków
Żyrardów
Otwock

Siedlce
Sokołów
Podlaski

Międzyrzec
Podlaski
Łuków
Biała
Podlaska

Brest
Malaryta

Zhabinka
Kobryn
Dragichyn

Pinsk
Ivanava
Stolin

David Harodok
Pripyat
Mazyr
Yelsk

Khoyniki
Loyew
Oster
Desna

Pripet
316
Ovruch
Chernobyl
Kiev
Res.
Dymer
Irpin
KIEV

C

POLAND
Łódź
Pabianice
Zduńska
Wola
Sieradz

Radom
Puławy
Lublin
Świdnik
Kraśnik

Chełm
Lyuboml
Kovel
Novovolynsk
Volodymyr-
Volynsky

Rozhyshche
Staryy
Chartoriysk

Lutsk
Rovno
Dubno
Ostroh
Zdolbuniv

Kivertsi
Kostopil
Korets
Slavuta
Shepetivka

Novohrad-
Volynskyy
Malyn
Radomyshl

Korosten
Belokorovichi

Zhitomir
Pershotravensk
Korostyshev
Fastiv
Vasylkiv

50

Wrocław
Oława
Opole

Ostrów
Wielkopolski
Oleśnica
Kluczbork
Wieluń

Częstochowa
Radomsko
Piotrków
Trybunalski
Kańsk
Myszków

Kielce
Skarżysko-
Kamienna
Starachowice
Ostrowiec-
Świętokrzyski

Radom
Stalowa Wola
Sandomierz
Tarnobrzeg

Zamość
Sokal
Chervonohrad
Rava-
Ruska
Radekhiv
Beresteckko
Brody

341
Dubno
Ostroh
Kremenets
Izyaslav
Polonne

Berdichev
Kozyatyn
Skvyra

Belaya Tserkov
Tarashcha

D

Tarnowskie
Góry
Zabrze
Gliwice
Bytom
Sosnowiec
Katowice
Chorzów
Tychy

Kraków
Oświęcim
Bochnia
Tarnów

Dębica
Mielec
Rzeszów
Jarosław
Przemyśl

Nesterov
Yavoriv
Mostyska
Horodok
Lvov

UKRAINE
Zolochiv
Zbarazh
Ternopol
Skalat
Khmelnik
Vinnitsa
Zhmerynka
327
270

Opava
Ostrava
Frýdek-
Místek
1324
Karviná
Bielsko-Biala

Żywiec
1725
Nowy
Targ
Zakopane
2655

Nowy
Sącz
Krosno
Sanok
Jasło

Dukelský
Priesmyk 502
1345

Drohobych
Borislav
Truskavets
Stryy
Skole
Bolekhiv

Rogatyn
Berezhany
Terebovlya
Kopychyntsi
Horodok

Khodoriv
Buchach
Chortkiv
Skala-Podilska
Kamyanets-
Podilskyy

Zalishchyky
Mohyliv-
Podilskyy
384
Bar
Tetiyev
Lipovets
Zhashkiv

Uman
Bershad
Balta

E

Povazská
Bystrica
Žilina
Ružomberok
2043
Poprad
1157
Prešov
Bardejov

Martin
Banská
Bystrica
1458
Zvolen

Košice
Michalovce
Uzhgorod

1725
Ivano-Frankovsk
1881
Pechenizhyn
Nadvirna
Kolomyya
Snyatyn

Khotyn
Novoselytsya
Chernovtsy
Hlyboka

Yaremche
Yasinya
Rakhiv

Dniester
Horodenka
Yaremche

Ocnita
Edineţ
Drochia
Soroca

Moldova
Floreşti
Rîbniţa
Ananyiv

Kotovsk

48

SLOVAK REP.
Prievidza
Trenčín
768
Topoľčany
Nitra
Levice
Lučenec
Zvolen

Sátoraljaújhely
Ózd
Chop
Vynohradiv
Berehovo
Mukachevo
Khust
Tyachiv
Rakhiv
Sighetu
Marmaţiei

Borşa
1665
2303
Pietrosul

Rădăuţi
Dorohoi
Botoşani

Edineţ
Bălţi
Ungheni

Beltsy
Orhei
Kishinev

Dubasari
Tiraspol
Tighina
Razdelnaya

F

Bratislava
Nové
Zámky
Komárno

Bruck
Mosonmagyaróvár

Győr
Tatabánya
Pápa 704
Veszprém

Esztergom
Dunakeszi
BUDAPEST
Érd
Cegléd

Vác
Gyöngyös
Eger
Mezőkövesd
Miskolc
Salgótarján

Nyíregyháza
Satu Mare
Carei
Baia Mare
1848
2100
Pietrosul 1804

Suceava
Fălticeni
Paşcani
Roman
Vaslui

Iaşi
Ungheni
Husi
Leova
Cimişlia
Cahul

Tighina
Leova
Comrat
Ceadâr-Lunga
Tatarbunary

Bilhorod-
Dnivstrovskyy
Artsyz

46

HUNGARY
Székesfehérvár
Balaton
Siófok
Dunaújváros

Nagykörös
Szolnok
Kecskemét
Kiskunfélegyháza

Karcag
Mezőtúr
Debrecen
Hajdúböszörmény
Zalău

Oradea
Salonta
Cluj-Napoca
1836
Turda

Dej
Bistriţa
Vatra-Dornei
2303
Reghin
Tîrgu
Mureş
1777

Odorheiu
Secuiesc
Miercurea Ciuc
Oneşti
Bacău
Bîrlad
Tecuci

Focşani

G

Nagykanizsa
Kaposvár 881
Pécs

Szekszárd
Baja
Kiskunhalas
Kalocsa

Csongrád
Békéscsaba
Szentes
Gyula
Hódmezővásárhely
Makó
Oroshaza

Arad
Brad
Abrud 2509
Munţii Bihor

Alba-Iulia
Deva
Simeria
Tîrnăveni
Mediaş
Sighişoara

Sibiu
Făgăraş
Braşov
Sfîntu
Gheorghe 1783
Săcele

Rîmnicu
Sărat
Buzău
Galaţi
Brăila

Focşani
Vulcăneşti

Reni
Izmail
Kiliya
Vylkove
Sulina

Virovitica
Osijek
989
Nova

Vukovar
Vinkovci
Sombor
Novi Sad
Sremska
Mitrovica
Zemun

Subotica
Senta
Kikinda
Zrenjanin
Bečej

Timişoara
Caransebeş
Lugoj
Reşiţa
1445
Vt. Peleaga
2509
Vulcan
Petroşani
Hunedoara

Poarta
de Fier
Bela Crkva
1226
Iron
Gate
Orşova
Drobeta-
Turnu-Severin

Cîmpulung
Vî. Omul
Cîmpina
Ploieşti
Piteşti
Tîrgovişte
Slobozia
Feteşti

Buzău
Brăila

Constanţa
Babadag
Tulcea

F

Bosanska
Gradiška
Banja Luka
Doboj

Brčko
Bijeljina
Tuzla

BELGRADE
Pančevo
Smederevo
Požarevac

YUGOSLAVIA
Negotin
Bor

Craiova
Rosiori-
de-Vede
Slatina
Drăgăşani
Rîmnicu
Vîlcea
Tîrgu-Jiu
Piteşti

Olteniţa
Alexandria
Giurgiu
Turnu
Măgurele
Zimnicea
Corabia

Silistra
Turtukan
Călăraşi
Medgidia
Năvodari

Dobrich
Balchik
Nos Kaliakra

44

BOSNIA-
HERZEGOVINA
1943
Žepče
Travnik
Zenica
2006 Cincar
Sarajevo
2112
Visegrad

Srebrnica
Titovo
Užice
Čačak
Kragujevac
Valjevo
Svetozarevo
Zaječar

Vidin
Lom
Oryakhovo

Bailesti
Corabia

Turnu
Măgurele

BULGARIA
Razgrad
Ruse
Varna

G

East from Greenwich
1 : 5 000 000
CARTOGRAPHY BY PHILIP'S.

9 18 **10** 20 **11** 22 **12** 24 **13** 26 **14** **15**

50   0   50   100 miles
50 0 50 100 150 km

SWITZERLAND

AUSTRIA

SLOVENIA

CROATIA

FRANCE

ITALY

ALGERIA

TUNISIA

MALTA

Seas and major water features:
LIGURIAN SEA
TYRRHENIAN SEA
ADRIATIC SEA
MEDITERRANEAN

Selected place names:

Lyon, Annecy, Chambéry, Aix-les-Bains, Grenoble, Massif du Pelvoux, Valence, Montélimar, Orange, Avignon, Carpentras, Manosque, Salon-de-Provence, Aix-en-Provence, Aubagne, Istres, Martigues, MARSEILLES, Toulon, La Seyne-sur-Mer, Hyères, Îles d'Hyères, Draguignan, Grasse, Cannes, Antibes, Fréjus, St-Tropez, Côte d'Azur, MONACO, Monte-Carlo, Menton, Nice, San Remo, Imperia

Mont Blanc 4807, Matterhorn, Monte Rosa, Domodossola, Aosta, Gran Paradiso 4061, Ivrea, Biella, TURIN, Chivasso, Pinerolo, Rivoli, Asti, Alba, Cuneo, Mondovi, Savona, Genoa, Rapallo, Chiavari, La Spezia, Carrara, Massa, Viareggio, Pisa, Livorno

MILAN, Monza, Bergamo, Brescia, Como, Lecco, Varese, Lodi, Pavia, Piacenza, Cremona, Mantova, Verona, Vicenza, Padova, Venice, Treviso, Trieste, Rovigo, Ferrara, Modena, Reggio nell'Emilia, Parma, Bologna, Ravenna, Forlì, Cesena, Rimini, Imola, Faenza

Bolzano, Trento, Rovereto, Belluno, Udine, Gorizia, LJUBLJANA, Maribor, Zagreb, Rijeka, Pula, Split

Florence, SAN MARINO, Pésaro, Fano, Ancona, Urbino, Perugia, Assisi, Arezzo, Siena, Grosseto, Orvieto, Viterbo, Terni, Rieti, ROME, VATICAN CITY, Tivoli, Frosinone, Latina, Anzio, Gaeta

Corsica, Ajaccio, Bastia, Bonifacio, Porto-Vecchio, Mte. Cinto 2710

Sardinia, Sássari, Alghero, Oristano, Nuoro, Cágliari, Iglésias, Carbonia, Sant'Antioco, San Pietro, Asinara, Olbia, Porto Torres

NAPLES, Caserta, Avellino, Salerno, Benevento, Campobasso, Foggia, Bari, Barletta, Trani, Andria, Altamura, Matera, Potenza, Táranto, Brindisi, Cosenza, Crotone, Catanzaro, Réggio di Calábria

SICILY, Palermo, Trápani, Marsala, Mazara del Vallo, Sciacca, Agrigento, Gela, Ragusa, Siracusa, Catánia, Messina, Etna 3340, Enna, Caltanissetta

ALGERIA: Constantine, Annaba, Skikda, Guelma, El Milia, Collo

TUNISIA: Tunis, Bizerte, Sousse, Kairouan, Pantelleria (Italy), Ísole Pelagie (Italy), Lampedusa, Linosa

MALTA, Valletta, Gozo

Projection: Conical with two standard parallels

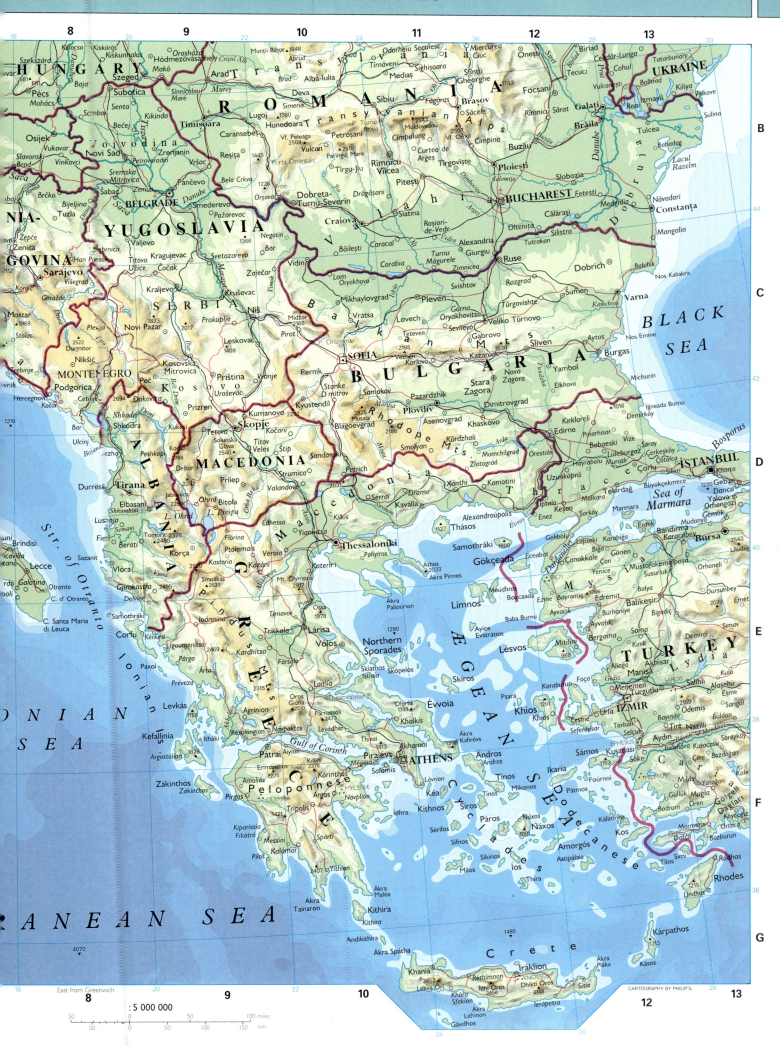

: 5 000 000

CARTOGRAPHY BY PHILIP'S

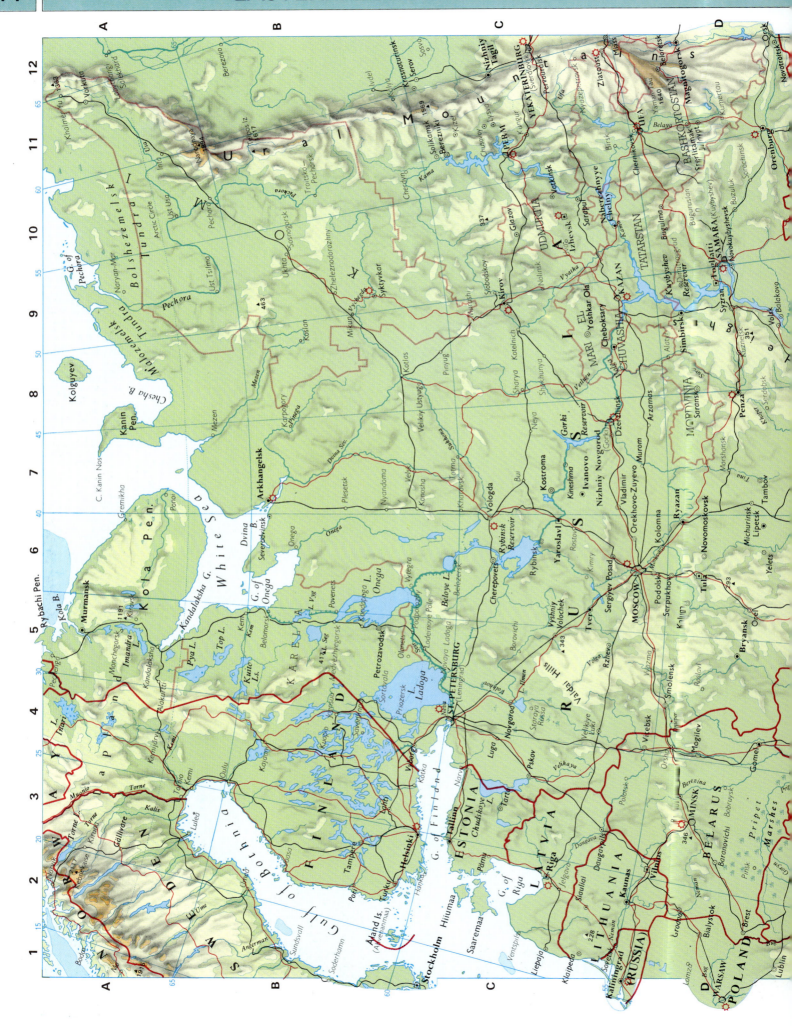

1:50 000 000

Projection: Bonne

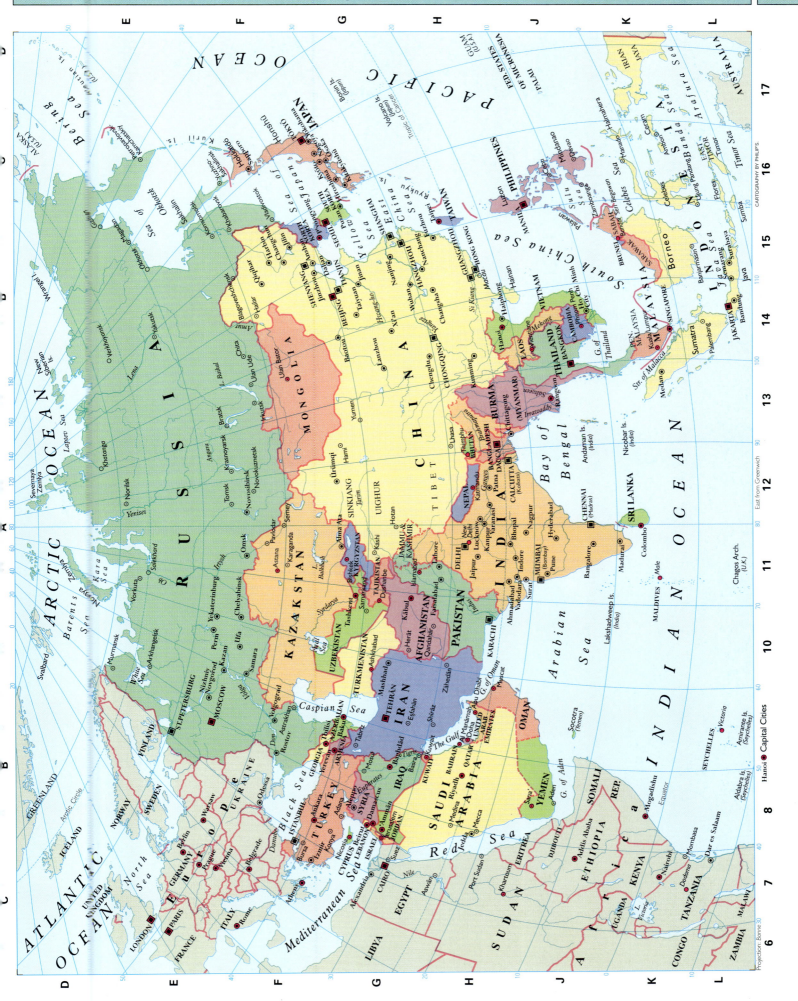

1 : 35 000 000

Projection: Lambert's Conical Orthomorphic
Copyright George Philip & Son Ltd.

SOUTHERN HONSHU, KYUSHU AND SHIKOKU

SEA OF JAPAN

PACIFIC OCEAN

Sea of Okhotsk

1:5 000 000

25 0 25 50 75 100 miles

25 0 25 50 75 100 km

Projection : Conical with two standard parallels

East from Greenwich

SOUTH KOREA

EAST CHINA SEA

SEA OF JAPAN

PACIFIC OCEAN

1:10 000 000

100 50 0 50 100 150 200 miles

100 0 100 200 300 km

Projection : Bonne

East from Greenwich

JAPAN

COPYRIGHT. GEORGE PHILIP & SON, LTD.

ft m
9000 3000
6000 2000
4500 1500
3000 1000
1200 400
600 200
0 0
200 600
2000 6000
4000 12,000
6000 18,000
8000 24,000
m ft

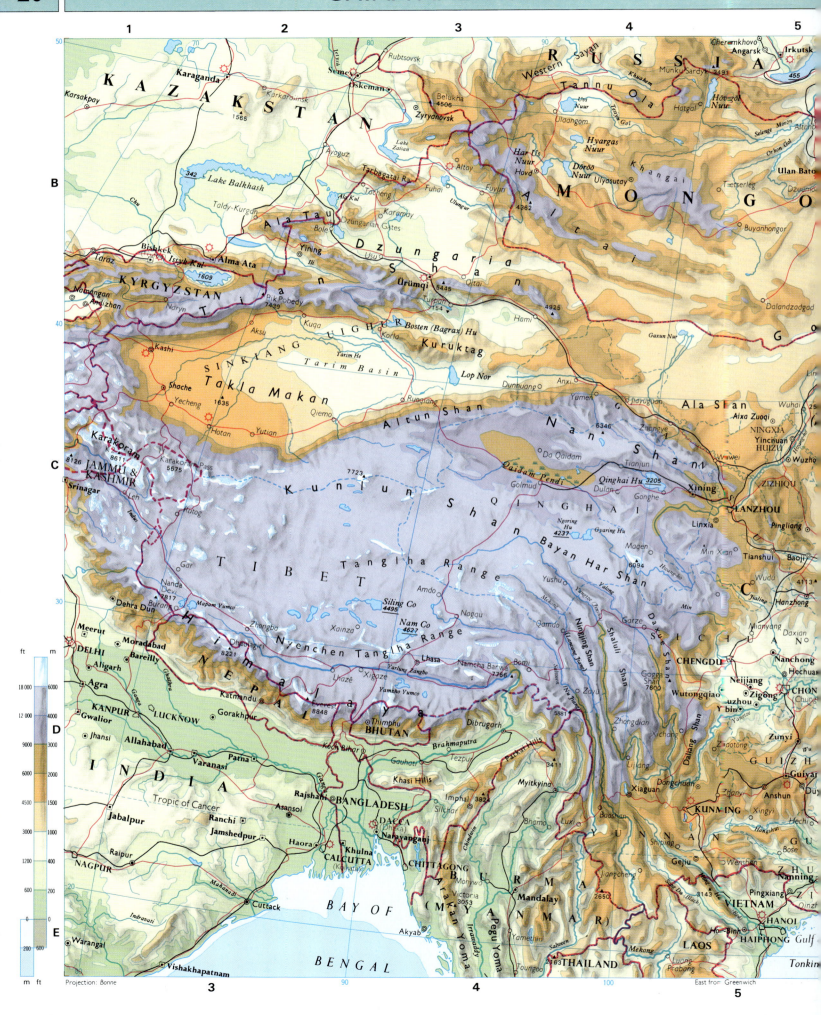

1:15 000 000

100   0   100   200   300   400 miles

100   0   100   200   300   400   500   600 km

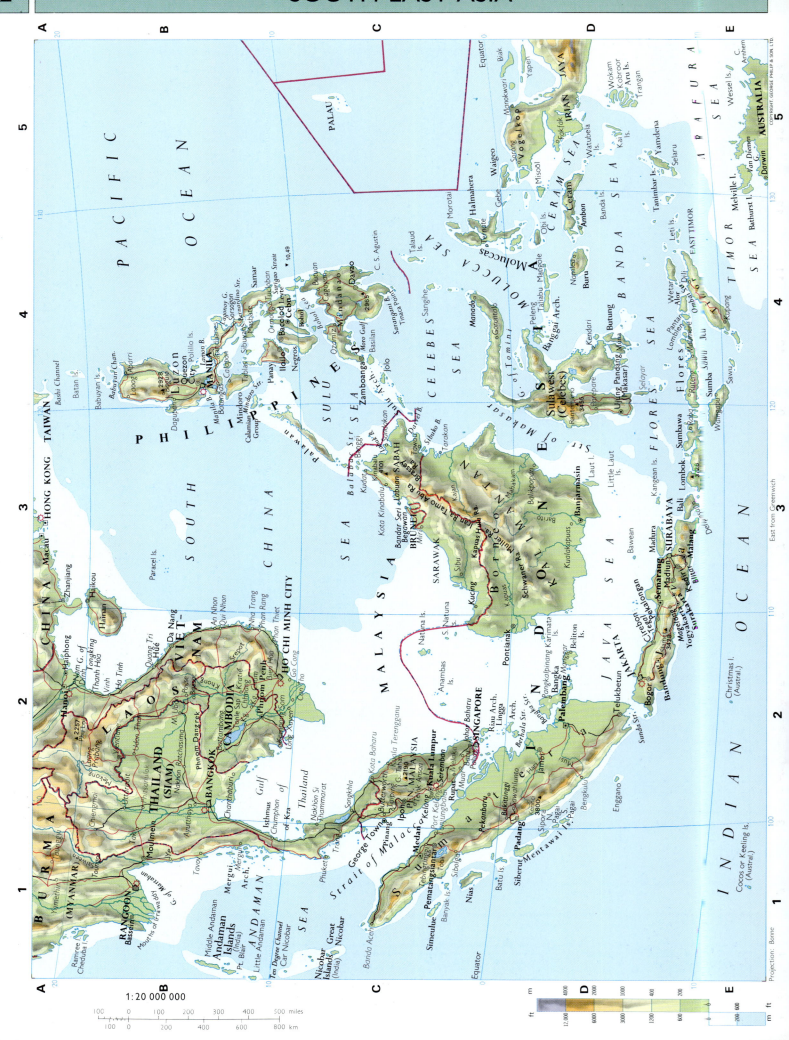

1:20 000 000

100   0   100   200   300   400   500 miles

100   0   200   400   600   800 km

Projection: Bonne

East from Greenwich

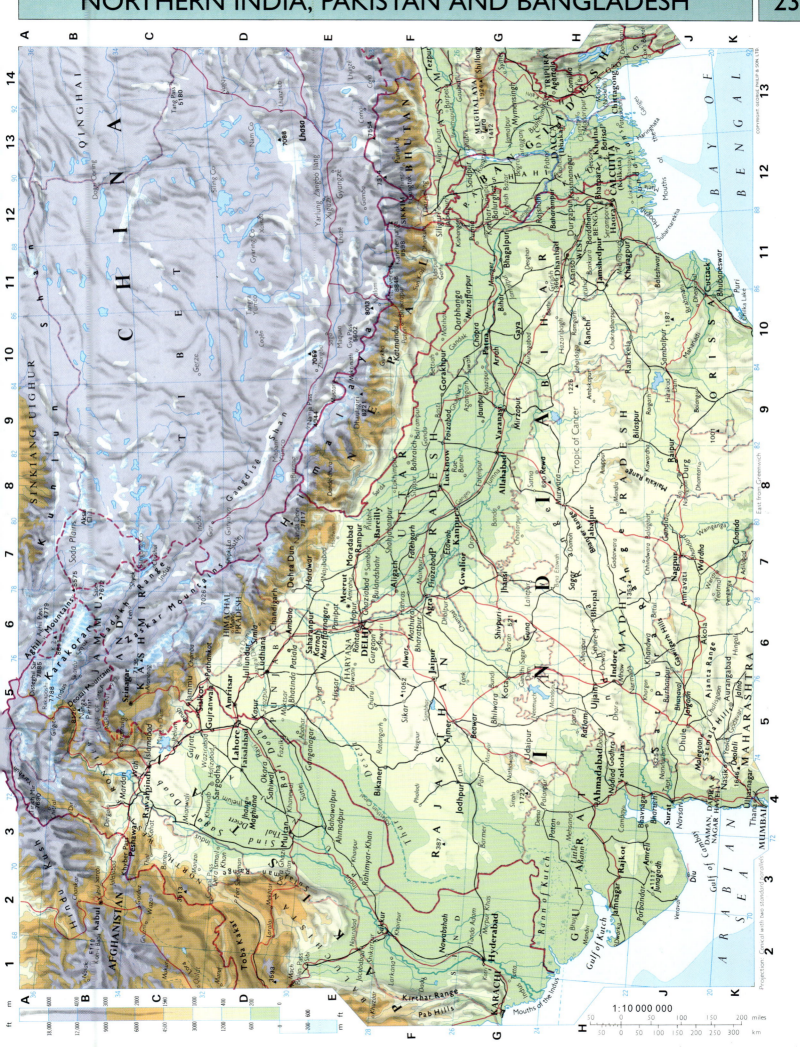

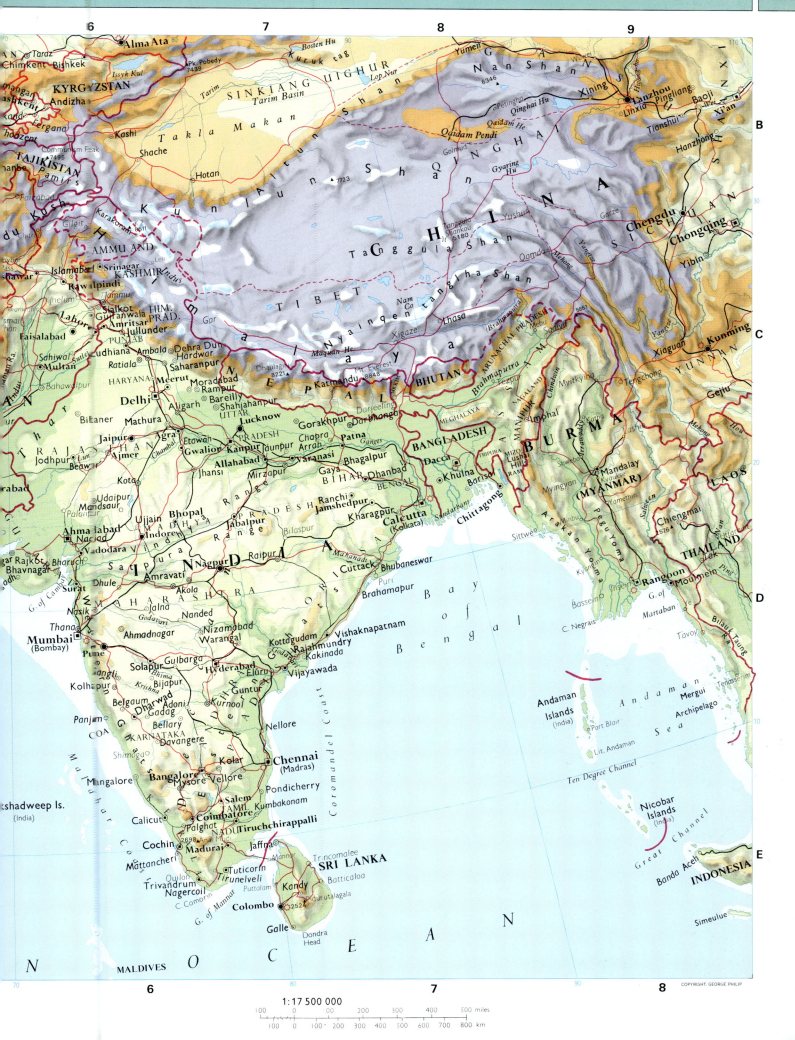

1:17 500 000

AFRICA : physical

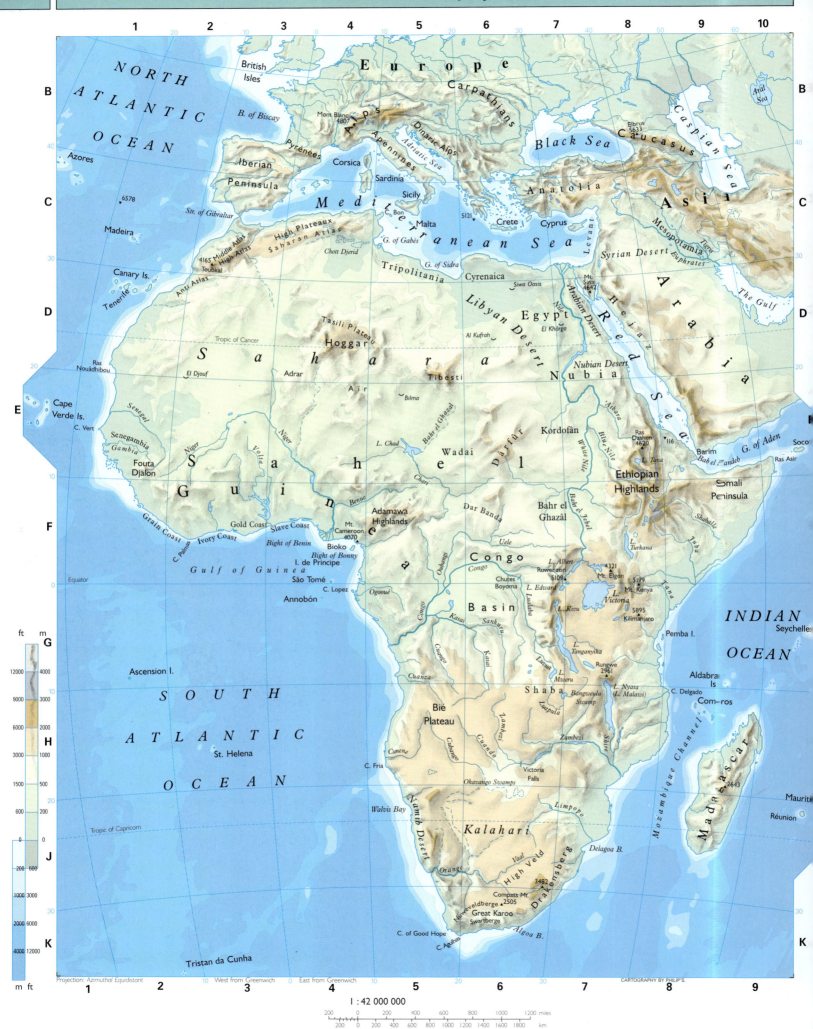

Projection: *Azimuthal Equidistant*

CARTOGRAPHY BY PHILIP'S.

1 : 42 000 000

AFRICA : *political*

1:15 000 000

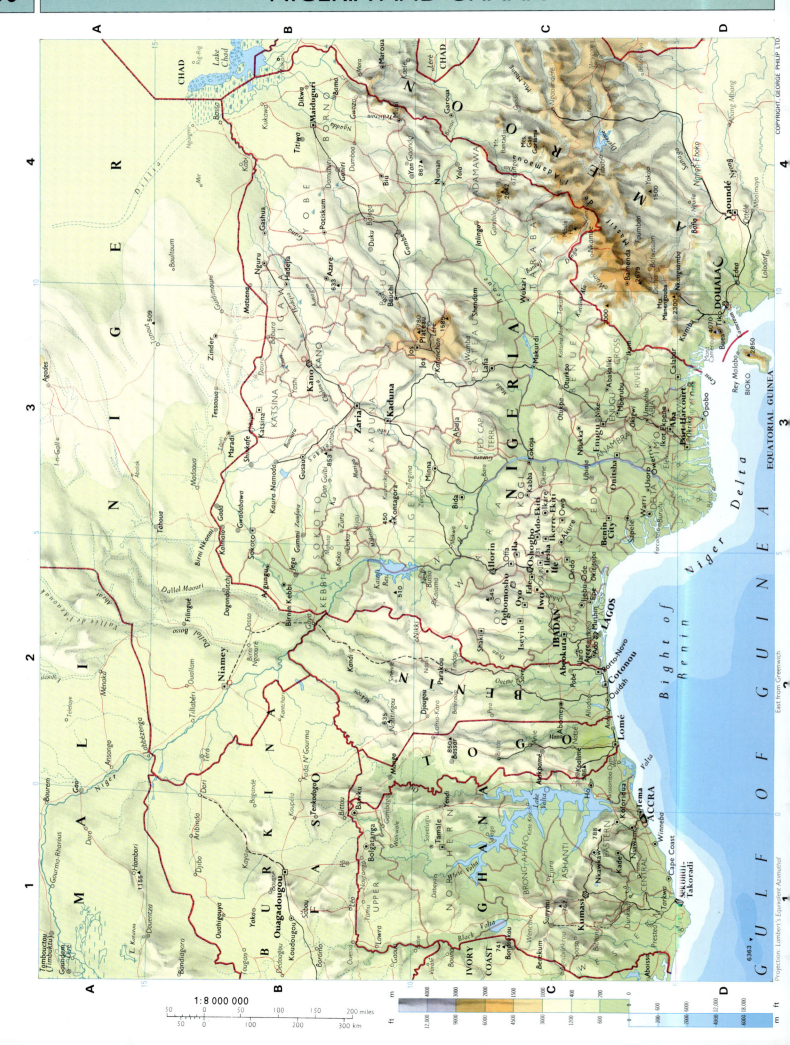

1:8 000 000

Projection: Lambert's Equivalent Azimuthal

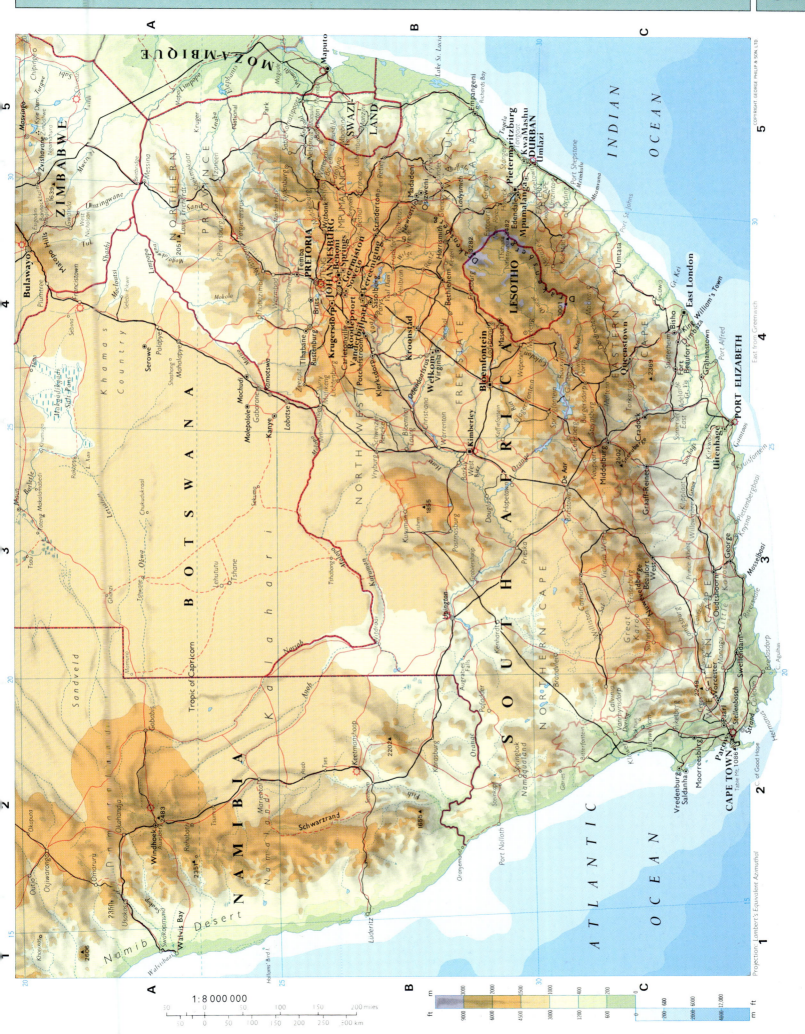

1 : 8 000 000

Projection Lambert's Equivalent Azimuthal

COPYRIGHT GEORGE PHILIP & SON LTD

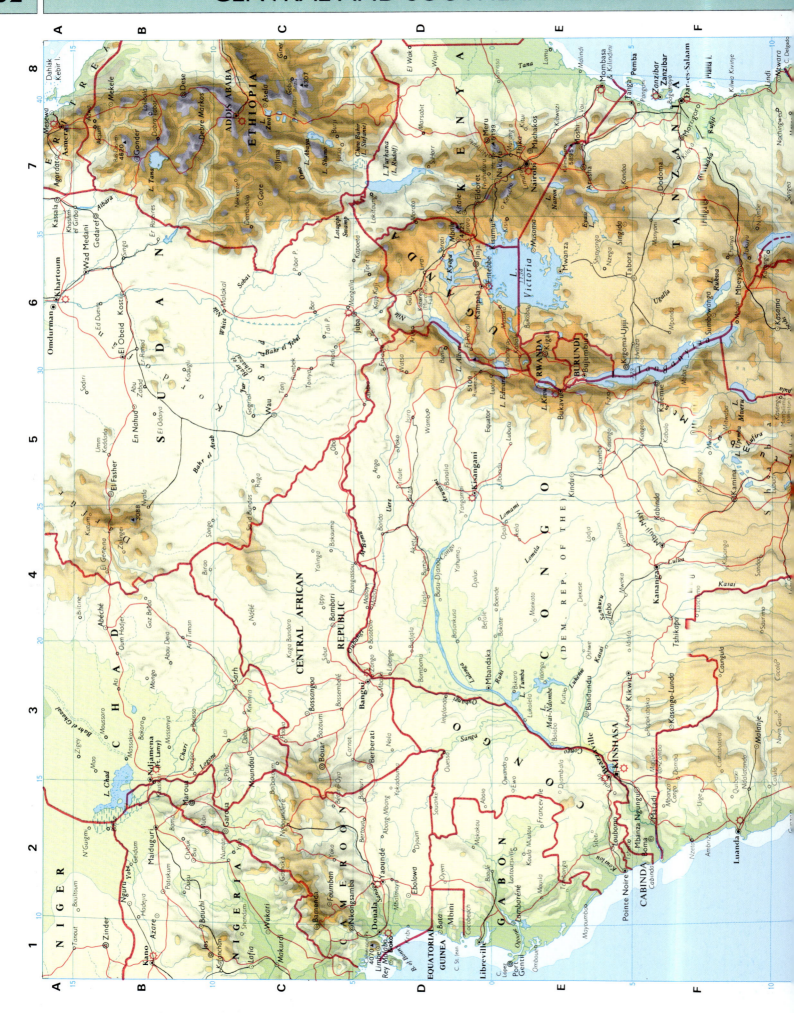

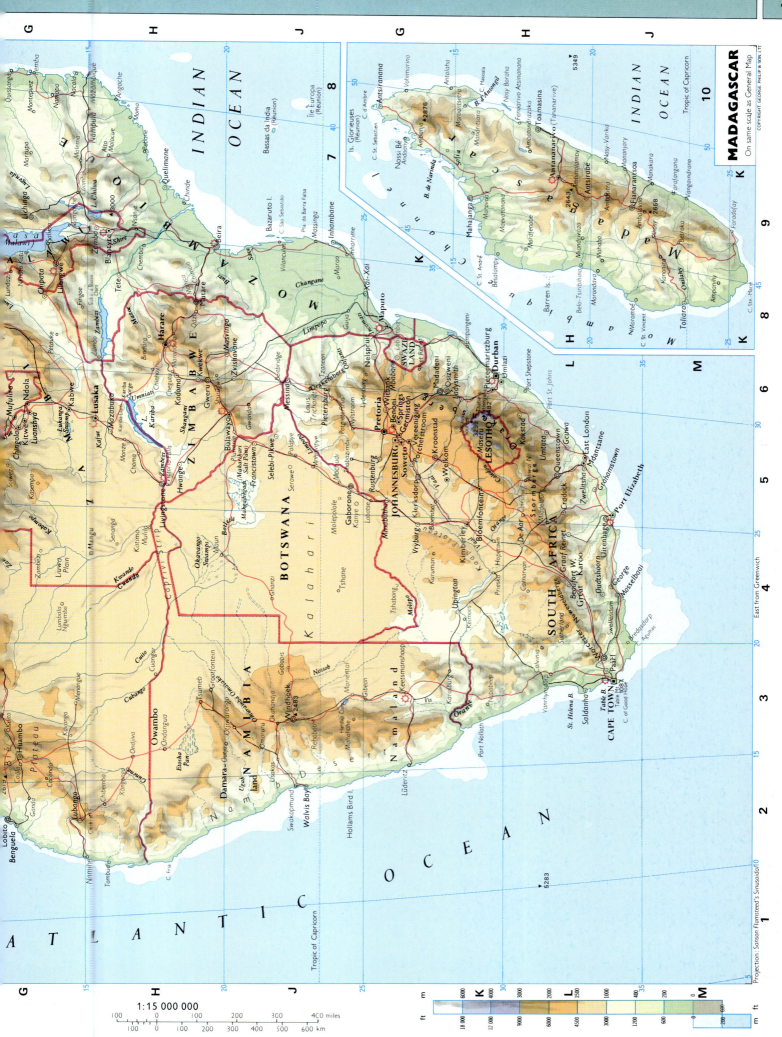

INDIAN OCEAN

ATLANTIC OCEAN

MADAGASCAR
On same scale as General Map

COPYRIGHT GEORGE PHILIP & SON LTD

1:15 000 000

Projection: Sanson Flamsteed's Sinusoidal

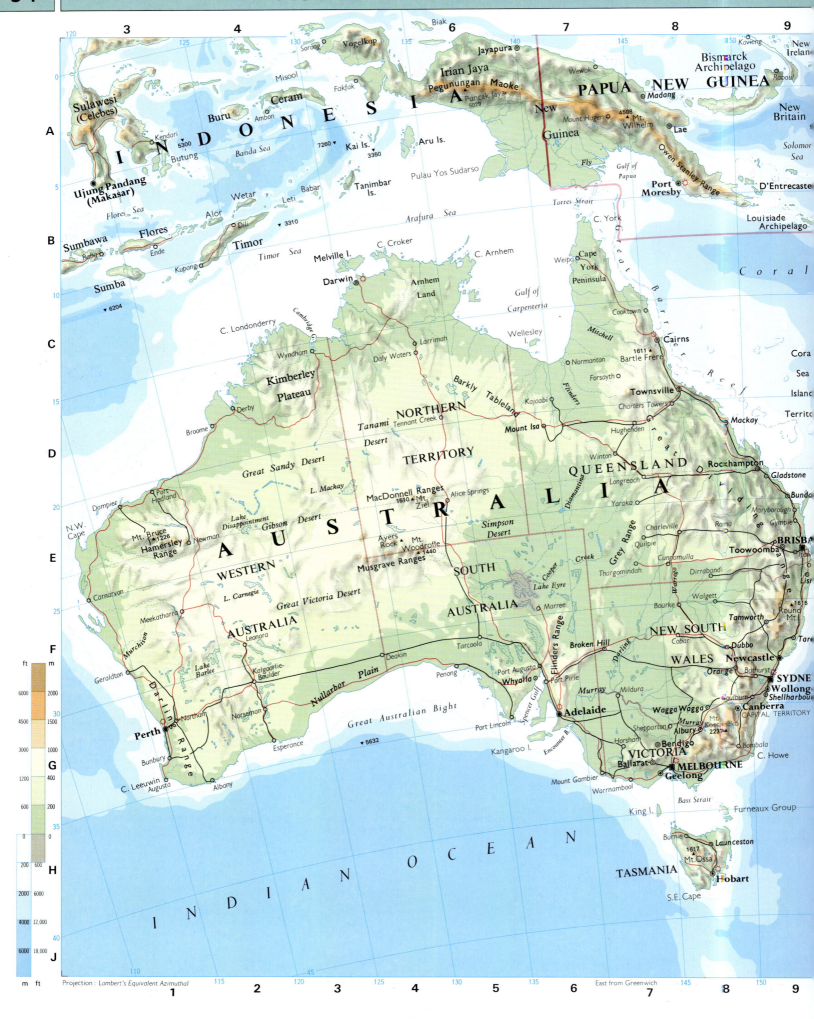

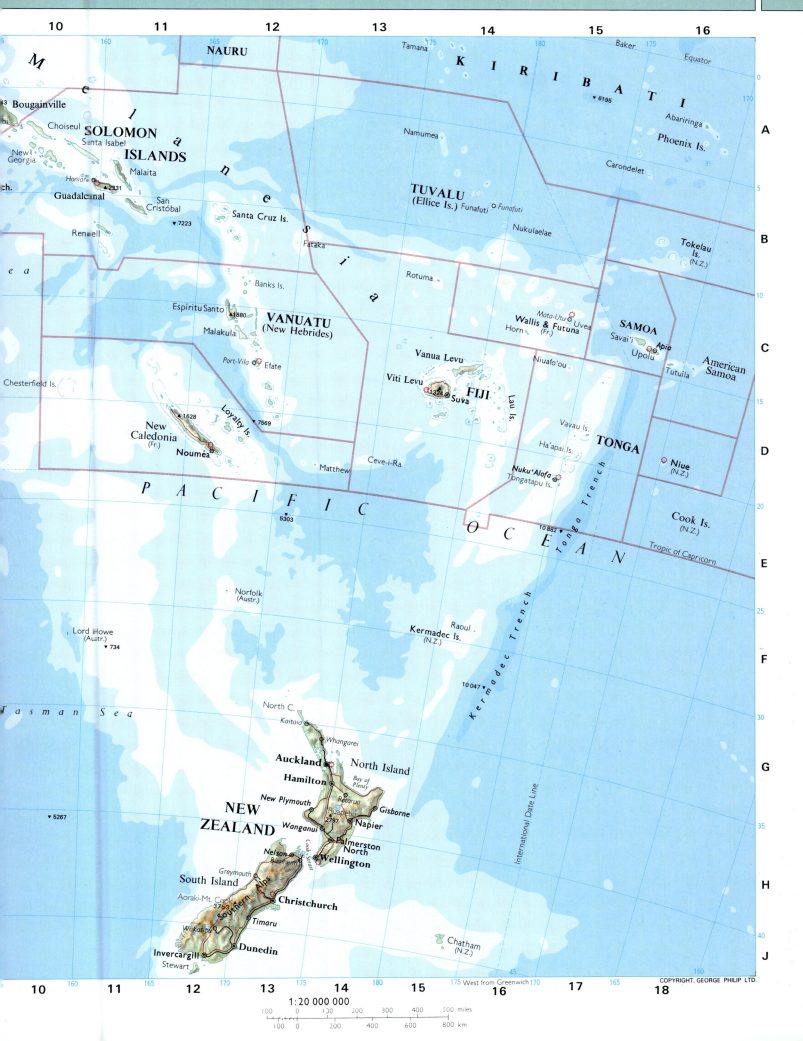

1:20 000 000

100   130 200   300   400   500 miles

100 0   200   400   600   800 km

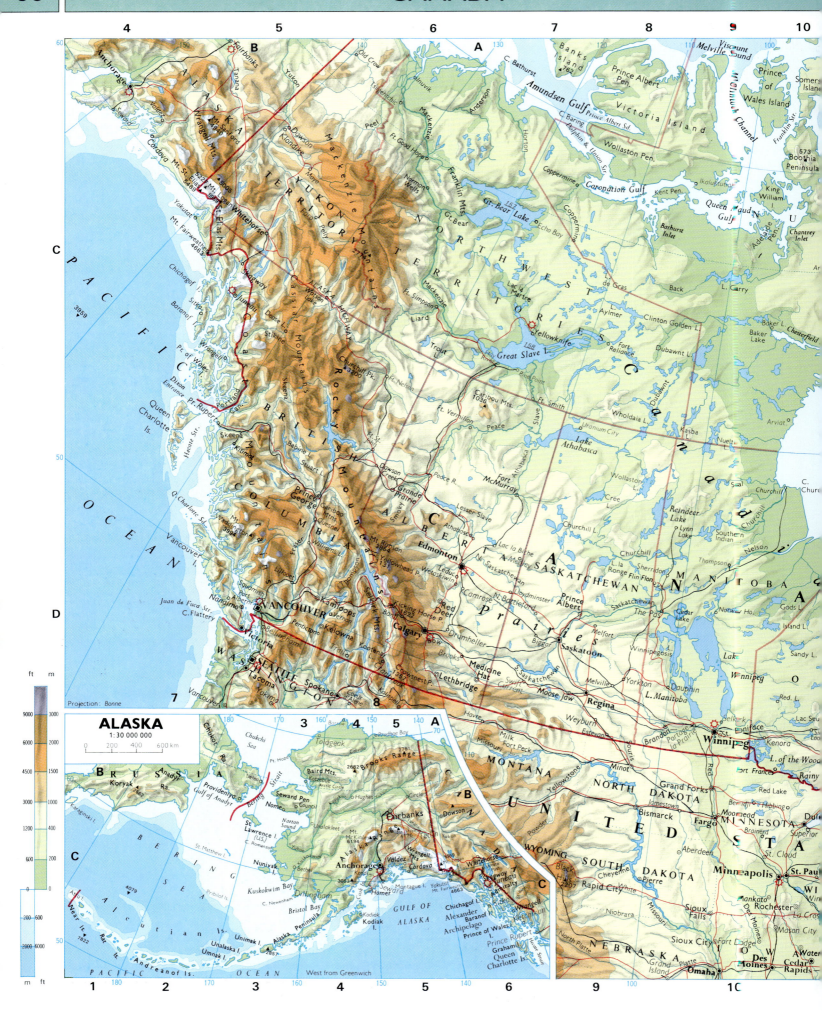

ALASKA
1:30 000 000
0 200 400 600 km

Projection : Bonne

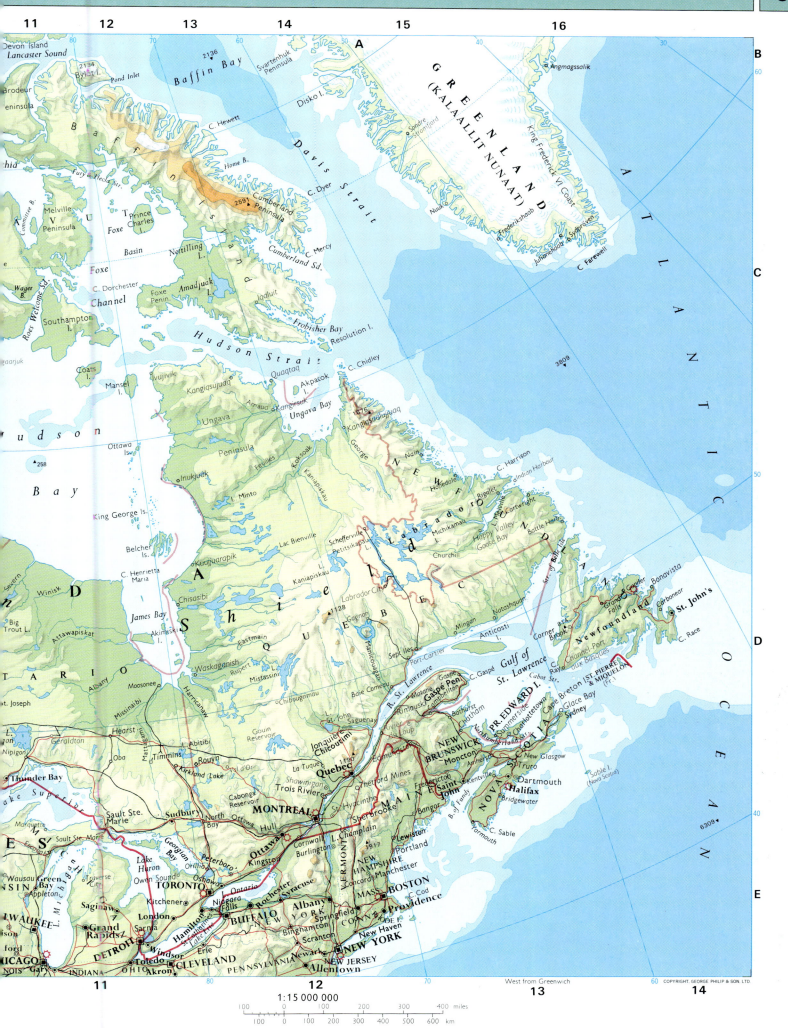

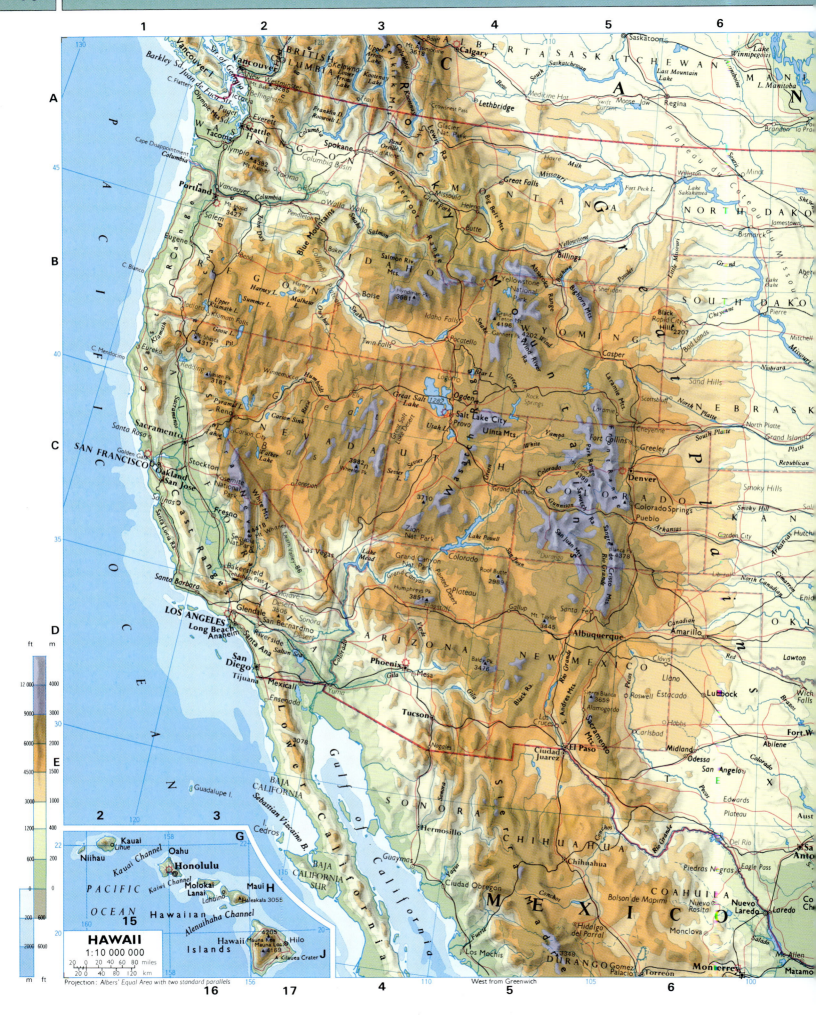

1:12 000 000

Projection: Albers' Equal Area with two standard parallels

1:6 000 000

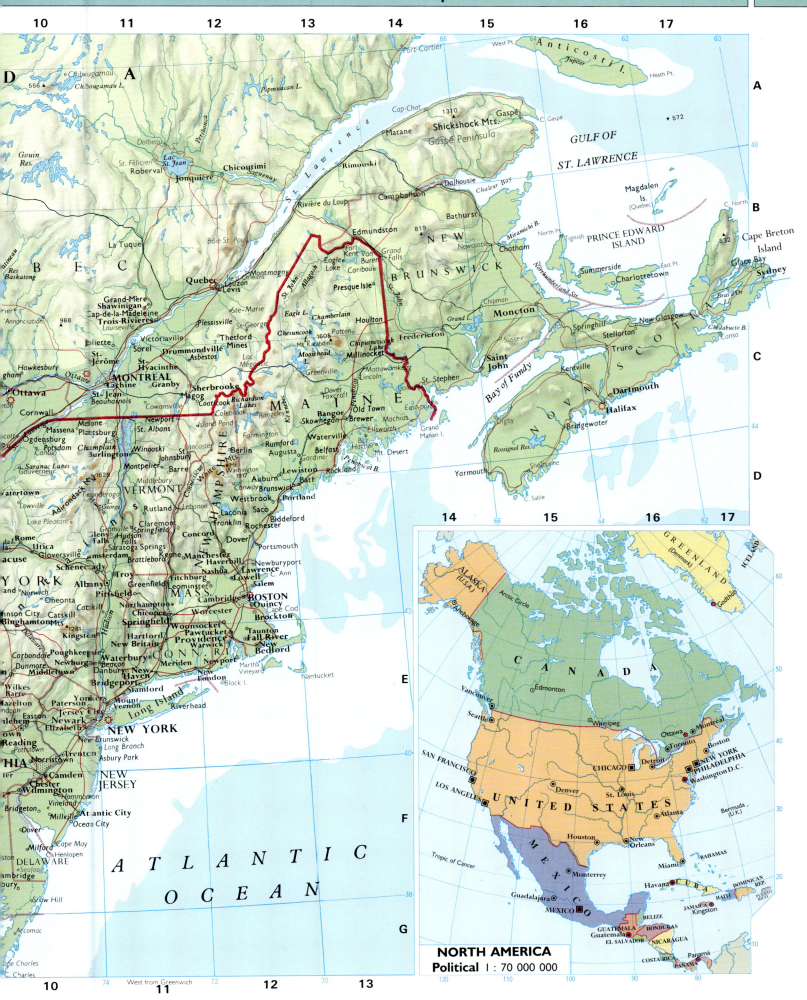

Port-Cartier
West Pt. *Anticosti I.*
Jupiter
Heath Pt.

D 556 ▲ Chibougamau
Chibougamau L.
Pipmuacan L.

A

GULF OF
ST. LAWRENCE

Cap-Chat
1310 Gaspé
Shickshock Mts. C. Gaspé
Gaspé Peninsula ▼ 572

Matane

Dolbeau
St. Félicien
Roberval
Lac
St. Jean
Jonquière
Chicoutimi
Saguenay

Rimouski

Gouin
Res.

Magdalen
Is.
(Quebec) C. North

B

Rivière du Loup
Campbellton
Dalhousie Chaleur Bay
Bathurst

B

La Tuque
Baie St. Paul

Edmundston
N E W
Miramichi B.
North Pt.
Newcastle
Tignish PRINCE EDWARD
ISLAND Cape Breton
Island

Grand-Mère
Shawinigan
Cap-de-la-Madeleine
Trois-Rivières
Louiseville

Kent
Eagle Van
Lake Buren
Grand
Falls
Caribou

B R U N S W I C K
Chatham

Summerside
Charlottetown East Pt.
Glace Bay
Sydney
Bras d'Or

Quebec Île d'Orléans
Lévis
Ste-Marie

Presque Isle

St. John
Allagash

Chipman

Springhill
Stellarton
New Glasgow

Annonciation
968 ▲
St-George
Thetford
Mines

Eagle L.
Chamberlain
L.
1605
Houlton
Moncton

N O V A

C. Gaspé
Chedabucto B.
Canso

Juliette
Victoriaville
Plessisville
Chesuncook
L.
Patten
Grand L.

Truro

Montmagny

Fredericton

Kentville

St-Jérôme
Drummondville
Asbestos

Mt. Katahdin
Moosehead
L.

Chiputneticook
Lakes
Millinocket

Saint
John

S C O T I A

Dartmouth

Sorel
St-
Hyacinthe

Lac-
Mégantic
Greenville

Lincoln
Mattawamkeag

Sussex

Dartmouth

MONTREAL
Granby
Sherbrooke
Magog

Richardson
Lakes

M A I N E

St. Stephen

Bay of Fundy

Halifax

Lachine
St-Jean
Beauharnois
Coaticook
Colebrook

Dover
Foxcroft

East-
Grand
port
Manan I.

Digby

Bridgewater

Cornwall
Cowansville
Newport
Island Pond

Rangeley
Old Town
Brewer

Machias

Yarmouth

Rossignol Res.

Shelburne

Malone
St. Albans
Bangor
Skowhegan

Ellsworth

C. Sable

Massena
Plattsburgh
Farmington

Waterville
Belfast
Bar
Harbor
Mt. Desert

Ogdensburg
Potsdam
Canton
Champlain
1629 ▲
Winooski
Burlington

Rumford
Augusta
Gardiner
Penobscot B.

Saranac Lakes
Gouverneur

Montpelier
Barre

N E W   H A M P S H I R E
Washington
1917

Auburn
Lewiston
Bath
Rockland

Watertown
Lowville
Lake Pleasant
Adirondack

Middlebury
V E R M O N T
Lebanon
Conway
Brunswick
Portland

D

Ticonderoga
L. George
Rutland

Berlin
Laconia
Franklin
Westbrook
Saco
Biddeford

Rome
Utica
Gloversville

Glens
Falls
Granville
Claremont
Springfield

Concord
Dover
Portsmouth

Amsterdam
Saratoga
Springs

Keene
Manchester

Y O R K
Schenectady
Troy
Albany

Greenfield

Fitchburg
Leominster
Nashua
Lawrence
Lowell
Salem
C. Ann
Newburyport

Norwich
Oneonta
Catskill

Pittsfield
Northampton
Chicopee
Springfield

M A S S.
Worcester
Cambridge
Quincy
Brockton

BOSTON

Cape Cod

Binghamton Mts.
1281 ▲
Kingston

Hartford
Woonsocket
Pawtucket
Providence
Warwick

Taunton
Fall River
New
Bedford

Johnson City
Catskill

Poughkeepsie
Newburgh

New Britain
Waterbury
Meriden
New
Haven

C O N N.   R. I.
Newport

Nantucket

Carbondale
Dunmore
Middletown
Beacon
Danbury
Bridgeport

New
London

Martha's
Vineyard

Wilkes-
Barre
Hazleton
Randolph
Bethlehem
town

Easton
Paterson
Jersey City

Stamford
Mount
Vernon
Long Island
Riverhead

Reading
Newark
Elizabeth

NEW YORK

Pottstown
New Brunswick
Long Branch

HIA
Norristown
Trenton
Asbury Park

Camden
Chester
Wilmington

NEW
JERSEY

Bridgeton
Hammonton
Vineland

Milford
Dover
Millville
Atlantic City
Ocean City

DELAWARE
Cape May
C. Henlopen

ton
ambridge
bury
Snow Hill
Seaford

E

A T L A N T I C

O C E A N

F

G

pe Charles
C. Charles
Accomac

West from Greenwich
74   72   70

--- Inset map ---

14   15   16   17

GREENLAND
(Denmark)
ICELAND

ALASKA
(USA)

Arctic Circle

Godthåb

Anchorage

60

C A N A D A

Edmonton

Vancouver
Seattle

Winnipeg

Ottawa
Montréal
Toronto
Boston

SAN FRANCISCO

U N I T E D   S T A T E S
CHICAGO
Detroit
NEW YORK
PHILADELPHIA
Washington D.C.

40

LOS ANGELES
Denver
St. Louis

Bermuda
(U.K.)

30

Atlanta

M E X I C O
Houston
New
Orleans

Miami
BAHAMAS

Tropic of Cancer

Monterrey

Havana
CUBA
DOMINICAN
REP.

20

Guadalajara
JAMAICA
HAITI
Kingston
PUERTO
RICO

MEXICO
BELIZE
GUATEMALA
HONDURAS

Guatemala
EL SALVADOR
NICARAGUA

COSTA RICA
Panamá
PANAMA

10

NORTH AMERICA
Political 1 : 70 000 000

120   110   100   90   80

ATLANTIC OCEAN

Bermuda (U.K.)
Hamilton

Columbus
C. Fear
Atlanta
Macon
mbus
Charleston
Savannah
hassee
Jacksonville
Daytona Beach
C. Canaveral
Orlando
West Palm Beach
Tampa
rsburg
L. Okeechobee
Grand Bahama I.
Freeport
Gt. Abaco I.
Miami
Fort Lauderdale
New Providence I.
C. Sable
Eleuthera I.
Key West
Nassau
Cat I.
S. Salvador
Andros I.
BAHAMAS
Tropic of Cancer
Havana
Matanzas
Cárd nas
Long I.
Sagua la Grande
Mayaguana
Key West
I. de Juventud
Cienfuegos
Sta Clara
Morón
Acklins I.
Turks & Caicos Is. (U.K.)
GR
Sancti Spiritus
Ciego de Avila
Camagüey
Holguin
Gt. Inagua I.
Grand Cayman (U.K.)
Bayamó
Santiago de Cuba
Guantánamo
Cap Haitien
Santiago
San Francisco de Macoris
PUERTO RICO (U.S.A.)
St. Thomas (U.S.A.)
Charlotte Amalie
Anguilla
St. Martin (Fr. & Neth.)
Montego Bay
Gonaives
San Juan
Virgin Is. (U.K.)
ST. KITTS – NEVIS
JAMAICA
Kingston
Port au Prince
La Romana
Mona Passage
Ponce
St. Croix (U.S.A.)
Aguas
St. John's
ANTIGUA & BARBUDA
Les Cayes
Santo Domingo
Mayagüez
Montserrat (U.K.)
Guadeloupe (Fr.)
Pointe à Pitre
DOMINICAN REP.
Bani
Barahona
Santo Domingo
Hispaniola
LESSER
DOMINICA
A N T I L L E S
Fort de France
Martinique (Fr.)
Caratasca Lagoon
A N T I L L E S
C. Gracias á Dios
Coast
Providencia (Col.)
Windward
ST. LUCIA
BARBADOS
ST. VINCENT
Bridgetown
San Andrés (Col.)
THE GRENADINES
Islands
GRENADA
Bluefields
ua
Pta. Gallinas
Gulf of Venezuela
Aruba (Neth.)
Curaçao
Willemstad
Bonaire
La Blanquilla (Ven.)
Margarita
Tobago
Santa Marta
Pen. de la Guajira
Pen. de NETH.
Paraguaná ANTILLES
La Tortuga (Ven.)
Carúpano
Port of Spain
TRINIDAD & TOBAGO
Barranquilla
Punto Fijo
Coro
Cumana
G. of Paria
San Fernando
Limón
Cartagena
Sincelejo
Maracaibo
Cabimas
Caracas
Maracay
Barcelona
Maturin
Delta of the Orinoco
Colón
G. of Darién
L. de Maracaibo
Valencia
Barquisimeto
El Tigre
Georgetown
Panama
Valera
Mérida
Barinas
Orinoco
Ciudad Guayana
David
Fzuero Pen.
Cord. de Mérida
Apure
San Fernando de Apure
Ciudad Bolívar
New Amsterdam
Coiba
G. of Panama
Cúcuta
San Cristóbal
Arauca
Angel Falls
Cuyuni
Barrancabermeja
Bucaramanga
VENEZUELA
Caura
Roraima
Quibdó
Medellín
Tunja
Pto. Ayacucho
Caroní
Sierra Pacaraima
Manizales
COLOMBIA
Meta
Essequibo
Pereira
Bogotá
GUYANA
Buenaventura
Armenia
Girardot
Guaviare
SURINAM
Cali
Guaviare
Casiquiare
Popayán
BRAZIL

1:15 000 000

100   0   100   200   300   400 miles
100   0   100 200 300 400 500 600 km

COPYRIGHT. GEORGE PHILIP & SON. LTD.

POLITICAL
1 : 70 000 000

1 : 20 000 000

100   0   100   200   300   400   500 miles
100   0   200   400   600   800 km

Projection : Lambert's Equivalent Azimuthal

The Arctic

NORTH AMERICA

CANADA

ASIA

RUSSIA

NORWAY

GREENLAND (KALAALLIT NUNAAT) (Denmark)

ARCTIC OCEAN

Beaufort Sea
Canada Basin
Alpha Cordillera
Makarov Basin
Lomonosov Ridge
Nansen Cordillera
Nansen Basin
Fram Basin
Mendeleyev Ridge
Laptev Sea
Kara Sea
Barents Sea
Greenland Sea
Denmark Strait
Hudson Bay
Baffin Bay
Davis Str.
Labrador

Great Bear Lake
Gt. Slave Lake
Victoria Island
Banks I.
Melville I.
Parry Is.
Ellesmere I.
Devon I.
Baffin I.
Melville Pen.
Southampton I.
Coats I.
King William I.

Magnetic Pole 1990

New Siberian Is.
Severnaya Zemlya
Novaya Zemlya
Franz Josef Land
Yamal
Kola Peninsula
Taimyr Peninsula
Central Siberian Plateau
Ural Mts.
Verkhoyansk Range

North Cape
Jan Mayen
Svalbard (Norway)
Vestspitsbergen
Bear I.

Murmansk
Arkhangelsk
Yekaterinburg

C. Columbia
Peary Ld.
McKinley Sea
Lincoln Sea
Mont Forel 3360
Gunnbjørn Field 3700

Projection: Zenithal Equidistant

Antarctica

ATLANTIC / INDIAN OCEAN
PACIFIC OCEAN

Weddell Sea
Ross Sea
Amundsen Sea
Bellingshausen Sea
Drake Passage

EAST ANTARCTICA
WEST ANTARCTICA

Antarctic Peninsula
Graham Land
Palmer Land
Ellsworth Land
Marie Byrd Land
Edward VII Pen.
Queen Maud Land
Enderby Ld.
Kemp Land
Mac-Robertson Land
Wilkes Land
Victoria Land
Coats Land
Ellsworth Mts.
Vinson Massif 4897
Transantarctic Mts.

Ross Ice Shelf
Ronne Ice Shelf
Larsen Ice Shelf
Amery Ice Shelf
Shackleton Ice Shelf
George VI Sound
Berkner I.

SOUTH POLE
Amundsen-Scott (U.S.A.) 2807

Mt. Erebus 3743
McMurdo
Roosevelt I.
Falkland Is. (U.K.)
Stanley (U.K.)
South Georgia
South Orkney Is. (U.K.)
South Shetland Is.
Tierra del Fuego
C. de Hornos

Mt. Markham 4349
Prince Charles Mts.
Lambert Glacier
Beardmore Glacier

Davis Sea
Prydz Bay
American Highland
Queen Mary Land
Budd Coast
Sabrina Coast
Banzare Coast
Terre Adélie
George V Land
Oates Land

Magnetic Pole 1990

Projection: Zenithal Equidistant
1:35 000 000

Legend
- Ice cap
- Permanent ice shelf
- Maximum extent of sea ice
- March (Summer) extent of sea ice
- ▲3488 / 3700 Surface elevation and depth of ice (in metres)
- ● Stanley (U.K.) Permanent bases

WORLD THEMES

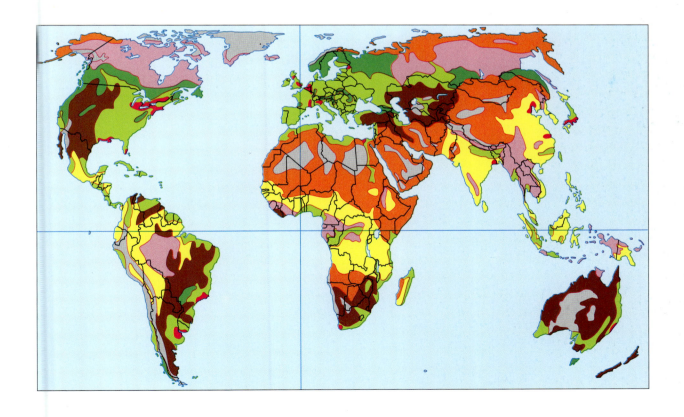

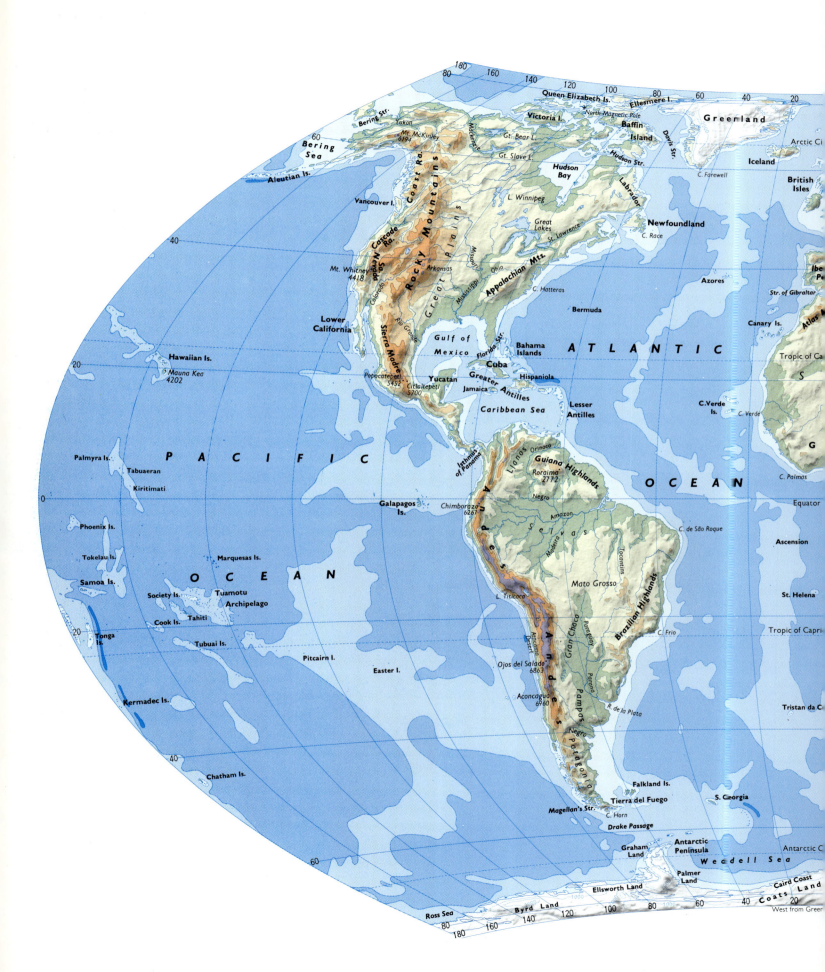

Projection: Hammer Equal Area

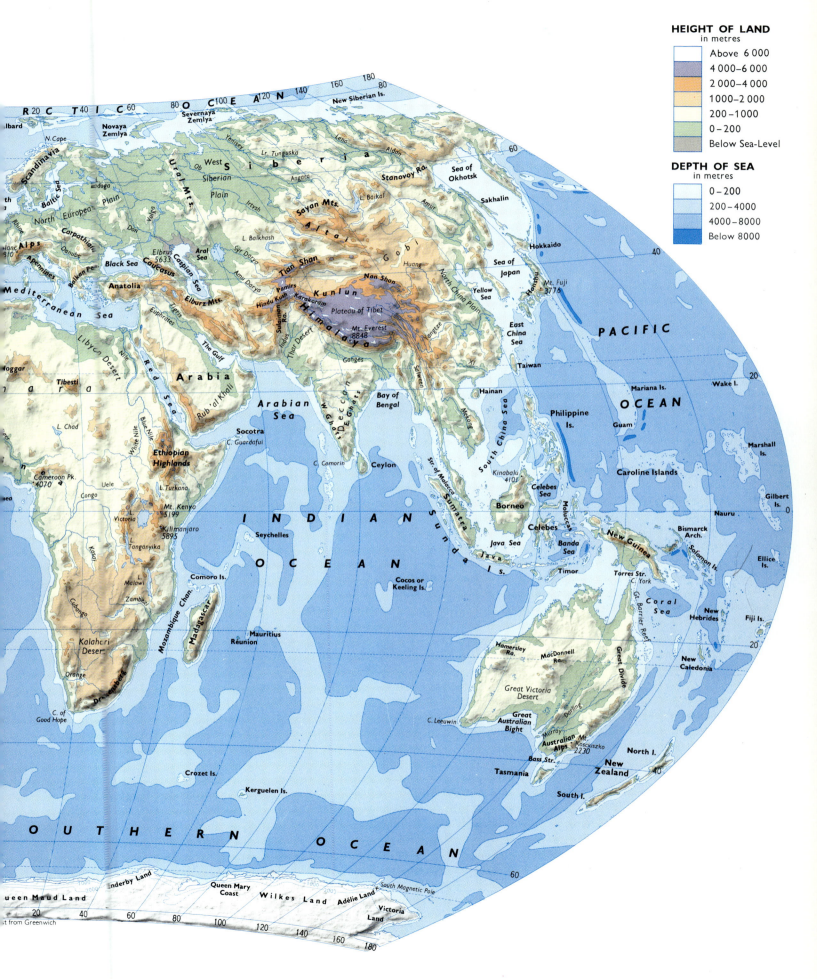

HEIGHT OF LAND
in metres

Above 6 000
4 000–6 000
2 000–4 000
1 000–2 000
200–1 000
0–200
Below Sea-Level

DEPTH OF SEA
in metres

0–200
200–4 000
4 000–8 000
Below 8 000

ARCTIC OCEAN

Spitsbergen 20 40 60 80 100 120 140 160 180 80
N. Cape Severnaya Zemlya
Novaya Zemlya New Siberian Is.
Scandinavia Yenisey Lena Aldan
Baltic Sea West Siberian Plain Stanovoy Ra.
Ladoga Ob Irtysh Siberia Sea of Okhotsk
North European Plain Angara Amur 60
Rhine Volga Don Danube Lr. Tunguska Sakhalin
Alps Carpathians L. Balkhash L. Baikal Hokkaido
3910 Apennines Balkan Pen. Black Sea Caucasus Elbrus 5633 Aral Sea Syr Darya Altai Gobi Sea of Japan 40
Mediterranean Sea Anatolia Caspian Sea Amu Darya Soyan Mts. Tian Shan North China Plain Honshu Mt. Fuji 3776
Elburz Mts. Pamirs Tigris Hindu Kush Karakoram Nan Shan Kunlun Huang Yellow Sea East China Sea
Libyan Desert Red Sea Euphrates Sulaiman Ra. Indus Plateau of Tibet Mt. Everest 8848 Yangtze Xi Taiwan PACIFIC
Hoggar Nile Arabia The Gulf Thar Desert Himalaya Ganges Hainan 20
Tibesti Arabian Rub'al Khali W. Ghats Deccan Bay of Bengal Mekong South China Sea Mariana Is. Wake I. OCEAN
Sahara L. Chad White Nile Blue Nile Sea Socotra C. Guardafui E. Ghats Philippine Is. Guam
Cameroon Pk. 4070 Uele Ethiopian Highlands C. Comorin Ceylon Kinabalu 4101 Celebes Sea Caroline Islands Marshall Is.
Congo L. Turkana Mt. Kenya 5199 Str. of Malacca Sumatra Borneo Celebes Moluccas Nauru Gilbert Is. 0
L. Victoria Kilimanjaro 5895 Seychelles INDIAN Java Sea Java Banda Sea New Guinea Bismarck Arch.
L. Tanganyika Comoro Is. Timor Torres Str. Solomon Is. Ellice Is.
Kasai Zambezi Mozambique Chan. Madagascar Cocos or Keeling Is. OCEAN C. York Coral Sea New Hebrides Fiji Is. 20
Cubango L. Malawi Mauritius Réunion Hamersley Ra. MacDonnell Ra. Great Dividing New Caledonia
Kalahari Desert Orange Drakensberg Comoro Is. Great Victoria Desert Murray Darling Australian Alps Mt. Kosciuszko 2230 North I.
C. of Good Hope Crozet Is. C. Leeuwin Great Australian Bight Bass Str. New Zealand 40
Kerguelen Is. Tasmania South I.

SOUTHERN OCEAN

Queen Maud Land Enderby Land Queen Mary Coast Wilkes Land Adélie Land Victoria Land 60
20 40 60 80 100 120 140 160 180
East from Greenwich South Magnetic Pole

1:80 000 000

Copyright, George Philip & Son, Ltd.

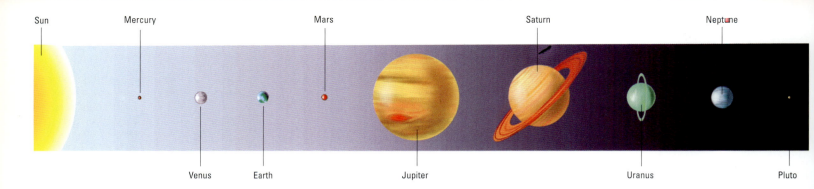

Sun · Mercury · Venus · Earth · Mars · Jupiter · Saturn · Uranus · Neptune · Pluto

The Solar System

A minute part of one of the billions of galaxies (collections of stars) that comprises the Universe, the Solar System lies some 27,000 light-years from the centre of our own galaxy, the 'Milky Way'. Thought to be over 4,700 million years old, it consists of a central sun with nine planets and their moons revolving around it, attracted by its gravitational pull. The planets orbit the Sun in the same direction – anti-clockwise when viewed from the Northern Heavens – and almost in the same plane. Their orbital paths, however, vary enormously.

The Sun's diameter is 109 times that of Earth, and the temperature at its core – caused by continuous thermonuclear fusions of hydrogen into helium – is estimated to be 15 million degrees Celsius. It is the Solar System's only source of light and heat.

Profile of the Planets

	Mean distance from Sun (million km)	Mass (Earth = 1)	Period of orbit (Earth years)	Period of rotation (Earth days)	Equatorial diameter (km)	Number of known satellites
Mercury	57.9	0.055	0.24 years	58.67	4,878	0
Venus	108.2	0.815	0.62 years	243.00	12,104	0
Earth	149.6	1.0	1.00 years	1.00	12,756	1
Mars	227.9	0.107	1.88 years	1.03	6,787	2
Jupiter	778.3	317.8	11.86 years	0.41	142,800	16
Saturn	1,427	95.2	29.46 years	0.43	120,000	20
Uranus	2,871	14.5	84.01 years	0.75	51,118	15
Neptune	4,497	17.1	164.80 years	0.80	49,528	8
Pluto	5,914	0.002	248.50 years	6.39	2,320	1

All planetary orbits are elliptical in form, but only Pluto and Mercury follow paths that deviate noticeably from a circular one. Near perihelion – its closest approach to the Sun – Pluto actually passes inside the orbit of Neptune, an event that last occurred in 1983. Pluto did not regain its station as outermost planet until February 1999.

The Seasons

Seasons occur because the Earth's axis is tilted at a constant angle of 23½°. When the northern hemisphere is tilted to a maximum extent towards the Sun, on 21 June, the Sun is overhead at the Tropic of Cancer (latitude 23½° North). This is midsummer, or the summer solstice, in the northern hemisphere.

On 22 or 23 September, the Sun is overhead at the Equator, and day and night are of equal length throughout the world. This is the autumn equinox in the northern hemisphere. On 21 or 22 December, the Sun is overhead at the Tropic of Capricorn (23½° South), the winter solstice in the northern hemisphere. The overhead Sun then tracks north until, on 21 March, it is overhead at the Equator. This is the spring (vernal) equinox in the northern hemisphere.

In the southern hemisphere, the seasons are the reverse of those in the north.

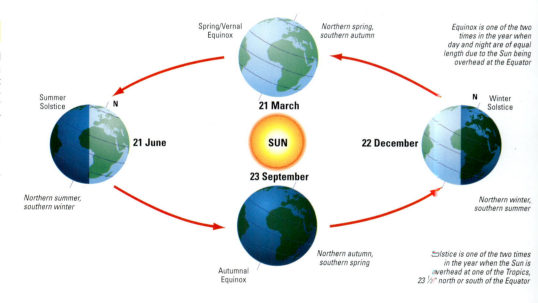

Spring/Vernal Equinox · Northern spring, southern autumn · 21 March · Summer Solstice · 21 June · Northern summer, southern winter · SUN · 23 September · Autumnal Equinox · Northern autumn, southern spring · Winter Solstice · 22 December · Northern winter, southern summer

Equinox is one of the two times in the year when day and night are of equal length due to the Sun being overhead at the Equator

Solstice is one of the two times in the year when the Sun is overhead at one of the Tropics, 23 ½° north or south of the Equator

Day and Night

The Sun appears to rise in the east, reach its highest point at noon, and then set in the west, to be followed by night. In reality, it is not the Sun that is moving but the Earth rotating from west to east. The moment when the Sun's upper limb first appears above the horizon is termed sunrise; the moment when the Sun's upper limb disappears below the horizon is sunset.

At the summer solstice in the northern hemisphere (21 June), the Arctic has total daylight and the Antarctic total darkness. The opposite occurs at the winter solstice (21 or 22 December). At the Equator, the length of day and night are almost equal all year.

21 June · N · N. Pole: 6 months daylight · 24 hours daylight · 66½° · SHORT NIGHT · 12 hours daylight · LONG DAY · 23½° · LONG NIGHT · 13½ hours daylight · Sun's rays · Equator · 12 hours daylight · 0° · SHORT DAY · 23½° · 10½ hours daylight · Antarctic Circle: 24 hours darkness · S. Pole: 6 months darkness

22 December · N. Pole: 6 months darkness Arctic Circle: 24 hours darkness · 10½ hours daylight · 23½° · SHORT DAY · 66½° · 0° · 23½° · LONG DAY · Equator · 24 hours daylight · Antarctic Circle: 24 hours daylight · S. Pole: 6 months daylight · S

Time

Year: The time taken by the Earth to revolve around the Sun, or 365.24 days.

Leap Year: A calendar year of 366 days, 29 February being the additional day. It offsets the difference between the calendar and the solar year.

Month: The approximate time taken by the Moon to revolve around the Earth. The 12 months of the year in fact vary from 28 (29 in a Leap Year) to 31 days.

Week: An artificial period of 7 days, not based on astronomical time

Day: The time taken by the Earth to complete one rotation on its axis

Hour: 24 hours make one day. Usually the day is divided into hours AM (ante meridiem or before noon) and PM (post meridiem or after noon), although most timetables now use the 24-hour system, from midnight to midnight.

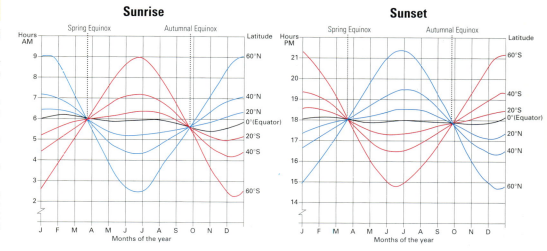

The Moon

The Moon rotates more slowly than the Earth, making one complete turn on its axis in just over 27 days. Since this corresponds to its period of revolution around the Earth, the Moon always presents the same hemisphere or face to us, and we never see 'the dark side'. The interval between one full Moon and the next (and between new Moons) is about 29½ days – a lunar month. The apparent changes in the shape of the Moon are caused by its changing position in relation to the Earth; like the planets, it produces no light of its own and shines only by reflecting the rays of the Sun.

Phases of the Moon

Distance from Earth: 356,410 km – 406,685 km; Mean diameter: 3,475.1 km; Mass: approx. 1/81 that of Earth; Surface gravity: one-sixth of Earth's; Daily range of temperature at lunar equator: 200°C; Average orbital speed: 3,683 km/h

New Moon | Crescent | First quarter | Gibbous | Full Moon | Gibbous | Last quarter | Crescent | New Moon

Eclipses

When the Moon passes between the Sun and the Earth it causes a partial eclipse of the Sun (1) if the Earth passes through the Moon's outer shadow (P), or a total eclipse (2) if the inner cone shadow crosses the Earth's surface. In a lunar eclipse, the Earth's shadow crosses the Moon and, again, provides either a partial or total eclipse.

Eclipses of the Sun and the Moon do not occur every month because of the 5° difference between the plane of the Moon's orbit and the plane in which the Earth moves. In the 1990s only 14 lunar eclipses were possible, for example, seven partial and seven total; each was visible only from certain, and variable, parts of the world. The same period witnessed 13 solar eclipses – six partial (or annular) and seven total.

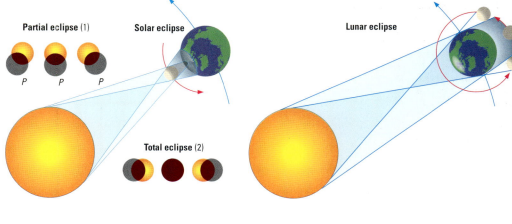

Tides

The daily rise and fall of the ocean's tides are the result of the gravitational pull of the Moon and that of the Sun, though the effect of the latter is only 46.6% as strong as that of the Moon. This effect is greatest on the hemisphere facing the Moon and causes a tidal 'bulge'. When the Sun, Earth and Moon are in line, tide-raising forces are at a maximum and Spring tides occur: high tide reaches the highest values, and low tide falls to low levels. When lunar and solar forces are least coincidental with the Sun and Moon at an angle (near the Moon's first and third quarters), Neap tides occur, which have a small tidal range.

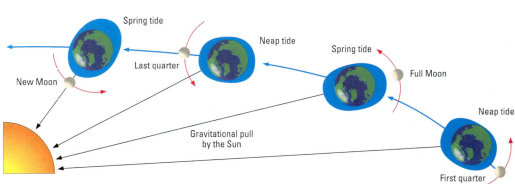

The Earth's Structure

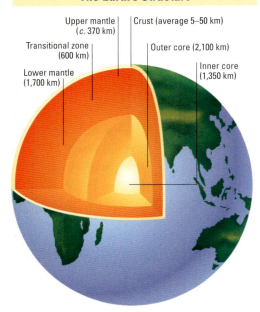

Upper mantle (c. 370 km)
Crust (average 5–50 km)
Transitional zone (600 km)
Outer core (2,100 km)
Lower mantle (1,700 km)
Inner core (1,350 km)

Continental Drift

About 200 million years ago the original Pangaea landmass began to split into two continental groups, which further separated over time to produce the present-day configuration.

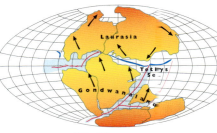

180 million years ago

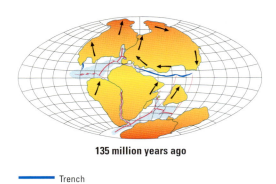

135 million years ago

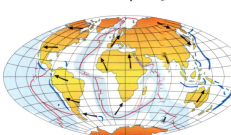

Present day

— Trench
— Rift
◯ New ocean floor
— Zones of slippage

Notable Earthquakes Since 1900

Year	Location	Richter Scale	Deaths
1906	San Francisco, USA	8.3	503
1906	Valparaiso, Chile	8.6	22,000
1908	Messina, Italy	7.5	83,000
1915	Avezzano, Italy	7.5	30,000
1920	Gansu (Kansu), China	8.6	180,000
1923	Yokohama, Japan	8.3	143,000
1927	Nan Shan, China	8.3	200,000
1932	Gansu (Kansu), China	7.6	70,000
1933	Sanriku, Japan	8.9	2,990
1934	Bihar, India/Nepal	8.4	10,700
1935	Quetta, India (now Pakistan)	7.5	60,000
1939	Chillan, Chile	8.3	28,000
1939	Erzincan, Turkey	7.9	30,000
1960	Agadir, Morocco	5.8	12,000
1962	Khorasan, Iran	7.1	12,230
1968	N.E. Iran	7.4	12,000
1970	N. Peru	7.7	66,794
1972	Managua, Nicaragua	6.2	5,000
1974	N. Pakistan	6.3	5,200
1976	Guatemala	7.5	22,778
1976	Tangshan, China	8.2	255,000
1978	Tabas, Iran	7.7	25,000
1980	El Asnam, Algeria	7.3	20,000
1980	S. Italy	7.2	4,800
1985	Mexico City, Mexico	8.1	4,200
1988	N.W. Armenia	6.8	55,000
1990	N. Iran	7.7	36,000
1993	Maharashtra, India	6.4	30,000
1994	Los Angeles, USA	6.6	51
1995	Kobe, Japan	7.2	5,000
1995	Sakhalin Is., Russia	7.5	2,000
1997	N.E. Iran	7.1	2,500
1998	Takhar, Afghanistan	6.1	4,200
1998	Rostaq, Afghanistan	7.0	5,000
1999	Izmit, Turkey	7.4	15,000
1999	Taipei, Taiwan	7.6	1,700

The highest magnitude recorded on the Richter scale is 8.9 in Japan on 2 March 1933 which killed 2,990 people.

Structure and Earthquakes

Mobile land areas
Submarine zones of mobile land areas
Stable land platforms
Submarine extensions of stable land platforms
Mid-oceanic volcanic ridges
Oceanic platforms

1976 ◯ Principal earthquakes and dates

Earthquakes are a series of rapid vibrations originating from the slipping or faulting of parts of the Earth's crust when stresses within build up to breaking point. They usually happen at depths varying from 8 km to 30 km. Severe earthquakes cause extensive damage when they take place in populated areas, destroying structures and severing communications. Most initial loss of life occurs due to secondary causes such as falling masonry, fires and flooding.

Earthquakes

Earthquake magnitude is usually rated according to either the Richter or the Modified Mercalli scale, both devised by seismologists in the 1930s. The Richter scale measures absolute earthquake power with mathematical precision: each step upwards represents a tenfold increase in shockwave amplitude. Theoretically, there is no upper limit, but the largest earthquakes measured have been rated at between 8.8 and 8.9. The 12–point Mercalli scale, based on observed effects, is often more meaningful, ranging from I (earthquakes noticed only by seismographs) to XII (total destruction); intermediate points include V (people awakened at night; unstable objects overturned), VII (collapse of ordinary buildings; chimneys and monuments fall) and IX (conspicuous cracks in ground; serious damage to reservoirs).

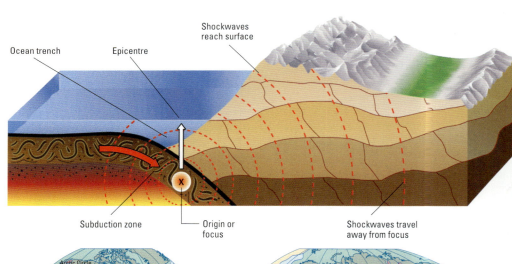

Ocean trench
Epicentre
Shockwaves reach surface
Subduction zone
Origin or focus
Shockwaves travel away from focus

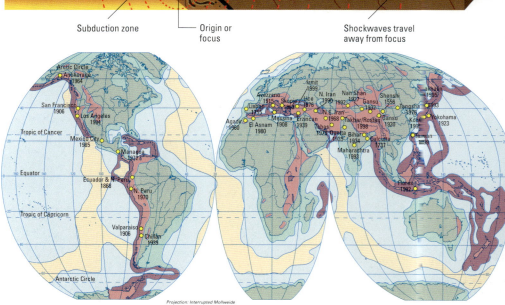

Projection: Interrupted Mollweide

Plate Tectonics

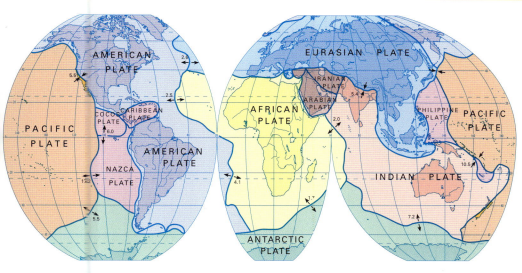

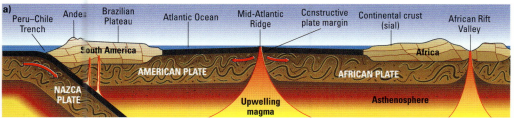

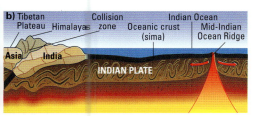

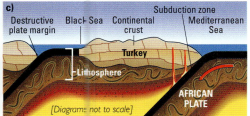

The drifting of the continents is a feature that is unique to Planet Earth. The complementary, almost jigsaw-puzzle fit of the coastlines on each side of the Atlantic Ocean inspired Alfred Wegener's theory of continental drift in 1915. The theory suggested that the ancient super-continent, which Wegener named Pangaea, incorporated all of the Earth's landmasses and gradually split up to form today's continents.

The original debate about continental drift was a prelude to a more radical idea: plate tectonics. The basic theory is that the Earth's crust is made up of a series of rigid plates which float on a soft layer of the mantle and are moved about by continental convection currents within the Earth's interior. These plates diverge and converge along margins marked by seismic activity. Plates diverge from mid-ocean ridges where molten lava pushes upwards and forces the plates apart at rates of up to 40 mm [1.6 in] a year.

The three diagrams, left, give some examples of plate boundaries from around the world. Diagram (a) shows sea-floor spreading at the Mid-Atlantic Ridge as the American and African plates slowly diverge. The same thing is happening in (b) where sea-floor spreading at the Mid-Indian Ocean Ridge is forcing the Indian plate to collide into the Eurasian plate. In (c) oceanic crust (sima) is being subducted beneath lighter continental crust (sial).

Volcanoes

Volcanoes occur when hot liquefied rock beneath the Earth's crust is pushed up by pressure to the surface as molten lava. Some volcanoes erupt in an explosive way, throwing out rocks and ash, whilst others are effusive and lava flows out of the vent. There are volcanoes which are both, such as Mount Fuji. An accumulation of lava and cinders creates cones of variable size and shape. As a result of many eruptions over centuries, Mount Etna in Sicily has a circumference of more than 120 km [75 miles].

Climatologists believe that volcanic ash, if ejected high into the atmosphere, can influence temperature and weather for several years afterwards. The 1991 eruption of Mount Pinatubo in the Philippines ejected more than 20 million tonnes of dust and ash 32 km [20 miles] into the atmosphere and is believed to have accelerated ozone depletion over a large part of the globe.

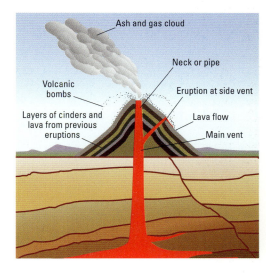

Distribution of Volcanoes

Volcanoes today may be the subject of considerable scientific study but they remain both dramatic and unpredictable: in 1991 Mount Pinatubo, 100 km [62 miles] north of the Philippines capital Manila, suddenly burst into life after lying dormant for more than six centuries. Most of the world's active volcanoes occur in a belt around the Pacific Ocean, on the edge of the Pacific plate, called the 'ring of fire'. Indonesia has the greatest concentration with 90 volcanoes, 12 of which are active. The most famous, Krakatoa, erupted in 1883 with such force that the resulting tidal wave killed 36,000 people and tremors were felt as far away as Australia.

- Submarine volcanoes
- Land volcanoes active since 1700
- Boundaries of tectonic plates

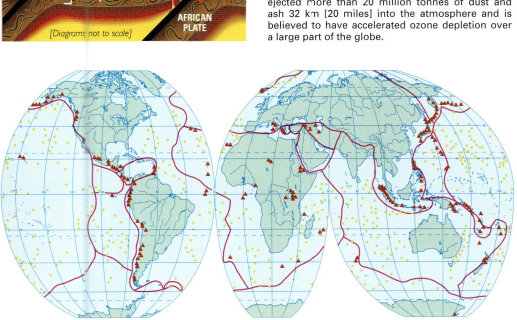

The Great Oceans

Relative sizes of the world's oceans

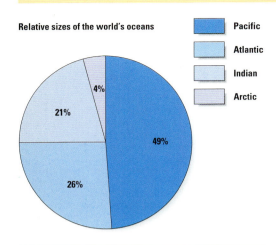

- Pacific
- Atlantic
- Indian
- Arctic

In a strict geographical sense there are only three true oceans – the Atlantic, Indian and Pacific. The legendary 'Seven Seas' would require these to be divided at the Equator and the addition of the Arctic Ocean – which accounts for less than 4% of the total sea area. The International Hydrographic Bureau does not recognize the Antarctic Ocean (even less the 'Southern Ocean') as a separate entity.

The Earth is a watery planet: more than 70% of its surface – over 360,000,000 sq km [140,000,000 sq miles] – is covered by the oceans and seas. The mighty Pacific alone accounts for nearly 36% of the total, and 49% of the sea area. Gravity holds in around 1,400 million cu. km [320 million cu. miles] of water, of which over 97% is saline.

The vast underwater world starts in the shallows of the seaside and plunges to depths of more than 11,000 m [36,000 ft]. The continental shelf, part of the landmass, drops gently to around 200 m [650 ft]; here the seabed falls away suddenly at an angle of 3° to 6° – the continental slope. The third stage, called the continental rise, is more gradual with gradients varying from 1 in 100 to 1 in 700. At an average depth of 5,000 m [16,500 ft] there begins the aptly-named abyssal plain – massive submarine depths where sunlight fails to penetrate and few creatures can survive.

From these plains rise volcanoes which, taken from base to top, rival and even surpass the tallest continental mountains in height. Mount Kea, on Hawaii, reaches a total of 10,203 m [33,400 ft], some 1,355 m [4,500 ft] more than Mount Everest, though scarcely 40% is visible above sea level.

In addition, there are underwater mountain chains up to 1,000 km [600 miles] across, whose peaks sometimes appear above sea level as islands such as Iceland and Tristan da Cunha.

The Ocean Depths

Average and maximum depths of the world's great oceans, in metres

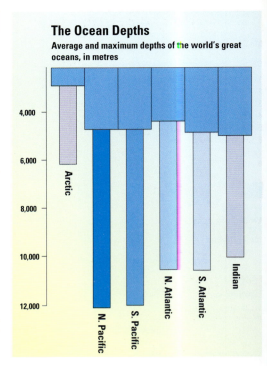

Ocean Currents

January temperatures and ocean currents

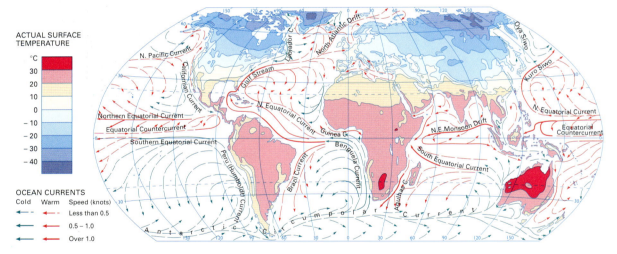

ACTUAL SURFACE TEMPERATURE

°C
30
20
10
0
-10
-20
-30
-40

OCEAN CURRENTS
Cold Warm Speed (knots)
Less than 0.5
0.5 – 1.0
Over 1.0

July temperatures and ocean currents

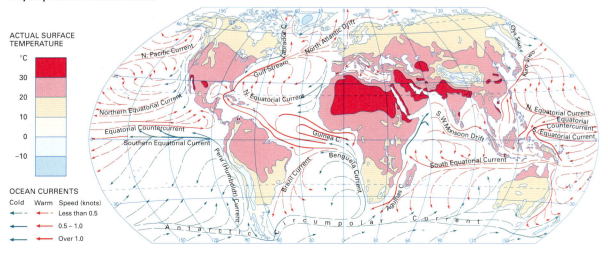

ACTUAL SURFACE TEMPERATURE

°C
30
20
10
0
-10

OCEAN CURRENTS
Cold Warm Speed (knots)
Less than 0.5
0.5 – 1.0
Over 1.0

Moving immense quantities of energy as well as billions of tonnes of water every hour, the ocean currents are a vital part of the great heat engine that drives the Earth's climate. They themselves are produced by a twofold mechanism. At the surface, winds push huge masses of water before them; in the deep ocean, below an abrupt temperature gradient that separates the churning surface waters from the still depths, density variations cause slow vertical movements.

The pattern of circulation of the great surface currents is determined by the displacement known as the Coriolis effect. As the Earth turns beneath a moving object – whether it is a tennis ball or a vast mass of water – it appears to be deflected to one side. The deflection is most obvious near the Equator, where the Earth's surface is spinning eastwards at 1,700 km/h [1,050 mph]; currents moving polewards are curved clockwise in the northern hemisphere and anti-clockwise in the southern.

The result is a system of spinning circles known as gyres. The Coriolis effect piles up water on the left of each gyre, creating a narrow, fast-moving stream that is matched by a slower, broader returning current on the right. North and south of the Equator, the fastest currents are located in the west and in the east respectively. In each case, warm water moves from the Equator and cold water returns to it. Cold currents often bring an upwelling of nutrients with them, supporting the world's most economically important fisheries.

Depending on the prevailing winds, some currents on or near the Equator may reverse their direction in the course of the year – a seasonal variation on which Asian monsoon rains depend, and whose occasional failure can bring disaster to millions.

World Fishing Areas

Main commercial fishing areas (numbered FAO regions)

Catch by top marine fishing areas, thousand tonnes (1992)

1.	Pacific, NW	61]	24,199	29.3%
2.	Pacific, SE	87]	13,899	16.8%
3.	Atlantic, NE	27]	11,073	13.4%
4.	Pacific, WC	71]	7,710	9.3%
5.	Indian, W	51]	3,747	4.5%
6.	Indian, E	57]	3,262	4.0%
7.	Atlantic, EC	34]	3,259	3.9%
8.	Pacific, NE	67]	3,149	3.8%

 Principal fishing areas

Leading fishing nations

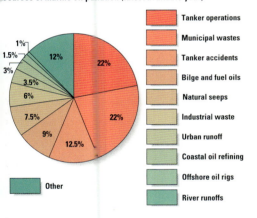

China 17.3% Peru 8.3% Japan 8.0% Chile 5.9% U.S.A. 5.9% Russia 4.4% India 4.3% Indonesia 3.6%

World total (1993): 101,417,500 tonnes
(Marine catch 83.1% Inland catch 16.9%)

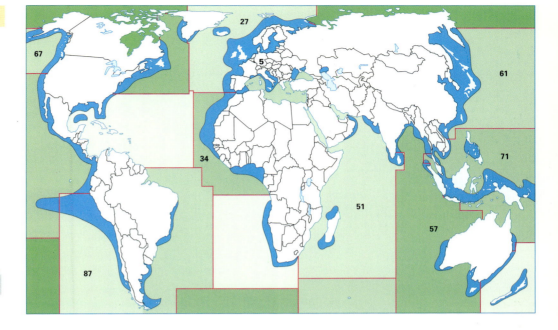

Marine Pollution

Sources of marine oil pollution (latest available year)

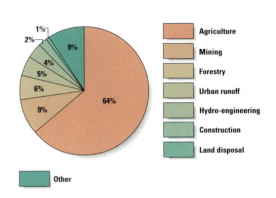

- Tanker operations
- Municipal wastes
- Tanker accidents
- Bilge and fuel oils
- Natural seeps
- Industrial waste
- Urban runoff
- Coastal oil refining
- Offshore oil rigs
- River runoffs
- Other

Oil Spills

Major oil spills from tankers and combined carriers

Year	Vessel	Location	Spill (barrels)**	Cause
1979	Atlantic Empress	West Indies	1,890,000	collision
1983	Castillo De Bellver	South Africa	1,760,000	fire
1978	Amoco Cadiz	France	1,628,000	grounding
1991	Haven	Italy	1,029,000	explosion
1988	Odyssey	Canada	1,000,000	fire
1967	Torrey Canyon	UK	909,000	grounding
1972	Sea Star	Gulf of Oman	902,250	collision
1977	Hawaiian Patriot	Hawaiian Is.	742,500	fire
1979	Independenta	Turkey	696,350	collision
1993	Braer	UK	625,000	grounding
1996	Sea Empress	UK	515,000	grounding

Other sources of major oil spills

Year	Source	Location	Spill (barrels)	Cause
1983	Nowruz oilfield	The Gulf	4,250,000†	war
1979	Ixtoc 1 oilwell	Gulf of Mexico	4,200,000	blow-out
1991	Kuwait	The Gulf	2,500,000†	war

** 1 barrel = 0.136 tonnes/159 lit./35 Imperial gal./42 US gal.   † estimated

River Pollution

Sources of river pollution, USA (latest available year)

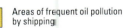

- Agriculture
- Mining
- Forestry
- Urban runoff
- Hydro-engineering
- Construction
- Land disposal
- Other

Water Pollution

- Severely polluted sea areas and lakes
- Polluted sea areas and lakes
- Areas of frequent oil pollution by shipping

- ◣ Major oil tanker spills
- ▲ Major oil rig blow-outs
- ▼ Offshore dumpsites for industrial and municipal waste
- — Severely polluted rivers and estuaries

The most notorious tanker spillage of the 1980s occurred when the *Exxon Valdez* ran aground in Prince William Sound, Alaska, in 1989, spilling 267,000 barrels of crude oil close to shore in a sensitive ecological area. This rates as the world's 28th worst spill in terms of volume.

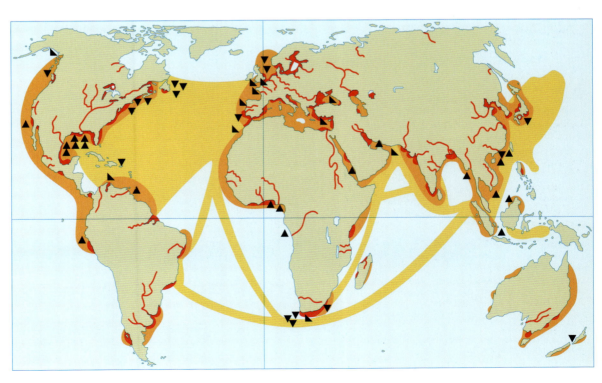

Climatic Regions

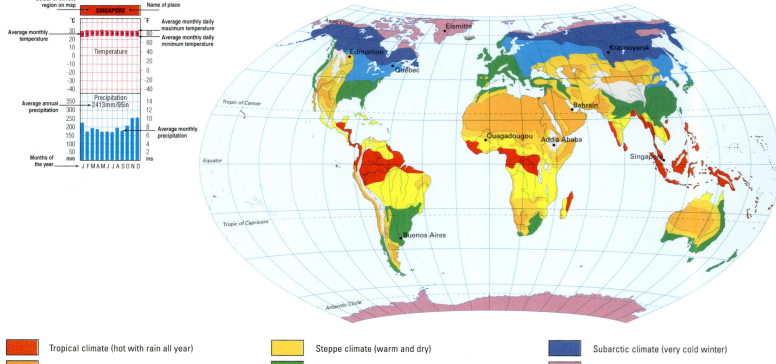

Tropical climate (hot with rain all year)

Desert climate (hot and very dry)

Savanna climate (hot with dry season)

Steppe climate (warm and dry)

Mild climate (warm and wet)

Continental climate (wet with cold winter)

Subarctic climate (very cold winter)

Polar climate (very cold and dry)

Mountainous climate (altitude affects climate)

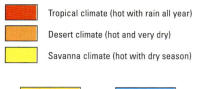

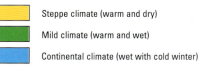

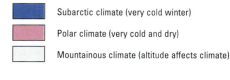

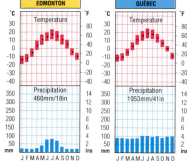

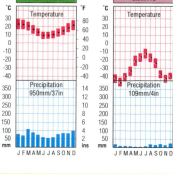

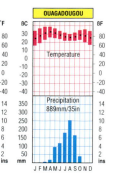

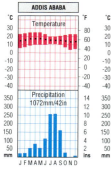

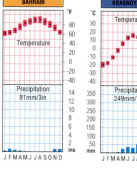

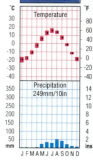

Climate Records

Temperature

Highest recorded shade temperature: Al Aziziyah, Libya, 58°C [136.4°F], 13 September 1922.

Highest mean annual temperature: Dallol, Ethiopia, 34.4°C [94°F], 1960–66.

Longest heatwave: Marble Bar, W. Australia, 162 days over 38°C [100°F], 23 October 1923 to 7 April 1924.

Lowest recorded temperature (outside poles): Verkhoyansk, Siberia, –68°C [–90°F], 6 February 1933.

Lowest mean annual temperature: Plateau Station, Antarctica, –56.6°C [–72.0°F]

Pressure

Longest drought: Calama, N. Chile, no recorded rainfall in 400 years to 1971.

Wettest place (12 months): Cherrapunji, Meghalaya, N. E. India, 26,470 mm [1,040 in], August 1860 to August 1861. Cherrapunji also holds the record for the most rainfall in one month: 2,930 mm [115 in], July 1861.

Wettest place (average): Mawsynram, India, mean annual rainfall 11,873 mm [467.4 in].

Wettest place (24 hours): Cilaos, Réunion, Indian Ocean, 1,870 mm [73.6 in], 15–16 March 1952.

Heaviest hailstones: Gopalganj, Bangladesh, up to 1.02 kg [2.25 lb], 14 April 1986 (killed 92 people).

Heaviest snowfall (continuous): Bessans, Savoie, France, 1,730 mm [68 in] in 19 hours, 5–6 April 1969.

Heaviest snowfall (season/year): Paradise Ranger Station, Mt Rainier, Washington, USA, 31,102 mm [1,224.5 in], 19 February 1971 to 18 February 1972.

Pressure and winds

Highest barometric pressure: Agata, Siberia (at 262 m [862 ft] altitude), 1,083.8 mb, 31 December 1968.

Lowest barometric pressure: Typhoon Tip, Guam, Pacific Ocean, 870 mb, 12 October 1979.

Highest recorded wind speed: Mt Washington, New Hampshire, USA, 371 km/h [231 mph], 12 April 1934. This is three times as strong as hurricane force on the Beaufort Scale.

Windiest place: Commonwealth Bay, Antarctica, where gales frequently reach over 320 km/h [200 mph].

Climate

Climate is weather in the long term: the seasonal pattern of hot and cold, wet and dry, averaged over time (usually 30 years). At the simplest level, it is caused by the uneven heating of the Earth. Surplus heat at the Equator passes towards the poles, levelling out the energy differential. Its passage is marked by a ceaseless churning of the atmosphere and the oceans, further agitated by the Earth's diurnal spin and the motion it imparts to moving air and water. The heat's means of transport – by winds and ocean currents, by the continual evaporation and recondensation of water molecules – is the weather itself. There are four basic types of climate, each of which can be further subdivided: tropical, desert (dry), temperate and polar.

Composition of Dry Air

Nitrogen	78.09%	Sulphur dioxide	trace
Oxygen	20.95%	Nitrogen oxide	trace
Argon	0.93%	Methane	trace
Water vapour	0.2–4.0%	Dust	trace
Carbon dioxide	0.03%	Helium	trace
Ozone	0.00006%	Neon	trace

El Niño

In a normal year, south-easterly trade winds drive surface waters westwards off the coast of South America, drawing cold, nutrient-rich water up from below. In an El Niño year (which occurs every 2–7 years), warm water from the west Pacific suppresses upwelling in the east, depriving the region of nutrients. The water is warmed by as much as 7°C [12°F], disturbing the tropical atmospheric circulation. During an intense El Niño, the south-east trade winds change direction and become equatorial westerlies, resulting in climatic extremes in many regions of the world, such as drought in parts of Australia and India, and heavy rainfall in south-eastern USA. An intense El Niño occurred in 1997–8, with resultant freak weather conditions across the entire Pacific region.

Normal year

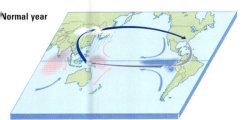

El Niño event

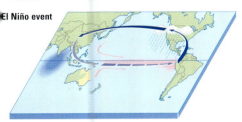

Beaufort Wind Scale

Named after the 19th-century British naval officer who devised it, the Beaufort Scale assesses wind speed according to its effects. It was originally designed as an aid for sailors, but has since been adapted for use on the land.

Scale	Wind speed km/h	mph	Effect
0	0–1	0–1	**Calm** Smoke rises vertically
1	1–5	1–3	**Light air** Wind direction shown only by smoke drift
2	6–11	4–7	**Light breeze** Wind felt on face; leaves rustle; vanes moved by wind
3	12–19	8–12	**Gentle breeze** Leaves and small twigs in constant motion; wind extends small flag
4	20–28	13–18	**Moderate** Raises dust and loose paper; small branches move
5	29–38	19–24	**Fresh** Small trees in leaf sway; wavelets on inland waters
6	39–49	25–31	**Strong** Large branches move; difficult to use umbrellas
7	50–61	32–38	**Near gale** Whole trees in motion; difficult to walk against wind
8	62–74	39–46	**Gale** Twigs break from trees; walking very difficult
9	75–88	47–54	**Strong gale** Slight structural damage
10	89–102	55–63	**Storm** Trees uprooted; serious structural damage
11	103–117	64–72	**Violent storm** Widespread damage
12	118+	73+	**Hurricane**

Conversions

°C = (°F − 32) × 5/9; °F = (°C × 9/5) + 32; 0°C = 32°F
1 in = 25.4 mm; 1 mm = 0.0394 in; 100 mm = 3.94 in

Temperature

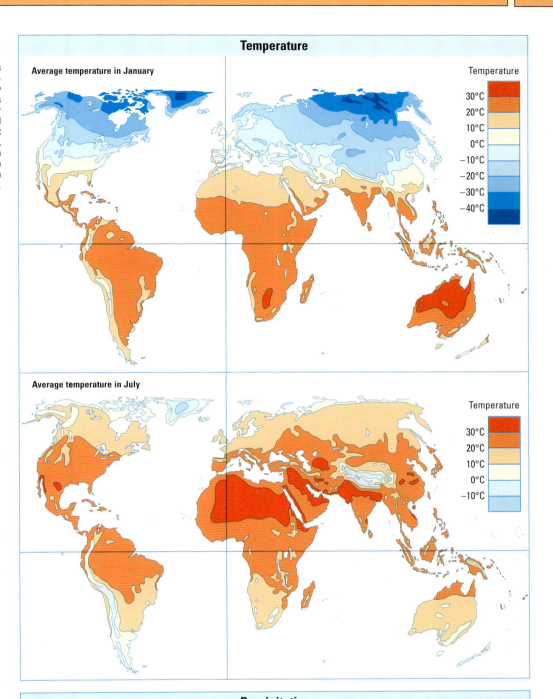

Average temperature in January

Average temperature in July

Temperature
30°C
20°C
10°C
0°C
−10°C
−20°C
−30°C
−40°C

Temperature
30°C
20°C
10°C
0°C
−10°C

Precipitation

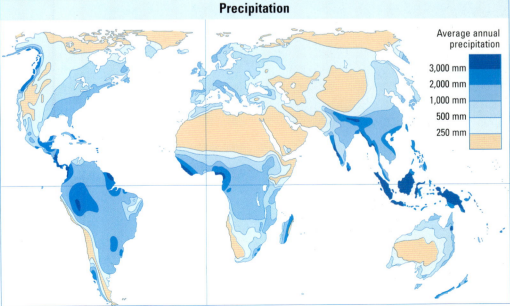

Average annual precipitation
3,000 mm
2,000 mm
1,000 mm
500 mm
250 mm

The Hydrological Cycle

The world's water balance is regulated by the constant recycling of water between the oceans, atmosphere and land. The movement of water between these three reservoirs is known as the hydrological cycle. The oceans play a vital role in the hydrological cycle: 74% of the total precipitation falls over the oceans and 84% of the total evaporation comes from the oceans.

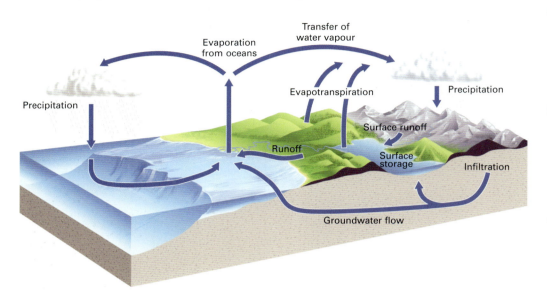

Water Distribution

The distribution of planetary water, by percentage. Oceans and ice-caps together account for more than 99% of the total; the breakdown of the remainder is estimated.

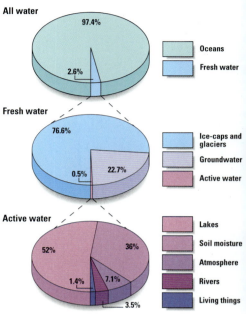

All water
- 97.4%
- 2.6%
- Oceans
- Fresh water

Fresh water
- 76.6%
- 0.5%
- 22.7%
- Ice-caps and glaciers
- Groundwater
- Active water

Active water
- 52%
- 36%
- 1.4%
- 7.1%
- 3.5%
- Lakes
- Soil moisture
- Atmosphere
- Rivers
- Living things

Water Utilization

Domestic **Industrial** **Agriculture**

The percentage breakdown of water usage by sector, selected countries (1996)

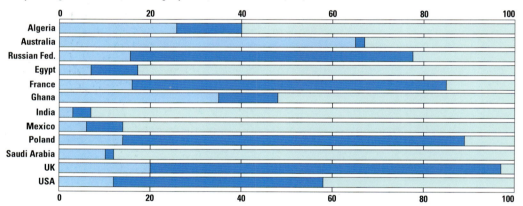

Algeria
Australia
Russian Fed.
Egypt
France
Ghana
India
Mexico
Poland
Saudi Arabia
UK
USA

Water Usage

Almost all the world's water is 3,000 million years old, and all of it cycles endlessly through the hydrosphere, though at different rates. Water vapour circulates over days, even hours, deep ocean water circulates over millennia, and ice-cap water remains solid for millions of years.

Fresh water is essential to all terrestrial life. Humans cannot survive more than a few days without it, and even the hardiest desert plants and animals could not exist without some water. Agriculture requires huge quantities of fresh water: without large-scale irrigation most of the world's people would starve. In the USA, agriculture uses 42% and industry 45% of all water withdrawals.

The United States is one of the heaviest users of water in the world. According to the latest figures the average American uses 380 litres a day and the average household uses 415,000 litres a year. This is two to four times more than in Western Europe.

Water Supply

Percentage of total population with access to safe drinking water (1995)

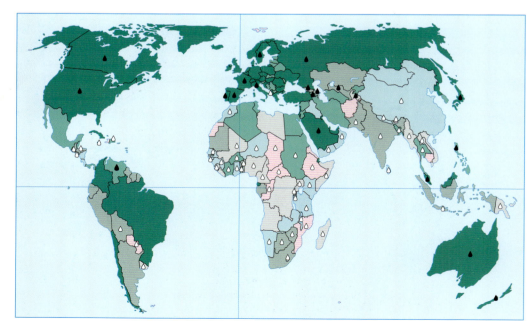

- Over 90% with safe water
- 75 – 90% with safe water
- 60 – 75% with safe water
- 45 – 60% with safe water
- 30 – 45% with safe water
- Under 30% with safe water

△ Under 80 litres per person per day domestic water consumption

◆ Over 320 litres per person per day domestic water consumption

NB: 80 litres of water a day is considered necessary for a reasonable quality of life.

Least well-provided countries

Paraguay	8%	Central Afr. Rep.	18%
Afghanistan	10%	Bhutan	21%
Cambodia	13%	Congo (Dem. Rep.)	25%

Natural Vegetation

Regional variation in vegetation

- Tundra and mountain vegetation
- Needleleaf evergreen forest
- Mixed needleleaf evergreen & broadleaf deciduous trees
- Broadleaf deciduous woodland
- Mid-latitude grassland
- Evergreen broadleaf and deciduous trees & shrubs
- Semi-desert scrub
- Desert
- Tropical grassland (savanna)
- Tropical broadleaf rainforest and monsoon forest
- Subtropical broadleaf and needleleaf forest

The map shows the natural 'climax vegetation' of regions, as dictated by climate and topography. In most cases, however, agricultural activity has drastically altered the vegetation pattern. Western Europe, for example, lost most of its broadleaf forest many centuries ago, while irrigation has turned some natural semi-desert into productive land.

Land Use by Continent

- Forest
- Permanent pasture and rough grazing
- Permanent crops and plantations
- Arable
- Non-productive

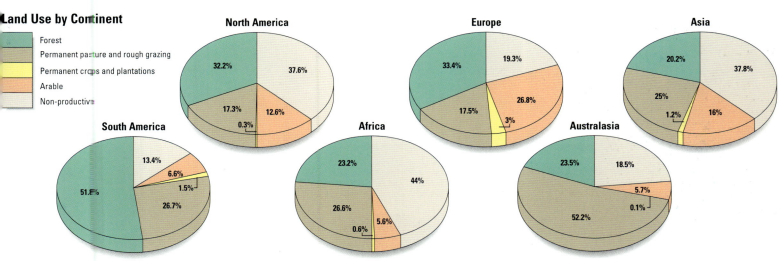

North America: 32.2%, 37.6%, 17.3%, 0.3%, 12.6%

Europe: 33.4%, 19.3%, 17.5%, 3%, 26.8%

Asia: 20.2%, 37.8%, 25%, 1.2%, 16%

South America: 13.4%, 6.6%, 1.5%, 51.8%, 26.7%

Africa: 23.2%, 44%, 26.6%, 0.6%, 5.6%

Australasia: 23.5%, 18.5%, 5.7%, 0.1%, 52.2%

Forestry: Production

Forest and woodland (million hectares)	Annual production (1996, million cubic metres) Fuelwood and charcoal	Industrial roundwood*
World **3,98 .9**	**1,864.8**	**1,489.5**
S. America 82 .3	193.0	129.9
N. & C. America 70 .8	155.4	600.4
Africa 68 .6	519.9	67.9
Asia 13 .8	905.2	280.2
Europe 15 .3	82.4	369.7
Australasia 15 .2	8.7	41.5

Paper and Board

Top producers (1996)**		Top exporters (1996)**	
USA	85 173	Canada	13,393
China	30 253	USA	9,113
Japan	30 14	Finland	8,529
Canada	18 14	Sweden	7,483
Germany	14 33	Germany	6,319

* roundwood is timber as it is felled
** in thousand tonnes

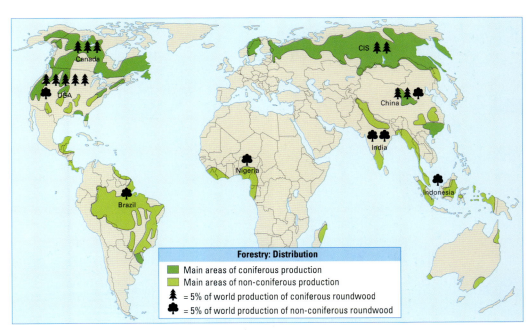

Forestry: Distribution

- Main areas of coniferous production
- Main areas of non-coniferous production
- 🌲 = 5% of world production of coniferous roundwood
- ♣ = 5% of world production of non-coniferous roundwood

Humans have always had a dramatic effect on their environment, at least since the development of agriculture almost 10,000 years ago. Generally, the Earth has accepted human interference without obvious ill effects: the complex systems that regulate the global environment have been able to absorb substantial damage while maintaining a stable and comfortable home for the planet's trillions of lifeforms. But advancing human technology and the rapidly-expanding populations it supports are now threatening to overwhelm the Earth's ability to compensate.

Industrial wastes, acid rainfall, desertification and large-scale deforestation all combine to create environmental change at a rate far faster than the great slow cycles of planetary evolution can accommodate. As a result of overcultivation, overgrazing and overcutting of groundcover for firewood, desertification is affecting as much as 60% of the world's croplands. In addition, with fire and chain-saws, humans are destroying more forest in a day than their ancestors could have done in a century, upsetting the balance between plant and animal, carbon dioxide and oxygen, on which all life ultimately depends.

The fossil fuels that power industrial civilization have pumped enough carbon dioxide and other so-called greenhouse gases into the atmosphere to make climatic change a near certainty. As a result of the combination of these factors, the Earth's average temperature has risen by approximately 0.5°C [1°F] since the beginning of the 20th century, and it is still rising.

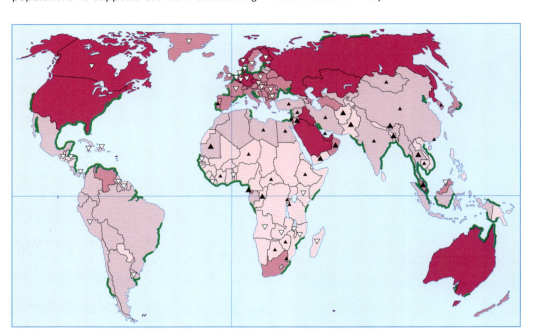

Global Warming

Carbon dioxide emissions in tonnes per person per year (1995)

- Over 10 tonnes of CO_2
- 5 – 10 tonnes of CO_2
- 1 – 5 tonnes of CO_2
- Under 1 tonne of CO_2

Changes in CO_2 emissions 1980–90

- ▲ Over 100% increase in emissions
- ▲ 50–100% increase in emissions
- ▽ Reduction in emissions
- ── Coastal areas in danger of flooding from rising sea levels caused by global warming

High atmospheric concentrations of heat-absorbing gases, especially carbon dioxide, appear to be causing a steady rise in average temperatures worldwide – up to 1.5°C [3°F] by the year 2020, according to some estimates. Global warming is likely to bring with it a rise in sea levels that may flood some of the Earth's most densely populated coastal areas.

Greenhouse Power

Relative contributions to the Greenhouse Effect by the major heat-absorbing gases in the atmosphere.

The chart combines greenhouse potency and volume. Carbon dioxide has a greenhouse potential of only 1, but its concentration of 350 parts per million makes it predominate. CFC 12, with 25,000 times the absorption capacity of CO_2, is present only as 0.00044 ppm.

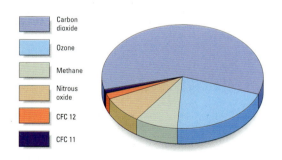

- Carbon dioxide
- Ozone
- Methane
- Nitrous oxide
- CFC 12
- CFC 11

Ozone Layer

The ozone 'hole' over the northern hemisphere on 12 March 1995.

The colours represent Dobson Units (DU). The ozone 'hole' is seen as the dark blue and purple patch in the centre, where ozone values are around 120 DU or lower. Normal levels are around 280 DU. The ozone 'hole' over Antarctica is much larger.

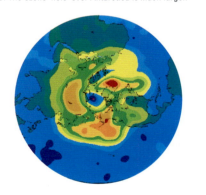

Courtesy: Science Photo Library/NOAA

Carbon Dioxide

Carbon dioxide released in millions of tonnes (1992)

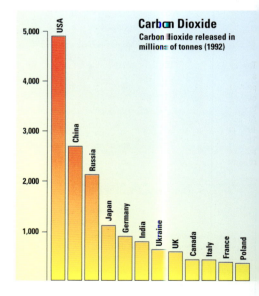

The Greenhouse Effect

Carbon dioxide is increased by burning fossil fuels and cutting forests

Carbon Dioxide

Carbon dioxide and other greenhouse gases trap the heat being reflected from the Earth, although some heat is lost

The warming increases water vapour in the air, leading to even greater absorption of heat

Rising temperatures would melt snow and ice causing oceans to rise

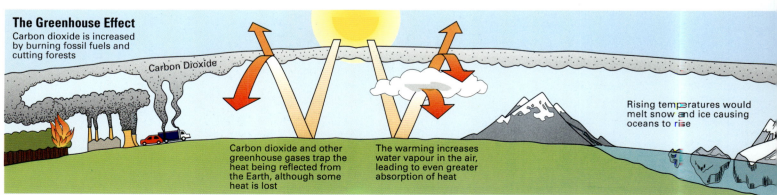

Desertification

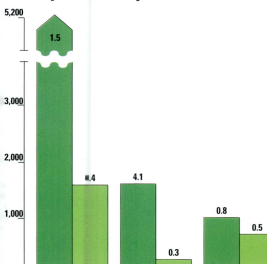

- Existing deserts
- Areas with a high risk of desertification
- Areas with a moderate risk of desertification
- Former areas of rainforest
- Existing rainforest

Forest Clearance

Thousands of hectares of forest cleared annually, tropical countries surveyed 1981–85 and 1987–90. Loss as a percentage of remaining stocks is shown in figures on each column.

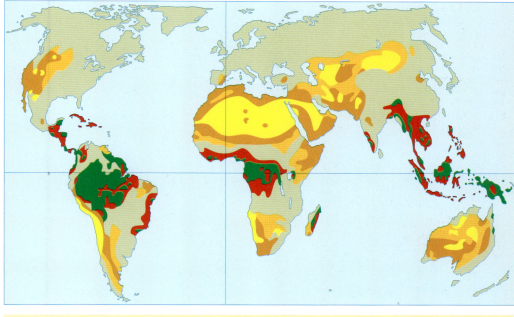

Chart values (1987–90 / 1981–85):
- Brazil: 1.5 / 0.4
- India: 4.1 / 0.3
- Indonesia: 0.8 / 0.5
- Burma: 2.1 / 0.3
- Thailand: 2.5 / 2.4
- Vietnam: 2.0 / 0.7
- Philippines: 1.5 / 1.0
- Costa Rica: 7.6 / 4.0
- Cameroon: 0.6 / 0.4

Legend: 1987–90, 1981–85

Deforestation

The Earth's remaining forests are under attack from three directions: expanding agriculture, logging, and growing consumption of fuelwood, often in combination. Sometimes deforestation is the direct result of government policy, as in the efforts made to resettle the urban poor in some parts of Brazil; just as often, it comes about despite state attempts at conservation. Loggers, licensed or unlicensed, blaze a trail into virgin forest, often destroying twice as many trees as they harvest. Landless farmers follow, burning away most of what remains to plant their crops, completing the destruction.

Ozone Depletion

The ozone layer, 25–30 km [15–18 miles] above sea level, acts as a barrier to most of the Sun's harmful ultra-violet radiation, protecting us from the ionizing radiation that can cause skin cancer and cataracts. In recent years, however, two holes in the ozone layer have been observed during winter: one over the Arctic and the other the size of the USA, over Antarctica. By 1996, ozone had been reduced to around a half of its 1970 amount. The ozone (O_3) is broken down by chlorine released into the atmosphere as CFCs (chlorofluorocarbons) – chemicals used in refrigerators, packaging and aerosols.

Air Pollution

Sulphur dioxide is the main pollutant associated with industrial cities. According to the World Health Organization, at least 600 million people live in urban areas where sulphur dioxide concentrations regularly reach damaging levels. One of the world's most dangerously polluted urban areas is Mexico City, due to a combination of its enclosed valley location, 3 million cars and 60,000 factories. In May 1998, this lethal cocktail was added to by nearby forest fires and the resultant air pollution led to over 20% of the population (3 million people) complaining of respiratory problems.

Acid Rain

Killing trees, poisoning lakes and rivers and eating away buildings, acid rain is mostly produced by sulphur dioxide emissions from industry and volcanic eruptions. By the mid 1990s, acid rain had sterilized 4,000 or more of Sweden's lakes and left 45% of Switzerland's alpine conifers dead or dying, while the monuments of Greece were dissolving in Athens' smog. Prevailing wind patterns mean that the acids often fall many hundred kilometres from where the original pollutants were discharged. In parts of Europe acid deposition has slightly decreased, following reductions in emissions, but not by enough.

World Pollution

Acid rain and sources of acidic emissions (latest available year)

Acid rain is caused by high levels of sulphur and nitrogen in the atmosphere. They combine with water vapour and oxygen to form acids (H_2SO_4 and HNO_3) which fall as precipitation.

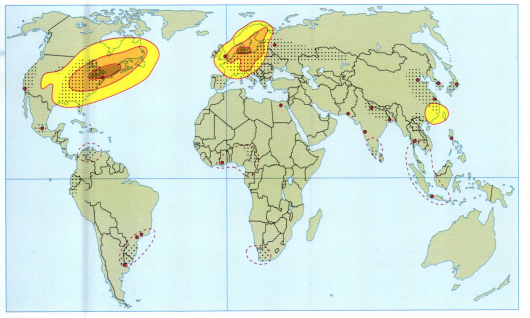

- Regions where sulphur and nitrogen oxides are released in high concentrations, mainly from fossil fuel combustion
- Major cities with high levels of air pollution (including nitrogen and sulphur emissions)

Areas of heavy acid deposition

pH numbers indicate acidity, decreasing from a neutral 7. Normal rain, slightly acid from dissolved carbon dioxide, never exceeds a pH of 5.6.

- pH less than 4.0 (most acidic)
- pH 4.0 to 4.5
- pH 4.5 to 5.0
- Areas where acid rain is a potential problem

Demographic Profiles

Developed nations such as the UK have populations evenly spread across the age groups and, usually, a growing proportion of elderly people. The great majority of the people in developing nations, however, are in the younger age groups, about to enter their most fertile years. In time, these population profiles should resemble the world profile (even Kenya has made recent progress with reducing its birth rate), but the transition will come about only after a few more generations of rapid population growth.

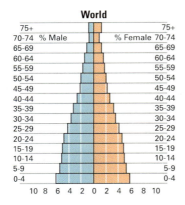

World

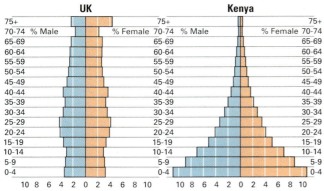

UK

Kenya

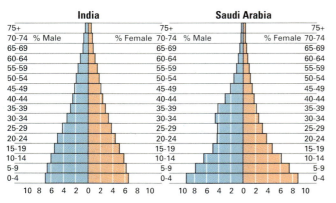

India

Saudi Arabia

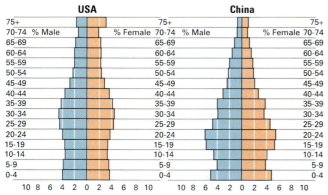

USA

China

Most Populous Nations [in millions (1998 estimates)]

1.	China	1,237	9. Bangladesh	125	17. Iran	64
2.	India	984	10. Nigeria	111	18. Thailand	60
3.	USA	270	11. Mexico	99	19. France	59
4.	Indonesia	213	12. Germany	82	20. UK	59
5.	Brazil	170	13. Philippines	78	21. Ethiopia	58
6.	Russia	147	14. Vietnam	76	22. Italy	57
7.	Pakistan	135	15. Egypt	66	23. Ukraine	50
8.	Japan	126	16. Turkey	65	24. Congo (= Zaïre)	49

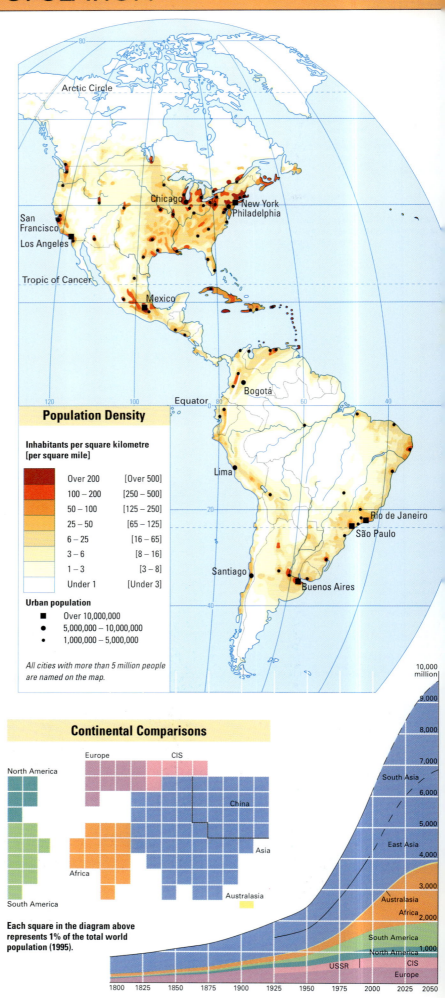

Population Density

Inhabitants per square kilometre
[per square mile]

Over 200	[Over 500]
100 – 200	[250 – 500]
50 – 100	[125 – 250]
25 – 50	[65 – 125]
6 – 25	[16 – 65]
3 – 6	[8 – 16]
1 – 3	[3 – 8]
Under 1	[Under 3]

Urban population

■ Over 10,000,000
● 5,000,000 – 10,000,000
• 1,000,000 – 5,000,000

All cities with more than 5 million people are named on the map.

Continental Comparisons

Each square in the diagram above represents 1% of the total world population (1995).

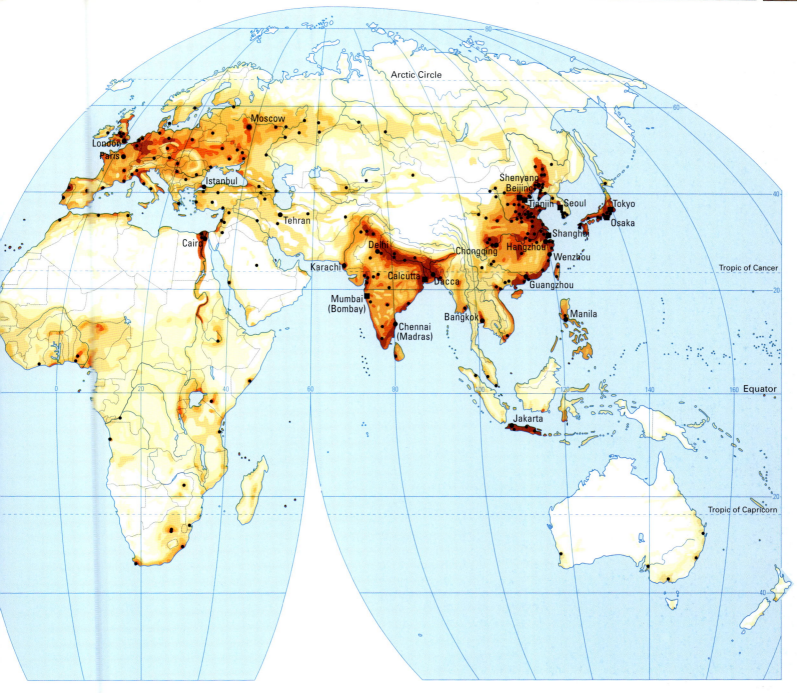

Arctic Circle

Moscow

London
Paris

Istanbul

Tehran

Cairo

Karachi

Delhi

Calcutta

Mumbai
(Bombay)

Chennai
(Madras)

Bangkok

Shenyang
Beijing

Tianjin Seoul Tokyo
Osaka
Shanghai
Chongqing Hangzhou
Wenzhou
Dacca
Guangzhou

Manila

Jakarta

Tropic of Cancer

Equator

Tropic of Capricorn

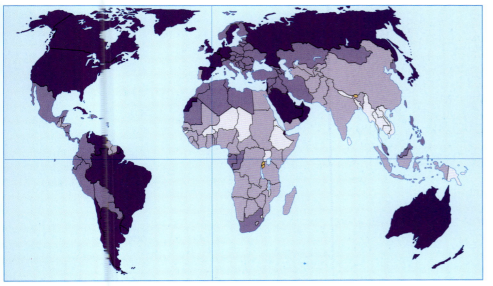

Urban Population

Percentage of total population living in towns and cities (1997)

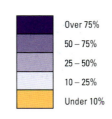

Over 75%

50 – 75%

25 – 50%

10 – 25%

Under 10%

Most urbanized		Least urbanized	
Singapore	100%	Rwanda	6%
Belgium	97%	Bhutan	8%
Israel	91%	Burundi	8%
Uruguay	91%	Nepal	11%
Netherlands	89%	Swaziland	12%

[UK 89%]

Predominant Languages

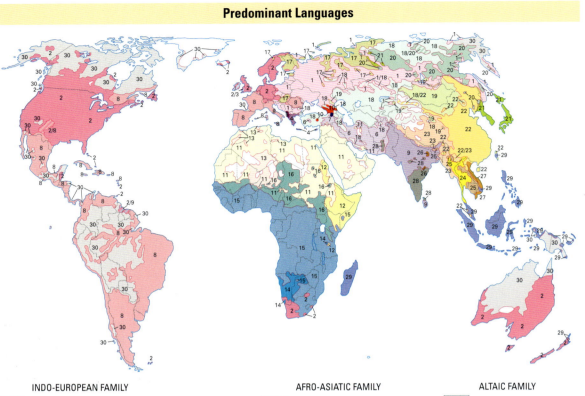

Languages of the World

Language can be classified by ancestry and structure. For example, the Romance and Germanic groups are both derived from an Indo-European language believed to have been spoken 5,000 years ago.

Mother tongues (in millions)
Chinese 1,069 (Mandarin 864), English 443, Hindi 352, Spanish 341, Russian 293, Arabic 197, Bengali 184, Portuguese 173, Malay-Indonesian 142, Japanese 125, French 121, German 118, Urdu 92, Punjabi 84, Korean 71.

Official languages (% of total population)
English 27%, Chinese 19%, Hindi 13.5%, Spanish 5.4%, Russian 5.2%, French 4.2%, Arabic 3.3%, Portuguese 3%, Malay 3%, Bengali 2.9%, Japanese 2.3%.

INDO-EUROPEAN FAMILY

1 Balto-Slavic group (incl. Russian, Ukrainian)
2 Germanic group (incl. English, German)
3 Celtic group
4 Greek
5 Albanian
6 Iranian group
7 Armenian
8 Romance group (incl. Spanish, Portuguese, French, Italian)
9 Indo-Aryan group (incl. Hindi, Bengali, Urdu, Punjabi, Marathi)
10 CAUCASIAN FAMILY

AFRO-ASIATIC FAMILY

11 Semitic group (incl. Arabic)
12 Kushitic group
13 Berber group

14 KHOISAN FAMILY
15 NIGER-CONGO FAMILY
16 NILO-SAHARAN FAMILY
17 URALIC FAMILY

ALTAIC FAMILY

18 Turkic group
19 Mongolian group
20 Tungus-Manchu group
21 Japanese and Korean

SINO-TIBETAN FAMILY

22 Sinitic (Chinese) languages
23 Tibetic-Burmic languages

24 TAI FAMILY

AUSTRO-ASIATIC FAMILY

25 Mon-Khmer group
26 Munda group
27 Vietnamese

28 DRAVIDIAN FAMILY (incl. Telugu, Tamil)

29 AUSTRONESIAN FAMILY (incl. Malay-Indonesian)

30 OTHER LANGUAGES

Predominant Religions

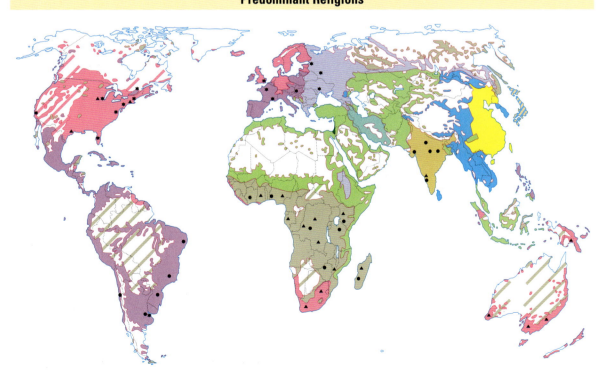

Religious Adherents

Religious adherents in millions:

Christian	1,669	Hindu	663
Roman Catholic	952	Buddhist	312
Protestant	337	Chinese Folk	172
Orthodox	162	Tribal	92
Anglican	70	Jewish	18
Other Christian	148	Sikhs	17
Muslim	866		
Sunni	841		
Shia	125		

- Roman Catholicism
- Orthodox and other Eastern Churches
- Protestantism
- Sunni Islam
- Shia Islam
- Buddhism
- Hinduism
- Confucianism
- Judaism
- Shintoism
- Tribal Religions

United Nations

Created in 1945 to promote peace and co-operation and based in New York, the United Nations is the world's largest international organization, with 185 members and an annual budget of US $2.6 billion (1996–97). Each member of the General Assembly has one vote, while the permanent members of the 15-nation Security Council – USA, Russia, China, UK and France – hold a veto. The Secretariat is the UN's principal administrative arm. The 54 members of the Economic and Social Council are responsible for economic, social, cultural, educational, health and related matters. The UN has 16 specialized agencies – based in Canada, France, Switzerland and Italy, as well as the USA – which help members in fields such as education (UNESCO), agriculture (FAO), medicine (WHO) and finance (IFC). By the end of 1994, all the original 11 trust territories of the Trusteeship Council had become independent.

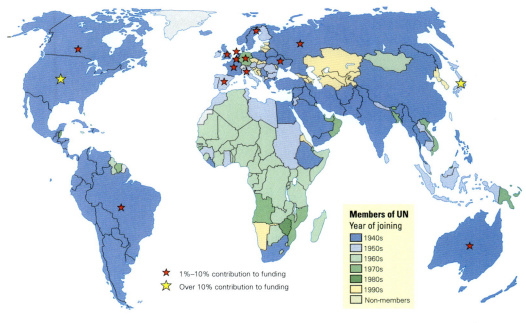

Members of UN
Year of joining
- 1940s
- 1950s
- 1960s
- 1970s
- 1980s
- 1990s
- Non-members

★ 1%–10% contribution to funding
★ Over 10% contribution to funding

MEMBERSHIP OF THE UN In 1945 there were 51 members; by December 1994 membership had increased to 185 following the admission of Palau. There are 7 independent states which are not members of the UN – Kiribati, Nauru, Switzerland, Taiwan, Tonga, Tuvalu and the Vatican City. All the successor states of the former USSR had joined by the end of 1992. The official languages of the UN are Chinese, English, French, Russian, Spanish and Arabic.

FUNDING The UN budget for 1996–97 was US $2.6 billion. Contributions are assessed by the members' ability to pay, with the maximum 25% of the total, the minimum 0.01%. Contributions for 1996 were: USA 25.0%, Japan 15.4%, Germany 9.0%, France 6.4%, UK 5.3%, Italy 5.2%, Russia 4.5%, Canada 3.1%, Spain 2.4%, Brazil 1.6%, Netherlands 1.6%, Australia 1.5%, Sweden 1.2%, Ukraine 1.1%, Belgium 1.0%.

International Organizations

EU European Union (evolved from the European Community in 1993). The 15 members – Austria, Belgium, Denmark, Finland, France, Germany, Greece, Ireland, Italy, Luxembourg, Netherlands, Portugal, Spain, Sweden and the UK – aim to integrate economies, co-ordinate social developments and bring about political union. These members of what is now the world's biggest market share agricultural and industrial policies and tariffs on trade. The original body, the European Coal and Steel Community (ECSC), was created in 1951 following the signing of the Treaty of Paris.

EFTA European Free Trade Association (formed in 1960). Portugal left the original 'Seven' in 1989 to join what was then the EC, followed by Austria, Finland and Sweden in 1995. Only 4 members remain: Norway, Iceland, Switzerland and Liechtenstein.

ACP African-Caribbean-Pacific (formed in 1963). Members have economic ties with the EU.

NATO North Atlantic Treaty Organization (formed in 1949). It continues after 1991 despite the winding up of the Warsaw Pact. The Czech Republic, Hungary and Poland were the latest members to join in 1999.

OAS Organization of American States (formed in 1948). It aims to promote social and economic co-operation between developed countries of North America and developing nations of Latin America.

ASEAN Association of South-east Asian Nations (formed in 1967). Burma and Laos joined in 1997.

OAU Organization of African Unity (formed in 1963). Its 53 members represent over 94% of Africa's population. Arabic, French, Portuguese and English are recognized as working languages.

LAIA Latin American Integration Association (1980). Its aim is to promote freer regional trade.

OECD Organization for Economic Co-operation and Development (formed in 1961). It comprises the 29 major Western free-market economies. Poland, Hungary and South Korea joined in 1996. 'G8' is its 'inner group' comprising Canada, France, Germany, Italy, Japan, Russia, the UK and the USA.

COMMONWEALTH The Commonwealth of Nations evolved from the British Empire; it comprises 16 Queen's realms, 32 republics and 5 indigenous monarchies, giving a total of 53.

OPEC Organization of Petroleum Exporting Countries (formed in 1960). It controls about three-quarters of the world's oil supply. Gabon left the organization in 1996.

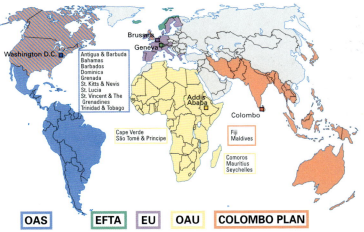

OAS EFTA EU OAU COLOMBO PLAN

ARAB LEAGUE (formed in 1945). The League's aim is to promote economic, social, political and military co-operation. There are 21 member nations.

COLOMBO PLAN (formed in 1951). Its 26 members aim to promote economic and social development in Asia and the Pacific.

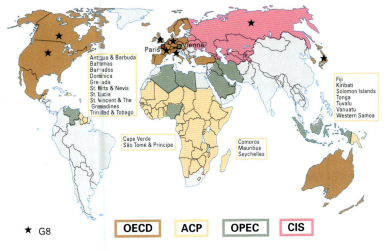

★ G8

OECD ACP OPEC CIS

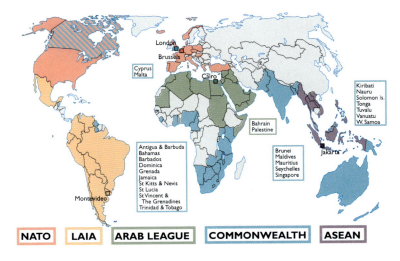

NATO LAIA ARAB LEAGUE COMMONWEALTH ASEAN

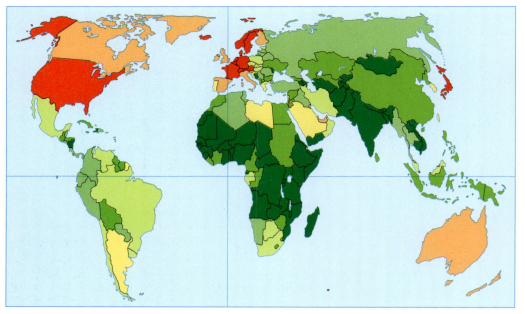

Levels of Income

Gross National Product per capita: the value of total production divided by the population (1997)

▮ (red)	Over 400% of world average
▮ (orange)	200 – 400% of world average
▮ (yellow)	100 – 200% of world average

[World average wealth per person US $6,316]

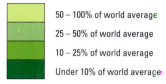

▮	50 – 100% of world average
▮	25 – 50% of world average
▮	10 – 25% of world average
▮	Under 10% of world average

GNP per capita growth rate (%), selected countries, 1985–94

Thailand	8.2	Brazil	–0.4
Chile	6.9	Zimbabwe	–0.6
Japan	3.2	USA	–1.3
Germany	1.9	UK	–1.4
Australia	1.2	Armenia	–12.9

Wealth Creation

The Gross National Product (GNP) of the world's largest economies, US $ million (1997)

1.	USA	7,690,100	23.	Turkey	199,500
2.	Japan	4,772,300	24.	Denmark	171,400
3.	Germany	2,319,300	25.	Thailand	169,600
4.	France	1,526,400	26.	Hong Kong	164,400
5.	UK	1,220,200	27.	Norway	158,900
6.	Italy	1,155,400	28.	Poland	138,900
7.	China	1,055,400	29.	South Africa	130,200
8.	Brazil	773,400	30.	Saudi Arabia	128,900
9.	Canada	583,900	31.	Greece	126,200
10.	Spain	570,100	32.	Finland	123,800
11.	South Korea	485,200	33.	Portugal	103,900
12.	Russia	403,500	34.	Singapore	101,800
13.	Netherlands	402,700	35.	Malaysia	98,200
14.	Australia	380,000	36.	Philippines	89,300
15.	India	373,900	37.	Israel	87,600
16.	Mexico	348,600	38.	Colombia	86,800
17.	Switzerland	313,500	39.	Venezuela	78,700
18.	Argentina	305,700	40.	Chile	73,300
19.	Belgium	268,400	41.	Egypt	71,200
20.	Sweden	232,000	42.	Pakistan	67,200
21.	Austria	225,900	43.	Ireland	66,400
22.	Indonesia	221,900	44.	Peru	60,800

The Wealth Gap

The world's richest and poorest countries, by Gross National Product per capita in US $ (1997)

1.	Luxembourg	45,360	1.	Mozambique	90
2.	Switzerland	44,220	2.	Ethiopia	110
3.	Japan	37,850	3.	Congo (D. Rep.)	110
4.	Norway	36,090	4.	Burundi	180
5.	Liechtenstein	33,000	5.	Sierra Leone	200
6.	Singapore	32,940	6.	Niger	200
7.	Denmark	32,500	7.	Rwanda	210
8.	Bermuda	31,870	8.	Tanzania	210
9.	USA	28,740	9.	Nepal	210
10.	Germany	28,260	10.	Malawi	220
11.	Austria	27,980	11.	Chad	240
12.	Iceland	26,580	12.	Madagascar	250
13.	Belgium	26,420	13.	Mali	260
14.	Sweden	26,220	14.	Yemen	270
15.	France	26,050	15.	Cambodia	300
16.	Netherlands	25,820	16.	Bosnia-Herzegovina	300
17.	Monaco	25,000	17.	Gambia, The	320
18.	Hong Kong	22,990	18.	Haiti	330
19.	Finland	20,580	19.	Kenya	330
20.	UK	18,700	20.	Angola	340

GNP per capita is calculated by dividing a country's Gross National Product by its total population.

Continental Shares

Shares of population and of wealth (GNP) by continent

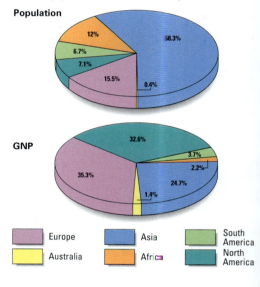

Population

GNP

▮ Europe	▮ Asia	▮ South America
▮ Australia	▮ Africa	▮ North America

Inflation

Average annual rate of inflation (1990–96)

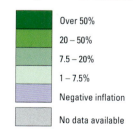

▮	Over 50%
▮	20 – 50%
▮	7.5 – 20%
▮	1 – 7.5%
▮	Negative inflation
▮	No data available

Highest average inflation		Lowest average inflation	
Congo (Dem. Rep.)	2747%	Oman	–3.0%
Georgia	2279%	Bahrain	–0.5%
Angola	1103%	Brunei	–0.0%
Turkmenistan	1074%	Saudi Arabia	1.0%
Armenia	897%	Japan	1.0%

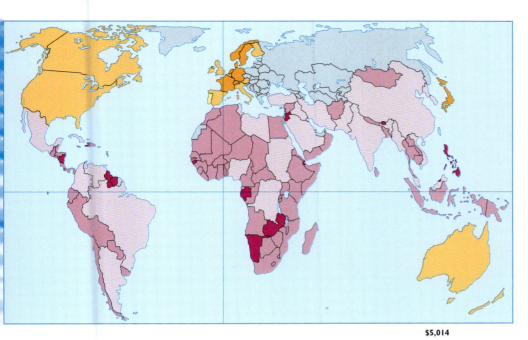

International Aid

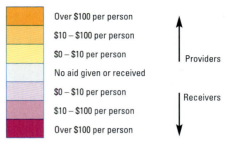

Aid provided or received, divided by the total population, in US $ (1995)

- Over $100 per person
- $10 – $100 per person
- $0 – $10 per person — Providers
- No aid given or received
- $0 – $10 per person
- $10 – $100 per person — Receivers
- Over $100 per person

Top 5 providers per capita (1994)		Top 5 receivers per capita (1994)	
France	$279	São Tomé & P.	$378
Denmark	$260	Cape Verde	$314
Norway	$247	Djibouti	$235
Sweden	$201	Surinam	$198
Germany	$166	Mauritania	$153

Debt and Aid

International debtors and the aid they receive (1996)

Although aid grants make a vital contribution to many of the world's poorer countries, they are usually dwarfed by the burden of debt that the developing economies are expected to repay. In 1992, they had to pay US $160,000 million in debt service charges alone – more than two and a half times the amount of Official Development Assistance (ODA) the developing countries were receiving, and US $60,000 million more than total private flows of aid in the same year. In 1990, the debts of Mozambique, one of the world's poorest countries, were estimated to be 75 times its entire earnings from exports.

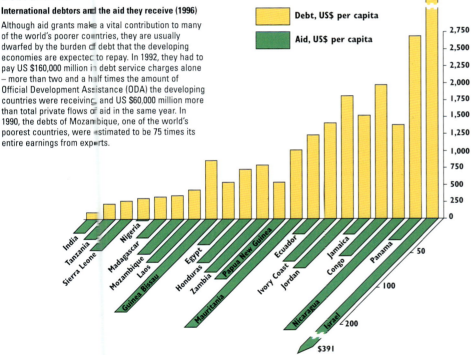

- Debt, US$ per capita
- Aid, US$ per capita

$5,014

$391

Distribution of Spending

Percentage share of household spending, selected countries

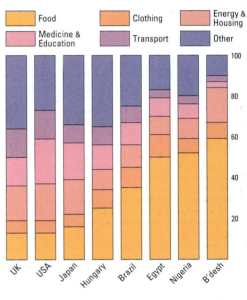

- Food
- Clothing
- Energy & Housing
- Medicine & Education
- Transport
- Other

UK, USA, Japan, Hungary, Brazil, Egypt, Nigeria, B'desh

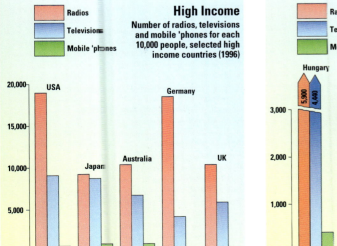

High Income

Number of radios, televisions and mobile 'phones for each 10,000 people, selected high income countries (1996)

- Radios
- Televisions
- Mobile 'phones

USA, Japan, Australia, Germany, UK

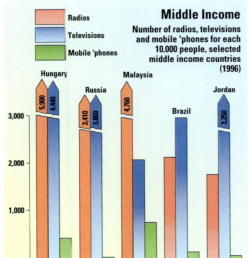

Middle Income

Number of radios, televisions and mobile 'phones for each 10,000 people, selected middle income countries (1996)

- Radios
- Televisions
- Mobile 'phones

Hungary 5,900 / 4,440
Russia 3,410 / 3,860
Malaysia 4,760
Brazil
Jordan 3,250

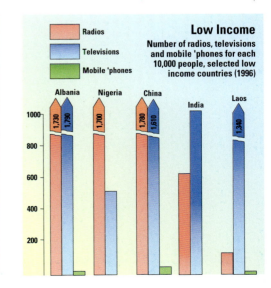

Low Income

Number of radios, televisions and mobile 'phones for each 10,000 people, selected low income countries (1996)

- Radios
- Televisions
- Mobile 'phones

Albania 1,730 / 1,750
Nigeria 1,700
China 1,780 / 1,610
India
Laos 1,340

Daily Food Consumption

Average daily food intake in calories per person (1995)

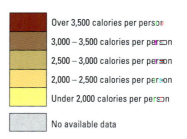

▨	Over 3,500 calories per person
▨	3,000 – 3,500 calories per person
▨	2,500 – 3,000 calories per person
▨	2,000 – 2,500 calories per person
▨	Under 2,000 calories per person
▨	No available data

Top 5 countries		Bottom 5 countries	
Cyprus	3,708 cal.	Congo (Dem. Rep.)	1,879 cal.
Denmark	3,704 cal.	Djibouti	1,831 cal.
Portugal	3,639 cal.	Togo	1,754 cal.
Ireland	3,638 cal.	Burundi	1,749 cal.
USA	3,603 cal.	Mozambique	1,678 cal.

[UK 3,149 calories]

Hospital Capacity

Hospital beds available for each 1,000 people (1996)

Highest capacity		Lowest capacity	
Switzerland	20.8	Benin	0.2
Japan	16.2	Nepal	0.2
Tajikistan	16.0	Afghanistan	0.3
Norway	13.5	Bangladesh	0.3
Belarus	12.4	Ethiopia	0.3
Kazakstan	12.2	Mali	0.4
Moldova	12.2	Burkina Faso	0.5
Ukraine	12.2	Niger	0.5
Latvia	11.9	Guinea	0.6
Russia	11.8	India	0.6

[UK 4.9] [USA 4.2]

Although the ratio of people to hospital beds gives a good approximation of a country's health provision, it is not an absolute indicator. Raw numbers may mask inefficiency and other weaknesses: the high availability of beds in Kazakstan, for example, has not prevented infant mortality rates over three times as high as in the United Kingdom and the United States.

Life Expectancy

Years of life expectancy at birth, selected countries (1997)

The chart shows combined data for both sexes. On average, women live longer than men worldwide, even in developing countries with high maternal mortality rates. Overall, life expectancy is steadily rising, though the difference between rich and poor nations remains dramatic.

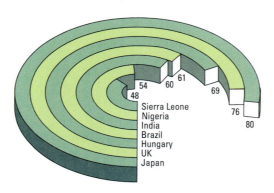

54 60 61
48 69
76
80

Sierra Leone
Nigeria
India
Brazil
Hungary
UK
Japan

Causes of Death

Causes of death for selected countries by % (1992–94)

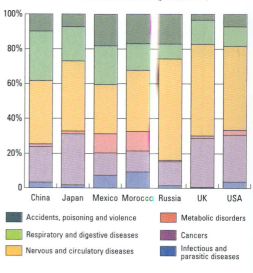

China Japan Mexico Morocco Russia UK USA

■ Accidents, poisoning and violence
■ Respiratory and digestive diseases
■ Nervous and circulatory diseases
■ Metabolic disorders
■ Cancers
■ Infectious and parasitic diseases

Child Mortality

Number of babies who will die under the age of one, per 1,000 births (average 1990–95)

▨	Over 150 deaths per 1,000 births
▨	100 – 150 deaths per 1,000 births
▨	50 – 100 deaths per 1,000 births
▨	20 – 50 deaths per 1,000 births
▨	10 – 20 deaths per 1,000 births
▨	Under 10 deaths per 1,000 births

Highest child mortality		Lowest child mortality	
Afghanistan	162	Hong Kong	6
Mali	159	Denmark	6
Sierra Leone	143	Japan	6
Guinea-Bissau	140	Iceland	5
Malawi	138	Finland	5

[UK 8 deaths]

Illiteracy

Percentage of the total population unable to read or write (latest available year)

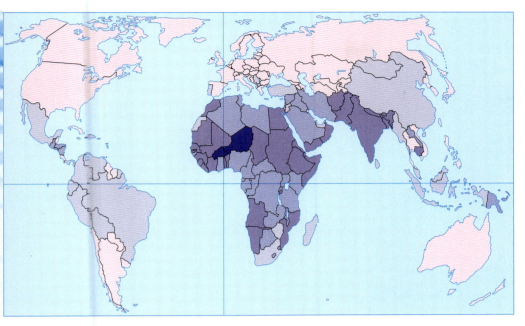

- Over 75% of population illiterate
- 50 – 75% of population illiterate
- 25 – 50% of population illiterate
- 10 – 25% of population illiterate
- Under 10% of population illiterate

Educational expenditure per person (latest available year)

Top 5 countries		Bottom 5 countries	
Sweden	$997	Chad	$2
Qatar	$989	Bangladesh	$3
Canada	$983	Ethiopia	$3
Norway	$971	Nepal	$4
Switzerland	$796	Somalia	$4

Fertility and Education

Fertility rates compared with female education, selected countries (1992–95)

Percentage of females aged 12–17 in secondary education

Fertility rate: average number of children borne per woman

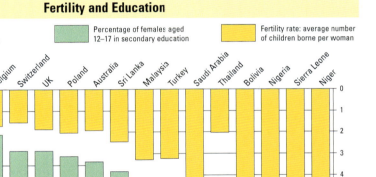

Living Standards

At first sight, most international contrasts in living standards are swamped by differences in wealth. The rich not only have more money, they have more of everything, including years of life. Those with only a little money are obliged to spend most of it on food and clothing, the basic maintenance costs of their existence; air travel and tourism are unlikely to feature on their expenditure lists. However, poverty and wealth are both relative: slum dwellers living on social security payments in an affluent industrial country have far more resources at their disposal than an average African peasant, but feel their own poverty nonetheless. A middle-class Indian lawyer cannot command a fraction of the earnings of a counterpart living in New York, London or Rome; nevertheless, he rightly sees himself as prosperous.

The rich not only live longer, on average, than the poor, they also die from different causes. Infectious and parasitic diseases, all but eliminated in the developed world, remain a scourge in the developing nations. On the other hand, more than two-thirds of the populations of OECD nations eventually succumb to cancer or circulatory disease.

Women in the Workforce

Women in paid employment as a percentage of the total workforce (latest available year)

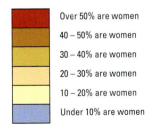

- Over 50% are women
- 40 – 50% are women
- 30 – 40% are women
- 20 – 30% are women
- 10 – 20% are women
- Under 10% are women

Most women in the workforce		Fewest women in the workforce	
Cambodia	56%	Saudi Arabia	4%
Kazakstan	54%	Oman	6%
Burundi	53%	Afghanistan	8%
Mozambique	53%	Algeria	9%
Turkmenistan	52%	Libya	9%

[USA 45] [UK 44]

CARTOGRAPHY BY PHILIP'S. COPYRIGHT GEORGE PHILIP LTD

Production

[Each square represents 1% of world energy production]

North America

Europe

CIS

Middle East

Africa

Asia

Japan

South America

Australasia

Consumption

[Each square represents 1% of world energy consumption]

North America

Europe

CIS

Middle East

Africa

Asia

Japan

South America

Australasia

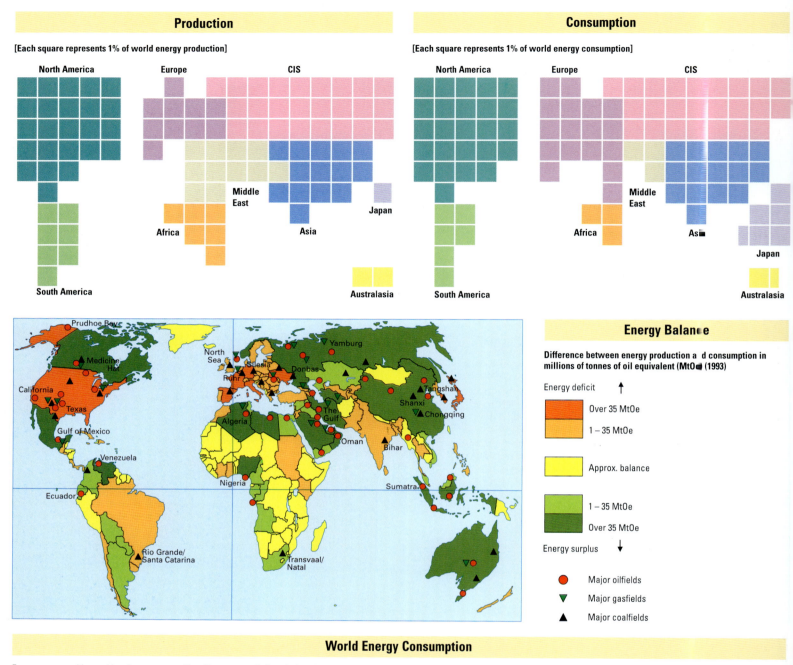

Energy Balance

Difference between energy production and consumption in millions of tonnes of oil equivalent (MtOe) (1993)

Energy deficit ↑

Over 35 MtOe

1 – 35 MtOe

Approx. balance

1 – 35 MtOe

Over 35 MtOe

Energy surplus ↓

● Major oilfields

▽ Major gasfields

▲ Major coalfields

Map labels: Prudhoe Bay, Medicine Hat, California, Texas, Gulf of Mexico, Venezuela, Ecuador, Rio Grande/Santa Catarina, North Sea, Silesia, Ruhr, Donbas, Algeria, Nigeria, Transvaal/Natal, Yamburg, The Gulf, Oman, Shanxi, Tangshan, Chongqing, Bihar, Sumatra

World Energy Consumption

Energy consumed by world regions, measured in million tonnes of oil equivalent in 1997. Total world consumption was 8,509 MtOe. Only energy from oil, gas, coal, nuclear and hydroelectric sources are

included. Excluded are fuels such as wood, peat, animal waste, wind, solar and geothermal which, though important in some countries, are unreliably documented in terms of consumption statistics.

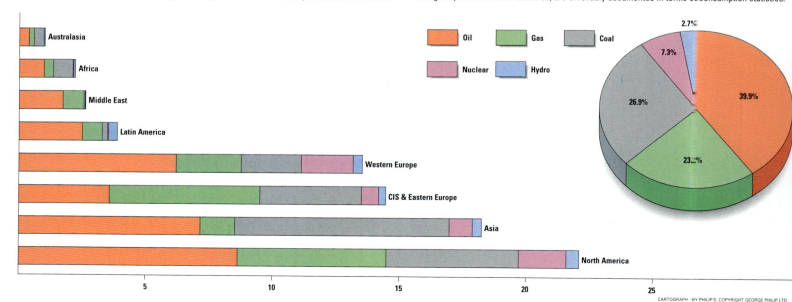

■ Oil   ■ Gas   ■ Coal

■ Nuclear   ■ Hydro

Australasia

Africa

Middle East

Latin America

Western Europe

CIS & Eastern Europe

Asia

North America

5   10   15   20   25

Pie chart: 39.9%, 23.2%, 26.9%, 7.3%, 2.7%

Energy

Energy is used to keep us warm or cool, fuel our industries and our transport systems, and even feed us; high-intensity agriculture, with its use of fertilizers, pesticides and machinery, is heavily energy-dependent. Although we live in a high-energy society, there are vast discrepancies between rich and poor; for example, a North American consumes 13 times as much energy as a Chinese person. But even developing nations have more power at their disposal than was imaginable a century ago.

The distribution of energy supplies, most importantly fossil fuels (coal, oil and natural gas), is very uneven. In addition, the diagrams and map opposite show that the largest producers of energy are not necessarily the largest consumers. The movement of energy supplies around the world is therefore an important component of international trade. In 1995, total world movements in oil amounted to 1,815 million tonnes.

As the finite reserves of fossil fuels are depleted, renewable energy sources, such as solar, hydro-thermal, wind, tidal and biomass, will become increasingly important around the world.

Nuclear Power

Percentage of electricity generated by nuclear power stations, leading nations (1995)

1. Lithuania	85%	11. Spain	33%
2. France	77%	12. Finland	30%
3. Belgium	56%	13. Germany	29%
4. Slovak Rep.	49%	14. Japan	29%
5. Sweden	48%	15. UK	27%
6. Bulgaria	41%	16. Ukraine	27%
7. Hungary	41%	17. Czech Rep.	22%
8. Switzerland	39%	18. Canada	19%
9. Slovenia	38%	19. USA	18%
10. South Korea	33%	20. Russia	12%

Although the 1980s were a bad time for the nuclear power industry (major projects ran over budget, and fears of long-term environmental damage were heavily reinforced by the 1986 disaster at Chernobyl), the industry picked up in the early 1990s. However, whilst the number of reactors is still increasing, orders for new plants have shrunk. This is partly due to the increasingly difficult task of disposing of nuclear waste.

Hydroelectricity

Percentage of electricity generated by hydroelectric power stations, leading nations (1995)

1. Paraguay	99.9%	11. Rwanda	97.6%
2. Congo (Zaïre)	99.7%	12. Malawi	97.6%
3. Bhutan	99.6%	13. Cameroon	96.9%
4. Zambia	99.5%	14. Nepal	96.7%
5. Norway	99.4%	15. Laos	95.3%
6. Ghana	99.3%	16. Albania	95.2%
7. Congo	99.3%	17. Iceland	94.0%
8. Uganda	99.1%	17. Brazil	92.2%
9. Burundi	98.3%	19. Honduras	87.6%
10. Uruguay	98.0%	20. Tanzania	87.1%

Countries heavily reliant on hydroelectricity are usually small and non-industrial: a high proportion of hydroelectric power more often reflects a modest energy budget than vast hydroelectric resources. The USA, for instance, produces only 9% of power requirements from hydroelectricity; yet that 9% amounts to more than three times the hydropower generated by all of Africa.

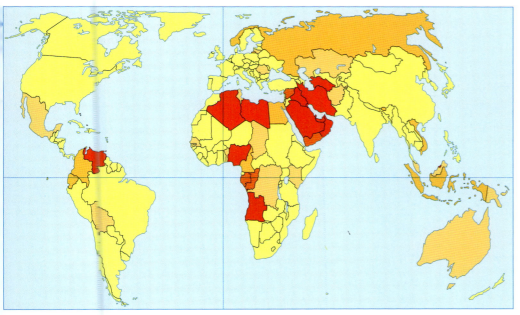

Fuel Exports

Fuels as a percentage of total value of exports (1990–94)

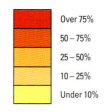

- Over 75%
- 50 – 75%
- 25 – 50%
- 10 – 25%
- Under 10%

Conversion Rates

1 barrel = 0.136 tonnes or 159 litres or 35 Imperial gallons or 42 US gallons

1 tonne = 7.33 barrels or 1,185 litres or 256 Imperial gallons or 261 US gallons

1 tonne oil = 1.5 tonnes hard coal or 3.0 tonnes lignite or 12,000 kWh

1 Imperial gallon = 1.201 US gallons or 4.546 litres or 277.4 cubic inches

Measurements

For historical reasons, oil is traded in 'barrels'. The weight and volume equivalents (shown right) are all based on average-density 'Arabian light' crude oil.

The energy equivalents given for a tonne of oil are also somewhat imprecise: oil and coal of different qualities will have varying energy contents, a fact usually reflected in their price on world markets.

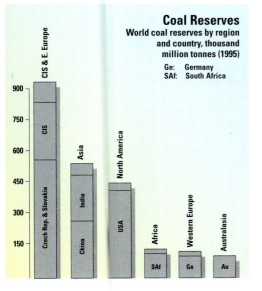

Coal Reserves
World coal reserves by region and country, thousand million tonnes (1995)

Ge: Germany
SAf: South Africa

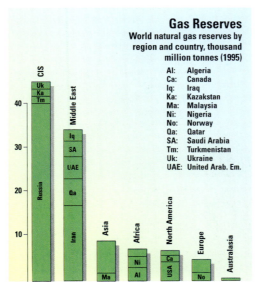

Gas Reserves
World natural gas reserves by region and country, thousand million tonnes (1995)

Al: Algeria
Ca: Canada
Iq: Iraq
Ka: Kazakstan
Ma: Malaysia
Ni: Nigeria
No: Norway
Qa: Qatar
SA: Saudi Arabia
Tm: Turkmenistan
Uk: Ukraine
UAE: United Arab. Em.

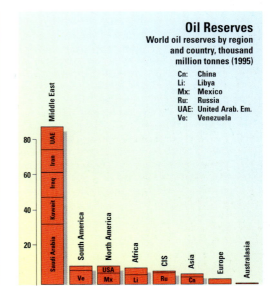

Oil Reserves
World oil reserves by region and country, thousand million tonnes (1995)

Cn: China
Li: Libya
Mx: Mexico
Ru: Russia
UAE: United Arab. Em.
Ve: Venezuela

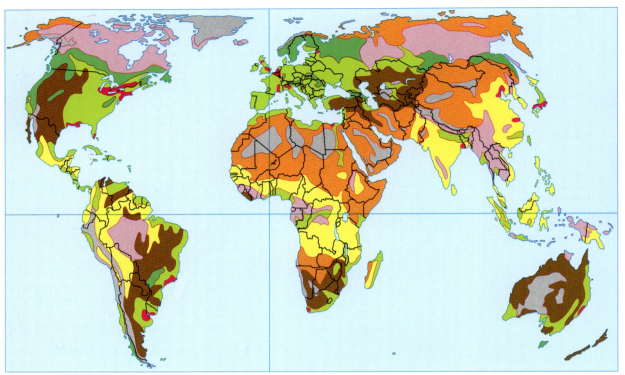

Agriculture

Predominant type of farming or land use.

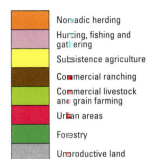

- Nomadic herding
- Hunting, fishing and gathering
- Subsistence agriculture
- Commercial ranching
- Commercial livestock and grain farming
- Urban areas
- Forestry
- Unproductive land

The development of agriculture has transformed human existence more than any other. The whole business of farming is constantly developing: due mainly to the new varieties of rice and wheat, world grain production has increased by over 70% since 1965. New machinery and modern agricultural techniques enable relatively few farmers to produce enough food for the world's 6 billion or so people.

Staple Crops

Wheat

China 18.9%
India 12.2%
USA 11.0%
France 5.7%
Russia 5.6%
Canada 4.6%

World total (1996): 584,874,000 tonnes

Maize

USA 36.4%
China 21.8%
Brazil 7.0%

World total (1996): 576,821,000 tonnes

Oats

Russia 29.7%
Canada 9.9%
USA 8.2%
Australia 6.7%
Germany 5.6%

World total (1996): 28,794,000 tonnes

Millet

India 33.2%
Nigeria 18.3%
China 16.1%
Niger 6.4%

World total (1996): 29,563,000 tonnes

Rice

China 34.0%
India 21.7%
Indonesia 9.0%
Bangladesh 4.8%
Vietnam 4.4%
Thailand 3.8%

World total (1996): 562,259,000 tonnes

Potatoes

China 16.0%
Russia 14.0%
Poland 8.7%
India 6.3%
Ukraine 5.2%

World total (1996): 294,834,000 tonnes

Soya

USA 47.1%
Brazil 20.4%
China 10.7%
Argentina 9.6%

World total (1996): 130,302,000 tonnes

Cassava

Nigeria 19.2%
Brazil 15.6%
Thailand 11.1%
Congo (Zaire) 10.7%
Indonesia 9.4%
Ghana 4.2%

World total (1996): 162,942,000 tonnes

Sugars

Sugar cane

Brazil 26.0%
India 22.2%
China 6.0%
Thailand 5.0%
Pakistan 4.0%
Mexico 3.6%

World total (1996): 1,192,555,000 tonnes

Sugar beet

France 11.5%
Ukraine 11.1%
Germany 9.8%
USA 9.6%
Russia 7.2%
Italy 5.0%
Poland 5.0%
Turkey 4.2%

World total (1996): 255,500,000 tonnes

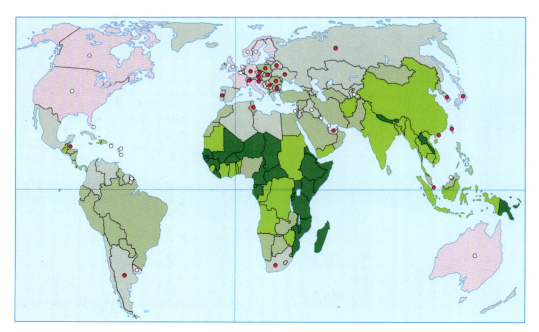

Balance of Employment

Percentage of total workforce employed in agriculture, including forestry and fishing (1990–92)

- Over 75% in agriculture
- 50 – 75% in agriculture
- 25 – 50% in agriculture
- 10 – 25% in agriculture
- Under 10% in agriculture

Employment in industry and services

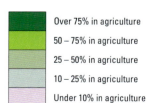

- Over a third of total workforce employed in manufacturing

- Over two-thirds of total workforce employed in service industries (work in offices, shops, tourism, transport, construction and government)

Mineral Production

*Figures for aluminium are for refined metal; all other figures refer to ore production.

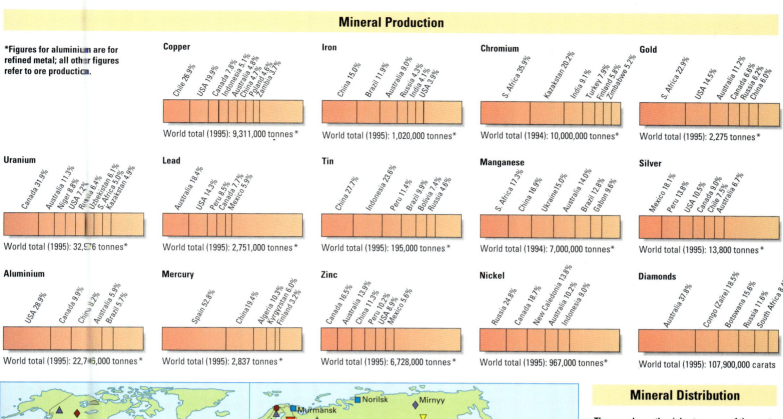

Copper
Chile 26.9% · USA 19.9% · Canada 7.8% · Indonesia 5.1% · Australia 4.8% · China 4.7% · Poland 4.6% · Zambia 3.7%
World total (1995): 9,311,000 tonnes *

Iron
China 15.0% · Brazil 11.9% · Australia 9.0% · Russia 4.3% · India 4.1% · USA 3.9%
World total (1995): 1,020,000 tonnes *

Chromium
S. Africa 35.9% · Kazakstan 20.2% · India 9.1% · Turkey 7.9% · Finland 5.8% · Zimbabwe 5.2%
World total (1994): 10,000,000 tonnes *

Gold
S. Africa 22.9% · USA 14.5% · Australia 11.2% · Canada 6.6% · Russia 6.2% · China 6.0%
World total (1995): 2,275 tonnes *

Uranium
Canada 31.9% · Australia 11.3% · Niger 8.8% · USA 7.2% · Russia 6.4% · Uzbekistan 6.1% · S. Africa 5.0% · Kazakstan 4.9%
World total (1995): 32,576 tonnes *

Lead
Australia 18.4% · USA 14.3% · Peru 8.5% · Canada 7.7% · Mexico 5.9%
World total (1995): 2,751,000 tonnes *

Tin
China 27.7% · Indonesia 23.6% · Peru 11.4% · Brazil 9.9% · Bolivia 7.4% · Russia 4.6%
World total (1995): 195,000 tonnes *

Manganese
S. Africa 17.3% · China 16.9% · Ukraine 15.0% · Australia 14.0% · Brazil 12.8% · Gabon 9.6%
World total (1994): 7,000,000 tonnes *

Silver
Mexico 18.1% · Peru 13.8% · USA 10.5% · Canada 9.0% · Chile 7.5% · Australia 6.7%
World total (1995): 13,800 tonnes *

Aluminium
USA 28.9% · Canada 9.9% · China 8.2% · Australia 5.9% · Brazil 5.7%
World total (1995): 22,765,000 tonnes *

Mercury
Spain 52.8% · China 19.4% · Algeria 10.3% · Kyrgyzstan 6.0% · Finland 3.2%
World total (1995): 2,837 tonnes *

Zinc
Canada 16.5% · Australia 13.9% · China 11.3% · Peru 10.2% · USA 8.9% · Mexico 5.6%
World total (1995): 6,728,000 tonnes *

Nickel
Russia 24.8% · Canada 18.7% · New Caledonia 13.8% · Australia 10.2% · Indonesia 9.0%
World total (1995): 967,000 tonnes *

Diamonds
Australia 37.8% · Congo (Zaire) 18.5% · Botswana 15.6% · Russia 11.6% · South Africa 8.4%
World total (1995): 107,900,000 carats

Map labels: Norilsk, Mirnyy, Murmansk, Urals, Sudbury, Donbas, Ukraine, Great Lakes, Kazakstan, Shanxi, Nevada, Bingham, Missouri, Hebei, Arizona, Charcas, Yunnan, Jamaica, Bihar, Sipalay, Guinea, Goa, Malay Peninsula, Carajas, Celebes, Pôrto Velho, Bangka, Weipa, Cerro de Pasco, Mbuji Mayi, Katanga, Copperbelt, Hamersley Range, Mt. Isa, Minas Gerais, Great Dyke, Kalgoorlie, Witwatersrand, Broken Hill, Kimberley

Mineral Distribution

The map shows the richest sources of the most important minerals. Major mineral locations are named.

Light metals
● Bauxite

Base metals
■ Copper
▲ Lead
▽ Mercury
▽ Tin
◆ Zinc

Iron and ferro-alloys
● Iron
◗ Chrome
▲ Manganese
■ Nickel

Precious metals
▽ Gold
◠ Silver

Precious stones
◆ Diamonds

The map does not show undersea deposits, most of which are considered inaccessible.

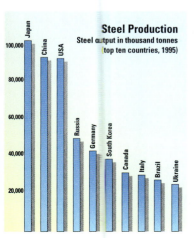

Steel Production
Steel output in thousand tonnes (top ten countries, 1995)

Japan, China, USA, Russia, Germany, South Korea, Canada, Italy, Brazil, Ukraine

Ship Building
Merchant vessels launched by the top ten countries, in thousand gross registered tonnes (1996)

Japan, South Korea, Germany, Taiwan, China, Italy, Spain, Poland, France, Finland

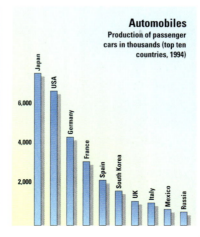

Automobiles
Production of passenger cars in thousands (top ten countries, 1994)

Japan, USA, Germany, France, Spain, South Korea, UK, Italy, Mexico, Russia

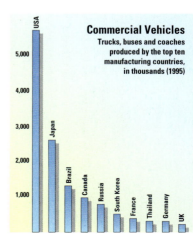

Commercial Vehicles
Trucks, buses and coaches produced by the top ten manufacturing countries, in thousands (1995)

USA, Japan, Brazil, Canada, Russia, South Korea, France, Thailand, Germany, UK

Share of World Trade

Percentage share of total world exports by value (1996)

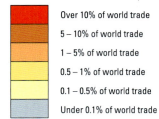

- Over 10% of world trade
- 5 – 10% of world trade
- 1 – 5% of world trade
- 0.5 – 1% of world trade
- 0.1 – 0.5% of world trade
- Under 0.1% of world trade

International trade is dominated by a handful of powerful maritime nations. The members of 'G8', the inner circle of OECD (see page 19), and the top seven countries listed in the diagram below, account for more than half the total. The majority of nations – including all but four in Africa – contribute less than one quarter of 1% to the worldwide total of exports; the EU countries account for 40%, the Pacific Rim nations over 35%.

The Main Trading Nations

The imports and exports of the top ten trading nations as a percentage of world trade (1994). Each country's trade in manufactured goods is shown in dark blue.

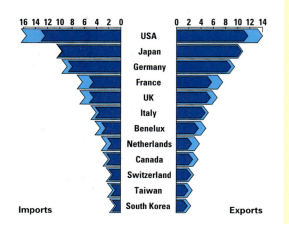

Imports		Exports
	USA	
	Japan	
	Germany	
	France	
	UK	
	Italy	
	Benelux	
	Netherlands	
	Canada	
	Switzerland	
	Taiwan	
	South Korea	

Patterns of Trade

Thriving international trade is the outward sign of a healthy world economy, the obvious indicator that some countries have goods to sell and others the means to buy them. Global exports expanded to an estimated US $3.92 trillion in 1994, an increase due partly to economic recovery in industrial nations but also to export-led growth strategies in many developing nations and lowered regional trade barriers. International trade remains dominated, however, by the rich, industrialized countries of the Organization for Economic Development: between them, OECD members account for almost 75% of world imports and exports in most years. However, continued rapid economic growth in some developing countries is altering global trade patterns. The 'tiger economies' of South-east Asia are particularly vibrant, averaging more than 8% growth between 1992 and 1994. The size of the largest trading economies means that imports and exports usually represent only a small percentage of their total wealth. In export-concious Japan, for example, trade in goods and services amounts to less than 18% of GDP. In poorer countries, trade – often in a single commodity – may amount to 50% of GDP.

Traded Products

Top ten manufactures traded, by value in billions of US $ (latest available year)

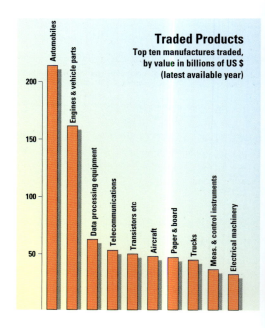

Automobiles; Engines & vehicle parts; Data processing equipment; Telecommunications; Transistors etc; Aircraft; Paper & board; Trucks; Meas. & control instruments; Electrical machinery

Balance of Trade

Value of exports in proportion to the value of imports (1995)

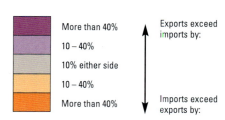

Exports exceed imports by:
- More than 40%
- 10 – 40%
- 10% either side
- 10 – 40%
- More than 40%

Imports exceed exports by:

The total world trade balance should amount to zero, since exports must equal imports on a global scale. In practice, at least $100 billion in exports go unrecorded, leaving the world with an apparent deficit and many countries in a better position than public accounting reveals. However, a favourable trade balance is not necessarily a sign of prosperity: many poorer countries must maintain a high surplus in order to service debts, and do so by restricting imports below the levels needed to sustain successful economies.

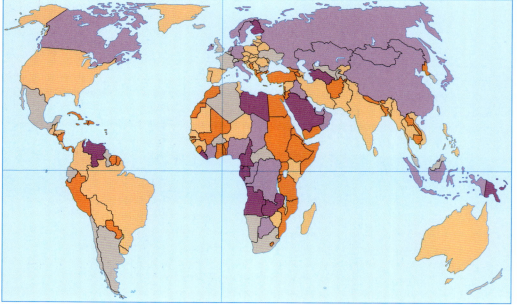

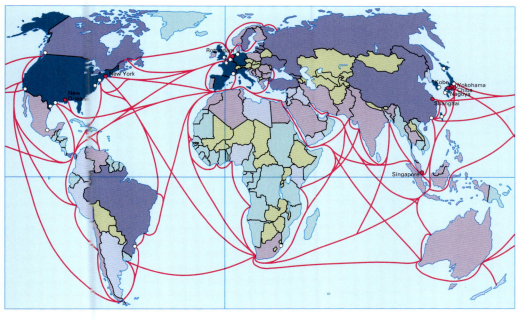

Seaborne Freight

Freight unloaded in millions of tonnes (latest available year)

- Over 100
- 50 – 100
- 10 – 50
- 5 – 10
- Under 5
- Landlocked countries

Major seaports

- Over 100 million tonnes per year
- 50–100 million tonnes per year
- Major shipping routes

Cargoes

Type of seaborne freight

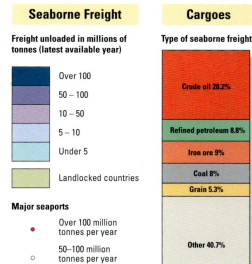

Crude oil 28.2%
Refined petroleum 8.8%
Iron ore 9%
Coal 8%
Grain 5.3%
Other 40.7%

Merchant Fleets

Merchant fleets in thousand gross tonnage (1996). A large number of vessels are registered in Liberia and Panama but they are not part of the national fleet.

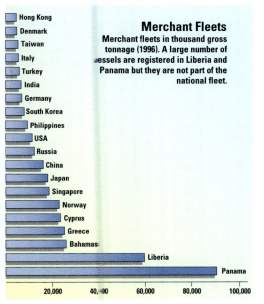

Hong Kong
Denmark
Taiwan
Italy
Turkey
India
Germany
South Korea
Philippines
USA
Russia
China
Japan
Singapore
Norway
Cyprus
Greece
Bahamas
Liberia
Panama

20,000   40,000   60,000   80,000   100,000

The Great Ports

Total Cargo Traffic (1995) '000 tonnes

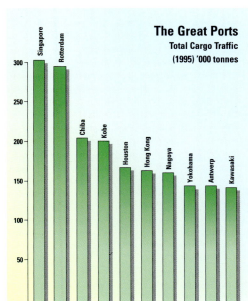

Singapore
Rotterdam
Chiba
Kobe
Houston
Hong Kong
Nagoya
Yokohama
Antwerp
Kawasaki

World Shipping

World merchant fleet by type of vessel and deadweight tonnage (latest available year)

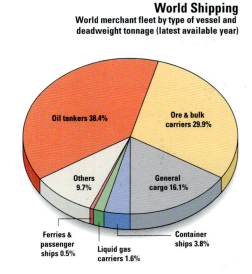

Oil tankers 38.4%
Ore & bulk carriers 29.9%
General cargo 16.1%
Others 9.7%
Ferries & passenger ships 0.5%
Liquid gas carriers 1.6%
Container ships 3.8%

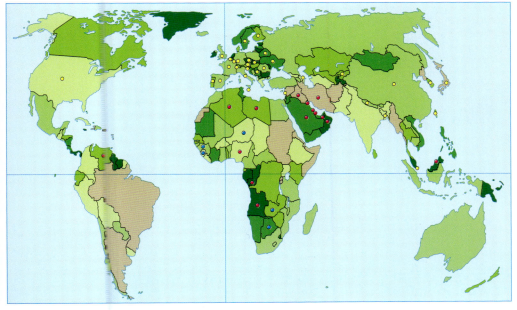

Dependence on Trade

Value of exports as a percentage of Gross Domestic Product (1997)

- Over 50% GDP from exports
- 40 – 50% GDP from exports
- 30 – 40% GDP from exports
- 20 – 30% GDP from exports
- 10 – 20% GDP from exports
- Under 10% GDP from exports

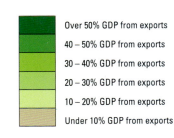

- Most dependent on industrial exports (over 75% of total exports)
- Most dependent on fuel exports (over 75% of total exports)
- Most dependent on mineral and metal exports (over 75% of total exports)

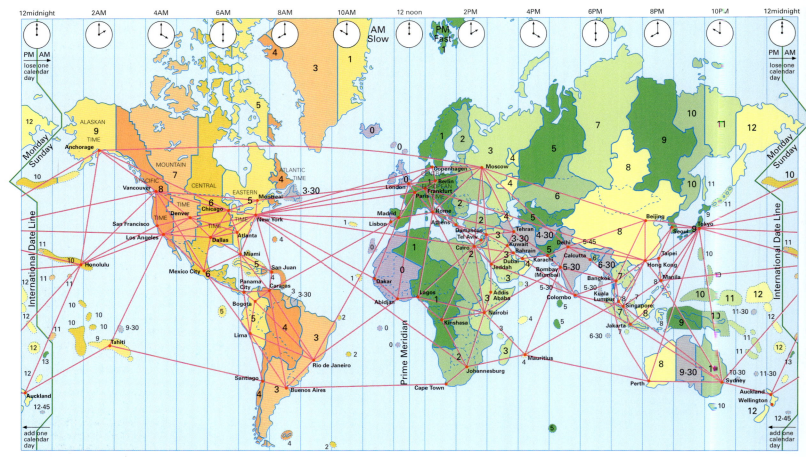

Time Zones

Zones using GMT
Zones slow of GMT
Zones fast of GMT
Half-hour zones

International boundaries
Time zone boundaries
International Date Line
Selected air routes

10   Hours slow or fast of GMT

Certain time zones are affected by the incidence of 'summer time' in countries where it is adopted.

Actual Solar Time, when it is noon at Greenwich, is shown along the top of the map.

The world is divided into 24 time zones, each centred on meridians at 15° intervals, which is the longitudinal distance the sun travels every hour. The meridian running through Greenwich, London, passes through the middle of the first zone.

Rail and Road: The Leading Nations

Total rail network ('000 km) (1995)	Passenger km per head per year	Total road network ('000 km)	Vehicle km per head per year	Number of vehicles per km of roads
1. USA 235.7	Japan 2,017	USA 6,277.9	USA 12,505	Hong Kong 284
2. Russia 87.4	Belarus 1,880	India 2,962.5	Luxembourg 7,989	Taiwan 211
3. India 62.7	Russia 1,826	Brazil 1,824.4	Kuwait 7,251	Singapore 152
4. China 54.6	Switzerland 1,769	Japan 1,130.9	France 7,142	Kuwait 140
5. Germany 41.7	Ukraine 1,456	China 1,041.1	Sweden 6,991	Brunei 96
6. Australia 35.8	Austria 1,168	Russia 884.0	Germany 6,806	Italy 91
7. Argentina 34.2	France 1,011	Canada 849.4	Denmark 6,764	Israel 87
8. France 31.9	Netherlands 994	France 811.6	Austria 6,518	Thailand 73
9. Mexico 26.5	Latvia 918	Australia 810.3	Netherlands 5,984	Ukraine 73
10. South Africa 26.3	Denmark 884	Germany 636.3	UK 5,738	UK 67
11. Poland 24.9	Slovak Rep. 862	Romania 461.9	Canada 5,493	Netherlands 66
12. Ukraine 22.6	Romania 851	Turkey 388.1	Italy 4,852	Germany 62

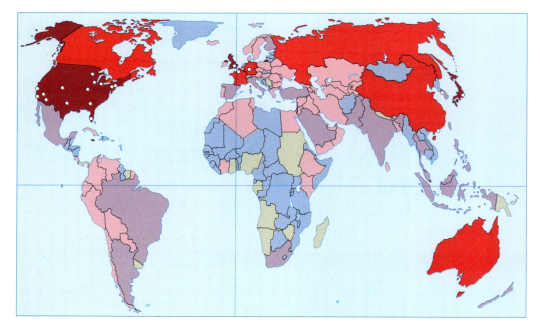

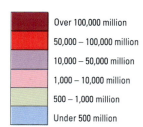

Air Travel

Passenger kilometres (the number of passengers – international and domestic – multiplied by the distance flown by each passenger from the airport of origin) (1996)

- Over 100,000 million
- 50,000 – 100,000 million
- 10,000 – 50,000 million
- 1,000 – 10,000 million
- 500 – 1,000 million
- Under 500 million

○   Major airports (handling over 25 million passengers in 1995)

World's busiest airports (total passengers)

1. Chicago (O'Hare)
2. Atlanta (Hatsfield)
3. Dallas (Dallas/Ft Worth)
4. Los Angeles (Intern'l)
5. London (Heathrow)

World's busiest airports (international passengers)

1. London (Heathrow)
2. London (Gatwick)
3. Frankfurt (International)
4. New York (Kennedy)
5. Paris (De Gaulle)

Destinations

- 🟥 Cultural and historical centres
- 🟨 Coastal resorts
- ⬜ Ski resorts
- 🟧 Centres of entertainment
- 🟦 Places of pilgrimage
- 🟩 Places of great natural beauty
- ～ Popular holiday cruise routes

Visitors to the USA

Overseas travellers to the USA, thousands (1997 estimates)

1. Canada 13,900
2. Mexico 12,370
3. Japan 4,640
4. UK 3,350
5. Germany 1,990
6. France 1,030
7. Taiwan 885
8. Venezuela 860
9. South Korea 800
10. Brazil 785

In 1996, the USA earned the most from tourism, with receipts of more than US $75 billion.

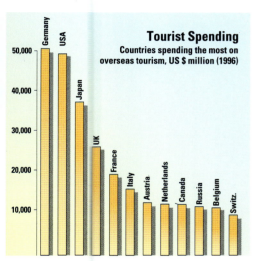

Tourist Spending

Countries spending the most on overseas tourism, US $ million (1996)

(Bars, left to right: Germany, USA, Japan, UK, France, Italy, Austria, Netherlands, Canada, Russia, Belgium, Switz.)

Importance of Tourism

	Arrivals from abroad (1996)	% of world total (1996)
1. France	66,800,000	10.2%
2. USA	49,038,000	7.5%
3. Spain	43,403,000	6.6%
4. Italy	34,087,000	5.2%
5. UK	25,960,000	3.9%
6. China	23,770,000	3.6%
7. Poland	19,514,000	3.0%
8. Mexico	18,667,000	2.9%
9. Canada	17,610,000	2.7%
10. Czech Republic	17,400,000	2.7%
11. Hungary	17,248,000	2.6%
12. Austra	16,642,000	2.5%

In 1996, there was a 4.6% rise, to 593 million, in the total number of people travelling abroad. Small economies in attractive areas are often completely dominated by tourism: in some West Indian islands, for example, tourist spending provides over 90% of total income.

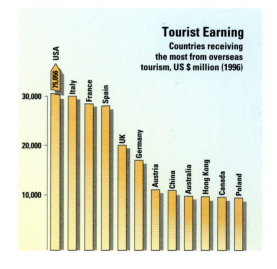

Tourist Earning

Countries receiving the most from overseas tourism, US $ million (1996)

(Bars, left to right: USA 75,056, Italy, France, Spain, UK, Germany, Austria, China, Australia, Hong Kong, Canada, Poland)

Tourism

Tourism receipts as a percentage of Gross National Product (1994)

- Over 10% of GNP from tourism
- 5 – 10% of GNP from tourism
- 2.5 – 5% of GNP from tourism
- 1 – 2.5% of GNP from tourism
- 0.5 – 1% of GNP from tourism
- Under 0.5% of GNP from tourism

Countries spending the most on promoting tourism, millions of US $ (1996)

Australia	88
Spain	79
UK	79
France	73
Singapore	54

Fastest growing tourist destinations, % change in receipts (1994–5)

South Korea	49%
Czech Republic	27%
India	21%
Russia	19%
Philippines	18%

This list shows the principal cities with more than 500,000 inhabitants (only cities with more than 1 million inhabitants are included for Brazil, China and India). The figures are taken from the most recent census or estimate available, and as far as possible are the population of the metropolitan area e.g. greater New York, Mexico or Paris. All the figures are in thousands. Local name forms have been used for the smaller cities (e.g. Kraków).

	Population *thousands*
Afghanistan	
Kabul	1,565
Algeria	
Algiers	2,168
Oran	916
Angola	
Luanda	2,418
Argentina	
Buenos Aires	11,256
Córdoba	1,208
Rosario	1,118
Mendoza	773
La Plata	642
San Miguel de Tucumán	622
Mar del Plata	512
Armenia	
Yerevan	1,248
Australia	
Sydney	3,770
Melbourne	3,217
Brisbane	1,489
Perth	1,262
Adelaide	1,080
Austria	
Vienna	1,595
Azerbaijan	
Baku	1,720
Bangladesh	
Dhaka	6,105
Chittagong	2,041
Khulna	877
Rajshahi	517
Belarus	
Minsk	1,700
Homyel	512
Belgium	
Brussels	948
Benin	
Cotonou	537
Bolivia	
La Paz	1,126
Santa Cruz	767
Bosnia-Herzegovina	
Sarajevo	526
Brazil	
São Paulo	16,417
Rio de Janeiro	9,888
Salvador	2,211
Belo Horizonte	2,091
Fortaleza	1,965
Brasília	1,821
Curitiba	1,476
Recife	1,346
Pôrto Alegre	1,288
Manaus	1,157
Belém	1,144
Goiânia	1,004
Bulgaria	
Sofia	1,116
Burkina Faso	
Ouagadougou	690
Burma (Myanmar)	
Rangoon	2,513
Mandalay	533
Cambodia	
Phnom Penh	920
Cameroon	
Douala	1,200
Yaoundé	800
Canada	
Toronto	4,344
Montréal	3,337
Vancouver	1,831
Ottawa–Hull	1,022
Edmonton	885
Calgary	831
Québec	693
Winnipeg	677
Hamilton	643
Central African Rep.	
Bangui	553
Chad	
Ndjaména	530
Chile	
Santiago	5,067
China	
Shanghai	15,082
Beijing	12,362
Tianjin	10,687
Hong Kong (SAR)*	6,502
Chongqing	3,870
Shenyang	3,860
Wuhan	3,520
Guangzhou	3,114
Harbin	2,505
Nanjing	2,211
Xi'an	2,115
Chengdu	1,933
Dalian	1,855
Changchun	1,810
Jinan	1,660
Taiyuan	1,642
Qingdao	1,584
Fuzhou, Fujian	1,380
Zibo	1,346
Zhengzhou	1,324
Lanzhou	1,296
Anshan	1,252
Fushun	1,246
Kunming	1,242
Changsha	1,198
Hangzhou	1,185
Nanchang	1,169
Shijiazhuang	1,159
Guiyang	1,131
Ürümqi	1,130
Jilin	1,118
Tangshan	1,110
Qiqihar	1,104
Baotou	1,033
Hefei	1,000
Colombia	
Bogotá	6,004
Cali	1,985
Medellín	1,970
Barranquilla	1,157
Cartagena	812
Congo	
Brazzaville	937
Pointe-Noire	576
Congo (Zaïre)	
Kinshasa	1,655
Lubumbashi	851
Mbuji-Mayi	806
Costa Rica	
San José	1,220
Croatia	
Zagreb	931
Cuba	
Havana	2,241
Czech Republic	
Prague	1,209
Denmark	
Copenhagen	1,362
Dominican Republic	
Santo Domingo	2,135
Santiago	691
Ecuador	
Guayaquil	1,973
Quito	1,487
Egypt	
Cairo	9,900
Alexandria	3,431
El Gîza	2,144
Shubra el Kheima	834
El Salvador	
San Salvador	1,522
Ethiopia	
Addis Ababa	2,112
Finland	
Helsinki	532
France	
Paris	9,319
Lyon	1,262
Marseille	1,087
Lille	959
Bordeaux	696
Toulouse	650
Nice	516
Georgia	
Tbilisi	1,300
Germany	
Berlin	3,470
Hamburg	1,706
Munich	1,240
Cologne	964
Frankfurt	651
Essen	616
Dortmund	600
Stuttgart	587
Düsseldorf	571
Bremen	549
Duisburg	535
Hanover	524
Ghana	
Accra	949
Greece	
Athens	3,097
Guatemala	
Guatemala	1,167
Guinea	
Conakry	1,508
Haiti	
Port-au-Prince	1,255
Honduras	
Tegucigalpa	813
Hungary	
Budapest	1,885
India	
Bombay (Mumbai)	12,572
Calcutta (Kolkata)	10,916
Delhi	7,207
Madras (Chennai)	5,361
Hyderabad	4,280
Bangalore	4,087
Ahmadabad	3,298
Pune	2,485
Kanpur	2,111
Nagpur	1,661
Lucknow	1,642
Surat	1,517
Jaipur	1,514
Coimbatore	1,136
Vadodara	1,115
Indore	1,104
Patna	1,099
Madurai	1,094
Bhopal	1,064
Vishakhapatnam	1,052
Varanasi	1,026
Ludhiana	1,012
Indonesia	
Jakarta	11,500
Surabaya	2,701
Bandung	2,368
Medan	1,910
Semarang	1,366
Palembang	1,352
Tangerang	1,198
Ujung Pandang	1,092
Bandar Lampung	832
Malang	763
Padang	721
Pakanbaru	558
Samarinda	536
Banjarmasin	535
Surakarta	516
Iran	
Tehran	6,750
Mashhad	1,964
Esfahan	1,221
Tabriz	1,166
Shiraz	1,043
Ahvaz	828
Qom	780
Bakhtaran	666
Karaj	588
Iraq	
Baghdad	3,841
Diyala	961
As Sulaymaniyah	952
Arbil	770
Al Mawsil	664
Kadhimain	521
Ireland	
Dublin	952
Israel	
Tel Aviv-Yafo	1,502
Jerusalem	591
Italy	
Rome	2,775
Milan	1,369
Naples	1,067
Turin	962
Palermo	698
Genoa	678
Ivory Coast	
Abidjan	2,500
Jamaica	
Kingston	644
Japan	
Tokyo–Yokohama	26,836
Osaka	10,601
Nagoya	2,152
Sapporo	1,757
Kyoto	1,464
Kobe	1,424
Fukuoka	1,285
Kawasaki	1,203
Hiroshima	1,109
Kitakyushu	1,020
Sendai	971
Chiba	857
Sakai	803
Kumamoto	650
Okayama	616
Sagamihara	571
Hamamatsu	562
Kagoshima	546
Funabashi	541
Higashiosaka	517
Hachioji	503
Jordan	
Amman	1,300
Az-Zarqā	609
Kazakstan	
Almaty	1,150
Qaraghandy	573
Kenya	
Nairobi	2,000
Mombasa	600
Korea, North	
Pyŏngyang	2,639
Hamhung	775
Chŏngjin	754
Chinnampo	691
Sinŭiju	500
Korea, South	
Seoul	11,641
Pusan	3,814
Taegu	2,449
Inchon	2,308
Taejŏn	1,272
Kwangju	1,258
Ulsan	967
Sŏngnam	869
Puch'on	779
Suwŏn	756
Anyang	590
Chŏnju	563
Chŏngju	531
Ansan	510
P'ohang	509
Kyrgyzstan	
Bishkek	584
Latvia	
Riga	846
Lebanon	
Beirut	1,900
Tripoli	500
Libya	
Tripoli	1,083
Lithuania	
Vilnius	580
Macedonia	
Skopje	541
Madagascar	
Antananarivo	1,053
Malaysia	
Kuala Lumpur	1,145
Mali	
Bamako	800
Mauritania	
Nouakchott	735
Mexico	
Mexico City	15,048
Guadalajara	2,847
Monterrey	2,522
Puebla	1,055
León	872
Ciudad Juárez	798
Tijuana	743
Culiacán Rosales	602
Mexicali	602
Acapulco de Juárez	592
Mérida	557
Chihuahua	530
San Luis Potosí	526
Aguascalientés	506
Moldova	
Chişinău	700
Mongolia	
Ulan Bator	627
Morocco	
Casablanca	3,079
Rabat-Salé	1,344
Fès	735
Marrakesh	621
Mozambique	
Maputo	2,000
Nepal	
Katmandu	535
Netherlands	
Amsterdam	1,101
Rotterdam	1,076
The Hague	694
Utrecht	548
New Zealand	
Auckland	997
Nicaragua	
Managua	864
Nigeria	
Lagos	10,287
Ibadan	1,365
Ogbomosho	712
Kano	657
Norway	
Oslo	714
Pakistan	
Karachi	9,863
Lahore	5,085
Faisalabad	1,875
Peshawar	1,676
Gujranwala	1,663
Rawalpindi	1,290
Multan	1,257
Hyderabad	1,107
Paraguay	
Asunción	945
Peru	
Lima–Callao	6,601
Callao	638
Arequipa	620
Trujillo	509
Philippines	
Manila	9,280
Quezon City	1,989
Davao	1,191
Caloocan	1,023
Cebu	662
Zamboanga	511
Poland	
Warsaw	1,638
Lódz	825
Kraków	745
Wroclaw	642
Poznań	581
Portugal	
Lisbon	2,561
Oporto	1,174
Romania	
Bucharest	2,060
Russia	
Moscow	9,233
St Petersburg	4,883
Nizhniy Novgorod	1,425
Novosibirsk	1,400
Yekaterinburg	1,300
Samara	1,200
Omsk	1,200
Chelyabinsk	1,100
Kazan	1,100
Ufa	1,100
Volgograd	1,003
Perm	1,000
Rostov	1,000
Voronezh	908
Saratov	895
Krasnoyarsk	869
Togliatti	689
Simbirsk	678
Izhevsk	654
Krasnodar	645
Vladivostok	632
Yaroslavl	629
Khabarovsk	618
Barnaul	596
Irkutsk	585
Novokuznetsk	572
Ryazan	536
Penza	534
Orenburg	532
Tula	532
Naberezhnyye-Chelny	526
Kemerovo	503
Saudi Arabia	
Riyadh	1,800
Jedda	1,500
Mecca	630
Senegal	
Dakar	1,571
Sierra Leone	
Freetown	505
Singapore	
Singapore	3,104
Somalia	
Mogadishu	1,000
South Africa	
Cape Town	2,350
East Rand	1,379
Johannesburg	1,196
Durban	1,137
Pretoria	1,080
West Rand	870
Port Elizabeth	853
Vanderbijlpark–Vereeniging	774
Soweto	597
Sasolburg	540
Spain	
Madrid	3,029
Barcelona	1,614
Valencia	763
Sevilla	719
Zaragoza	607
Málaga	532
Sri Lanka	
Colombo	1,863
Sudan	
Nyala	1,267
Khartoum	925
Sharg el Nil	879
Sweden	
Stockholm	1,744
Göteburg	775
Switzerland	
Zürich	1,175
Bern	942
Syria	
Aleppo	1,591
Damascus	1,549
Homs	644
Taiwan	
Taipei	2,653
Kaohsiung	1,405
Taichung	817
Tainan	700
Panchiao	544
Tajikistan	
Dushanbe	524
Tanzania	
Dar-es-Salaam	1,361
Thailand	
Bangkok	5,572
Togo	
Lomé	590
Tunisia	
Tunis	1,827
Turkey	
Istanbul	7,490
Ankara	3,028
Izmir	2,333
Adana	1,472
Bursa	1,317
Konya	1,040
Gaziantep	930
Icel	908
Antalya	734
Diyarbakir	677
Kocaeli	661
Urfa	649
Kayseri	648
Manisa	641
Hatay	561
Samsun	557
Eskisehir	508
Balikesir	501
Turkmenistan	
Ashkhabad	536
Uganda	
Kampala	773
Ukraine	
Kiev	2,630
Kharkiv	1,555
Dnipropetrovsk	1,147
Donetsk	1,088
Odesa	1,046
Zaporizhzhya	887
Lviv	802
Kryvyy Rih	720
Mariupol	510
Mykolaiv	508
United Kingdom	
London	8,089
Birmingham	2,373
Manchester	2,353
Liverpool	852
Glasgow	832
Sheffield	661
Nottingham	649
Newcastle	617
Bristol	552
Leeds	529
United States	
New York	16,329
Los Angeles	12,410
Chicago	7,668
Philadelphia	4,949
Washington, DC	4,466
Detroit	4,307
Houston	3,653
Atlanta	3,331
Boston	3,240
Dallas	2,898
Minneapolis–St Paul	2,688
San Diego	2,632
St Louis	2,536
Phoenix	2,473
Baltimore	2,458
Pittsburgh	2,402
Cleveland	2,222
San Francisco	2,182
Seattle	2,180
Tampa	2,157
Miami	2,025
Newark	1,934
Denver	1,796
Portland (Or.)	1,676
Kansas City (Mo.)	1,647
Cincinnati	1,581
San Jose	1,557
Norfolk	1,529
Indianapolis	1,462
Milwaukee	1,456
Sacramento	1,441
San Antonio	1,437
Columbus (Oh.)	1,423
New Orleans	1,309
Charlotte	1,260
Buffalo	1,189
Salt Lake City	1,178
Hartford	1,151
Oklahoma	1,007
Jacksonville (Fl.)	665
Omaha	663
Memphis	614
El Paso	579
Austin	514
Nashville	505
Uruguay	
Montevideo	1,378
Uzbekistan	
Tashkent	2,107
Venezuela	
Caracas	2,784
Maracaibo	1,364
Valencia	1,032
Maracay	800
Barquisimeto	745
Ciudad Guayana	524
Vietnam	
Ho Chi Minh City	4,322
Hanoi	3,056
Haiphong	783
Yemen	
Sana	972
Aden	562
Yugoslavia	
Belgrade	1,137
Zambia	
Lusaka	982
Zimbabwe	
Harare	1,189
Bulawayo	622

* SAR = Special Administrative Region of China

CXC STUDY MAPS

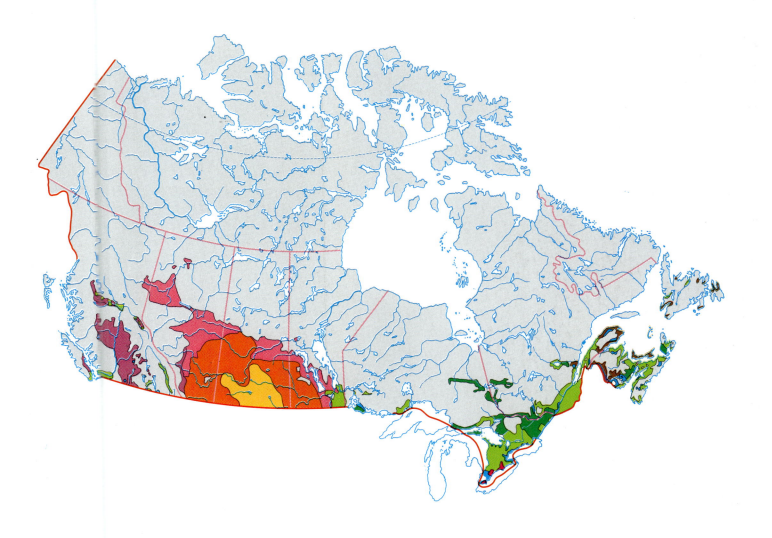

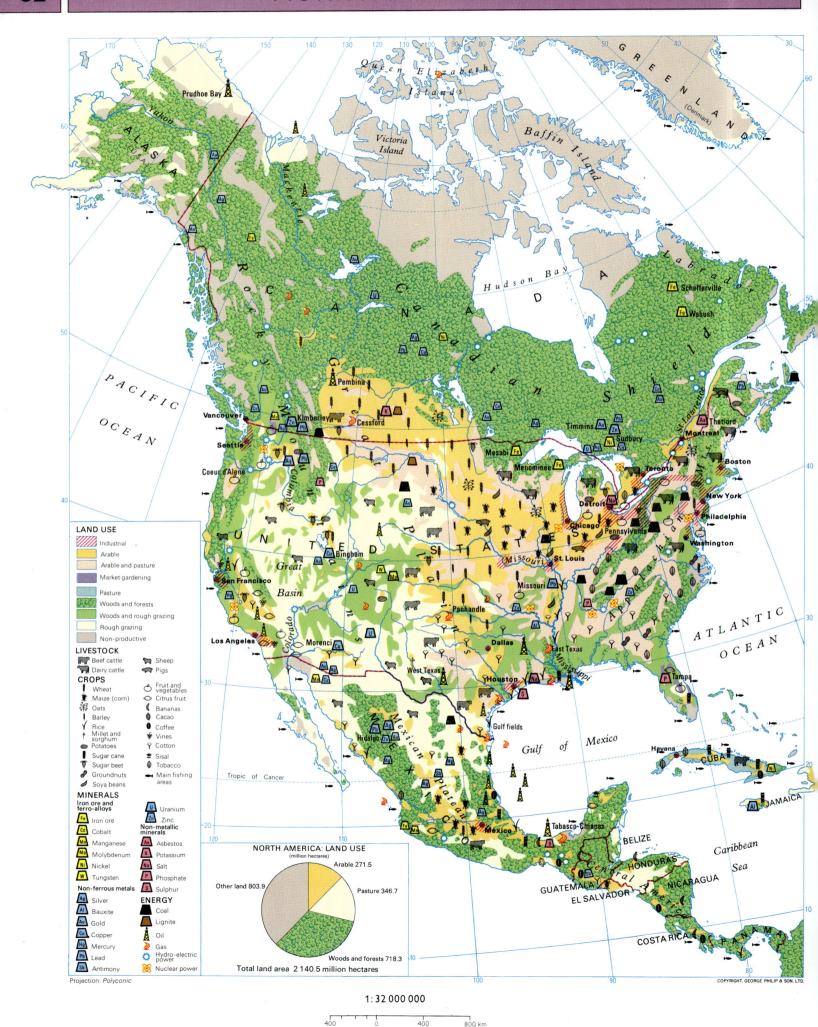

LAND USE

- Industrial
- Arable
- Arable and pasture
- Market gardening
- Pasture
- Woods and forests
- Woods and rough grazing
- Rough grazing
- Non-productive

LIVESTOCK

- Beef cattle
- Dairy cattle
- Sheep
- Pigs

CROPS

- Wheat
- Maize (corn)
- Oats
- Barley
- Rice
- Millet and sorghum
- Potatoes
- Sugar cane
- Sugar beet
- Groundnuts
- Soya beans
- Fruit and vegetables
- Citrus fruit
- Bananas
- Cacao
- Coffee
- Vines
- Cotton
- Sisal
- Tobacco
- Main fishing areas

MINERALS

Iron ore and ferro-alloys

- Fe Iron ore
- Co Cobalt
- Mn Manganese
- Mo Molybdenum
- Ni Nickel
- W Tungsten

Non-ferrous metals

- Ag Silver
- Al Bauxite
- Au Gold
- Cu Copper
- Hg Mercury
- Pb Lead
- Sb Antimony

- U Uranium
- Zn Zinc

Non-metallic minerals

- As Asbestos
- K Potassium
- Na Salt
- P Phosphate
- S Sulphur

ENERGY

- Coal
- Lignite
- Oil
- Gas
- Hydro-electric power
- Nuclear power

NORTH AMERICA: LAND USE
(million hectares)

- Arable 271.5
- Pasture 346.7
- Woods and forests 718.3
- Other land 803.9

Total land area 2 140.5 million hectares

Projection: *Polyconic*

COPYRIGHT. GEORGE PHILIP & SON. LTD.

1:32 000 000

400   0   400   800 km

SOUTH AMERICA: LAND USE
(million hectares)

Other land 283.5

Arable 104.1

Pasture 441.8

Woods and forests 924.3

Total land area 1 753.7 million hectares

LAND USE

- Industrial
- Arable
- Market gardening and plantations
- Pasture
- Woods and forests
- Rough grazing
- Non-productive

LIVESTOCK

- Beef cattle
- Dairy cattle
- Sheep
- Pigs

CROPS

- Wheat
- Maize (corn)
- Rice
- Millet and sorghum
- Potatoes
- Sugar cane
- Groundnuts
- Fruit and vegetables
- Citrus fruit
- Bananas
- Coconut palms
- Cacao
- Coffee
- Tea
- Vines
- Cotton
- Rubber
- Tobacco
- Main fishing areas

MINERALS

Iron ore and ferro-alloys
- Fe Iron ore
- Cr Chrome
- Mn Manganese
- Mo Molybdenum
- W Tungsten

Non-metallic minerals
- N Saltpetre

Non-ferrous metals
- Ag Silver
- Al Bauxite
- Au Gold
- Cu Copper
- Pb Lead
- Sb Antimony
- Sn Tin
- Zn Zinc

ENERGY

- Coal
- Oil
- Nuclear power
- Gas
- Hydro-electric power

Projection: *Lambert's Equivalent Azimuthal*

COPYRIGHT GEORGE PHILIP & SON LTD

1:30 000 000

200   0   200   400   600   800 km

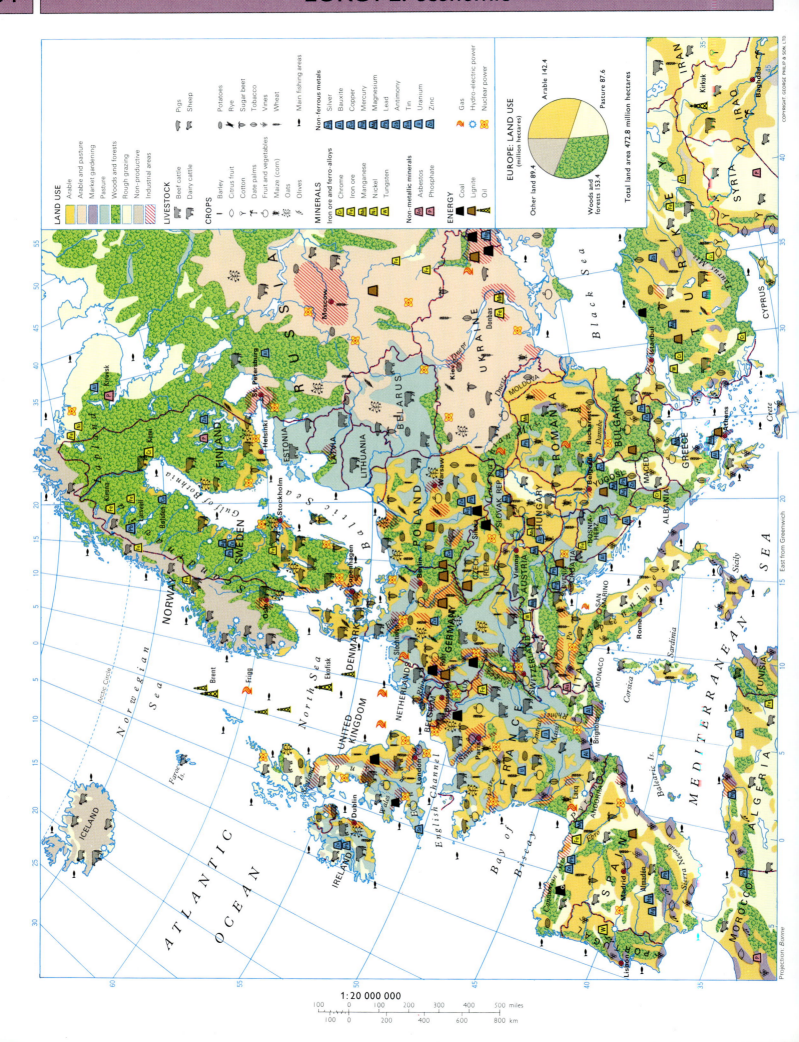

LAND USE

- Arable
- Arable and pasture
- Market gardening
- Pasture
- Woods and forests
- Rough grazing
- Non-productive
- Industrial areas

LIVESTOCK

- Beef cattle
- Dairy cattle
- Pigs
- Sheep

CROPS

- Barley
- Citrus fruit
- Cotton
- Date palms
- Fruit and vegetables
- Maize (corn)
- Oats
- Olives
- Potatoes
- Rye
- Sugar beet
- Tobacco
- Vines
- Wheat
- Main fishing areas

MINERALS

Non-ferrous metals
- Silver
- Bauxite
- Copper
- Mercury
- Magnesium
- Lead
- Antimony
- Tin
- Uranium
- Zinc

Iron ore and ferro-alloys
- Chrome
- Iron ore
- Manganese
- Nickel
- Tungsten

Non-metallic minerals
- Asbestos
- Phosphate

ENERGY
- Coal
- Lignite
- Oil
- Gas
- Hydro-electric power
- Nuclear power

EUROPE: LAND USE
(million hectares)

Arable 142.4
Pasture 87.6
Woods and forests 153.4
Other land 89.4

Total land area 472.8 million hectares

1:20 000 000

100   0   100   200   300   400   500 miles
100   0   200   400   600   800 km

Projection: Bonne

COPYRIGHT GEORGE PHILIP & SON LTD

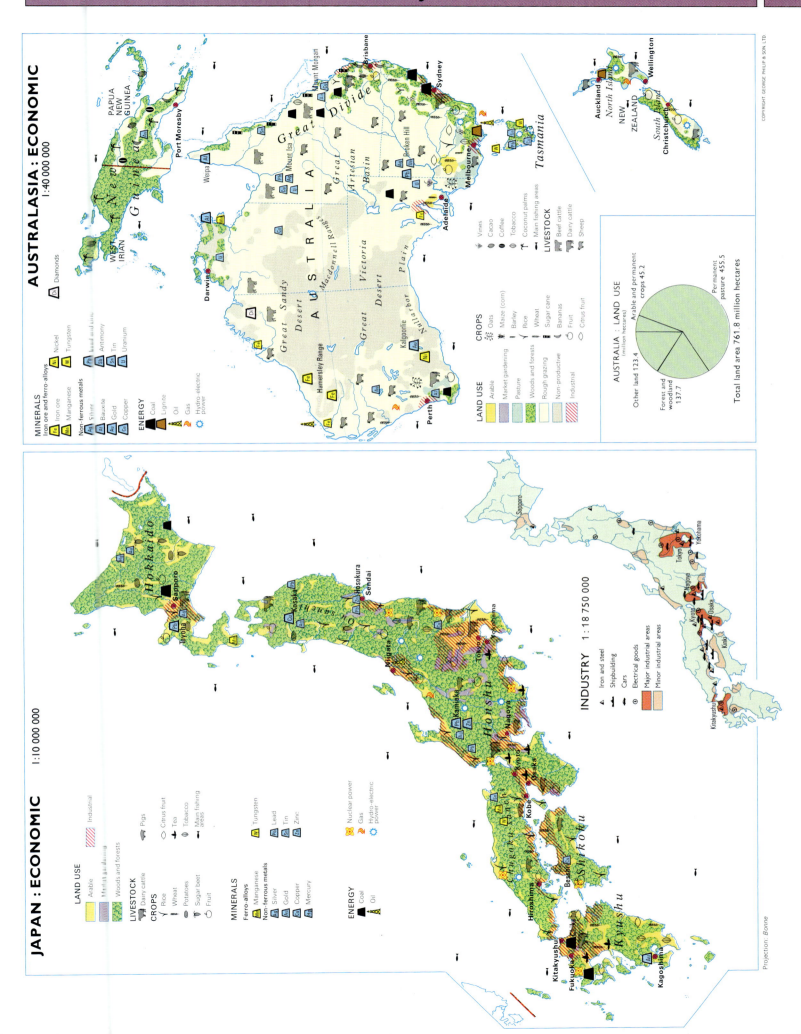

AUSTRALASIA: ECONOMIC

1:40 000 000

MINERALS
Iron ore and ferro-alloys
Fe Iron ore   Ni Nickel
Mn Manganese   W Tungsten

Non-ferrous metals
Ag Silver   Pb Lead and zinc
Al Bauxite   Sb Antimony
Au Gold   Sn Tin
Cu Copper   U Uranium

Di Diamonds

ENERGY
Coal
Lignite
Oil
Gas
Hydro electric power

CROPS
Oats   Maize (corn)
Barley   Rice
Wheat   Sugar cane
Bananas
Fruit
Citrus fruit

Vines   Cacao
Coffee
Tobacco
Coconut palms
Main fishing areas

LIVESTOCK
Beef cattle
Dairy cattle
Sheep

LAND USE
Arable
Market gardening
Pasture
Woods and forests
Rough grazing
Non-productive
Industrial

AUSTRALIA : LAND USE
(million hectares)

Arable and permanent crops 45.2
Permanent pasture 455.5
Forest and woodland 137.7
Other land 123.4

Total land area 761.8 million hectares

JAPAN : ECONOMIC

1:10 000 000

LAND USE
Arable
Market gardening
Woods and forests
Industrial

LIVESTOCK
Dairy cattle
Pigs

CROPS
Rice   Citrus fruit
Wheat   Tea
Potatoes   Tobacco
Sugar beet   Main fishing areas
Fruit

MINERALS
Ferro-alloys
Manganese   W Tungsten
Non-ferrous metals
Ag Silver   Pb Lead
Au Gold   Sn Tin
Cu Copper   Zn Zinc
Hg Mercury

ENERGY
Coal   Nuclear power
Oil   Gas
Hydro-electric power

INDUSTRY 1:18 750 000
Iron and steel
Shipbuilding
Cars
Electrical goods
Major industrial areas
Minor industrial areas

Projection: *Bonne*

COPYRIGHT GEORGE PHILIP & SON LTD

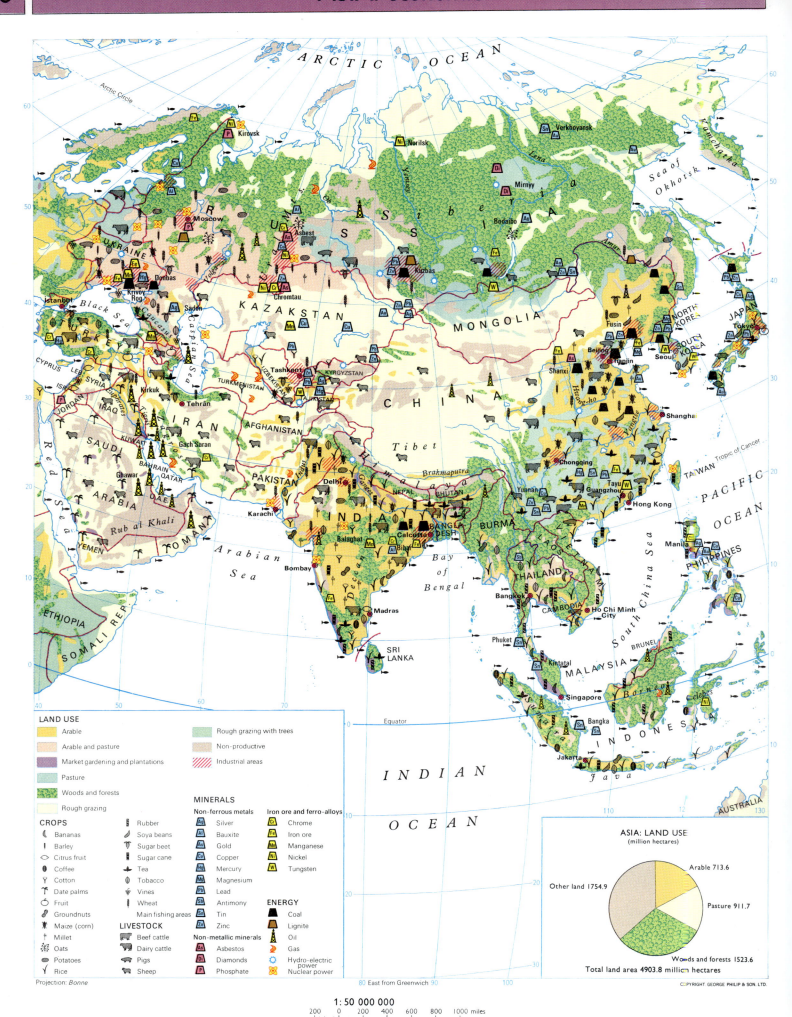

ASIA: LAND USE
(million hectares)

Arable 713.6
Pasture 911.7
Woods and forests 1523.6
Other land 1754.9
Total land area 4903.8 million hectares

LAND USE

- Arable
- Arable and pasture
- Market gardening and plantations
- Pasture
- Woods and forests
- Rough grazing
- Rough grazing with trees
- Non-productive
- Industrial areas

CROPS

- Bananas
- Barley
- Citrus fruit
- Coffee
- Cotton
- Date palms
- Fruit
- Groundnuts
- Maize (corn)
- Millet
- Oats
- Potatoes
- Rice
- Rubber
- Soya beans
- Sugar beet
- Sugar cane
- Tea
- Tobacco
- Vines
- Wheat
- Main fishing areas

LIVESTOCK

- Beef cattle
- Dairy cattle
- Pigs
- Sheep

MINERALS

Non-ferrous metals
- Ag Silver
- Al Bauxite
- Au Gold
- Cu Copper
- Hg Mercury
- Mg Magnesium
- Pb Lead
- Sb Antimony
- Sn Tin
- Zn Zinc

Non-metallic minerals
- As Asbestos
- Di Diamonds
- P Phosphate

Iron ore and ferro-alloys
- Cr Chrome
- Fe Iron ore
- Mn Manganese
- Ni Nickel
- W Tungsten

ENERGY
- Coal
- Lignite
- Oil
- Gas
- Hydro-electric power
- Nuclear power

Projection: *Bonne*

East from Greenwich

1:50 000 000

200 0 200 400 600 800 1000 miles
200 0 400 800 1200 1600 km

COPYRIGHT GEORGE PHILIP & SON, LTD.

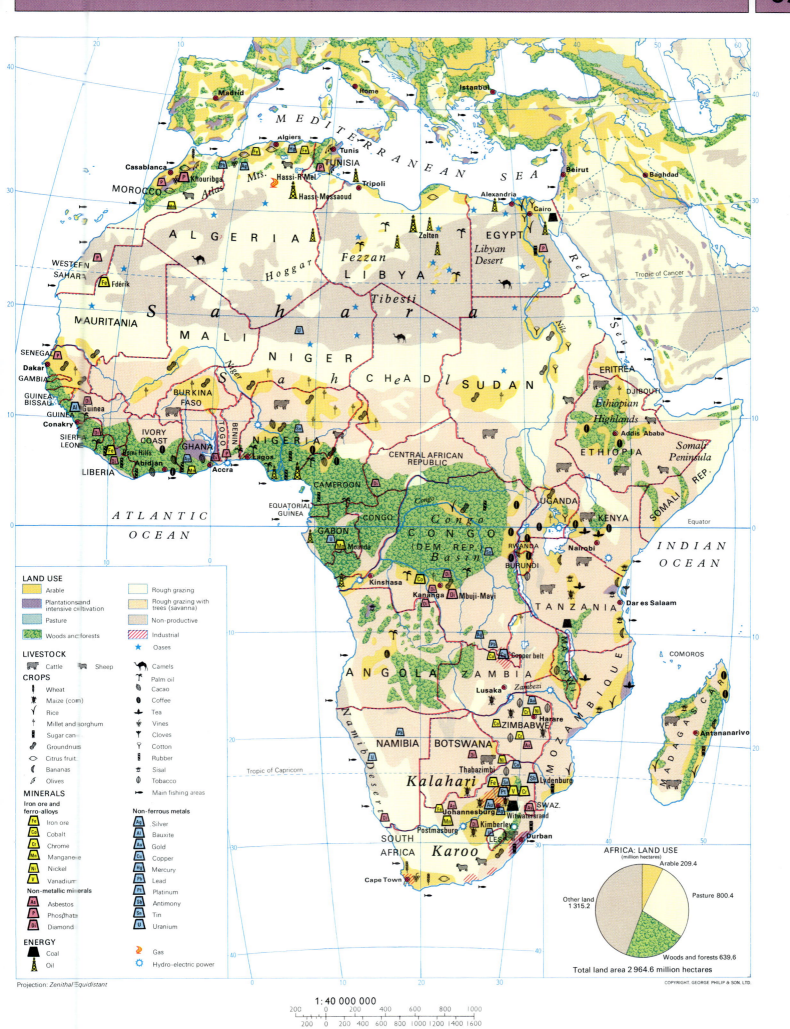

LAND USE
- Arable
- Plantations and intensive cultivation
- Pasture
- Woods and forests
- Rough grazing
- Rough grazing with trees (savanna)
- Non-productive
- Industrial
- ★ Oases

LIVESTOCK
- Cattle
- Sheep
- Camels

CROPS
- Wheat
- Maize (corn)
- Rice
- Millet and sorghum
- Sugar cane
- Groundnuts
- Citrus fruit
- Bananas
- Olives
- Palm oil
- Cacao
- Coffee
- Tea
- Vines
- Cloves
- Cotton
- Rubber
- Sisal
- Tobacco
- Main fishing areas

MINERALS

Iron ore and ferro-alloys
- Fe Iron ore
- Co Cobalt
- Cr Chrome
- Mn Manganese
- Ni Nickel
- V Vanadium

Non-metallic minerals
- As Asbestos
- P Phosphate
- Di Diamond

Non-ferrous metals
- Ag Silver
- Al Bauxite
- Au Gold
- Cu Copper
- Hg Mercury
- Pb Lead
- Pt Platinum
- Sb Antimony
- Sn Tin
- U Uranium

ENERGY
- Coal
- Oil
- Gas
- Hydro-electric power

AFRICA: LAND USE
(million hectares)

Arable 209.4
Pasture 800.4
Woods and forests 639.6
Other land 1 315.2

Total land area 2 964.6 million hectares

Projection: *Zenithal Equidistant*

COPYRIGHT. GEORGE PHILIP & SON. LTD.

1 : 40 000 000

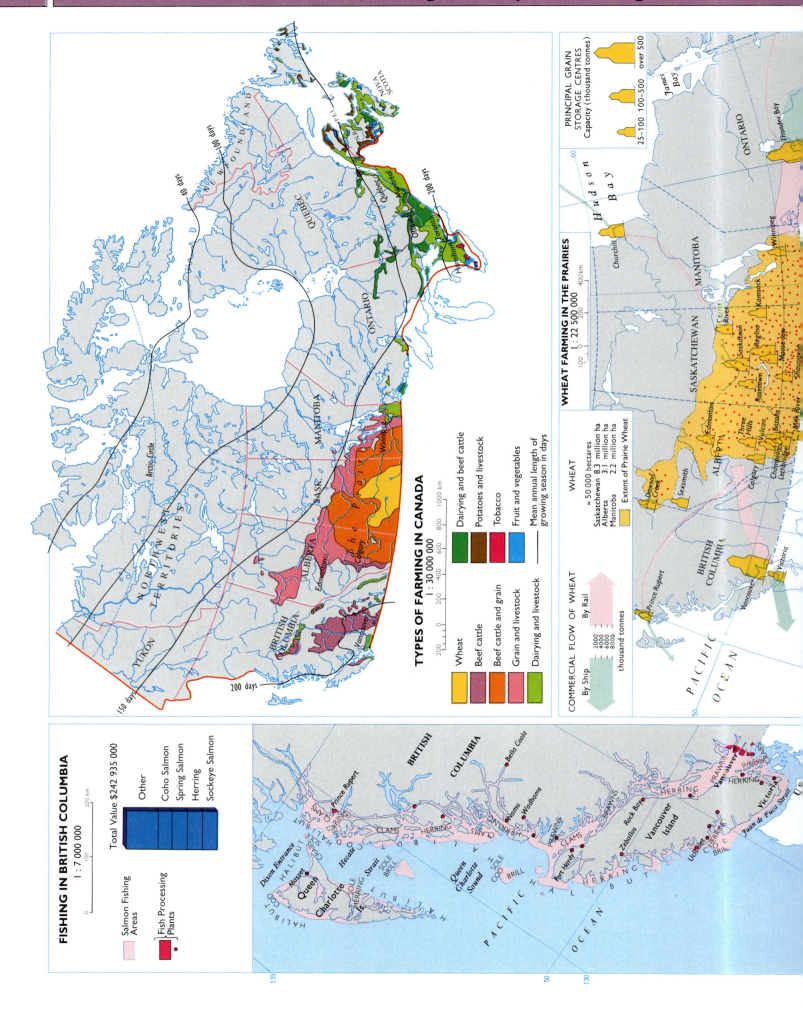

TYPES OF FARMING IN CANADA
1 : 30 000 000

- Wheat
- Beef cattle
- Beef cattle and grain
- Grain and livestock
- Dairying and livestock
- Dairying and beef cattle
- Potatoes and livestock
- Tobacco
- Fruit and vegetables
- Mean annual length of growing season in days

PRINCIPAL GRAIN STORAGE CENTRES
Capacity (thousand tonnes)
25–100 100–500 over 500

WHEAT FARMING IN THE PRAIRIES
1 : 22 500 000

WHEAT
= 50 000 hectares
Saskatchewan 8.3 million ha
Alberta 3.1 million ha
Manitoba 2.2 million ha

Extent of Prairie Wheat

COMMERCIAL FLOW OF WHEAT
By Ship — By Rail
2000
4000
8000
thousand tonnes

FISHING IN BRITISH COLUMBIA
1 : 7 000 000
0   100   200 km

Total Value $242 935 000

- Other
- Coho Salmon
- Spring Salmon
- Herring
- Sockeye Salmon

Salmon Fishing Areas

Fish Processing Plants

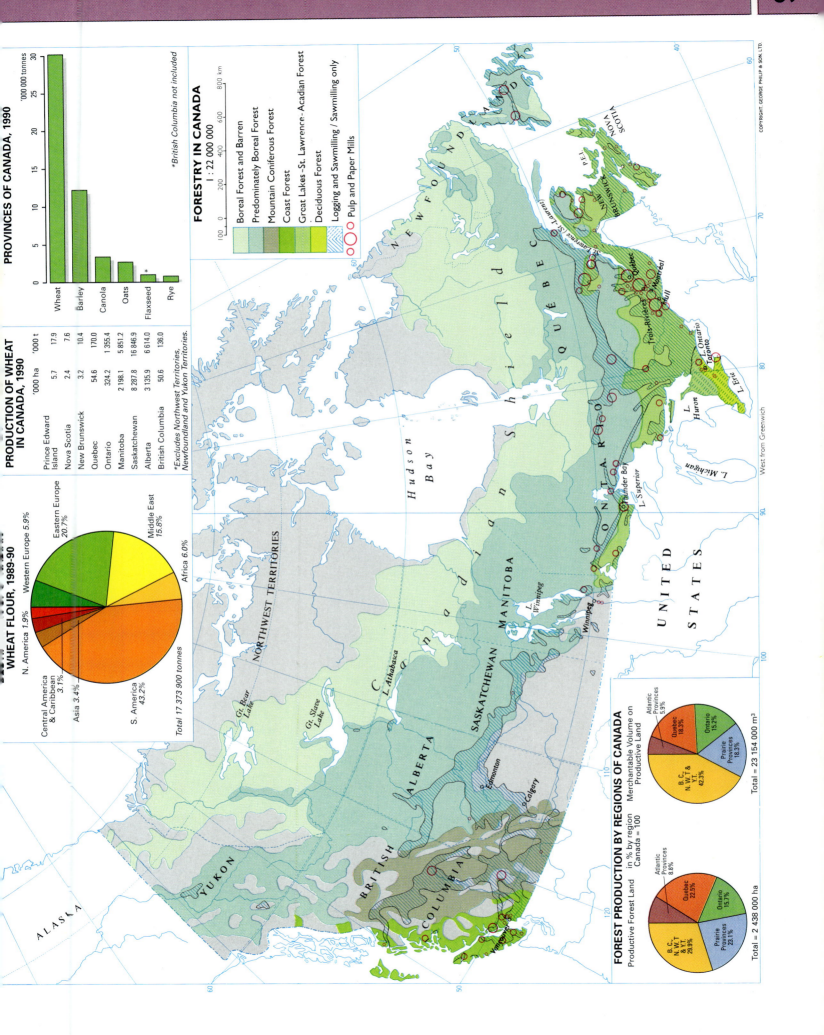

PROVINCES OF CANADA, 1990

'000 000 tonnes

- Wheat
- Barley
- Canola
- Oats
- Flaxseed *
- Rye

*British Columbia not included

PRODUCTION OF WHEAT IN CANADA, 1990

	'000 ha	'000 t
Prince Edward Island	5.7	17.9
Nova Scotia	2.4	7.6
New Brunswick	3.2	10.4
Quebec	54.6	170.0
Ontario	324.2	1 355.4
Manitoba	2 198.1	5 851.2
Saskatchewan	8 287.8	16 846.9
Alberta	3 135.9	6 614.0
British Columbia	50.6	136.0

*Excludes Northwest Territories, Newfoundland and Yukon Territories.

WHEAT FLOUR, 1989-90

- N. America 1.9%
- Western Europe 5.9%
- Eastern Europe 20.7%
- Middle East 15.8%
- Africa 6.0%
- S. America 43.2%
- Asia 3.4%
- Central America & Caribbean 3.1%

Total 17 373 900 tonnes

FORESTRY IN CANADA
1 : 22 000 000

- Boreal Forest and Barren
- Predominately Boreal Forest
- Mountain Coniferous Forest
- Coast Forest
- Great Lakes - St. Lawrence - Acadian Forest
- Deciduous Forest
- Logging and Sawmilling / Sawmilling only
- Pulp and Paper Mills

0 100 200 400 600 800 km

FOREST PRODUCTION BY REGIONS OF CANADA

Merchantable Volume on Productive Land
in % by region
Canada = 100

- Atlantic Provinces 5.9%
- Quebec 18.3%
- Ontario 15.2%
- Prairie Provinces 18.3%
- B.C., N.W.T. & Y.T. 42.3%

Total 23 154 000 m³

Productive Forest Land

- Atlantic Provinces 8.8%
- Quebec 22.5%
- Ontario 15.7%
- Prairie Provinces 23.1%
- B.C., N.W.T. & Y.T. 29.9%

Total 2 438 000 ha

COPYRIGHT GEORGE PHILIP & SON, LTD.

West from Greenwich

ALASKA

YUKON

NORTHWEST TERRITORIES

BRITISH COLUMBIA

ALBERTA

SASKATCHEWAN

MANITOBA

ONTARIO

QUEBEC

NEWFOUNDLAND

NOVA SCOTIA

NEW BRUNSWICK

P.E.I.

UNITED STATES

Hudson Bay

Gt. Bear Lake

Gt. Slave Lake

L. Athabasca

L. Winnipeg

L. Superior

L. Huron

L. Michigan

L. Erie

L. Ontario

Canadian Shield

Vancouver

Calgary

Edmonton

Winnipeg

Thunder Bay

Toronto

Hull

Montreal

Quebec

Trois-Rivières

St. Lawrence

SOIL EROSION AND CONSERVATION IN THE U.S.A.

PAST . . .

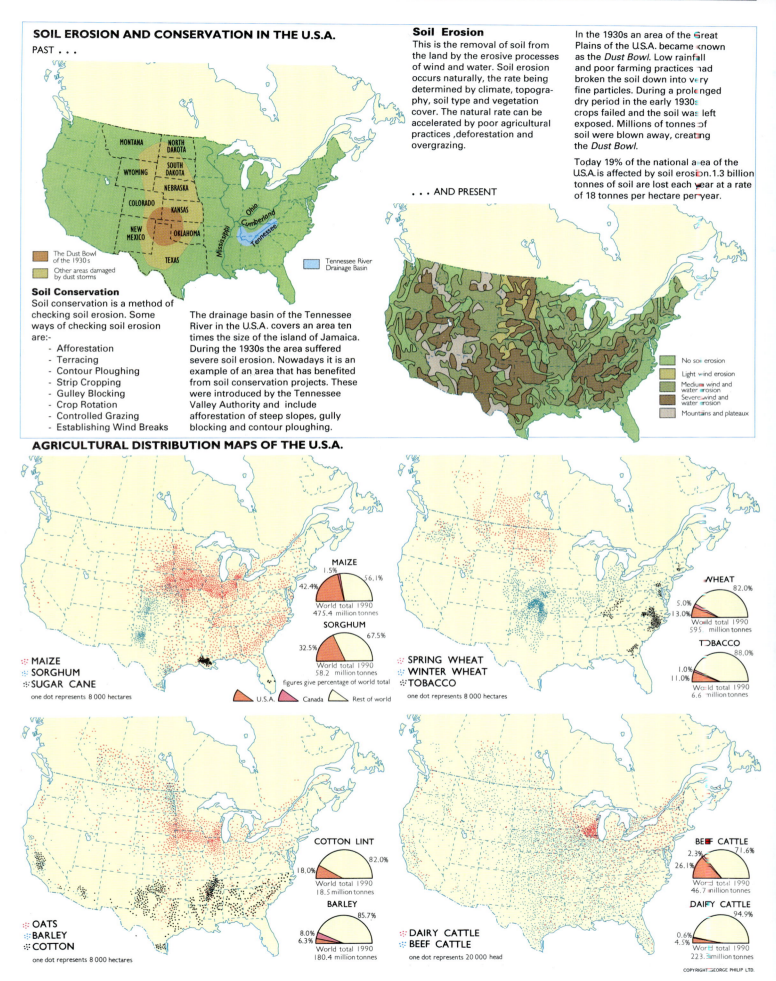

- ■ The Dust Bowl of the 1930s
- ■ Other areas damaged by dust storms
- ■ Tennessee River Drainage Basin

Soil Conservation

Soil conservation is a method of checking soil erosion. Some ways of checking soil erosion are:-

- Afforestation
- Terracing
- Contour Ploughing
- Strip Cropping
- Gulley Blocking
- Crop Rotation
- Controlled Grazing
- Establishing Wind Breaks

The drainage basin of the Tennessee River in the U.S.A. covers an area ten times the size of the island of Jamaica. During the 1930s the area suffered severe soil erosion. Nowadays it is an example of an area that has benefited from soil conservation projects. These were introduced by the Tennessee Valley Authority and include afforestation of steep slopes, gully blocking and contour ploughing.

Soil Erosion

This is the removal of soil from the land by the erosive processes of wind and water. Soil erosion occurs naturally, the rate being determined by climate, topography, soil type and vegetation cover. The natural rate can be accelerated by poor agricultural practices, deforestation and overgrazing.

. . . AND PRESENT

In the 1930s an area of the Great Plains of the U.S.A. became known as the *Dust Bowl*. Low rainfall and poor farming practices had broken the soil down into very fine particles. During a prolonged dry period in the early 1930s crops failed and the soil was left exposed. Millions of tonnes of soil were blown away, creating the *Dust Bowl*.

Today 19% of the national area of the U.S.A. is affected by soil erosion. 1.3 billion tonnes of soil are lost each year at a rate of 18 tonnes per hectare per year.

- No soil erosion
- Light wind erosion
- Medium wind and water erosion
- Severe wind and water erosion
- Mountains and plateaux

AGRICULTURAL DISTRIBUTION MAPS OF THE U.S.A.

MAIZE
1.5% 56.1%
42.4%
World total 1990
475.4 million tonnes

SORGHUM
32.5% 67.5%
World total 1990
58.2 million tonnes

figures give percentage of world total

- ■ MAIZE
- ■ SORGHUM
- ■ SUGAR CANE

one dot represents 8 000 hectares

■ U.S.A. ■ Canada ■ Rest of world

WHEAT
82.0%
5.0%
13.0%
World total 1990
595. million tonnes

TOBACCO
88.0%
1.0%
11.0%
World total 1990
6.6 million tonnes

- ■ SPRING WHEAT
- ■ WINTER WHEAT
- ■ TOBACCO

one dot represents 8 000 hectares

COTTON LINT
82.0%
18.0%
World total 1990
18.5 million tonnes

BARLEY
85.7%
8.0%
6.3%
World total 1990
180.4 million tonnes

- ■ OATS
- ■ BARLEY
- ■ COTTON

one dot represents 8 000 hectares

BEEF CATTLE
2.3% 71.6%
26.1%
World total 1990
46.7 million tonnes

DAIRY CATTLE
94.9%
0.6%
4.5%
World total 1990
223.3 million tonnes

- ■ DAIRY CATTLE
- ■ BEEF CATTLE

one dot represents 20 000 head

1:60 000 000

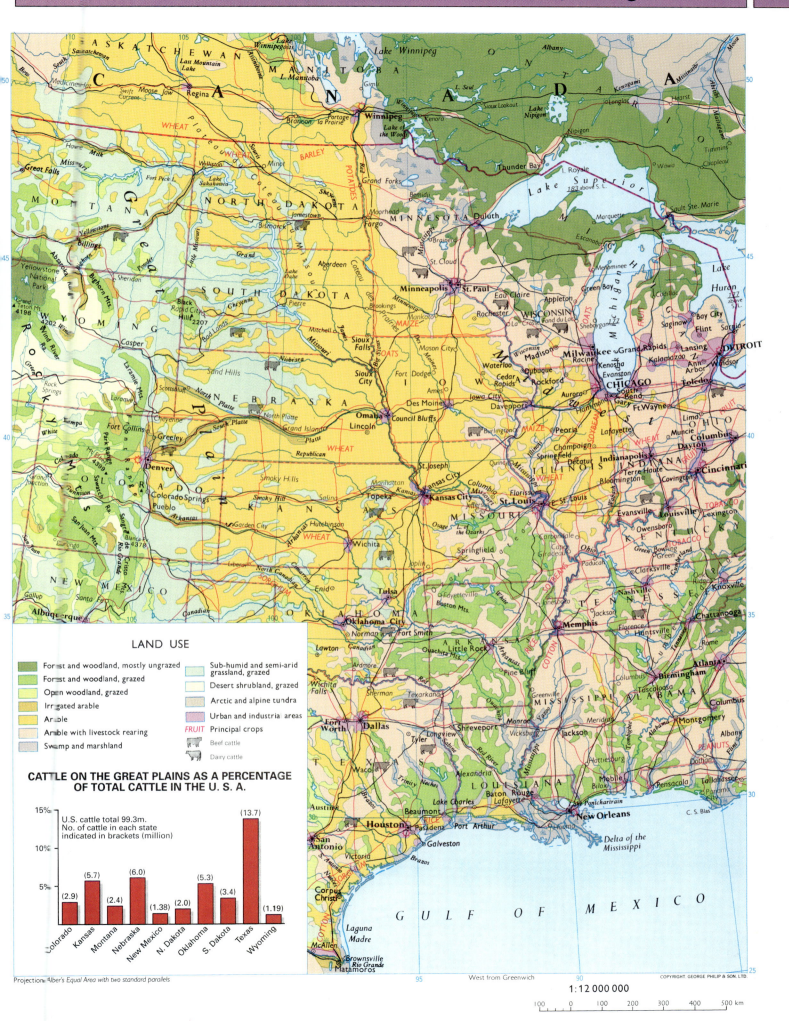

LAND USE

- Forest and woodland, mostly ungrazed
- Forest and woodland, grazed
- Open woodland, grazed
- Irrigated arable
- Arable
- Arable with livestock rearing
- Swamp and marshland
- Sub-humid and semi-arid grassland, grazed
- Desert shrubland, grazed
- Arctic and alpine tundra
- Urban and industrial areas
- *FRUIT* Principal crops
- Beef cattle
- Dairy cattle

CATTLE ON THE GREAT PLAINS AS A PERCENTAGE OF TOTAL CATTLE IN THE U.S.A.

U.S. cattle total 99.3m.
No. of cattle in each state indicated in brackets (million)

Colorado	(2.9)
Kansas	(5.7)
Montana	(2.4)
Nebraska	(6.0)
New Mexico	(1.38)
N. Dakota	(2.0)
Oklahoma	(5.3)
S. Dakota	(3.4)
Texas	(13.7)
Wyoming	(1.19)

Projection: Alber's Equal Area with two standard parallels

West from Greenwich

1:12 000 000

100 0 100 200 300 400 500 km

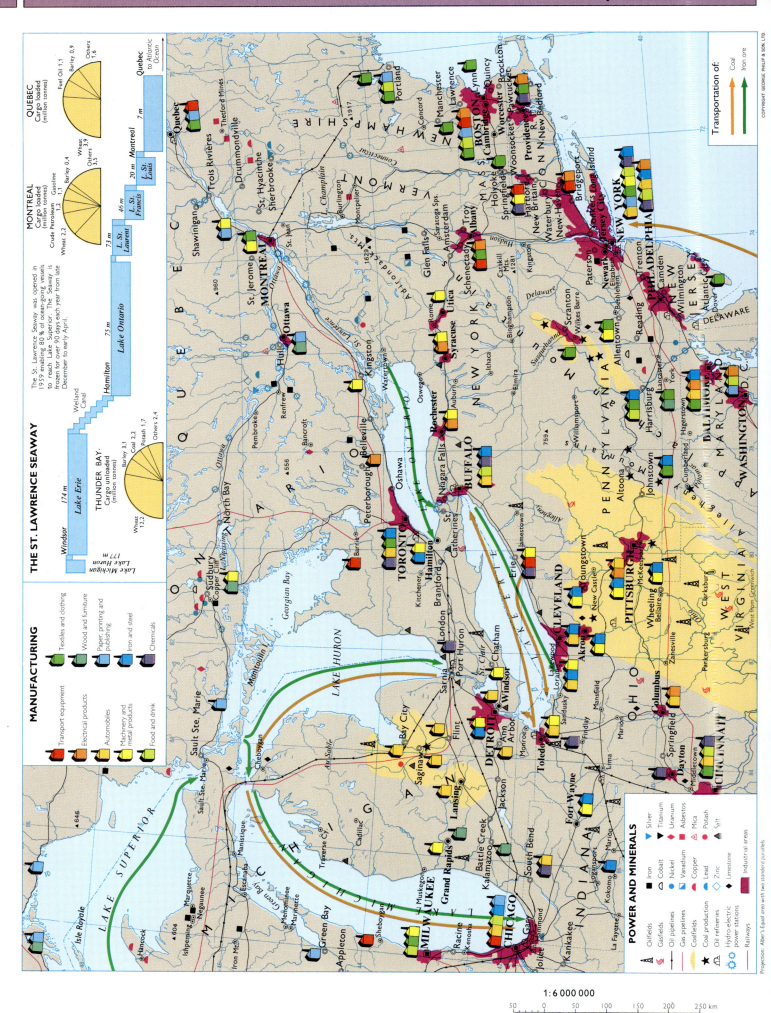

THE ST. LAWRENCE SEAWAY

The St. Lawrence Seaway was opened in 1959 enabling 80% of ocean-going vessels to reach Lake Superior. The Seaway is frozen for over 90 days each year from late December to early April.

QUEBEC
Cargo loaded
(million tonnes)
Fuel Oil 1.1
Barley 0.9
Others 1.6

MONTREAL
Cargo loaded
(million tonnes)
Crude Petroleum 1.2
Wheat 2.2
Gasoline 0.4
Barley 1.1
Wheat 3.9
Others 3.5

THUNDER BAY.
Cargo unloaded
(million tonnes)
Barley 3.1
Coal 1.7
Potash 2.2
Others 2.4
Wheat 12.2

MANUFACTURING

Textiles and clothing
Wood and furniture
Paper, printing and publishing
Iron and steel
Chemicals

Transport equipment
Electrical products
Automobiles
Machinery and metal products
Food and drink

POWER AND MINERALS

Oilfields
Gasfields
Oil pipelines
Gas pipelines
Coalfields
Oil refineries
Hydro-electric power stations
Railways

Iron
Cobalt
Nickel
Vanadium
Copper
Lead
Zinc
Limestone

Silver
Titanium
Uranium
Asbestos
Mica
Potash
Salt

Industrial areas

Transportation of:
Coal
Iron ore

Scale 1:6 000 000

50 0 50 100 150 200 250 km

COPYRIGHT GEORGE PHILIP & SON, LTD.

Projection: Alber's Equal area with two standard parallels.

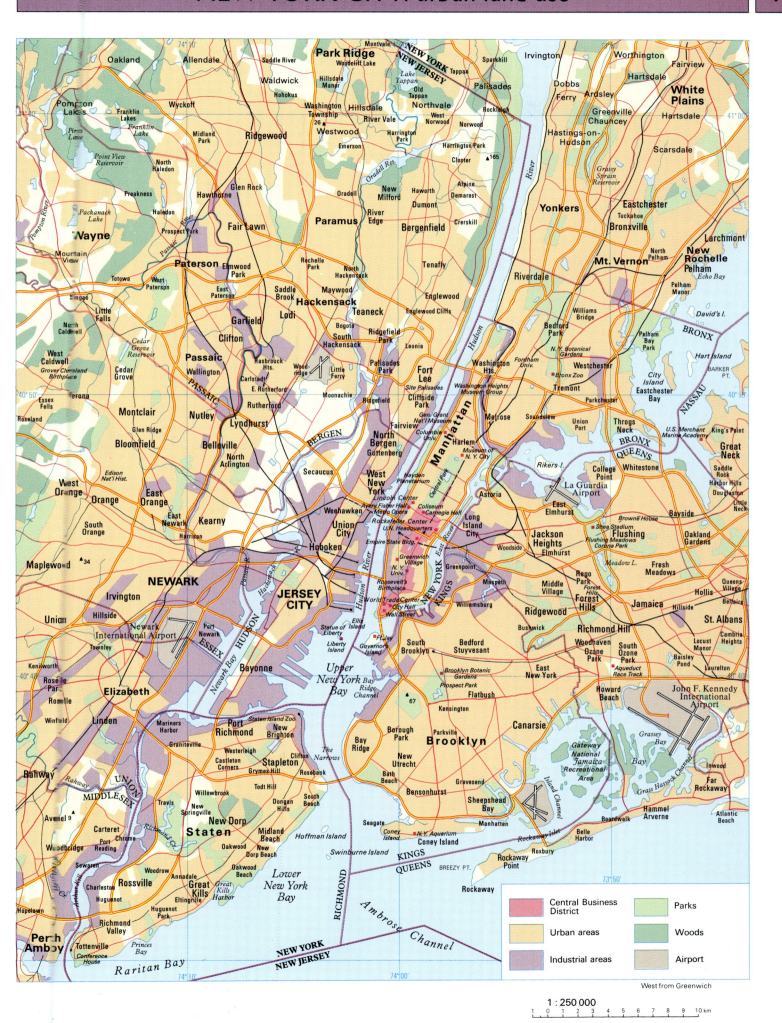

Central Business District		Parks
Urban areas		Woods
Industrial areas		Airport

West from Greenwich

1 : 250 000

1 0 1 2 3 4 5 6 7 8 9 10 km

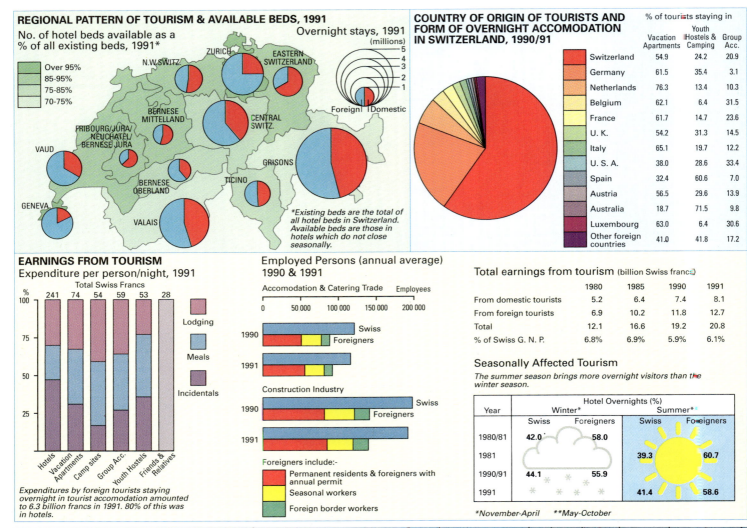

REGIONAL PATTERN OF TOURISM & AVAILABLE BEDS, 1991

No. of hotel beds available as a % of all existing beds, 1991*

- Over 95%
- 85–95%
- 75–85%
- 70–75%

Overnight stays, 1991 (millions)

5 4 3 2 1

Foreign | Domestic

ZURICH, N.W.SWITZ., EASTERN SWITZERLAND, BERNESE MITTELLAND, CENTRAL SWITZ., FRIBOURG/JURA/NEUCHATEL/BERNESE JURA, VAUD, GRISONS, BERNESE OBERLAND, TICINO, GENEVA, VALAIS

*Existing beds are the total of all hotel beds in Switzerland. Available beds are those in hotels which do not close seasonally.

COUNTRY OF ORIGIN OF TOURISTS AND FORM OF OVERNIGHT ACCOMODATION IN SWITZERLAND, 1990/91

	% of tourists staying in		
	Vacation Apartments	Youth Hostels & Camping	Group Acc.
Switzerland	54.9	24.2	20.9
Germany	61.5	35.4	3.1
Netherlands	76.3	13.4	10.3
Belgium	62.1	6.4	31.5
France	61.7	14.7	23.6
U. K.	54.2	31.3	14.5
Italy	65.1	19.7	12.2
U. S. A.	38.0	28.6	33.4
Spain	32.4	60.6	7.0
Austria	56.5	29.6	13.9
Australia	18.7	71.5	9.8
Luxembourg	63.0	6.4	30.6
Other foreign countries	41.0	41.8	17.2

EARNINGS FROM TOURISM

Expenditure per person/night, 1991

Total Swiss Francs: 241, 74, 54, 59, 53, 28

- Lodging
- Meals
- Incidentals

Hotels, Vacation Apartments, Camp sites, Group Acc., Youth Hostels, Friends & Relatives

Expenditures by foreign tourists staying overnight in tourist accomodation amounted to 6.3 billion francs in 1991. 80% of this was in hotels.

Employed Persons (annual average) 1990 & 1991

Accomodation & Catering Trade

Employees: 0, 50 000, 100 000, 150 000, 200 000

1990 — Swiss / Foreigners
1991 — Swiss / Foreigners

Construction Industry

1990 — Swiss / Foreigners
1991 — Swiss / Foreigners

Foreigners include:-
- Permanent residents & foreigners with annual permit
- Seasonal workers
- Foreign border workers

Total earnings from tourism (billion Swiss francs)

	1980	1985	1990	1991
From domestic tourists	5.2	6.4	7.4	8.1
From foreign tourists	6.9	10.2	11.8	12.7
Total	12.1	16.6	19.2	20.8
% of Swiss G. N. P.	6.8%	6.9%	5.9%	6.1%

Seasonally Affected Tourism

The summer season brings more overnight visitors than the winter season.

	Hotel Overnights (%)			
	Winter*		Summer**	
Year	Swiss	Foreigners	Swiss	Foreigners
1980/81	42.0	58.0		
1981			39.3	60.7
1990/91	44.1	55.9		
1991			41.4	58.6

*November–April   **May–October

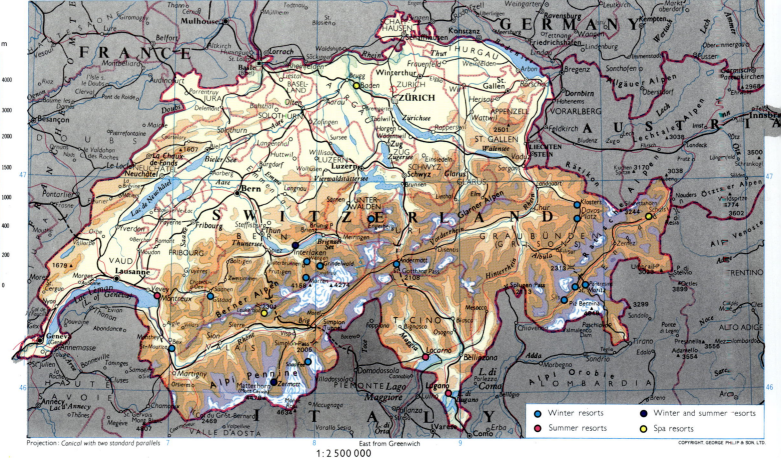

Winter resorts · Winter and summer resorts · Summer resorts · Spa resorts

Projection: Conical with two standard parallels

East from Greenwich

1 : 2 500 000

10 0 10 20 30 40 50 60 70 80 90 100 km

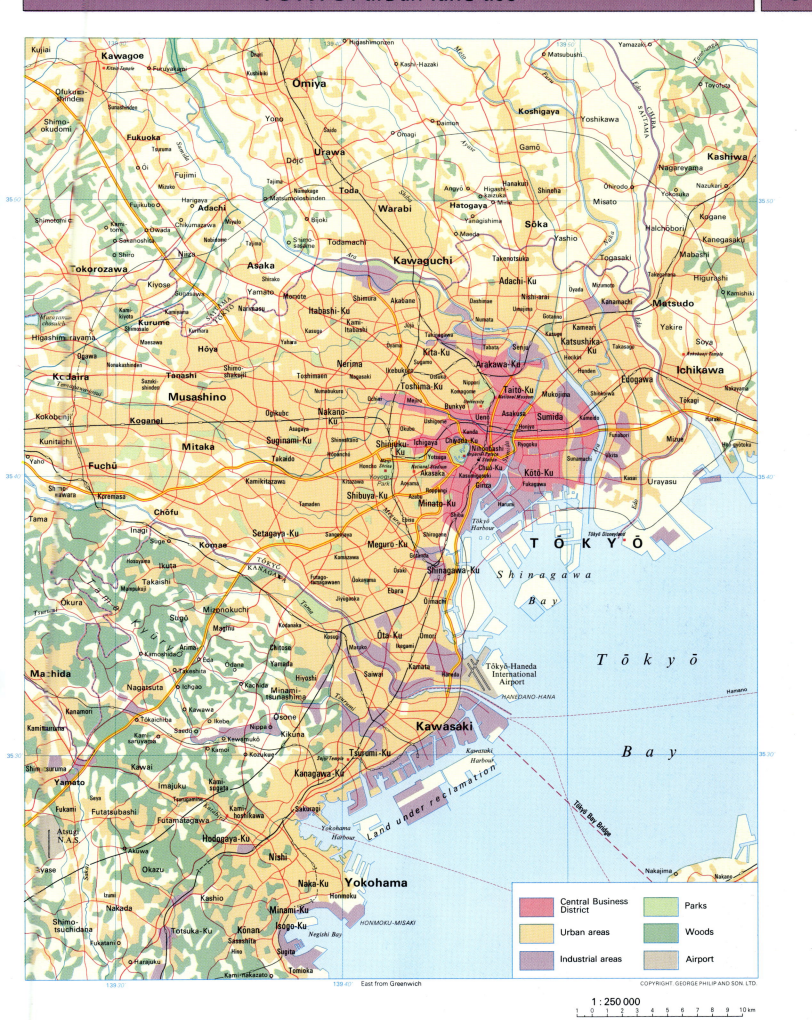

Central Business District

Urban areas

Industrial areas

Parks

Woods

Airport

COPYRIGHT. GEORGE PHILIP AND SON. LTD.

1 : 250 000

East from Greenwich

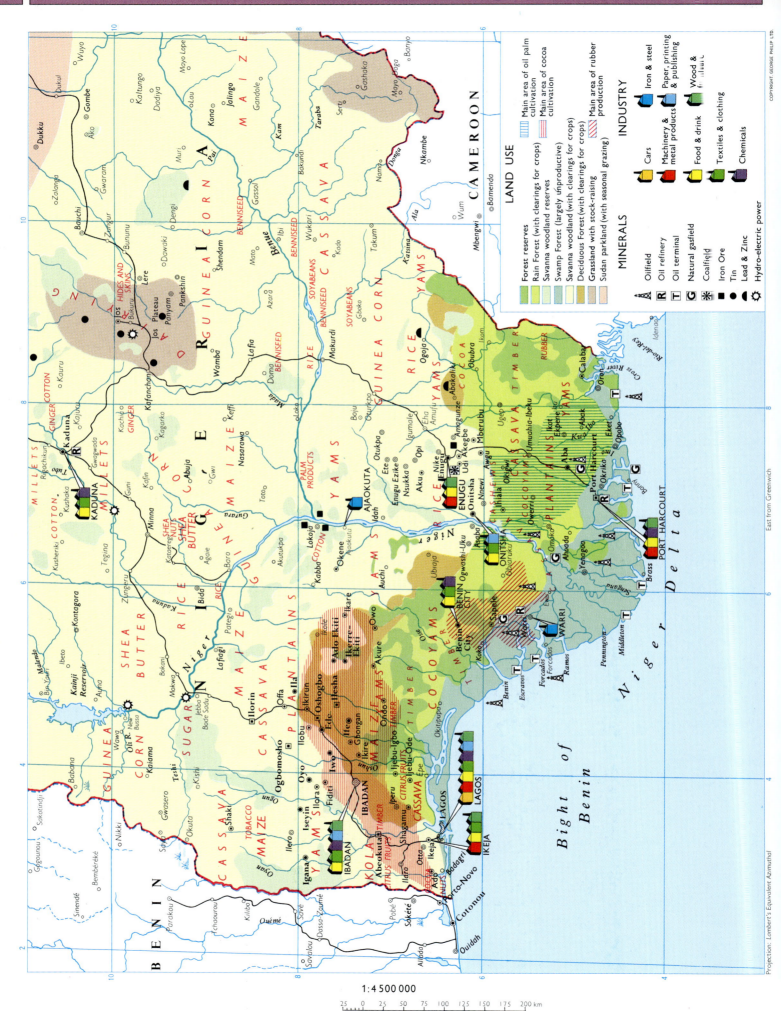

Projection: Lambert's Equivalent Azimuthal

East from Greenwich

COPYRIGHT GEORGE PHILIP LTD.

1:4 500 000

25 0 25 50 75 100 125 150 175 200 km

INDEX TO
WORLD MAPS

The index contains the names of all the principal places and features shown on the World Maps. Each name is followed by an additional entry in italics giving the country or region within which it is located. The alphabetical order of names composed of two or more words is governed primarily by the first word and then by the second. This is an example of the rule:

New South Wales □, *Australia*..	**34 G8**	33 0S	146 0E
New York □, *U.S.A.*	**43 D10**	42 40N	76 0W
New York City, *U.S.A.*	**43 E11**	40 45N	74 0W
New Zealand ■, *Oceania*	**35 J13**	40 0S	176 0E
Newark, *U.S.A.*	**43 F10**	39 42N	75 45W

Physical features composed of a proper name (Erie) and a description (Lake) are positioned alphabetically by the proper name. The description is positioned after the proper name and is usually abbreviated:

Erie, L., *N. Amer.*	**42 D7**	42 15N	81 0W

Where a description forms part of a settlement or administrative name, however, it is always written in full and put in its true alphabetical position:

Mount Isa, *Australia*	**34 E6**	20 42S	139 26E

Names beginning with M' and Mc are indexed as if they were spelt Mac. Names beginning St. are alphabetized under Saint, but Santa and San are all spelt in full and are alphabetized accordingly. If the same placename occurs two or more times in the index and all are in the same country, each is followed by the name of the administrative subdivision in which it is located. The names are placed in the alphabetical order of the subdivision. For example:

Columbus, Ga., *U.S.A.*	**41 D10**	32 30N	84 58W
Columbus, Ind., *U.S.A.*	**42 F5**	39 14N	85 55W
Columbus, Ohio, *U.S.A.*	**42 F6**	39 57N	83 1W

The number in bold type which follows each name in the index refers to the number of the map page where that feature or place will be found. This is usually the largest scale at which the place or feature appears.

The letter and figure which are in bold type immediately after the page number give the grid square on the map page, within which the feature is situated. The letter represents the latitude and the figure the longitude. In some cases the feature itself may fall within the specified square, while the name is outside.

For a more precise location, the geographical co-ordinates which follow the letter-figure references give the latitude and the longitude of each place. The first set of figures represent the latitude, which is the distance north or south of the Equator measured as an angle at the centre of the Earth. The Equator is latitude 0°, the North Pole is 90°N and the South Pole 90°S.

The second set of figures represent the longitude, which is the distance east or west of the prime meridian, which runs through Greenwich, England. Longitude is also measured as an angle at the centre of the Earth and is given east or west of the prime meridian, from 0° to 180° in either direction.

The unit of measurement for latitude and longitude is the degree, which is subdivided into 60 minutes. Each index entry states the position of a place in degrees and minutes, a space being left between the degrees and the minutes. The latitude is followed by N(orth) or S(outh) and the longitude by E(ast) or W(est).

Rivers are indexed to their mouths or confluences, and carry the symbol ⇝ after their names. A solid square ■ follows the name of a country, while an open square □ refers to a first order administrative area.

ABBREVIATIONS USED IN THE INDEX

Afghan. – Afghanistan	Conn. – Connecticut	Isla. Island, Isle(s)	Mo. – Missouri	Nebr. – Nebraska	Provincial	Sib. – Siberia
Ala. – Alabama	Cord. – Cordillera	Ill. – Illirois	Mont. – Montana	Neths. – Netherlands	Pt. – Point	St. – Saint, Sankt, Sint
Alta. – Alberta	Cr. – Creek	Ind. – Indiana	Mozam.– Mozambique	Nev. – Nevada	Pta. – Ponta, Punta	Str. – Strait, Stretto
Amer. – America(n)	D.C. – District of	Ind. Oc. – Indian Ocean	Mt.(s).– Mont, Monte,	Nfld. – Newfoundland	Pte. – Pointe	Switz. – Switzerland
Arch. – Archipelago	Columbia	Ivory C. – Ivory Coast	Monti, Montaña,	Nic. – Nicaragua	Qué. – Québec	Tas. – Tasmania
Ariz – Arizona	Del. – Delaware	Kans. – Kansas	Mountain		Queens. – Queensland	Tenn. – Tennessee
Ark – Arkansas	Domin. – Dominica	Ky. – Kentucky	N. – Nord, Norte, North,		R. – Rio, River	Tex. – Texas
Atl. Oc. – Atlantic Ocean	Dom. Rep. – Dominican	L. – Lac, Lacul, Lago,	Northern	Okla. – Oklahoma	R.I. – Rhode Island	Trin. & Tob. – Trinidad
B. – Baie, Bahia, Bay,	Republic	Lagoa, Lake, Limni,	N.B. – New Brunswick	Ont. – Ontario	Ra.(s). – Range(s)	& Tobago
Bucht, Bugt	E. – East	Loch, Lough	N.C. – North Carolina	Oreg. – Oregon	Reg. – Region	U.A.E. – United Arab
B.C. – British Columbia	El Salv. – El Salvador	La. – Louisiana	N. Cal. – New Caledonia	P.E.I. – Prince Edward	Rep. – Republic	Emirates
Bangla. – Bangladesh	Eq. Guin. – Equatorial	Lux. – Luxembourg	N. Dak. – North Dakota	Island	Res. – Reserve,	U.K. – United Kingdom
C. – Cabo, Cap, Cape,	Guinea	Madag. – Madagascar	N.H. – New Hampshire	Pa. – Pennsylvania	Reservoir	U.S.A. – United States
Coast	Fla. – Florida	Man. – Manitoba	N.J. – New Jersey	Pac. Oc. – Pacific Ocean	S. – San, South	of America
C.A.R. – Central African	Falk. Is. – Falkland Is.	Mass.– Massachusetts	N. Mex. – New Mexico	Papua N.G. – Papua	Si. Arabia – Saudi Arabia	Va. – Virginia
Republic	G. – Golfe, Golfo, Gulf	Md. – Maryland	N.S. – Nova Scotia	New Guinea	S.C. – South Carolina	Vic. – Victoria
C. Prov. – Cape	Ga. – Georgia	Me. – Maine	N.S.W. – New South	Pen. – Peninsula,	S. Dak. – South Dakota	Vol. – Volcano
Province	Guinea–Biss. –	Medit. S. –	Wales	Peninsule	S. Leone – Sierra Leone	Vt. – Vermont
Calif. – California	Guinea–Bissau	Mediterranean Sea	N.W.T. – North West	Phil. – Philippines	Sa. – Serra, Sierra	W. – West
Cent. – Central	Hd. – Head	Mich. – Michigan	Territory	Pk. – Park, Peak	Sask. – Saskatchewan	W. Va. – West Virginia
Chan. – Channel	Hts. – Heights	Minn. – Minnesota	N.Y. – New York	Plat. – Plateau	Scot. – Scotland	Wash. – Washington
Colo. – Colorado	I.(s). – Ile, Ilha, Insel,	Miss. – Mississippi	N.Z. – New Zealand	Prov. – Province,	Sd. – Sound	Wis. – Wisconsin

INDEX TO WORLD MAPS

Place names on the yellow-coded large scale map section are to be found in the index at the end of that section

INDEX TO WORLD MAPS

Brunei

Comilla

Brunei ■, *Asia* 22 C3 4 50N 115 0 E
Brunswick, *Germany* 10 B6 52 15N 10 31 E
Brunswick, *U.S.A.* 43 D13 43 55N 69 58W
Brussels, *Belgium* 10 C3 50 51N 4 21 E
Bryan, *U.S.A.* 42 E5 41 28N 84 33W
Bryansk, *Russia* 14 D5 53 13N 34 25 E
Bucaramanga, *Colombia* 46 B2 7 0N 73 0W
Bucharest, *Romania* 11 F14 44 27N 26 10 E
Buckhannon, *U.S.A.* 42 F7 39 0N 80 8W
Buckingham, *Canada* 43 C10 45 37N 75 24W
Bucyrus, *U.S.A.* 42 E6 40 48N 82 59W
Budapest, *Hungary* 11 E10 47 29N 19 5 E
Buena Vista, *U.S.A.* 42 G8 37 44N 79 21W
Buenos Aires, *Argentina* 47 F4 34 30S 58 20W
Buffalo, *U.S.A.* 42 D8 42 53N 78 53W
Bug →, *Poland* 11 B11 52 31N 21 5 E
Buh →, *Ukraine* 15 E5 46 59N 31 58 E
Bujumbura, *Burundi* 32 E5 3 16S 29 18 E
Bukavu, *Congo (D.R.)* 32 E5 2 20S 28 52 E
Bukittinggi, *Indonesia* 22 D2 0 20S 100 20 E
Bulandshahr, *India* 23 E6 28 28N 77 51 E
Bulawayo, *Zimbabwe* 33 J5 20 7S 28 32 E
Bulgaria ■, *Europe* 13 C11 42 35N 25 30 E
Bunbury, *Australia* 34 G2 33 20S 115 35 E
Bundaberg, *Australia* 34 E9 24 54S 152 22 E
Bundi, *India* 23 G5 25 30N 75 35 E
Buraydah, *Si. Arabia* 24 C3 26 20N 44 8 E
Burgas, *Bulgaria* 13 C12 42 33N 27 29 E
Burgersdorp, *S. Africa* 31 C4 31 0S 26 20 E
Burgos, *Spain* 9 A4 42 21N 3 41W
Burgundy = Bourgogne, *France* 8 C6 47 0N 4 50 E
Burkina Faso ■, *Africa* 30 B1 12 0N 1 0W
Burlington, *Vt., U.S.A.* 43 C11 44 29N 73 12W
Burlington, *Wis., U.S.A.* 42 D3 42 41N 88 17W
Burlyu-Tyube, *Kazakstan* 18 E9 46 30N 79 10 E
Burma ■, *Asia* 25 C8 21 0N 96 30 E
Burnie, *Australia* 34 J8 41 4S 145 56 E
Bursa, *Turkey* 13 D13 40 15N 29 5 E
Buru, *Indonesia* 22 D4 3 30S 126 30 E
Burundi ■, *Africa* 32 E5 3 15S 30 0 E
Bushehr, *Iran* 24 C4 28 55N 50 55 E
Butler, *U.S.A.* 42 E8 40 52N 79 54W
Buton, *Indonesia* 22 D4 5 0S 122 45 E
Butterworth, *Malaysia* 22 C2 5 24N 100 23 E
Butuan, *Phil.* 22 C4 8 57N 125 33 E
Buzău, *Romania* 11 F14 45 10N 26 50 E
Bydgoszcz, *Poland* 11 B9 53 10N 18 0 E
Byelorussia = Belarus ■, *Europe* 11 B14 53 30N 27 0 E
Bytom, *Poland* 11 C10 50 25N 18 54 E

C

Cabinda □, *Angola* 32 F2 5 0S 12 30 E
Cabonga, Réservoir, *Canada* 42 B9 47 20N 76 40W
Čačak, *Serbia, Yug.* 13 C9 43 54N 20 20 E
Cáceres, *Spain* 9 C2 39 26N 6 23W
Cadillac, *U.S.A.* 42 C5 44 15N 85 24W
Cádiz, *Spain* 9 D2 36 30N 6 20W
Caen, *France* 8 B3 49 10N 0 22W
Cagayan de Oro, *Phil.* 22 C4 8 30N 124 40 E
Cágliari, *Italy* 12 E3 39 13N 9 7 E
Cahors, *France* 8 D4 44 27N 1 27 E
Caicos Is., *W. Indies* 45 C10 21 40N 71 40W
Cairns, *Australia* 34 D8 16 57S 145 45 E
Cairo, *Egypt* 29 B11 30 1N 31 14 E
Calabar, *Nigeria* 30 D3 4 57N 8 20 E
Calábria □, *Italy* 12 E7 39 0N 16 30 E
Calais, *France* 8 A4 50 57N 1 56 E
Calais, *U.S.A.* 43 C14 45 11N 67 17W
Calamian Group, *Phil.* 22 B3 11 50N 119 55 E
Calapan, *Phil.* 22 B4 13 25N 121 7 E
Calcutta, *India* 23 H12 22 36N 88 24 E
Caledon, *S. Africa* 31 C2 34 14S 19 26 E
Caledon →, *S. Africa* 31 C4 30 31S 26 5 E
Calgary, *Canada* 38 C8 51 0N 114 10W
Cali, *Colombia* 46 B2 3 25N 76 35W
Calicut, *India* 25 D6 11 15N 75 43 E
California □, *U.S.A.* 40 C2 37 30N 119 30W
California, G. of, *Mexico* 44 B2 27 0N 111 0W
Calitzdorp, *S. Africa* 31 C3 33 33S 21 42 E
Callao, *Peru* 46 D2 12 0S 77 0W
Caltanissetta, *Italy* 12 F6 37 29N 14 4 E
Calvi, *France* 8 E8 42 34N 8 45 E
Calvinia, *S. Africa* 31 C2 31 28S 19 45 E
Camagüey, *Cuba* 45 C9 21 20N 78 0W
Camargue, *France* 8 E6 43 34N 4 34 E
Cambay, G. of, *India* 23 J4 20 45N 72 30 E
Cambodia ■, *Asia* 22 B2 12 15N 105 0 E
Cambrai, *France* 8 A5 50 11N 3 14 E
Cambrian Mts., *U.K.* 7 E5 52 3N 3 57W
Cambridge, *U.K.* 7 E7 52 12N 0 8 E
Cambridge, *Mass., U.S.A.* 43 D12 42 22N 71 6W
Cambridge, *Md., U.S.A.* 43 F9 38 34N 76 5W
Cambridge, *Ohio, U.S.A.* 42 E7 40 2N 81 35W
Cambridge Bay = Ikaluktutiak, *Canada* 38 B9 69 10N 105 0W
Camden, *U.S.A.* 43 F10 39 56N 75 7W
Cameroon ■, *Africa* 30 C4 6 0N 12 30 E
Cameroun, Mt., *Cameroon* 30 D3 4 13N 9 10 E
Campánia □, *Italy* 12 D6 41 0N 14 30 E
Campbellsville, *U.S.A.* 42 G5 37 21N 85 20W
Campbellton, *Canada* 43 B14 47 57N 66 43W
Campeche, *Mexico* 44 D6 19 50N 90 32W
Campeche, G. of, *Mexico* 44 D6 19 30N 93 0W
Campina Grande, *Brazil* 46 C6 7 20S 35 47W
Campinas, *Brazil* 47 E5 22 50S 47 0W
Campo Grande, *Brazil* 46 E4 20 25S 54 40W
Campos, *Brazil* 46 E5 21 50S 41 20W
Camrose, *Canada* 38 C8 53 0N 112 50W
Can Tho, *Vietnam* 22 B2 10 2N 105 46 E
Canada ■, *N. Amer.* 38 C10 60 0N 100 0W
Canadian Shield, *Canada* 39 C10 53 0N 75 0W
Canandaigua, *U.S.A.* 42 D9 42 54N 77 17W
Canary Is., *Atl. Oc.* 28 C1 28 30N 16 0W
Canaveral, C., *U.S.A.* 41 E10 28 27N 80 32W
Canberra, *Australia* 34 H8 35 15S 149 8 E
Cannes, *France* 8 E7 43 32N 7 1 E
Canso, *Canada* 43 C17 45 20N 61 0W
Cantabria □, *Spain* 9 A4 43 10N 4 0W
Cantabrian Mts., *Spain* 9 A3 43 0N 5 10W
Canterbury, *U.K.* 7 F7 51 16N 1 6 E
Canton, *N.Y., U.S.A.* 43 C10 44 36N 75 10W
Canton, *Ohio, U.S.A.* 42 E7 40 48N 81 23W
Cap-Chat, *Canada* 43 A14 49 6N 66 40W
Cap-de-la-Madeleine, *Canada* 43 B11 46 22N 72 31W
Cape Breton I., *Canada* 43 B17 46 0N 60 30W
Cape Charles, *U.S.A.* 43 G10 37 16N 76 1W
Cape Coast, *Ghana* 30 C1 5 5N 1 15W
Cape May, *U.S.A.* 43 F10 38 56N 74 56W
Cape Town, *S. Africa* 31 C2 33 55S 18 22 E
Cape Verde Is. ■, *Atl. Oc.* 27 E1 17 10N 25 20W
Cape York Peninsula, *Australia* 34 C7 12 0S 142 30 E
Capreol, *Canada* 42 B7 46 43N 80 56W
Capri, *Italy* 12 D6 40 33N 14 14 E
Caracas, *Venezuela* 46 A3 10 30N 66 55W
Carbondale, *U.S.A.* 43 E10 41 35N 75 30W
Carcassonne, *France* 8 E5 43 13N 2 20 E
Cardiff, *U.K.* 7 F5 51 29N 3 10W
Caribbean Sea, *W. Indies* 45 E10 15 0N 75 0W
Caribou, *U.S.A.* 43 B13 46 52N 68 1W
Carleton Place, *Canada* 43 C9 45 8N 76 9W
Carletonville, *S. Africa* 31 B4 26 23S 27 22 E
Carlisle, *U.S.A.* 42 E9 40 12N 77 12W
Carmaux, *France* 8 D5 44 3N 2 10 E
Carmi, *U.S.A.* 42 F3 38 5N 88 10W
Carnarvon, *Australia* 34 E1 24 51S 113 42 E
Carnarvon, *S. Africa* 31 C3 30 56S 22 8 E
Carnegie, L., *Australia* 34 F3 26 5S 122 30 E
Caro, *U.S.A.* 42 D6 43 29N 83 24W
Carolina, *S. Africa* 31 B5 26 5S 30 6 E
Caroline Is., *Pac. Oc.* 36 G6 8 0N 150 0 E
Carpathians, *Europe* 11 D11 49 30N 21 0 E
Carpentaria, G. of, *Australia* 34 C6 14 0S 139 0 E
Carpentras, *France* 8 D6 44 3N 5 2 E
Cartagena, *Colombia* 46 A2 10 25N 75 33W
Cartagena, *Spain* 9 D5 37 38N 0 59W
Casablanca, *Morocco* 28 B3 33 36N 7 36W
Cascade Ra., *U.S.A.* 40 A2 47 0N 121 30W
Casper, *U.S.A.* 40 B5 42 51N 106 19W
Caspian Sea, *Eurasia* 15 F9 43 0N 50 0 E
Cass City, *U.S.A.* 42 D6 43 36N 83 11W
Castellón de la Plana, *Spain* 9 C5 39 58N 0 3W
Castelsarrasin, *France* 8 E4 44 2N 1 7 E
Castilla La Mancha □, *Spain* 9 C4 39 30N 3 30W
Castilla y Leon □, *Spain* 9 B3 42 0N 5 0W
Castres, *France* 8 E5 43 37N 2 13 E
Castries, *St. Lucia* 44 N21 14 2N 60 58W
Cataluña □, *Spain* 9 B6 41 40N 1 15 E
Catanduanes, *Phil.* 22 B4 13 50N 124 20 E
Catánia, *Italy* 12 F6 37 30N 15 6 E
Catanzaro, *Italy* 12 E7 38 54N 16 35 E
Catskill, *U.S.A.* 43 D11 42 14N 73 52W
Catskill Mts., *U.S.A.* 43 D10 42 10N 74 25W
Caucasus Mountains, *Eurasia* 15 F7 42 50N 44 0 E
Caxias do Sul, *Brazil* 47 E4 29 10S 51 10W
Cayenne, *Fr. Guiana* 46 B4 5 5N 52 18W
Cayuga L., *U.S.A.* 42 D9 42 41N 76 41W
Cedar Rapids, *U.S.A.* 41 B8 41 59N 91 40W
Cegléd, *Hungary* 11 E10 47 11N 19 47 E
Celebes Sea, *Indonesia* 22 C4 3 0N 123 0 E
Celina, *U.S.A.* 42 E5 40 33N 84 35W
Central African Rep. ■, *Africa* 32 C4 7 0N 20 0 E
Central Makran Range, *Pakistan* 24 C5 26 30N 64 15 E
Cephalonia = Kefallinía, *Greece* 13 E9 38 20N 20 30 E
Ceram, *Indonesia* 22 D4 3 10S 129 0 E
Ceram Sea, *Indonesia* 22 D4 2 30S 128 30 E
Ceres, *S. Africa* 31 C2 33 21S 19 18 E
Cerignola, *Italy* 12 D6 41 17N 15 53 E
České Budějovice, *Czech Rep.* 10 D8 48 55N 14 25 E
Ceuta, *N. Afr.* 9 E3 35 52N 5 18W
Cévennes, *France* 8 D5 44 10N 3 50 E
Chad ■, *Africa* 29 E8 15 0N 17 15 E
Chakradharpur, *India* 23 H10 22 45N 85 40 E
Chaleur B., *Canada* 43 B15 47 55N 65 30W
Chalisgaon, *India* 23 J5 20 30N 75 10 E
Chalon-sur-Saône, *France* 8 C6 46 48N 4 50 E
Châlons-en-Champagne, *France* 8 B6 48 58N 4 20 E
Chamba, *India* 23 C6 32 35N 76 10 E
Chambal →, *India* 23 F7 26 29N 79 15 E
Chambersburg, *U.S.A.* 42 F9 39 56N 77 40W
Chambéry, *France* 8 D6 45 34N 5 55 E
Champagne, *France* 8 B6 48 40N 4 20 E
Champaign, *U.S.A.* 42 E3 40 7N 88 15W
Champlain, L., *U.S.A.* 43 C11 44 40N 73 20W
Chandigarh, *India* 23 D6 30 43N 76 47 E
Chandpur, *Bangla.* 23 H13 23 8N 90 45 E
Changchun, *China* 21 B7 43 57N 125 17 E
Changde, *China* 21 D6 29 4N 111 35 E
Changsha, *China* 21 D6 28 12N 113 0 E
Changzhou, *China* 21 C6 31 47N 119 58 E
Chanthaburi, *Thailand* 22 B2 12 38N 102 12 E
Chapleau, *Canada* 42 B6 47 50N 83 24W
Chapra, *India* 23 G10 25 48N 84 44 E
Chardzhou, *Turkmenistan* 18 F8 39 6N 63 34 E
Chārīkār, *Afghan.* 23 B2 35 0N 69 10 E
Charleroi, *Belgium* 10 C3 50 24N 4 27 E
Charles, C., *U.S.A.* 43 G10 37 7N 75 58W
Charleston, *Ill., U.S.A.* 42 F3 39 30N 88 10W
Charleston, *S.C., U.S.A.* 41 D11 32 46N 79 56W
Charleston, *W. Va., U.S.A.* 42 F7 38 21N 81 38W
Charleville, *Australia* 34 F8 26 24S 146 15 E
Charleville-Mézières, *France* 8 B6 49 44N 4 40 E
Charlevoix, *U.S.A.* 42 C5 45 19N 85 16W
Charlotte, *Mich., U.S.A.* 42 D5 42 34N 84 50W
Charlotte, *N.C., U.S.A.* 41 C10 35 13N 80 51W
Charlottesville, *U.S.A.* 42 F8 38 2N 78 30W
Charlottetown, *Canada* 43 B16 46 14N 63 8W
Charolles, *France* 8 C6 46 27N 4 16 E
Charters Towers, *Australia* 34 E8 20 5S 146 13 E
Chartres, *France* 8 B4 48 29N 1 30 E
Châteaubriant, *France* 8 C3 47 43N 1 23W
Châteaulin, *France* 8 B1 48 11N 4 8W
Châteauroux, *France* 8 C4 46 50N 1 40 E
Châtellerault, *France* 8 C4 46 50N 0 30 E
Chatham, *N.B., Canada* 43 B15 47 2N 65 28W
Chatham, *Ont., Canada* 42 D6 42 24N 82 11W
Chattanooga, *U.S.A.* 41 C9 35 3N 85 19W
Chaumont, *France* 8 B6 48 7N 5 8 E
Cheb, *Czech Rep.* 10 C7 50 9N 12 28 E
Cheboksary, *Russia* 14 C8 56 8N 47 12 E
Cheboygan, *U.S.A.* 42 C5 45 39N 84 29W
Chechenia □, *Russia* 15 F8 43 30N 45 29 E
Chedabucto B., *Canada* 43 C17 45 25N 61 8W
Chełm, *Poland* 11 C12 51 8N 23 30 E
Chelyabinsk, *Russia* 18 D8 55 10N 61 24 E
Chelyuskin, C., *Russia* 18 B12 77 30N 103 0 E
Chemnitz, *Germany* 10 C7 50 51N 12 54 E
Chenab →, *Pakistan* 23 D3 30 23N 71 2 E
Chengdu, *China* 20 C5 30 38N 104 2 E
Chennai, *India* 25 D7 13 8N 80 19 E
Cher →, *France* 8 C4 47 21N 0 29 E
Cherbourg, *France* 8 B3 49 39N 1 40W
Cheremkhovo, *Russia* 18 D12 53 8N 103 1 E
Cherepovets, *Russia* 14 C6 59 5N 37 55 E
Cherkassy, *Ukraine* 15 E5 49 27N 32 4 E
Chernigov, *Ukraine* 14 D5 51 28N 31 20 E
Chernobyl, *Ukraine* 11 C16 51 20N 30 15 E
Chernovtsy, *Ukraine* 11 D13 48 15N 25 52 E
Cherski Ra., *Russia* 18 C16 65 0N 143 0 E
Chesapeake B., *U.S.A.* 42 F9 38 0N 76 10W
Chester, *U.S.A.* 43 F10 39 51N 75 22W
Chesterfield Inlet = Igluligaarjuk, *Canada* 38 B10 63 30N 90 45W
Chesuncook L., *U.S.A.* 43 B13 46 0N 69 21W
Chhatarpur, *India* 23 G7 24 55N 79 35 E
Chiai, *Taiwan* 21 D7 23 29N 120 25 E
Chiba, *Japan* 19 B7 35 30N 140 7 E
Chibougamau, *Canada* 43 A10 49 56N 74 24W
Chibougamau L., *Canada* 43 A10 49 50N 74 20W
Chicago, *U.S.A.* 42 E4 41 53N 87 38W
Chiclayo, *Peru* 46 C2 6 42S 79 50W
Chicopee, *U.S.A.* 43 D11 42 9N 72 37W
Chicoutimi, *Canada* 43 A12 48 28N 71 5W
Chidley, C., *Canada* 39 B13 60 23N 64 26W
Chieti, *Italy* 12 C6 42 21N 14 10 E
Chihli, G. of, *China* 21 C6 39 0N 119 0 E
Chihuahua, *Mexico* 44 B3 28 40N 106 3W
Chile ■, *S. Amer.* 47 F2 35 0S 72 0W
Chilka L., *India* 23 K10 19 40N 85 25 E
Chillán, *Chile* 47 F2 36 40S 72 10W
Chillicothe, *U.S.A.* 42 F6 39 20N 82 59W
Chilpancingo, *Mexico* 44 D5 7 30N 99 30W
Chilton, *U.S.A.* 42 C3 44 2N 88 10W
Chilung, *Taiwan* 21 D7 25 3N 121 45 E
Chimborazo, *Ecuador* 46 C2 1 29S 78 55W
Chimbote, *Peru* 46 C2 9 0S 78 35W
Chimkent, *Kazakstan* 18 E8 42 18N 69 36 E
China ■, *Asia* 21 C6 30 0N 110 0 E
Chindwin →, *Burma* 25 C8 21 26N 95 15 E
Chingola, *Zambia* 33 G5 12 31S 27 53 E
Chinon, *France* 8 C4 47 10N 0 15 E
Chíos, *Greece* 13 E12 38 27N 26 9 E
Chipata, *Zambia* 33 G6 13 38S 32 28 E
Chipman, *Canada* 43 B15 46 6N 65 53W
Chita, *Russia* 18 D13 52 0N 113 35 E
Chitral, *Pakistan* 23 B3 35 50N 71 56 E
Chittagong, *Bangla.* 23 H13 22 19N 91 48 E
Cholet, *France* 8 C3 47 4N 0 52W
Chŏngjin, *N. Korea* 21 B7 41 47N 129 50 E
Chongqing, *China* 20 D5 29 35N 106 25 E
Chorzów, *Poland* 11 C10 50 18N 18 57 E
Choybalsan, *Mongolia* 21 B6 48 4N 114 30 E
Christchurch, *N.Z.* 35 J13 43 33S 172 47 E
Christiana, *S. Africa* 31 B4 27 52S 25 8 E
Chukot Ra., *Russia* 18 C19 68 0N 175 0 E
Chumphon, *Thailand* 22 B1 10 35N 99 14 E
Chur, *Switz.* 10 E5 46 52N 9 32 E
Churchill →, *Man., Canada* 38 C10 58 47N 94 12W
Churchill →, *Nfld., Canada* 39 C13 53 9N 60 10W
Churu, *India* 23 E5 28 20N 74 50 E
Chushal, *India* 23 C7 33 40N 78 40 E
Chuvashia □, *Russia* 14 C8 55 30N 47 0 E
Cicero, *U.S.A.* 42 E4 41 48N 87 48W
Ciechanów, *Poland* 11 B11 52 52N 20 38 E
Ciénaga, *Colombia* 46 A2 11 1N 74 15W
Cienfuegos, *Cuba* 45 C8 22 10N 80 30W
Cincinnati, *U.S.A.* 42 F5 39 6N 84 31W
Cinto, Mte., *France* 8 E8 42 24N 8 54 E
Circleville, *U.S.A.* 42 F6 39 36N 82 57W
Cirebon, *Indonesia* 22 D2 6 45S 108 32 E
Citlaltépetl, *Mexico* 44 D5 19 0N 97 20W
Ciudad Bolívar, *Venezuela* 46 B3 8 5N 63 36W
Ciudad Guayana, *Venezuela* 46 B3 8 0N 62 30W
Ciudad Juárez, *Mexico* 44 A3 31 40N 106 28W
Ciudad Madero, *Mexico* 44 C5 22 19N 97 50W
Ciudad Obregón, *Mexico* 44 B3 27 28N 109 59W
Ciudad Real, *Spain* 9 C4 38 59N 3 55W
Ciudad Victoria, *Mexico* 44 C5 23 41N 99 9W
Clanwilliam, *S. Africa* 31 C2 32 11S 18 52 E
Claremont, *U.S.A.* 43 D11 43 23N 72 20W
Clarksburg, *U.S.A.* 42 F7 39 17N 80 30W
Clarksville, *U.S.A.* 41 C9 36 32N 87 21W
Clearfield, *U.S.A.* 42 E8 41 2N 78 27W
Clermont-Ferrand, *France* 8 D5 45 46N 3 4 E
Cleveland, *U.S.A.* 42 E7 41 30N 81 42W
Clifton Forge, *U.S.A.* 42 G8 37 49N 79 50W
Cluj-Napoca, *Romania* 11 E12 46 47N 23 38 E
Clyde →, *U.K.* 7 D4 55 55N 4 30W
Coast Mts., *Canada* 38 C7 55 0N 129 20W
Coast Ranges, *U.S.A.* 40 B2 39 0N 123 0W
Coaticook, *Canada* 43 C12 45 10N 71 46W
Coatzacoalcos, *Mexico* 44 D6 18 7N 94 25W
Cobourg, *Canada* 42 D8 43 58N 78 10W
Cochabamba, *Bolivia* 46 D3 17 26S 66 10W
Cochin, *India* 25 E6 9 59N 76 22 E
Cochrane, *Canada* 42 A7 49 0N 81 0W
Cockburn I., *Canada* 42 C6 45 55N 83 22W
Cod, C., *U.S.A.* 41 B13 42 5N 70 10W
Cognac, *France* 8 D3 45 41N 0 20W
Coimbatore, *India* 25 D6 11 2N 76 59 E
Coimbra, *Portugal* 9 B1 40 15N 8 27W
Colebrook, *U.S.A.* 43 C12 44 54N 71 30W
Colesberg, *S. Africa* 31 C4 30 45S 25 5 E
Colima, *Mexico* 44 D4 19 14N 103 43W
Collingwood, *Canada* 42 C7 44 29N 80 13W
Colmar, *France* 8 B7 48 5N 7 20 E
Cologne, *Germany* 10 C4 50 56N 6 57 E
Colombia ■, *S. Amer.* 46 B2 3 45N 73 0W
Colombo, *Sri Lanka* 25 E6 6 56N 79 58 E
Colón, *Panama* 44 H14 9 20N 79 54W
Colonial Heights, *U.S.A.* 42 G9 37 15N 77 25W
Colorado □, *U.S.A.* 40 C5 39 30N 105 30W
Colorado →, *N. Amer.* 40 D4 31 45N 114 40W
Colorado →, *U.S.A.* 41 E7 28 36N 95 59W
Colorado Plateau, *U.S.A.* 40 C4 37 0N 111 0W
Colorado Springs, *U.S.A.* 40 C6 38 50N 104 49W
Columbia, *U.S.A.* 41 D10 34 0N 81 2W
Columbia →, *U.S.A.* 40 A2 46 15N 124 5W
Columbia, District of □, *U.S.A.* 42 F9 38 55N 77 0W
Columbus, *Ga., U.S.A.* 41 D10 32 28N 84 59W
Columbus, *Ind., U.S.A.* 42 F5 39 13N 85 55W
Columbus, *Ohio, U.S.A.* 42 F6 39 58N 83 0W
Comilla, *Bangla.* 23 H13 23 28N 91 10 E

Place names on the yellow-coded large scale map section are to be found in the index at the end of that section

INDEX TO WORLD MAPS

Place names on the yellow-coded large scale map section are to be found in the index at the end of that section

INDEX TO WORLD MAPS

Erie — Greenville

Erie, *U.S.A.* **42 D7** 42 8N 80 5W
Erie, L., *N. Amer.* **42 D7** 42 15N 81 0W
Eritrea ■, *Africa* **29 F12** 14 0N 38 30 E
Erlangen, *Germany* **10 D6** 49 36N 11 0 E
Ermelo, *S. Africa* **31 B4** 26 31S 29 59 E
Erode, *India* **25 D6** 11 24N 77 45 E
Erzgebirge, *Germany* **10 C7** 50 27N 12 55 E
Erzurum, *Turkey* **15 G7** 39 57N 41 15 E
Esbjerg, *Denmark* **6 G9** 55 29N 8 29 E
Escanaba, *U.S.A.* **42 C4** 45 45N 87 4W
Esch-sur-Alzette, *Lux.* **10 D3** 49 32N 6 0 E
Esfahan, *Iran* **24 B4** 32 39N 51 43 E
Eskilstuna, *Sweden* **6 G11** 59 22N 16 32 E
Eskimo Pt. = Arviat, *Canada* **38 B10** 61 10N 94 15W
Eskişehir, *Turkey* **15 G5** 39 50N 30 35 E
Esperance, *Australia* **34 G3** 33 45S 121 55 E
Essen, *Germany* **10 C4** 51 28N 7 0 E
Estcourt, *S. Africa* **31 B4** 29 0S 29 53 E
Estonia ■, *Europe* **14 C4** 58 30N 25 30 E
Etawah, *India* **23 F7** 26 48N 79 6 E
Ethiopia ■, *Africa* **32 C7** 8 0N 40 0 E
Ethiopian Highlands, *Ethiopia* **26 E7** 10 0N 37 0 E
Etna, *Italy* **12 F6** 37 50N 14 55 E
Euclid, *U.S.A.* **42 E7** 41 34N 81 32W
Eugene, *U.S.A.* **40 B2** 44 5N 123 4W
Euphrates →, *Asia* **24 B3** 31 0N 47 25 E
Evanston, *U.S.A.* **42 D4** 42 3N 87 41W
Evansville, *U.S.A.* **42 G4** 37 58N 87 35W
Everest, Mt., *Nepal* **23 E11** 28 5N 86 58 E
Évora, *Portugal* **9 C2** 38 33N 7 57W
Évreux, *France* **8 B4** 49 3N 1 8 E
Évvoia, *Greece* **13 E11** 38 30N 24 0 E
Exeter, *U.K.* **7 F5** 50 43N 3 31W
Extremadura □, *Spain* **9 C2** 39 30N 6 5W
Eyre, L., *Australia* **34 F6** 29 30S 137 26 E

F

Færoe Is., *Atl. Oc.* **5 C4** 62 0N 7 0W
Fairbanks, *U.S.A.* **38 B5** 64 51N 147 43W
Fairfield, *U.S.A.* **42 F3** 38 23N 88 22W
Fairmont, *U.S.A.* **42 F7** 39 29N 80 9W
Faisalabad, *Pakistan* **23 D4** 31 30N 73 5 E
Faizabad, *India* **23 F9** 26 45N 82 10 E
Fakfak, *Indonesia* **22 D5** 3 0S 132 15 E
Falkland Is. □, *Atl. Oc.* **47 H4** 51 30S 59 0W
Fall River, *U.S.A.* **43 E12** 41 43N 71 10W
Falmouth, *U.S.A.* **42 F5** 38 41N 84 20W
Falun, *Sweden* **6 F11** 60 37N 15 37 E
Farah, *Afghan.* **24 B5** 32 20N 62 7 E
Farmville, *U.S.A.* **42 G8** 37 18N 78 24W
Fatehgarh, *India* **23 F7** 27 25N 79 35 E
Fatehpur, *India* **23 G8** 25 56N 81 13 E
Faya-Largeau, *Chad* **29 E8** 17 58N 19 6 E
Fayetteville, *U.S.A.* **41 C11** 35 3N 78 53W
Fazilka, *India* **23 D5** 30 27N 74 2 E
Fdérik, *Mauritania* **28 D2** 22 40N 12 45W
Fécamp, *France* **8 B4** 49 45N 0 22 E
Fehmarn, *Germany* **10 A6** 54 27N 11 7 E
Feira de Santana, *Brazil* **46 D6** 12 15S 38 57W
Fernando Póo = Bioko, *Eq. Guin.* **30 D3** 3 30N 8 40 E
Ferrara, *Italy* **12 B4** 44 50N 11 35 E
Ferret, C., *France* **8 D3** 44 38N 1 15W
Fès, *Morocco* **28 B4** 34 0N 5 0W
Fianarantsoa, *Madag.* **33 J9** 21 26S 47 5 E
Ficksburg, *S. Africa* **31 B4** 28 51S 27 53 E
Figeac, *France* **8 D5** 44 37N 2 2 E
Fiji ■, *Pac. Oc.* **35 D14** 17 20S 179 0 E
Findlay, *U.S.A.* **42 E6** 41 2N 83 39W
Finisterre, C., *Spain* **9 A1** 42 50N 9 19W
Finland ■, *Europe* **6 F13** 63 0N 27 0 E
Finland, G. of, *Europe* **6 G12** 60 0N 26 0 E
Firozabad, *India* **23 F7** 27 10N 78 25 E
Firozpur, *India* **23 D5** 30 55N 74 40 E
Fish →, *Namibia* **31 B2** 28 7S 17 10 E
Fitchburg, *U.S.A.* **43 D12** 42 35N 71 48W
Flandre, *Europe* **10 C2** 51 0N 3 0 E
Flensburg, *Germany* **10 A5** 54 47N 9 27 E
Flers, *France* **8 B3** 48 47N 0 33W
Flinders →, *Australia* **34 D7** 17 36S 140 36 E
Flinders Ras., *Australia* **34 G6** 31 30S 138 30 E
Flint, *U.S.A.* **42 D6** 43 1N 83 41W
Flint →, *U.S.A.* **41 D10** 30 57N 84 34W
Flora, *U.S.A.* **42 F3** 38 40N 88 29W
Florence, *Italy* **12 C4** 43 46N 11 15 E
Flores, *Indonesia* **22 D4** 8 35S 121 0 E
Florianópolis, *Brazil* **47 E5** 27 30S 48 30W
Florida □, *U.S.A.* **41 E10** 28 0N 82 0W
Florida, Straits of, *U.S.A.* **45 C9** 25 0N 80 0W
Florida Keys, *U.S.A.* **41 F10** 24 40N 81 0W
Florø, *Norway* **6 F9** 61 35N 5 1 E
Focşani, *Romania* **11 F14** 45 41N 27 15 E
Fóggia, *Italy* **12 D6** 41 27N 15 34 E
Foix, *France* **8 E4** 42 58N 1 38 E
Fontainebleau, *France* **8 B5** 48 24N 2 40 E
Fontenay-le-Comte, *France* **8 C3** 46 28N 0 48W
Forlì, *Italy* **12 B5** 44 13N 12 3 E
Fort Beaufort, *S. Africa* **31 C4** 32 46S 26 40 E
Fort Collins, *U.S.A.* **40 B5** 40 35N 105 5W
Fort-Coulonge, *Canada* **42 C9** 45 50N 76 45W
Fort-de-France, *Martinique* **44 N20** 14 36N 61 2W
Fort Kent, *U.S.A.* **43 B13** 47 15N 68 36W
Fort Lauderdale, *U.S.A.* **41 E10** 26 7N 80 8W
Fort McMurray, *Canada* **38 C8** 56 44N 111 7W
Fort Sandeman, *Pakistan* **23 D2** 31 20N 69 31 E
Fort Smith, *U.S.A.* **41 C8** 35 23N 94 25W
Fort Wayne, *U.S.A.* **42 E5** 41 4N 85 9W
Fort Worth, *U.S.A.* **41 D7** 32 45N 97 18W
Fortaleza, *Brazil* **46 C6** 3 45S 38 35W
Foshan, *China* **21 D6** 23 4N 113 5 E
Fostoria, *U.S.A.* **42 E6** 41 10N 83 25W
Fougères, *France* **8 B3** 48 21N 1 14W
Foxe Chan., *Canada* **39 B11** 65 0N 80 0W
France ■, *Europe* **8 C5** 47 0N 3 0 E
Franche-Comté, *France* **8 C6** 46 50N 5 55 E
Francistown, *Botswana* **31 A4** 21 7S 27 33 E
Frankfort, *S. Africa* **31 B4** 27 17S 28 30 E
Frankfort, *Ind., U.S.A.* **42 E4** 40 17N 86 31W
Frankfort, *Ky., U.S.A.* **42 F5** 38 12N 84 52W
Frankfort, *Mich., U.S.A.* **42 C4** 44 38N 86 14W
Frankfurt, *Brandenburg, Germany* **10 B8** 52 20N 14 32 E
Frankfurt, *Hessen, Germany* **10 C5** 50 7N 8 41 E
Franklin, *N.H., U.S.A.* **43 D12** 43 27N 71 39W
Franklin, *Pa., U.S.A.* **42 E8** 41 24N 79 50W
Franz Josef Land, *Russia* **18 A7** 82 0N 55 0 E
Fraser →, *Canada* **38 D7** 49 7N 123 11W
Fraserburg, *S. Africa* **31 C3** 31 55S 21 30 E
Frederick, *U.S.A.* **42 F9** 39 25N 77 25W
Fredericksburg, *U.S.A.* **42 F9** 38 18N 77 28W
Fredericton, *Canada* **43 C14** 45 57N 66 40W
Fredonia, *U.S.A.* **42 D8** 42 26N 79 20W
Fredrikstad, *Norway* **6 G10** 59 13N 10 57 E
Free State □, *S. Africa* **31 B4** 28 30S 27 0 E
Freetown, *S. Leone* **28 G2** 8 30N 13 17W
Freiburg, *Germany* **10 E4** 47 59N 7 51 E
Fremont, *U.S.A.* **42 E6** 41 21N 83 7W
French Creek →, *U.S.A.* **42 E8** 41 24N 79 50W
French Guiana □, *S. Amer.* **46 B4** 4 0N 53 0W
French Polynesia □, *Pac. Oc.* **37 J13** 20 0S 145 0W
Fresnillo, *Mexico* **44 C4** 23 10N 103 0W
Fresno, *U.S.A.* **40 C3** 36 44N 119 47W
Frobisher B., *Canada* **39 B13** 62 30N 66 0W
Front Royal, *U.S.A.* **42 F8** 38 55N 78 12W
Frunze = Bishkek, *Kyrgyzstan* **18 E9** 42 54N 74 46 E
Frýdek-Místek, *Czech Rep.* **11 D10** 49 40N 18 20 E
Fuji-San, *Japan* **19 B6** 35 22N 138 44 E
Fujian □, *China* **21 D6** 26 0N 118 0 E
Fukui, *Japan* **19 A5** 36 5N 136 10 E
Fukuoka, *Japan* **19 C2** 33 39N 130 21 E
Fukushima, *Japan* **19 A7** 37 44N 140 28 E
Fukuyama, *Japan* **19 B3** 34 35N 133 20 E
Fulda, *Germany* **10 C5** 50 32N 9 40 E
Fulda →, *Germany* **10 C5** 51 25N 9 39 E
Fulton, *U.S.A.* **42 D9** 43 19N 76 25W
Funafuti, *Pac. Oc.* **35 B14** 8 30S 179 0 E
Fundy, B. of, *Canada* **43 C15** 45 0N 66 0W
Furneaux Group, *Australia* **34 J8** 40 10S 147 50 E
Fürth, *Germany* **10 D6** 49 28N 10 59 E
Fury and Hecla Str., *Canada* **39 B11** 69 56N 84 0W
Fushun, *China* **21 B7** 41 50N 123 56 E
Fuxin, *China* **21 B7** 42 5N 121 48 E
Fuzhou, *China* **21 D6** 26 5N 119 16 E
Fyn, *Denmark* **6 G10** 55 20N 10 30 E

G

Gabès, *Tunisia* **28 B7** 33 53N 10 2 E
Gabon ■, *Africa* **32 E2** 0 10S 10 0 E
Gaborone, *Botswana* **31 A4** 24 45S 25 57 E
Gabrovo, *Bulgaria* **13 C11** 42 52N 25 19 E
Gadag, *India* **25 D6** 15 30N 75 45 E
Gadarwara, *India* **23 H7** 22 50N 78 50 E
Gainesville, *U.S.A.* **41 E10** 29 40N 82 20W
Galápagos, *Pac. Oc.* **37 H18** 0 0 91 0W
Galaţi, *Romania* **11 F15** 45 27N 28 2 E
Galdhøpiggen, *Norway* **6 F9** 61 38N 8 18 E
Galicia □, *Spain* **9 A2** 42 43N 7 45W
Galle, *Sri Lanka* **25 E7** 6 5N 80 10 E
Gallipoli, *Turkey* **13 D12** 40 28N 26 43 E
Gallipolis, *U.S.A.* **42 F6** 38 49N 82 12W
Gällivare, *Sweden* **6 E12** 67 9N 20 40 E
Galveston, *U.S.A.* **41 E8** 29 18N 94 48W
Galway, *Ireland* **7 E2** 53 17N 9 3W
Gambia ■, *W. Afr.* **28 F1** 13 25N 16 0W
Gan Jiang →, *China* **21 D6** 29 15N 116 0 E
Gananoque, *Canada* **43 C9** 44 20N 76 10W
Gandak →, *India* **23 G10** 25 39N 85 13 E
Gandhi Sagar Dam, *India* **23 G5** 24 40N 75 40 E
Ganganagar, *India* **23 E4** 29 56N 73 56 E
Gangdisê Shan, *China* **23 D8** 31 20N 81 0 E
Ganges →, *India* **23 H13** 23 20N 90 30 E
Gangtok, *India* **23 F12** 27 20N 88 37 E
Gansu □, *China* **20 C5** 36 0N 104 0 E
Gap, *France* **8 D7** 44 33N 6 5 E
Garda, L. di, *Italy* **12 B4** 45 40N 10 41 E
Gardēz, *Afghan.* **23 C2** 33 37N 69 9 E
Garies, *S. Africa* **31 C2** 30 32S 17 59 E
Garonne →, *France* **8 D3** 45 2N 0 36W
Garoua, *Cameroon* **30 C4** 9 19N 13 21 E
Gary, *U.S.A.* **42 E4** 41 36N 87 20W
Garzê, *China* **20 C5** 31 38N 100 1 E
Gascogne, *France* **8 E4** 43 45N 0 20 E
Gascogne, G. de, *Europe* **8 D2** 44 0N 2 0W
Gaspé, *Canada* **43 A15** 48 52N 64 30W
Gaspé, C., *Canada* **43 A15** 48 48N 64 7W
Gaspé Pen., *Canada* **43 A15** 48 45N 65 40W
Gatineau →, *Canada* **43 C10** 45 27N 75 42W
Gatun, *Panama* **44 H14** 9 16N 79 55W
Gatun, L., *Panama* **44 H14** 9 7N 79 56W
Gauhati, *India* **23 F13** 26 10N 91 45 E
Gävle, *Sweden* **6 F11** 60 40N 17 9 E
Gawilgarh Hills, *India* **23 J6** 21 15N 76 45 E
Gaya, *India* **23 G10** 24 47N 85 4 E
Gaylord, *U.S.A.* **42 C5** 45 2N 84 41W
Gaziantep, *Turkey* **15 G6** 37 6N 37 23 E
Gcuwa, *S. Africa* **31 C4** 32 20S 28 11 E
Gdańsk, *Poland* **11 A10** 54 22N 18 40 E
Gdynia, *Poland* **11 A10** 54 35N 18 33 E
Gebe, *Indonesia* **22 C4** 0 5N 129 25 E
Gedser, *Denmark* **6 H10** 54 35N 11 55 E
Geelong, *Australia* **34 H7** 38 10S 144 22 E
Gejiu, *China* **20 D5** 23 20N 103 10 E
Gelsenkirchen, *Germany* **10 C4** 51 32N 7 1 E
Geneva, *Switz.* **10 E4** 46 12N 6 9 E
Geneva, *U.S.A.* **42 D9** 42 52N 76 59W
Geneva, L. = Léman, L., *Europe* **10 E4** 46 26N 6 30 E
Gennargentu, Mti. del, *Italy* **12 D3** 40 1N 9 19 E
Genoa, *Italy* **12 B3** 44 25N 8 57 E
Gent, *Belgium* **10 C2** 51 2N 3 42 E
George, *S. Africa* **31 C3** 33 58S 22 29 E
George Town, *Malaysia* **22 C2** 5 25N 100 15 E
Georgetown, *Guyana* **46 B4** 6 50N 58 12W
Georgetown, *U.S.A.* **42 F5** 38 13N 84 33W
Georgia □, *U.S.A.* **41 D10** 32 50N 83 15W
Georgia ■, *Asia* **15 F7** 42 0N 43 0 E
Georgian B., *Canada* **42 C7** 45 15N 81 0W
Gera, *Germany* **10 C7** 50 53N 12 4 E
Geraldton, *Australia* **34 F1** 28 48S 114 32 E
Geraldton, *Canada* **42 A4** 49 44N 86 59W
Germany ■, *Europe* **10 C6** 51 0N 10 0 E
Germiston, *S. Africa* **31 B4** 26 15S 28 10 E
Gerona, *Spain* **9 B7** 41 58N 2 46 E
Getafe, *Spain* **9 B4** 40 18N 3 44W
Ghaghara →, *India* **23 G10** 25 45N 84 40 E
Ghana ■, *W. Afr.* **30 C1** 8 0N 1 0W
Ghanzi, *Botswana* **31 A3** 21 50S 21 34 E
Ghazâl, Bahr el →, *Sudan* **32 C6** 9 31N 30 25 E
Ghaziabad, *India* **23 E6** 28 42N 77 26 E
Ghazipur, *India* **23 G9** 25 38N 83 35 E
Ghazni, *Afghan.* **23 C2** 33 30N 68 28 E
Ghent = Gent, *Belgium* **10 C2** 51 2N 3 42 E
Gibraltar □, *Europe* **9 D3** 36 7N 5 22W
Gibraltar, Str. of, *Medit. S.* **9 E3** 35 55N 5 40W
Gibson Desert, *Australia* **34 E4** 24 0S 126 0 E
Gifu, *Japan* **19 B5** 35 30N 136 45 E
Gijón, *Spain* **9 A3** 43 32N 5 42W
Gilgit, *India* **23 B5** 35 50N 74 15 E
Giridih, *India* **23 G11** 24 10N 86 21 E
Gironde →, *France* **8 D3** 45 32N 1 7W
Gisborne, *N.Z.* **35 H14** 38 39S 178 5 E
Giza, *Egypt* **29 C11** 30 0N 31 10 E
Gizhiga, *Russia* **18 C18** 62 3N 160 30 E
Glace Bay, *Canada* **43 B18** 46 11N 59 58W
Gladstone, *Australia* **34 E9** 23 52S 151 16 E
Gladstone, *U.S.A.* **42 C4** 45 51N 87 1W
Gladwin, *U.S.A.* **42 D5** 43 59N 84 29W
Glasgow, *U.K.* **7 D4** 55 51N 4 15W
Glasgow, *U.S.A.* **42 G5** 37 0N 85 55W
Glencoe, *S. Africa* **31 B5** 28 11S 30 11 E
Glendale, *U.S.A.* **40 D3** 34 9N 118 15W
Glens Falls, *U.S.A.* **43 D11** 43 19N 73 39W
Gliwice, *Poland* **11 C10** 50 22N 18 41 E
Głogów, *Poland* **10 C9** 51 37N 16 5 E
Glomma →, *Norway* **6 G10** 59 12N 10 57 E
Gloversville, *U.S.A.* **43 D10** 43 3N 74 21W
Gniezno, *Poland* **11 B9** 52 30N 17 35 E
Go Cong, *Vietnam* **22 B2** 10 22N 106 40 E
Goa □, *India* **25 D6** 15 33N 73 59 E
Gobabis, *Namibia* **31 A2** 22 30S 19 0 E
Gobi, *Asia* **21 B6** 44 0N 111 0 E
Godavari →, *India* **25 D7** 16 25N 82 18 E
Goderich, *Canada* **42 D7** 43 45N 81 41W
Godhra, *India* **23 H4** 22 49N 73 40 E
Godthåb = Nuuk, *Greenland* **48 C4** 64 10N 51 35W
Gogama, *Canada* **42 B7** 47 35N 81 43W
Goiânia, *Brazil* **46 D5** 16 43S 49 20W
Gold Coast, *Australia* **34 F9** 28 0S 153 25 E
Gomel, *Belarus* **11 B16** 52 28N 31 0 E
Gómez Palacio, *Mexico* **44 B4** 25 40N 104 0W
Gonabad, *Iran* **24 B4** 34 15N 58 45 E
Gonda, *India* **23 F8** 27 9N 81 58 E
Gonder, *Ethiopia* **29 F12** 12 39N 37 30 E
Gondia, *India* **23 J8** 21 23N 80 10 E
Good Hope, C. of, *S. Africa* **31 C2** 34 24S 18 30 E
Gorakhpur, *India* **23 F9** 26 47N 83 23 E
Gorkiy = Nizhniy Novgorod, *Russia* **14 C7** 56 20N 44 0 E
Görlitz, *Germany* **10 C8** 51 9N 14 58 E
Gorontalo, *Indonesia* **22 C4** 0 35N 123 5 E
Gorzów Wielkopolski, *Poland* **10 B8** 52 43N 15 15 E
Gota Canal, *Sweden* **6 G11** 58 30N 15 58 E
Gotha, *Germany* **10 C6** 50 56N 10 42 E
Gothenburg, *Sweden* **6 G10** 57 43N 11 59 E
Gotland, *Sweden* **6 G11** 57 30N 18 33 E
Göttingen, *Germany* **10 C5** 51 31N 9 55 E
Gouda, *Neths.* **10 B3** 52 1N 4 42 E
Gouin Res., *Canada* **43 A10** 48 35N 74 40W
Goulburn, *Australia* **34 G8** 34 44S 149 44 E
Governador Valadares, *Brazil* **46 D5** 18 15S 41 57W
Gozo, *Malta* **12 F6** 36 3N 14 13 E
Graaff-Reinet, *S. Africa* **31 C3** 32 13S 24 32 E
Grahamstown, *S. Africa* **31 C4** 33 19S 26 31 E
Grampian Mts., *U.K.* **7 C4** 56 50N 4 0W
Gran Canaria, *Canary Is.* **28 C1** 27 55N 15 35W
Gran Chaco, *S. Amer.* **47 E3** 25 0S 61 0W
Granada, *Spain* **9 D4** 37 10N 3 35W
Granby, *Canada* **43 C11** 45 25N 72 45W
Grand Bahama I., *Bahamas* **45 B9** 26 40N 78 30W
Grand Canyon, *U.S.A.* **40 C4** 36 3N 112 9W
Grand Canyon National Park, *U.S.A.* **40 C4** 36 15N 112 30W
Grand Cayman, *Cayman Is.* **45 D8** 19 20N 81 20W
Grand Haven, *U.S.A.* **42 D4** 43 4N 86 13W
Grand L., *Canada* **43 C14** 45 57N 66 7W
Grand Manan I., *Canada* **43 C14** 44 45N 66 52W
Grand-Mère, *Canada* **43 B11** 46 36N 72 40W
Grand Rapids, *U.S.A.* **42 D4** 42 58N 85 40W
Grand St.-Bernard, Col du, *Europe* **10 F4** 45 50N 7 10 E
Grande, Rio →, *U.S.A.* **41 E7** 25 58N 97 9W
Grande de Santiago →, *Mexico* **44 C3** 21 36N 105 26W
Grande Prairie, *Canada* **38 C8** 55 10N 118 50W
Granville, *U.S.A.* **43 D11** 43 24N 73 16W
Grasse, *France* **8 E7** 43 38N 6 56 E
Graulhet, *France* **8 E4** 43 45N 1 59 E
Grayling, *U.S.A.* **42 C5** 44 40N 84 43W
Graz, *Austria* **10 E8** 47 4N 15 27 E
Great Abaco I., *Bahamas* **45 B9** 26 25N 77 10W
Great Australian Bight, *Australia* **34 G4** 33 30S 130 0 E
Great Barrier Reef, *Australia* **34 D8** 18 0S 146 50 E
Great Basin, *U.S.A.* **40 B3** 40 0N 117 0W
Great Bear L., *Canada* **38 B7** 65 30N 120 0W
Great Belt, *Denmark* **6 G10** 55 20N 11 0 E
Great Dividing Ra., *Australia* **34 E8** 23 0S 146 0 E
Great Falls, *U.S.A.* **40 A4** 47 30N 111 17W
Great Inagua I., *Bahamas* **45 C10** 21 0N 73 20W
Great Karoo, *S. Africa* **31 C3** 31 55S 21 0 E
Great Plains, *N. Amer.* **40 A6** 47 0N 105 0W
Great Salt L., *U.S.A.* **40 B4** 41 15N 112 40W
Great Sandy Desert, *Australia* **34 E3** 21 0S 124 0 E
Great Sangi, *Indonesia* **22 C4** 3 45N 125 30 E
Great Slave L., *Canada* **38 B8** 61 23N 115 38W
Great Victoria Desert, *Australia* **34 F4** 29 30S 126 30 E
Greater Antilles, *W. Indies* **45 D10** 17 40N 74 0W
Greece ■, *Europe* **13 E9** 40 0N 23 0 E
Greeley, *U.S.A.* **40 B6** 40 25N 104 42W
Green →, *U.S.A.* **42 G4** 37 54N 87 30W
Green B., *U.S.A.* **42 C4** 45 0N 87 30W
Green Bay, *U.S.A.* **42 C4** 44 31N 88 0W
Greencastle, *U.S.A.* **42 F4** 39 38N 86 52W
Greenfield, *Ind., U.S.A.* **42 F5** 39 47N 85 46W
Greenfield, *Mass., U.S.A.* **43 D11** 42 35N 72 36W
Greenland □, *N. Amer.* **48 C4** 66 0N 45 0W
Greensboro, *U.S.A.* **41 C11** 36 4N 79 48W
Greensburg, *Ind., U.S.A.* **42 F5** 39 20N 85 29W
Greensburg, *Pa., U.S.A.* **42 E8** 40 18N 79 33W
Greenville, *Maine, U.S.A.* **43 C13** 45 28N 69 35W
Greenville, *Mich., U.S.A.* **42 D5** 43 11N 85 15W

Place names on the yellow-coded large scale map section are to be found in the index at the end of that section

INDEX TO WORLD MAPS

Greenville **Jakarta**

Greenville, *Ohio, U.S.A.* **42 E5** 40 6N 84 38W
Grenada ■, *W. Indies* **44 Q20** 12 10N 61 40W
Grenoble, *France* **8 D6** 45 12N 5 42 E
Grey Ra., *Australia* **34 F7** 27 0S 143 30 E
Greymouth, *N.Z.* **35 J13** 42 29S 171 13 E
Greytown, *S. Africa* **31 B5** 29 1S 30 36 E
Gris-Nez, C., *France* **8 A4** 50 52N 1 35 E
Grodno, *Belarus* **11 B12** 53 42N 23 52 E
Groningen, *Neths.* **10 B4** 53 15N 6 35 E
Groot →, *S. Africa* **31 C3** 33 45S 24 36 E
Groot Vis →, *S. Africa* **31 C4** 33 28S 27 5 E
Gross Glockner, *Austria* **10 E7** 47 5N 12 40 E
Groundhog →, *Canada* **42 A6** 48 45N 82 58W
Groznyy, *Russia* **15 F8** 43 20N 45 45 E
Grudziądz, *Poland* **11 B10** 53 30N 18 47 E
Guadalajara, *Mexico* **44 C4** 20 40N 103 20W
Guadalajara, *Spain* **9 B4** 40 37N 3 12W
Guadalete →, *Spain* **9 D2** 36 35N 6 13W
Guadalquivir →, *Spain* **9 D2** 36 47N 6 22W
Guadarrama, Sierra de, *Spain* **9 B4** 41 0N 4 0W
Guadeloupe □, *W. Indies* **44 L20** 16 20N 61 40W
Guadiana →, *Portugal* **9 D2** 37 14N 7 22W
Guadix, *Spain* **9 D4** 37 18N 3 11W
Guam ■, *Pac. Oc.* **36 F6** 13 27N 144 45 E
Guangdong □, *China* **21 D6** 23 0N 113 0 E
Guangxi Zhuangzu Zizhiqu □, *China* **21 D5** 24 0N 109 0 E
Guangzhou, *China* **21 D6** 23 5N 113 10 E
Guantánamo, *Cuba* **45 C9** 20 10N 75 14W
Guaporé →, *Brazil* **46 D3** 11 55S 65 4W
Guatemala, *Guatemala* **44 E6** 14 40N 90 22W
Guatemala ■, *Cent. Amer.* **44 D6** 15 40N 90 30W
Guayaquil, *Ecuador* **46 C2** 2 15S 79 52W
Guaymas, *Mexico* **44 B2** 27 59N 110 54W
Guelph, *Canada* **42 D7** 43 35N 80 20W
Guéret, *France* **8 C4** 46 11N 1 51 E
Guilin, *China* **21 D6** 25 18N 110 15 E
Guinea ■, *W. Afr.* **28 F2** 10 20N 11 30W
Guinea, Gulf of, *Atl. Oc.* **26 F3** 3 0N 2 30 E
Guinea-Bissau ■, *Africa* **28 F2** 12 0N 15 0W
Guingamp, *France* **8 B2** 48 34N 3 10W
Guiyang, *China* **20 D5** 26 32N 106 40 E
Guizhou □, *China* **20 D5** 27 0N 107 0 E
Gujarat □, *India* **23 H3** 23 20N 71 0 E
Gujranwala, *Pakistan* **23 C5** 32 10N 74 12 E
Gujrat, *Pakistan* **23 C5** 32 40N 74 2 E
Gulbarga, *India* **25 D6** 17 20N 76 50 E
Gulf, The, *Asia* **24 C4** 27 0N 50 0 E
Guna, *India* **23 G6** 24 40N 77 19 E
Guntur, *India* **25 D7** 16 23N 80 30 E
Gurgaon, *India* **23 E6** 28 27N 77 1 E
Gurkha, *Nepal* **23 E10** 28 5N 84 40 E
Guyana ■, *S. Amer.* **46 B4** 5 0N 59 0W
Guyenne, *France* **8 D4** 44 30N 0 40 E
Gwadar, *Pakistan* **24 C5** 25 10N 62 18 E
Gwalior, *India* **23 F7** 26 12N 78 10 E
Gweru, *Zimbabwe* **33 H5** 19 28S 29 45 E
Gyandzha, *Azerbaijan* **15 F8** 40 45N 46 20 E
Gympie, *Australia* **34 F9** 26 11S 152 38 E
Györ, *Hungary* **11 E9** 47 41N 17 40 E
Gyumri, *Armenia* **15 F7** 40 47N 43 50 E

H

Haarlem, *Neths.* **10 B3** 52 23N 4 39 E
Hachinohe, *Japan* **19 F12** 40 30N 141 29 E
Hadd, Ras al, *Oman* **24 C4** 22 35N 59 50 E
Haeju, *N. Korea* **21 C7** 38 3N 125 45 E
Hafizabad, *Pakistan* **23 C4** 32 5N 73 40 E
Hafnarfjörður, *Iceland* **6 B3** 64 4N 21 57W
Hagen, *Germany* **10 C4** 51 21N 7 27 E
Hagerstown, *U.S.A.* **42 F9** 39 39N 77 43W
Hague, C. de la, *France* **8 B3** 49 44N 1 56W
Haguenau, *France* **8 B7** 48 49N 7 47 E
Haifa, *Israel* **24 B2** 32 46N 35 0 E
Haikou, *China* **21 D6** 20 1N 110 16 E
Hail, *Si. Arabia* **24 C3** 27 28N 41 45 E
Hailar, *China* **21 B6** 49 10N 119 38 E
Haileybury, *Canada* **42 B8** 47 30N 79 38W
Hainan □, *China* **21 E5** 19 0N 109 30 E
Haiphong, *Vietnam* **20 D5** 20 47N 106 41 E
Haiti ■, *W. Indies* **45 D10** 19 0N 72 30W
Hakodate, *Japan* **19 F12** 41 45N 140 44 E
Halab, *Syria* **24 B2** 36 10N 37 15 E
Halberstadt, *Germany* **10 C6** 51 54N 11 3 E
Halden, *Norway* **6 G10** 59 9N 11 23 E
Haldwani, *India* **23 E7** 29 31N 79 30 E
Halifax, *Canada* **43 C16** 44 38N 63 35W
Halle, *Germany* **10 C6** 51 30N 11 56 E
Halmahera, *Indonesia* **22 C4** 0 40N 128 0 E
Halmstad, *Sweden* **6 G10** 56 41N 12 52 E
Hama, *Syria* **24 B2** 35 5N 36 40 E
Hamadan, *Iran* **24 B3** 34 52N 48 32 E
Hamamatsu, *Japan* **19 B5** 34 45N 137 45 E
Hamar, *Norway* **6 F10** 60 48N 11 7 E
Hamburg, *Germany* **10 B5** 53 33N 9 59 E
Hämeenlinna, *Finland* **6 F12** 61 0N 24 28 E
Hameln, *Germany* **10 B5** 52 6N 9 21 E
Hamersley Ra., *Australia* **34 E2** 22 0S 117 45 E
Hamilton, *Bermuda* **45 A12** 32 15N 64 45W
Hamilton, *Canada* **42 D8** 43 15N 79 50W
Hamilton, *N.Z.* **35 H14** 37 47S 175 19 E
Hamilton, *U.S.A.* **42 F5** 39 24N 84 34W
Hamm, *Germany* **10 C4** 51 40N 7 50 E
Hammerfest, *Norway* **6 D12** 70 39N 23 41 E
Hammond, *U.S.A.* **42 E4** 41 38N 87 30W
Hammonton, *U.S.A.* **43 F10** 39 39N 74 48W
Hancock, *U.S.A.* **42 B3** 47 8N 88 35W
Hangzhou, *China* **21 C7** 30 18N 120 11 E
Hannover, *Germany* **10 B5** 52 22N 9 46 E
Hanoi, *Vietnam* **20 D5** 21 5N 105 55 E
Hanover, *U.S.A.* **42 F9** 39 48N 76 59W
Haora, *India* **23 H12** 22 37N 88 20 E
Haparanda, *Sweden* **6 E12** 65 52N 24 8 E
Happy Valley-Goose Bay, *Canada* **39 C13** 53 15N 60 20W
Hapur, *India* **23 E6** 28 45N 77 45 E
Harare, *Zimbabwe* **33 H6** 17 43S 31 2 E
Harbin, *China* **21 B7** 45 48N 126 40 E
Harbor Beach, *U.S.A.* **42 D6** 43 51N 82 39W
Hardanger Fjord, *Norway* **6 F9** 60 5N 6 0 E
Harding, *S. Africa* **31 C4** 30 35S 29 55 E
Hari →, *Indonesia* **22 D2** 1 16S 104 5 E
Haridwar, *India* **23 E7** 29 58N 78 9 E
Haringhata →, *Bangla.* **23 J12** 22 0N 89 58 E
Härnösand, *Sweden* **6 F11** 62 38N 17 55 E
Harrisburg, *U.S.A.* **42 E9** 40 16N 76 53W
Harrismith, *S. Africa* **31 B4** 28 15S 29 8 E
Harrisonburg, *U.S.A.* **42 F8** 38 27N 78 52W
Harrisville, *U.S.A.* **42 C6** 44 39N 83 17W
Hart, *U.S.A.* **42 D4** 43 42N 86 22W
Hartford, *Conn., U.S.A.* **43 E11** 41 46N 72 41W
Hartford, *Ky., U.S.A.* **42 G4** 37 27N 86 55W
Harts →, *S. Africa* **31 B3** 28 24S 24 17 E
Harvey, *U.S.A.* **42 E4** 41 36N 87 50W
Haryana □, *India* **23 E6** 29 0N 76 10 E
Harz, *Germany* **10 C6** 51 38N 10 44 E
Hasa, *Si. Arabia* **24 C3** 26 0N 49 0 E
Hastings, *U.S.A.* **42 D5** 42 39N 85 17W
Hathras, *India* **23 F7** 27 36N 78 6 E
Hatteras, C., *U.S.A.* **41 C11** 35 14N 75 32W
Haugesund, *Norway* **6 G9** 59 23N 5 13 E
Havana, *Cuba* **45 C8** 23 8N 82 22W
Havel →, *Germany* **10 B7** 52 50N 12 3 E
Haverhill, *U.S.A.* **43 D12** 42 47N 71 5W
Hawaiian Is., *Pac. Oc.* **40 H17** 20 30N 156 0W
Hawkesbury, *Canada* **43 C10** 45 37N 74 37W
Hay River, *Canada* **38 B8** 60 51N 115 44W
Hazard, *U.S.A.* **42 G6** 37 15N 83 12W
Hazaribag, *India* **23 H10** 23 58N 85 26 E
Hazleton, *U.S.A.* **42 E10** 40 57N 75 59W
Hearst, *Canada* **42 A6** 49 40N 83 41W
Heath Pt., *Canada* **43 A17** 49 8N 61 40W
Hebei □, *China* **21 C6** 39 0N 116 0 E
Hechuan, *China* **20 C5** 30 2N 106 12 E
Heerlen, *Neths.* **10 C3** 50 55N 5 58 E
Hefei, *China* **21 C6** 31 52N 117 18 E
Hegang, *China* **21 B8** 47 20N 130 19 E
Heidelberg, *Germany* **10 D5** 49 24N 8 42 E
Heilbron, *S. Africa* **31 B4** 27 16S 27 59 E
Heilbronn, *Germany* **10 D5** 49 9N 9 13 E
Heilongjiang □, *China* **21 B7** 48 0N 126 0 E
Hejaz, *Si. Arabia* **24 C2** 26 0N 37 30 E
Helgoland, *Germany* **10 A4** 54 10N 7 53 E
Helmand →, *Afghan.* **24 B5** 31 12N 61 34 E
Helsingborg, *Sweden* **6 G10** 56 3N 12 42 E
Helsinki, *Finland* **6 F13** 60 15N 25 3 E
Henan □, *China* **21 C6** 34 0N 114 0 E
Henderson, *U.S.A.* **42 G4** 37 50N 87 35W
Hengyang, *China* **21 D6** 26 52N 112 33 E
Henlopen, C., *U.S.A.* **43 F10** 38 48N 75 6W
Herat, *Afghan.* **24 B5** 34 20N 62 7 E
Herford, *Germany* **10 B5** 52 7N 8 39 E
Hermanus, *S. Africa* **31 C2** 34 27S 19 12 E
Hermosillo, *Mexico* **44 B2** 29 10N 111 0W
Hernád →, *Hungary* **11 D11** 47 56N 21 8 E
's-Hertogenbosch, *Neths.* **10 C3** 51 42N 5 17 E
Hessen □, *Germany* **10 C5** 50 30N 9 0 E
High Atlas, *Morocco* **28 B3** 32 30N 5 0W
Hildesheim, *Germany* **10 B5** 52 9N 9 56 E
Hillsdale, *U.S.A.* **42 E5** 41 56N 84 38W
Hilo, *U.S.A.* **40 J17** 19 44N 155 5W
Hilversum, *Neths.* **10 B3** 52 14N 5 10 E
Himachal Pradesh □, *India* **23 D6** 31 30N 77 0 E
Himalaya, *Asia* **23 E10** 29 0N 84 0 E
Himeji, *Japan* **19 B4** 34 50N 134 40 E
Hindu Kush, *Asia* **23 B2** 36 0N 71 0 E
Hingoli, *India* **23 K6** 19 41N 77 15 E
Hinton, *U.S.A.* **42 G7** 37 40N 80 54W
Hiroshima, *Japan* **19 B3** 34 24N 132 30 E
Hisar, *India* **23 E5** 29 12N 75 45 E
Hispaniola, *W. Indies* **45 D10** 19 0N 71 0W
Hjälmaren, *Sweden* **6 G11** 59 18N 15 40 E
Ho Chi Minh City, *Vietnam* **22 B2** 10 58N 106 40 E
Hobart, *Australia* **34 J8** 42 50S 147 21 E
Hódmezövásárhely, *Hungary* **11 E11** 46 28N 20 22 E
Hoggar, *Algeria* **28 D6** 23 0N 6 30 E
Hohhot, *China* **21 B6** 40 52N 111 40 E
Hokkaidō □, *Japan* **19 F12** 43 30N 143 0 E
Holguín, *Cuba* **45 C9** 20 50N 76 20W
Hollams Bird I., *Namibia* **31 A1** 24 40S 14 30 E
Holland, *U.S.A.* **42 D4** 42 47N 86 7W
Homs, *Syria* **24 B2** 34 40N 36 45 E
Honduras ■, *Cent. Amer.* **44 E7** 14 40N 86 30W
Honduras, G. de, *Caribbean* **44 D7** 16 50N 87 0W
Hong Kong, *China* **21 D6** 22 11N 114 14 E
Hongha →, *Vietnam* **20 D5** 22 0N 104 0 E
Honiara, *Solomon Is.* **35 B10** 9 27S 159 57 E
Honolulu, *U.S.A.* **40 H16** 21 19N 157 52W
Honshū, *Japan* **19 B6** 36 0N 138 0 E
Hooghly →, *India* **23 J12** 21 56N 88 4 E
Hoopeston, *U.S.A.* **42 E4** 40 28N 87 40W
Hoorn, *Neths.* **10 B3** 52 38N 5 4 E
Hopetown, *S. Africa* **31 B3** 29 34S 24 3 E
Hopkinsville, *U.S.A.* **42 G4** 36 52N 87 29W
Hormuz, Str. of, *The Gulf* **24 C4** 26 30N 56 30 E
Horn, C., *Chile* **47 H3** 55 50S 67 30W
Hornavan, *Sweden* **6 E11** 66 15N 17 30 E
Hornell, *U.S.A.* **42 D9** 42 20N 77 40W
Hornepayne, *Canada* **42 A5** 49 14N 84 48W
Horsham, *Australia* **34 H7** 36 44S 142 13 E
Hospitalet de Llobregat, *Spain* **9 B7** 41 21N 2 6 E
Hotan, *China* **20 C2** 37 25N 79 55 E
Houghton, *U.S.A.* **42 B3** 47 7N 88 34W
Houghton L., *U.S.A.* **42 C5** 44 21N 84 44W
Houlton, *U.S.A.* **43 B14** 46 8N 67 51W
Houston, *U.S.A.* **41 E7** 29 46N 95 22W
Hovd, *Mongolia* **20 B4** 48 2N 91 37 E
Hövsgöl Nuur, *Mongolia* **20 A5** 51 0N 100 30 E
Howell, *U.S.A.* **42 D6** 42 36N 83 56W
Howick, *S. Africa* **31 B5** 29 28S 30 14 E
Howrah = Haora, *India* **23 H12** 22 37N 88 20 E
Høyanger, *Norway* **6 F9** 61 13N 6 4 E
Hradec Králové, *Czech Rep.* **10 C8** 50 15N 15 50 E
Hron →, *Slovak Rep.* **11 E10** 47 49N 18 45 E
Huainan, *China* **21 C6** 32 38N 116 58 E
Huambo, *Angola* **33 G3** 12 42S 15 54 E
Huancayo, *Peru* **46 D2** 12 5S 75 12W
Huangshi, *China* **21 C6** 30 10N 115 3 E
Hubei □, *China* **21 C6** 31 0N 112 0 E
Hudiksvall, *Sweden* **6 F11** 61 43N 17 10 E
Hudson →, *U.S.A.* **43 E10** 40 42N 74 2W
Hudson Bay, *Canada* **39 C11** 60 0N 86 0W
Hudson Falls, *U.S.A.* **43 D11** 43 18N 73 35W
Hudson Str., *Canada* **39 B13** 62 0N 70 0W
Hue, *Vietnam* **22 B2** 16 30N 107 35 E
Huelva, *Spain* **9 D2** 37 18N 6 57W
Huesca, *Spain* **9 A5** 42 8N 0 25W
Hughenden, *Australia* **34 E7** 20 52S 144 10 E
Hull = Kingston upon Hull, *U.K.* **7 E6** 53 45N 0 21W
Hull, *Canada* **43 C10** 45 25N 75 44W
Humboldt →, *U.S.A.* **40 B3** 39 59N 118 36W
Húnaflói, *Iceland* **6 B3** 65 50N 20 50W
Hunan □, *China* **21 D6** 27 30N 112 0 E
Hungary ■, *Europe* **11 E10** 47 20N 19 20 E
Hungnam, *N. Korea* **21 C7** 39 49N 127 45 E
Hunsrück, *Germany* **10 D4** 49 56N 7 27 E
Huntington, *Ind., U.S.A.* **42 E5** 40 53N 85 30W
Huntington, *W. Va., U.S.A.* **42 F6** 38 25N 82 27W
Huntsville, *Canada* **42 C8** 45 20N 79 14W
Huntsville, *U.S.A.* **41 D9** 34 44N 86 35W
Huron, L., *U.S.A.* **42 C6** 44 30N 82 40W
Húsavík, *Iceland* **6 A5** 66 3N 17 21W
Hwang-ho →, *China* **21 C6** 37 55N 118 50 E
Hyderabad, *India* **25 D6** 17 22N 78 29 E
Hyderabad, *Pakistan* **23 G2** 25 23N 68 24 E
Hyères, *France* **8 E7** 43 8N 6 9 E
Hyères, Is. d', *France* **8 E7** 43 0N 6 20 E

I

Ialomiţa →, *Romania* **11 F14** 44 42N 27 51 E
Iaşi, *Romania* **11 E14** 47 10N 27 40 E
Ibadan, *Nigeria* **30 C2** 7 22N 3 58 E
Ibagué, *Colombia* **46 B2** 4 20N 75 20W
Iberian Peninsula, *Europe* **4 H5** 40 0N 5 0W
Ibiza, *Spain* **9 C6** 38 54N 1 26 E
Iceland ■, *Europe* **6 B4** 64 45N 19 0W
Ichinomiya, *Japan* **19 B5** 35 18N 136 48 E
Idaho □, *U.S.A.* **40 B4** 45 0N 115 0W
Idar-Oberstein, *Germany* **10 D4** 49 43N 7 16 E
Ife, *Nigeria* **30 C2** 7 30N 4 31 E
Iglésias, *Italy* **12 E3** 39 19N 8 32 E
Igluligaarjuk, *Canada* **38 B10** 63 30N 90 45W
Ignace, *Canada* **42 A2** 49 30N 91 40W
Iguaçu Falls, *Brazil* **47 E4** 25 41S 54 26W
Iisalmi, *Finland* **6 F13** 63 32N 27 10 E
IJsselmeer, *Neths.* **10 B3** 52 45N 5 20 E
Ikaluktutiak, *Canada* **38 B9** 69 10N 105 0W
Ikerre-Ekiti, *Nigeria* **30 C3** 7 25N 5 19 E
Ila, *Nigeria* **30 C2** 8 0N 4 39 E
Île-de-France, *France* **8 B5** 49 0N 2 20 E
Ilesha, *Nigeria* **30 C2** 7 37N 4 40 E
Ilhéus, *Brazil* **46 D6** 14 49S 39 2W
Ili →, *Kazakstan* **18 E9** 45 53N 77 10 E
Iller →, *Germany* **10 D6** 48 23N 9 58 E
Illinois □, *U.S.A.* **41 C9** 40 15N 89 30W
Iloilo, *Phil.* **22 B4** 10 45N 122 33 E
Ilorin, *Nigeria* **30 C2** 8 30N 4 35 E
Imperatriz, *Brazil* **46 C5** 5 30S 47 29W
Imphal, *India* **25 C8** 24 48N 93 56 E
Inari, L., *Finland* **6 E13** 69 0N 28 0 E
Inchon, *S. Korea* **21 C7** 37 27N 126 40 E
Incomáti →, *Mozam.* **31 B5** 25 46S 32 43 E
Indals →, *Sweden* **6 F11** 62 36N 17 30 E
India ■, *Asia* **23 K7** 20 0N 78 0 E
Indiana, *U.S.A.* **42 E8** 40 37N 79 9W
Indiana □, *U.S.A.* **42 E4** 40 0N 86 0W
Indianapolis, *U.S.A.* **42 F4** 39 46N 86 9W
Indigirka →, *Russia* **18 B16** 70 48N 148 54 E
Indonesia ■, *Asia* **22 D3** 5 0S 115 0 E
Indore, *India* **23 H5** 22 42N 75 53 E
Indre →, *France* **8 C4** 47 16N 0 11 E
Indus →, *Pakistan* **23 G1** 24 20N 67 47 E
Ingolstadt, *Germany* **10 D6** 48 46N 11 26 E
Inn →, *Austria* **10 D7** 48 35N 13 28 E
Inner Mongolia □, *China* **21 B6** 42 0N 112 0 E
Innsbruck, *Austria* **10 E6** 47 16N 11 23 E
Inowrocław, *Poland* **11 B10** 52 50N 18 12 E
Insein, *Burma* **25 D8** 16 50N 96 5 E
Interlaken, *Switz.* **10 E4** 46 41N 7 50 E
Inuvik, *Canada* **38 B6** 68 16N 133 40W
Invercargill, *N.Z.* **35 K12** 46 24S 168 24 E
Inverness, *U.K.* **7 C4** 57 29N 4 13W
Ionia, *U.S.A.* **42 D5** 42 59N 85 4W
Ionian Is., *Greece* **13 E9** 38 40N 20 0 E
Ionian Sea, *Medit. S.* **13 E7** 37 30N 17 30 E
Iowa □, *U.S.A.* **41 B8** 42 18N 93 30W
Iowa City, *U.S.A.* **41 B8** 41 40N 91 32W
Ipoh, *Malaysia* **22 C2** 4 35N 101 5 E
Ipswich, *U.K.* **7 E7** 52 4N 1 10 E
Iquique, *Chile* **46 E2** 20 19S 70 5W
Iquitos, *Peru* **46 C2** 3 45S 73 10W
Iráklion, *Greece* **13 G11** 35 20N 25 12 E
Iran ■, *Asia* **24 B4** 33 0N 53 0 E
Iran Ra., *Malaysia* **22 C3** 2 20N 114 50 E
Irapuato, *Mexico* **44 C4** 20 40N 101 30W
Iraq ■, *Asia* **24 B3** 33 0N 44 0 E
Ireland ■, *Europe* **7 E2** 53 50N 7 52W
Irian Jaya □, *Indonesia* **22 D5** 4 0S 137 0 E
Iringa, *Tanzania* **32 F7** 7 48S 35 43 E
Irish Sea, *U.K.* **7 E4** 53 38N 4 48W
Irkutsk, *Russia* **18 D12** 52 18N 104 20 E
Iron Gate, *Europe* **11 F12** 44 42N 22 30 E
Iron Mountain, *U.S.A.* **42 C3** 45 49N 88 4W
Ironton, *U.S.A.* **42 F6** 38 32N 82 41W
Irrawaddy →, *Burma* **25 D8** 15 50N 95 6 E
Irtysh →, *Russia* **18 C8** 61 4N 68 52 E
Ísafjörður, *Iceland* **6 A2** 66 5N 23 9W
Isar →, *Germany* **10 D7** 48 48N 12 57 E
Isère →, *France* **8 D6** 44 59N 4 51 E
Iseyin, *Nigeria* **30 C2** 8 0N 3 36 E
Ishpeming, *U.S.A.* **42 B4** 46 29N 87 40W
İskenderun, *Turkey* **15 G6** 36 32N 36 10 E
Islamabad, *Pakistan* **23 C4** 33 40N 73 10 E
Island Pond, *U.S.A.* **43 C12** 44 49N 71 53W
Ismâ'ilîya, *Egypt* **29 B11** 30 37N 32 18 E
Israel ■, *Asia* **24 B2** 32 0N 34 50 E
Issoire, *France* **8 D5** 45 32N 3 15 E
İstanbul, *Turkey* **13 D13** 41 0N 29 0 E
Istres, *France* **8 E6** 43 31N 4 59 E
Istria, *Croatia* **10 F7** 45 10N 14 0 E
Itaipu Dam, *Brazil* **47 E4** 25 30S 54 30W
Italy ■, *Europe* **12 C5** 42 0N 13 0 E
Ithaca, *U.S.A.* **42 D9** 42 27N 76 30W
Ivanava, *Belarus* **11 B13** 52 7N 25 29 E
Ivano-Frankovsk, *Ukraine* **11 D13** 48 40N 24 40 E
Ivanovo, *Russia* **14 C7** 57 5N 41 0 E
Ivory Coast ■, *Africa* **28 G3** 7 30N 5 0W
Ivujivik, *Canada* **39 B12** 62 24N 77 55W
Iwaki, *Japan* **19 A7** 37 3N 140 55 E
Iwo, *Nigeria* **30 C2** 7 39N 4 9 E
Ixopo, *S. Africa* **31 C5** 30 11S 30 5 E
Izhevsk, *Russia* **14 C9** 56 51N 53 14 E
İzmir, *Turkey* **13 E12** 38 25N 27 8 E

J

Jabalpur, *India* **23 H7** 23 9N 79 58 E
Jackson, *Ky., U.S.A.* **42 G6** 37 33N 83 23W
Jackson, *Mich., U.S.A.* **42 D5** 42 15N 84 24W
Jackson, *Miss., U.S.A.* **41 D8** 32 18N 90 12W
Jacksonville, *U.S.A.* **41 D10** 30 20N 81 39W
Jacobabad, *Pakistan* **23 E2** 28 20N 68 29 E
Jaén, *Spain* **9 D4** 37 44N 3 43W
Jaffna, *Sri Lanka* **25 E7** 9 45N 80 2 E
Jagersfontein, *S. Africa* **31 B4** 29 44S 25 27 E
Jahrom, *Iran* **24 C4** 28 30N 53 31 E
Jaipur, *India* **23 F5** 27 0N 75 50 E
Jakarta, *Indonesia* **22 D2** 6 9S 106 49 E

Place names on the yellow-coded large scale map section are to be found in the index at the end of that section

INDEX TO WORLD MAPS

Jalalabad **Kür**

Jalalabad, *Afghan.* 23 B3 34 30N 70 29 E
Jalgaon, *India* 23 J5 21 0N 75 42 E
Jalna, *India* 23 K5 19 48N 75 38 E
Jalpaiguri, *India* 23 F12 26 32N 88 46 E
Jamaica ■, *W. Indies* 44 J16 18 10N 77 30W
Jamalpur, *Bangla.* 23 G12 24 52N 89 56 E
Jamalpur, *India* 23 G11 25 18N 86 28 E
Jambi, *Indonesia* 22 D2 1 38S 103 30 E
James B., *Canada* 39 C11 51 30N 80 0W
Jamestown, *Ky., U.S.A.* 42 G5 36 59N 85 4W
Jamestown, *N.Y., U.S.A.* 42 D8 42 6N 79 14W
Jammu, *India* 23 C5 32 43N 74 54 E
Jammu & Kashmir □, *India* 23 B6 34 25N 77 0 E
Jamnagar, *India* 23 H3 22 30N 70 6 E
Jamshedpur, *India* 23 H11 22 44N 86 12 E
Jaora, *India* 23 H5 23 40N 75 10 E
Japan ■, *Asia* 19 G11 36 0N 136 0 E
Japan, Sea of, *Asia* 19 G11 40 0N 135 0 E
Japurá →, *Brazil* 46 C3 3 8S 65 46W
Jask, *Iran* 24 C4 25 38N 57 45 E
Jaunpur, *India* 23 G9 25 46N 82 44 E
Java, *Indonesia* 22 D3 7 0S 110 0 E
Java Sea, *Indonesia* 22 D2 4 35S 107 15 E
Jedda, *Si. Arabia* 24 C2 21 29N 39 10 E
Jeffersonville, *U.S.A.* 42 F5 38 17N 85 44W
Jelenia Góra, *Poland* 10 C8 50 50N 15 45 E
Jena, *Germany* 10 C6 50 54N 11 35 E
Jerez de la Frontera, *Spain* 9 D2 36 41N 6 7W
Jersey City, *U.S.A.* 43 E10 40 44N 74 4W
Jerusalem, *Israel* 24 B2 31 47N 35 10 E
Jessore, *Bangla.* 23 H12 23 10N 89 10 E
Jhang Maghiana, *Pakistan* 23 D4 31 15N 72 22 E
Jhansi, *India* 23 G7 25 30N 78 36 E
Jhelum, *Pakistan* 23 C4 33 0N 73 45 E
Jhelum →, *Pakistan* 23 D4 31 20N 72 10 E
Jiamusi, *China* 21 B8 46 40N 130 26 E
Jian, *China* 21 D6 27 6N 114 59 E
Jiangsu □, *China* 21 C7 33 0N 120 0 E
Jiangxi □, *China* 21 D6 27 30N 116 0 E
Jihlava →, *Czech Rep.* 11 D9 48 55N 16 36 E
Jilin, *China* 21 B7 43 44N 126 30 E
Jilin □, *China* 21 B7 44 0N 127 0 E
Jima, *Ethiopia* 29 G12 7 40N 36 47 E
Jinan, *China* 21 C6 36 38N 117 1 E
Jinja, *Uganda* 32 D6 0 25N 33 12 E
Jinzhou, *China* 21 B7 41 5N 121 3 E
Jixi, *China* 21 B8 45 20N 130 50 E
João Pessoa, *Brazil* 46 C6 7 10S 34 52W
Jodhpur, *India* 23 F4 26 23N 73 8 E
Johannesburg, *S. Africa* 31 B4 26 10S 28 2 E
Johnson City, *U.S.A.* 43 D10 42 7N 75 58W
Johnstown, *U.S.A.* 42 E8 40 20N 78 55W
Johor Baharu, *Malaysia* 22 C2 1 28N 103 46 E
Joliet, *U.S.A.* 42 E3 41 32N 88 5W
Joliette, *Canada* 43 B11 46 3N 73 24W
Jolo, *Phil.* 22 C4 6 0N 121 0 E
Jönköping, *Sweden* 6 G10 57 45N 14 10 E
Jonquière, *Canada* 43 A12 48 27N 71 14W
Jordan ■, *Asia* 24 B2 31 0N 36 0 E
Jos, *Nigeria* 30 C3 9 53N 8 51 E
Juan de Fuca Str., *Canada* 40 A2 48 15N 124 0W
Juiz de Fora, *Brazil* 46 E5 21 43S 43 19W
Jullundur, *India* 23 D5 31 20N 75 40 E
Junagadh, *India* 23 J3 21 30N 70 30 E
Juneau, *U.S.A.* 38 C6 58 18N 134 25W
Junggar Pendi, *China* 20 B3 44 30N 86 0 E
Jupiter →, *Canada* 43 A16 49 29N 63 37W
Jura, *Europe* 8 C7 46 40N 6 5 E
Jutland, *Denmark* 6 G9 56 25N 9 30 E
Jyväskylä, *Finland* 6 F13 62 14N 25 50 E

K

K2, *Pakistan* 23 B6 35 58N 76 32 E
Kabardino Balkaria □, *Russia* 15 F7 43 30N 43 30 E
Kābul, *Afghan.* 23 B2 34 28N 69 11 E
Kabwe, *Zambia* 33 G5 14 30S 28 29 E
Kachin □, *Burma* 25 C8 26 0N 97 30 E
Kaduna, *Nigeria* 30 B3 10 30N 7 21 E
Kaesong, *N. Korea* 21 C7 37 58N 126 35 E
Kagoshima, *Japan* 19 D2 31 35N 130 33 E
Kai Is., *Indonesia* 22 D5 5 55S 132 45 E
Kaifeng, *China* 21 C6 34 48N 114 21 E
Kaiserslautern, *Germany* 10 D4 49 26N 7 45 E
Kaitaia, *N.Z.* 35 H13 35 8S 173 17 E
Kajaani, *Finland* 6 F13 64 17N 27 46 E
Kakinada, *India* 25 D7 16 57N 82 11 E
Kalaallit Nunaat = Greenland □, *N. Amer.* 48 C4 66 0N 45 0W
Kalahari, *Africa* 31 A3 24 0S 21 30 E
Kalamazoo, *U.S.A.* 42 D5 42 17N 85 35W
Kalamazoo →, *U.S.A.* 42 D4 42 40N 86 10W
Kalemie, *Congo (D.R.)* 32 F5 5 55S 29 9 E
Kalgoorlie-Boulder, *Australia* 34 G3 30 40S 121 22 E
Kalimantan, *Indonesia* 22 D3 0 0 114 0 E
Kaliningrad, *Russia* 14 D3 54 42N 20 32 E
Kalisz, *Poland* 11 C10 51 45N 18 8 E
Kalkaska, *U.S.A.* 42 C5 44 44N 85 11W
Kalmar, *Sweden* 6 G11 56 40N 16 20 E
Kalmykia □, *Russia* 15 E8 46 5N 46 1 E
Kaluga, *Russia* 14 D6 54 35N 36 10 E
Kama →, *Russia* 14 C9 55 45N 52 0 E
Kamchatka, *Russia* 18 D18 57 0N 160 0 E
Kamina, *Congo (D.R.)* 32 F5 8 45S 25 0 E
Kamloops, *Canada* 38 C7 50 40N 120 20W
Kampala, *Uganda* 32 D6 0 20N 32 30 E
Kampuchea = Cambodia ■, *Asia* 22 B2 12 15N 105 0 E
Kamyanets-Podilskyy, *Ukraine* 11 D14 48 45N 26 40 E
Kananga, *Congo (D.R.)* 32 F4 5 55S 22 18 E
Kanawha →, *U.S.A.* 42 F6 38 50N 82 9W
Kanazawa, *Japan* 19 A5 36 30N 136 38 E
Kanchenjunga, *Nepal* 23 F12 27 50N 88 10 E
Kanchipuram, *India* 25 D6 12 52N 79 45 E
Kandy, *Sri Lanka* 25 E7 7 18N 80 43 E
Kane, *U.S.A.* 42 E8 41 40N 78 49W
Kangean Is., *Indonesia* 22 D3 6 55S 115 23 E
Kanin Pen., *Russia* 14 A8 68 0N 45 0 E
Kankakee, *U.S.A.* 42 E4 41 7N 87 52W
Kankakee →, *U.S.A.* 42 E3 41 23N 88 15W
Kankan, *Guinea* 28 F3 10 23N 9 15W
Kano, *Nigeria* 30 B3 12 2N 8 30 E
Kanpur, *India* 23 F8 26 28N 80 20 E
Kansas □, *U.S.A.* 40 C7 38 30N 99 0W
Kansas City, *Kans., U.S.A.* 41 C8 39 7N 94 38W
Kansas City, *Mo., U.S.A.* 41 C8 39 6N 94 35W
Kanye, *Botswana* 31 A4 24 55S 25 28 E
Kaohsiung, *Taiwan* 21 D7 22 35N 120 16 E
Kaolack, *Senegal* 28 F1 14 5N 16 8W
Kaposvár, *Hungary* 11 E9 46 25N 17 47 E
Kapuas →, *Indonesia* 22 D2 0 25S 109 20 E
Kapuas Hulu Ra., *Malaysia* 22 C3 1 30N 113 30 E
Kapuskasing, *Canada* 42 A6 49 25N 82 30W
Kara Bogaz Gol, *Turkmenistan* 15 F9 41 0N 53 30 E
Kara Kum, *Turkmenistan* 18 F8 39 30N 60 0 E
Kara Sea, *Russia* 18 B8 75 0N 70 0 E
Karachi, *Pakistan* 23 G1 24 53N 67 0 E
Karaganda, *Kazakstan* 18 E9 49 50N 73 10 E
Karakoram Ra., *Pakistan* 23 B6 35 30N 77 0 E
Karasburg, *Namibia* 31 B2 28 0S 18 44 E
Karbala, *Iraq* 24 B3 32 36N 44 3 E
Karelia □, *Russia* 14 A5 65 30N 32 30 E
Karimata Is., *Indonesia* 22 D2 1 25S 109 0 E
Karimunjawa Is., *Indonesia* 22 D3 5 50S 110 30 E
Karlskrona, *Sweden* 6 G11 56 10N 15 35 E
Karlsruhe, *Germany* 10 D5 49 0N 8 23 E
Karlstad, *Sweden* 6 G10 59 23N 13 30 E
Karnal, *India* 23 E6 29 42N 77 2 E
Karnataka □, *India* 25 D6 13 15N 77 0 E
Kärnten □, *Austria* 10 E8 46 52N 13 30 E
Karsakpay, *Kazakstan* 18 E8 47 55N 66 40 E
Kasai →, *Congo (D.R.)* 32 E3 3 30S 16 10 E
Kashan, *Iran* 24 B4 34 5N 51 30 E
Kashi, *China* 20 C2 39 30N 76 2 E
Kassalâ, *Sudan* 29 E12 15 30N 36 0 E
Kassel, *Germany* 10 C5 51 18N 9 26 E
Kasur, *Pakistan* 23 D5 31 5N 74 25 E
Katha, *Burma* 25 C8 24 10N 96 30 E
Katihar, *India* 23 G11 25 34N 87 36 E
Katmandu, *Nepal* 23 F10 27 45N 85 20 E
Katowice, *Poland* 11 C10 50 17N 19 5 E
Katsina, *Nigeria* 30 B3 13 0N 7 32 E
Kattegat, *Denmark* 6 G10 57 0N 11 20 E
Kauai, *U.S.A.* 40 H15 22 3N 159 30W
Kaukauna, *U.S.A.* 42 C3 44 17N 88 17W
Kaunas, *Lithuania* 14 D3 54 54N 23 54 E
Kavála, *Greece* 13 D11 40 57N 24 28 E
Kawagoe, *Japan* 19 B6 35 55N 139 29 E
Kawardha, *India* 23 J8 22 0N 81 17 E
Kawasaki, *Japan* 19 B6 35 35N 139 42 E
Kayes, *Mali* 28 F2 14 25N 11 30W
Kayseri, *Turkey* 15 G6 38 45N 35 30 E
Kazakstan ■, *Asia* 18 E9 50 0N 70 0 E
Kazan, *Russia* 14 C8 55 50N 49 10 E
Kazerun, *Iran* 24 C4 29 38N 51 40 E
Kebnekaise, *Sweden* 6 E11 67 53N 18 33 E
Kecskemét, *Hungary* 11 E10 46 57N 19 42 E
Kediri, *Indonesia* 22 D3 7 51S 112 1 E
Keene, *U.S.A.* 43 D11 42 56N 72 17W
Keetmanshoop, *Namibia* 31 B2 26 35S 18 8 E
Kefallinía, *Greece* 13 E9 38 20N 20 30 E
Keflavík, *Iceland* 6 B2 64 2N 22 35W
Kelang, *Malaysia* 22 C2 3 2N 101 26 E
Kelowna, *Canada* 38 D8 49 50N 119 25W
Kemerovo, *Russia* 18 D10 55 20N 86 5 E
Kemi, *Finland* 6 E12 65 44N 24 34 E
Kemi →, *Finland* 6 E12 65 47N 24 32 E
Kendari, *Indonesia* 22 D4 3 50S 122 30 E
Kenhardt, *S. Africa* 31 B3 29 19S 21 12 E
Kenitra, *Morocco* 28 B3 34 15N 6 40W
Kenosha, *U.S.A.* 42 D4 42 35N 87 49W
Kent, *U.S.A.* 42 E7 41 9N 81 22W
Kenton, *U.S.A.* 42 E6 40 39N 83 37W
Kentucky □, *U.S.A.* 42 G5 37 0N 84 0W
Kentucky →, *U.S.A.* 42 F5 38 41N 85 11W
Kentville, *Canada* 43 C15 45 6N 64 29W
Kenya ■, *Africa* 32 D7 1 0N 38 0 E
Kenya, Mt., *Kenya* 32 E7 0 10S 37 18 E
Kerala □, *India* 25 D6 11 0N 76 15 E
Kerch, *Ukraine* 15 E6 45 20N 36 20 E
Kerinci, *Indonesia* 22 D2 1 40S 101 15 E
Kermadec Trench, *Pac. Oc.* 35 G15 30 30S 176 0W
Kerman, *Iran* 24 B4 30 15N 57 1 E
Kestell, *S. Africa* 31 B4 28 17S 28 42 E
Ketchikan, *U.S.A.* 38 C6 55 21N 131 39W
Kewaunee, *U.S.A.* 42 C4 44 27N 87 31W
Keweenaw B., *U.S.A.* 42 B3 47 0N 88 15W
Keweenaw Pen., *U.S.A.* 42 B3 47 30N 88 0W
Keweenaw Pt., *U.S.A.* 42 B4 47 25N 87 43W
Key West, *U.S.A.* 41 F10 24 33N 81 48W
Keyser, *U.S.A.* 42 F8 39 26N 78 59W
Khabarovsk, *Russia* 18 E15 48 30N 135 5 E
Khairpur, *Pakistan* 23 F2 27 32N 68 49 E
Khamas Country, *Botswana* 31 A4 21 45S 26 30 E
Khandwa, *India* 23 J6 21 49N 76 22 E
Khanewal, *Pakistan* 23 D3 30 20N 71 55 E
Khaniá, *Greece* 13 G11 35 30N 24 4 E
Kharagpur, *India* 23 H11 22 20N 87 25 E
Khargon, *India* 23 J5 21 45N 75 40 E
Kharkov, *Ukraine* 15 E6 49 58N 36 20 E
Khartoum, *Sudan* 29 E11 15 31N 32 35 E
Khaskovo, *Bulgaria* 13 D11 41 56N 25 30 E
Khatanga, *Russia* 18 B12 72 0N 102 20 E
Kherson, *Ukraine* 15 E5 46 35N 32 35 E
Khmelnitskiy, *Ukraine* 11 D14 49 23N 27 0 E
Khorixas, *Namibia* 31 A1 20 16S 14 59 E
Khorramshahr, *Iran* 24 B3 30 29N 48 15 E
Khouribga, *Morocco* 28 B3 32 58N 6 57W
Khulna, *Bangla.* 23 H12 22 45N 89 34 E
Khulna □, *Bangla.* 23 H12 22 25N 89 35 E
Khumago, *Botswana* 31 A3 20 26S 24 32 E
Khushab, *Pakistan* 23 C4 32 20N 72 20 E
Khuzdar, *Pakistan* 23 F1 27 52N 66 30 E
Kicking Horse Pass, *Canada* 38 C8 51 28N 116 16W
Kiel, *Germany* 10 A6 54 19N 10 8 E
Kiel Canal = Nord-Ostsee-Kanal →, *Germany* 10 A5 54 12N 9 32 E
Kielce, *Poland* 11 C11 50 52N 20 42 E
Kieler Bucht, *Germany* 10 A6 54 35N 10 25 E
Kiev, *Ukraine* 11 C16 50 30N 30 28 E
Kigali, *Rwanda* 32 E6 1 59S 30 4 E
Kigoma-Ujiji, *Tanzania* 32 E5 4 55S 29 36 E
Kikwit, *Congo (D.R.)* 32 E3 5 0S 18 45 E
Kilimanjaro, *Tanzania* 32 E7 3 7S 37 20 E
Kimberley, *S. Africa* 31 B3 28 43S 24 46 E
Kimberley Plateau, *Australia* 34 D4 16 20S 127 0 E
Kincardine, *Canada* 42 C7 44 10N 81 40W
Kindu, *Congo (D.R.)* 32 E5 2 55S 25 50 E
King William's Town, *S. Africa* 31 C4 32 51S 27 22 E
Kingston, *Canada* 42 C9 44 14N 76 30W
Kingston, *Jamaica* 44 K17 18 0N 76 50W
Kingston, *N.Y., U.S.A.* 43 E10 41 56N 73 59W
Kingston, *Pa., U.S.A.* 43 E10 41 16N 75 54W
Kingston upon Hull, *U.K.* 7 E6 53 45N 0 21W
Kingstown, *St. Vincent* 44 P20 13 10N 61 10W
Kinshasa, *Congo (D.R.)* 32 E3 4 20S 15 15 E
Kirensk, *Russia* 18 D12 57 50N 107 55 E
Kirgiz Steppe, *Eurasia* 15 D10 50 0N 55 0 E
Kiribati ■, *Pac. Oc.* 36 H10 5 0S 180 0 E
Kirkenes, *Norway* 6 E14 69 40N 30 5 E
Kirkland Lake, *Canada* 42 A7 48 9N 80 2W
Kirkuk, *Iraq* 24 B3 35 30N 44 21 E
Kirkwood, *S. Africa* 31 C4 33 22S 25 15 E
Kirov, *Russia* 14 C8 58 35N 49 40 E
Kirovograd, *Ukraine* 15 E5 48 35N 32 20 E
Kirthar Range, *Pakistan* 23 F1 27 0N 67 0 E
Kiruna, *Sweden* 6 E12 67 52N 20 15 E
Kisangani, *Congo (D.R.)* 32 D5 0 35N 25 15 E
Kishanganj, *India* 23 F12 26 3N 88 14 E
Kishinev, *Moldova* 11 E15 47 0N 28 50 E
Kisumu, *Kenya* 32 E6 0 3S 34 45 E
Kitakyūshū, *Japan* 19 C2 33 50N 130 50 E
Kitchener, *Canada* 42 D7 43 27N 80 29W
Kíthira, *Greece* 13 F10 36 8N 23 0 E
Kitimat, *Canada* 38 C7 54 3N 128 38W
Kittanning, *U.S.A.* 42 E8 40 49N 79 31W
Kitwe, *Zambia* 33 G5 12 54S 28 13 E
Kivu, L., *Congo (D.R.)* 32 E5 1 48S 29 0 E
Kladno, *Czech Rep.* 10 C8 50 10N 14 7 E
Klagenfurt, *Austria* 10 E8 46 38N 14 20 E
Klar →, *Sweden* 6 G10 59 23N 13 32 E
Klawer, *S. Africa* 31 C2 31 44S 18 36 E
Klerksdorp, *S. Africa* 31 B4 26 53S 26 38 E
Klipplaat, *S. Africa* 31 C3 33 1S 24 22 E
Klondike, *Canada* 38 B6 64 0N 139 26W
Klyuchevsk Vol., *Russia* 18 D18 55 50N 160 30 E
Knossós, *Greece* 13 G11 35 16N 25 10 E
Knoxville, *U.S.A.* 41 C10 35 58N 83 55W
Knysna, *S. Africa* 31 C3 34 2S 23 2 E
Kōbe, *Japan* 19 B4 34 45N 135 10 E
Koblenz, *Germany* 10 C4 50 21N 7 36 E
Kobroor, *Indonesia* 22 D5 6 10S 134 30 E
Koch Bihar, *India* 23 F12 26 22N 89 29 E
Kodiak I., *U.S.A.* 38 C4 57 30N 152 45W
Koffiefontein, *S. Africa* 31 B4 29 30S 25 0 E
Koforidua, *Ghana* 30 C1 6 3N 0 17W
Koh-i-Bābā, *Afghan.* 23 B1 34 30N 67 0 E
Kohat, *Pakistan* 23 C3 33 40N 71 29 E
Kokchetav, *Kazakstan* 18 D8 53 20N 69 25 E
Kokomo, *U.S.A.* 42 E4 40 29N 86 8W
Kokstad, *S. Africa* 31 C4 30 32S 29 29 E
Kola Pen., *Russia* 14 A6 67 30N 38 0 E
Kolar, *India* 25 D6 13 12N 78 15 E
Kolguyev I., *Russia* 14 A8 69 20N 48 30 E
Kolhapur, *India* 25 D6 16 43N 74 15 E
Kolkata = Calcutta, *India* 23 H12 22 36N 88 24 E
Kolomna, *Russia* 14 C6 55 8N 38 45 E
Kolwezi, *Congo (D.R.)* 32 G5 10 40S 25 25 E
Kolyma →, *Russia* 18 C18 69 30N 161 0 E
Kolyma Ra., *Russia* 18 C17 63 0N 157 0 E
Komandorskiye Is., *Russia* 18 D18 55 0N 167 0 E
Komatipoort, *S. Africa* 31 B5 25 25S 31 55 E
Komi □, *Russia* 14 B10 64 0N 55 0 E
Kompong Cham, *Cambodia* 22 B2 12 0N 105 30 E
Kompong Chhnang, *Cambodia* 22 B2 12 20N 104 35 E
Kompong Som, *Cambodia* 22 B2 10 38N 103 30 E
Komsomolets I., *Russia* 18 A11 80 30N 95 0 E
Komsomolsk, *Russia* 18 D15 50 30N 137 0 E
Konin, *Poland* 11 B10 52 12N 18 15 E
Konya, *Turkey* 15 G5 37 52N 32 35 E
Korce, *Albania* 13 D9 40 37N 20 50 E
Korea, North ■, *Asia* 21 C7 40 0N 127 0 E
Korea, South ■, *Asia* 21 C7 36 0N 128 0 E
Korea Strait, *Asia* 21 C7 34 0N 129 30 E
Kōriyama, *Japan* 19 A7 37 24N 140 23 E
Korla, *China* 20 B3 41 45N 86 4 E
Körös →, *Hungary* 11 E11 46 43N 20 12 E
Kortrijk, *Belgium* 10 C2 50 50N 3 17 E
Kos, *Greece* 13 F12 36 50N 27 15 E
Košice, *Slovak Rep.* 11 D11 48 42N 21 15 E
Kosovo □, *Serbia, Yug.* 13 C9 42 30N 21 0 E
Kosti, *Sudan* 29 F11 13 8N 32 43 E
Kostroma, *Russia* 14 C7 57 50N 40 58 E
Koszalin, *Poland* 10 A9 54 11N 16 8 E
Kota, *India* 23 G5 25 14N 75 49 E
Kota Baharu, *Malaysia* 22 C2 6 7N 102 14 E
Kota Kinabalu, *Malaysia* 22 C3 6 0N 116 4 E
Kotka, *Finland* 6 F13 60 28N 26 58 E
Kotri, *Pakistan* 23 G2 25 22N 68 22 E
Kotuy →, *Russia* 18 B12 71 54N 102 6 E
Kounradskiy, *Kazakstan* 18 E9 46 59N 75 0 E
Kra, Isthmus of, *Thailand* 22 B1 10 15N 99 30 E
Kragujevac, *Serbia, Yug.* 13 B9 44 2N 20 56 E
Krajina, *Bos.-H.* 12 B7 44 45N 16 35 E
Kraków, *Poland* 11 C10 50 4N 19 57 E
Krasnodar, *Russia* 15 E6 45 5N 39 0 E
Krasnoturinsk, *Russia* 14 C11 59 46N 60 12 E
Krasnovodsk, *Turkmenistan* 15 F9 40 5N 53 5 E
Krasnoyarsk, *Russia* 18 D11 56 8N 93 0 E
Kratie, *Cambodia* 22 B2 12 32N 106 10 E
Krefeld, *Germany* 10 C4 51 20N 6 33 E
Kremenchug, *Ukraine* 15 E5 49 5N 33 25 E
Krishna →, *India* 25 D7 15 57N 80 59 E
Krishnanagar, *India* 23 H12 23 24N 88 33 E
Kristiansand, *Norway* 6 G9 58 8N 8 1 E
Kristiansund, *Norway* 6 F9 63 7N 7 45 E
Krivoy Rog, *Ukraine* 15 E5 47 51N 33 20 E
Kroonstad, *S. Africa* 31 B4 27 43S 27 19 E
Krosno, *Poland* 11 D11 49 42N 21 46 E
Kruger Nat. Park, *S. Africa* 31 A5 23 30S 31 40 E
Krugersdorp, *S. Africa* 31 B4 26 5S 27 46 E
Kruisfontein, *S. Africa* 31 C3 33 59S 24 43 E
Kruševac, *Serbia, Yug.* 13 C9 43 35N 21 28 E
Kuala Lumpur, *Malaysia* 22 C2 3 9N 101 41 E
Kuala Terengganu, *Malaysia* 22 C2 5 20N 103 8 E
Kualakapuas, *Indonesia* 22 D3 2 55S 114 20 E
Kucing, *Malaysia* 22 C3 1 33N 110 25 E
Kudat, *Malaysia* 22 C3 6 55N 116 55 E
Kugluktuk, *Canada* 38 B8 67 50N 115 5W
Kumanovo, *Macedonia* 13 C9 42 9N 21 42 E
Kumasi, *Ghana* 30 C1 6 41N 1 38W
Kumayri = Gyumri, *Armenia* 15 F7 40 47N 43 50 E
Kumbakonam, *India* 25 D6 10 58N 79 25 E
Kunlun Shan, *Asia* 20 C3 36 0N 86 30 E
Kunming, *China* 20 D5 25 1N 102 41 E
Kuopio, *Finland* 6 F13 62 53N 27 35 E
Kupang, *Indonesia* 22 E4 10 19S 123 39 E
Kür →, *Azerbaijan* 15 G8 39 29N 49 15 E

Place names on the yellow-coded large scale map section are to be found in the index at the end of that section

Place names on the yellow-coded large scale map section are to be found in the index at the end of that section

INDEX TO WORLD MAPS

Place names on the yellow-coded large scale map section are to be found in the index at the end of that section

Nagaoka

O

Oshogbo

Place names on the yellow-coded large scale map section are to be found in the index at the end of that section

INDEX TO WORLD MAPS

Osijek

Queensland

Osijek, Croatia 13 B8 45 34N 18 41 E
Osizweni, S. Africa 31 B5 27 49S 30 7 E
Oskarshamn, Sweden 6 G11 57 15N 16 27 E
Oslo, Norway 6 G10 59 55N 10 45 E
Oslo Fjord, Norway 6 G10 59 20N 10 35 E
Osnabrück, Germany 10 B5 52 17N 8 3 E
Osorno, Chile 47 G2 40 25S 73 0W
Ostend = Oostende, Belgium 10 C2 51 15N 2 54 E
Österdalälven, Sweden 6 F10 61 30N 13 45 E
Östersund, Sweden 6 F10 63 10N 14 38 E
Ostfriesische Inseln, Germany 10 B4 53 42N 7 0 E
Ostrava, Czech Rep. 11 D10 49 51N 18 18 E
Ostrołęka, Poland 11 B11 53 4N 21 32 E
Ostrów Wielkopolski, Poland 11 C9 51 36N 17 44 E
Ostrowiec-Świętokrzyski, Poland 11 C11 50 55N 21 22 E
Oswego, U.S.A. 42 D9 43 27N 76 31W
Otaru, Japan 19 F12 43 10N 141 0 E
Otjiwarongo, Namibia 31 A2 20 30S 16 33 E
Otranto, Str. of, Italy 13 D8 40 15N 18 40 E
Ōtsu, Japan 19 B4 35 0N 135 50 E
Ottawa, Canada 43 C10 45 27N 75 42W
Ottawa →, Canada 43 C10 45 27N 74 8W
Ouagadougou, Burkina Faso 30 B1 12 25N 1 30W
Oubangi →, Congo (D.R.) 32 E3 0 30S 17 50 E
Oudtshoorn, S. Africa 31 C3 33 35S 22 14 E
Oujda, Morocco 28 B4 34 41N 1 55W
Oulu, Finland 6 E13 65 1N 25 29 E
Oulu →, Finland 6 E13 65 1N 25 30 E
Oulu, L., Finland 6 F13 64 25N 27 15 E
Outer Hebrides, U.K. 7 C3 57 30N 7 40W
Outjo, Namibia 31 A2 20 5S 16 7 E
Oviedo, Spain 9 A3 43 25N 5 50W
Owen Sound, Canada 42 C7 44 35N 80 55W
Owensboro, U.S.A. 42 G4 37 46N 87 7W
Owo, Nigeria 30 C3 7 10N 5 39 E
Owosso, U.S.A. 42 D5 43 0N 84 10W
Oxford, U.K. 7 F6 51 46N 1 15W
Oyo, Nigeria 30 C2 7 46N 3 56 E
Ozamiz, Phil. 22 C4 8 15N 123 50 E
Ozark Plateau, U.S.A. 41 C8 37 20N 91 40W

P

Paarl, S. Africa 31 C2 33 45S 18 56 E
Pab Hills, Pakistan 23 F1 26 30N 66 45 E
Pabna, Bangla. 23 G12 24 1N 89 18 E
Pacaraima, Sierra, Venezuela 46 B3 4 0N 62 30W
Pachuca, Mexico 44 C5 20 10N 98 40W
Pacific Ocean, Pac. Oc. 37 G14 10 0N 140 0W
Padang, Indonesia 22 D2 1 0S 100 20 E
Paderborn, Germany 10 C5 51 42N 8 45 E
Padua, Italy 12 B4 45 25N 11 53 E
Paducah, U.S.A. 42 G3 37 5N 88 37W
Painesville, U.S.A. 42 E7 41 43N 81 15W
Paintsville, U.S.A. 42 G6 37 49N 82 48W
País Vasco □, Spain 9 A4 42 50N 2 45W
Pakistan ■, Asia 23 D3 30 0N 70 0 E
Pakse, Laos 22 B2 15 5N 105 52 E
Palanpur, India 23 G4 24 10N 72 25 E
Palapye, Botswana 31 A4 22 30S 27 7 E
Palau ■, Pac. Oc. 36 G5 7 30N 134 30 E
Palawan, Phil. 22 C3 9 30N 118 30 E
Palembang, Indonesia 22 D2 3 0S 104 50 E
Palencia, Spain 9 A3 42 1N 4 34W
Palermo, Italy 12 E5 38 7N 13 22 E
Palghat, India 25 D6 10 46N 76 42 E
Pali, India 23 G4 25 50N 73 20 E
Palma de Mallorca, Spain 9 C7 39 35N 2 39 E
Palmerston North, N.Z. 35 J14 40 21S 175 39 E
Palmira, Colombia 46 B2 3 32N 76 16W
Pamiers, France 8 E4 43 7N 1 39 E
Pamirs, Tajikistan 25 B6 37 40N 73 0 E
Pamlico Sd., U.S.A. 41 C11 35 20N 76 0W
Pampas, Argentina 47 F3 35 0S 63 0W
Pamplona, Spain 9 A5 42 48N 1 38W
Panamá, Panama 44 H14 9 0N 79 25W
Panama ■, Cent. Amer. 45 F9 8 48N 79 55W
Panamá, G. de, Panama 45 F9 8 4N 79 20W
Panama Canal, Panama 44 H14 9 10N 79 37W
Panay, Phil. 22 B4 11 10N 122 30 E
Pančevo, Serbia, Yug. 13 B9 44 52N 20 41 E
Pangkalpinang, Indonesia 22 D2 2 0S 106 0 E
Panjim, India 25 D6 15 25N 73 50 E
Pantar, Indonesia 22 D4 8 28S 124 10 E
Pantelleria, Italy 12 F4 36 50N 11 57 E
Papua New Guinea ■, Oceania 34 B8 8 0S 145 0 E
Pará □, Brazil 46 C4 3 20S 52 0W
Paracel Is., Pac. Oc. 22 B3 15 50N 112 0 E
Paraguay ■, S. Amer. 47 E4 23 0S 57 0W
Paraguay →, Paraguay 47 E4 27 18S 58 38W
Paramaribo, Surinam 46 B4 5 50N 55 10W
Paraná, Argentina 47 F3 31 45S 60 30W
Paraná →, Argentina 47 F4 33 43S 59 15W
Parbhani, India 23 K6 19 8N 76 52 E
Pardubice, Czech Rep. 10 C8 50 3N 15 45 E
Paris, France 8 B5 48 50N 2 20 E
Parkersburg, U.S.A. 42 F7 39 16N 81 34W
Parma, Italy 12 B4 44 48N 10 20 E
Parnaíba →, Brazil 46 C5 3 0S 41 50W
Parry Sound, Canada 42 C7 45 20N 80 0W
Parys, S. Africa 31 B4 26 52S 27 29 E
Pasni, Pakistan 24 C5 25 15N 63 27 E
Passau, Germany 10 D7 48 34N 13 28 E
Pasto, Colombia 46 B2 1 13N 77 17W
Patagonia, Argentina 47 G3 45 0S 69 0W
Patan, India 23 H4 23 54N 72 14 E
Patan, Nepal 23 F10 27 40N 85 20 E
Paterson, U.S.A. 43 E10 40 55N 74 11W
Pathankot, India 23 C5 32 18N 75 45 E
Patiala, India 23 D6 30 23N 76 26 E
Patna, India 23 G10 25 35N 85 12 E
Patos, L. dos, Brazil 47 F4 31 20S 51 0W
Patras, Greece 13 E9 38 14N 21 47 E
Patten, U.S.A. 43 C13 46 0N 68 38W
Patuakhali, Bangla. 23 H13 22 20N 90 25 E
Pau, France 8 E3 43 19N 0 25W
Pavia, Italy 12 B3 45 7N 9 8 E
Pavlodar, Kazakstan 18 D9 52 33N 77 0 E
Pawtucket, U.S.A. 43 E12 41 53N 71 23W
Paxton, U.S.A. 42 E3 40 27N 88 6W
Pazardzhik, Bulgaria 13 C11 42 12N 24 20 E
Peace →, Canada 38 C8 59 0N 111 25W
Pechora →, Russia 14 A9 68 13N 54 15 E
Pécs, Hungary 11 E10 46 5N 18 15 E
Pegu Yoma, Burma 25 D8 19 0N 96 0 E
Pekalongan, Indonesia 22 D2 6 53S 109 40 E
Pekanbaru, Indonesia 22 C2 0 30N 101 15 E
Peking = Beijing, China 21 C6 39 55N 116 20 E
Peleng, Indonesia 22 D4 1 20S 123 30 E
Peloponnese □, Greece 13 F10 37 10N 22 0 E
Pelotas, Brazil 47 F4 31 42S 52 23W
Pelvoux, Massif du, France 8 D7 44 52N 6 20 E
Pematangsiantar, Indonesia 22 C1 2 57N 99 5 E
Pemba I., Tanzania 32 F7 5 0S 39 45 E
Pembroke, Canada 42 C9 45 50N 77 7W
Penetanguishene, Canada 42 C8 44 50N 79 55W
Peninsular Malaysia □, Malaysia 22 C2 4 0N 102 0 E
Penmarch, Pte. de, France 8 C1 47 48N 4 22W
Penn Yan, U.S.A. 42 D9 42 40N 77 3W
Pennines, U.K. 7 D5 54 45N 2 27W
Pennsylvania □, U.S.A. 42 E8 40 45N 77 30W
Pensacola, U.S.A. 41 D9 30 25N 87 13W
Penza, Russia 14 D8 53 15N 45 5 E
Peoria, U.S.A. 41 B9 40 42N 89 36W
Perdido, Mte., Spain 9 A6 42 40N 0 5 E
Péribonca →, Canada 43 A11 48 45N 72 5W
Périgueux, France 8 D4 45 10N 0 42 E
Perm, Russia 14 C10 58 0N 56 10 E
Perpignan, France 8 E5 42 42N 2 53 E
Perth, Australia 34 G2 31 57S 115 52 E
Perth, Canada 42 C9 44 55N 76 15W
Perth, U.K. 7 C5 56 24N 3 26W
Peru, U.S.A. 42 E4 40 45N 86 4W
Peru ■, S. Amer. 46 C2 4 0S 75 0W
Perúgia, Italy 12 C5 43 7N 12 23 E
Pescara, Italy 12 C6 42 28N 14 13 E
Peshawar, Pakistan 23 B3 34 2N 71 37 E
Peterborough, Canada 39 D12 44 20N 78 20W
Petersburg, U.S.A. 42 G9 37 14N 77 24W
Petoskey, U.S.A. 42 C5 45 22N 84 57W
Petropavlovsk-Kamchatskiy, Russia 18 D17 53 3N 158 43 E
Petrópolis, Brazil 47 E5 22 33S 43 9W
Petrovsk, Russia 18 D12 51 20N 108 55 E
Petrozavodsk, Russia 14 B5 61 41N 34 20 E
Pforzheim, Germany 10 D5 48 52N 8 41 E
Phalodi, India 23 F4 27 12N 72 24 E
Phan Rang, Vietnam 22 B2 11 34N 109 0 E
Philadelphia, U.S.A. 43 E10 39 57N 75 10W
Philippines ■, Asia 22 B4 12 0N 123 0 E
Phitsanulok, Thailand 22 B2 16 50N 100 12 E
Phnom Penh, Cambodia 22 B2 11 33N 104 55 E
Phoenix, U.S.A. 40 D4 33 27N 112 4W
Phoenix Is., Kiribati 35 A16 3 30S 172 0W
Phuket, Thailand 22 C1 7 52N 98 22 E
Piacenza, Italy 12 B3 45 1N 9 40 E
Piatra Neamţ, Romania 11 E14 46 56N 26 21 E
Picardie, France 8 B5 49 50N 3 0 E
Picton, Canada 42 C9 44 1N 77 9W
Pidurutalagala, Sri Lanka 25 E7 7 10N 80 50 E
Piedmont □, Italy 12 B2 45 0N 8 0 E
Piedras Negras, Mexico 44 B4 28 42N 100 31W
Piet Retief, S. Africa 31 B5 27 1S 30 50 E
Pietermaritzburg, S. Africa 31 B5 29 35S 30 25 E
Pietersburg, S. Africa 31 A4 23 54S 29 25 E
Pigeon, U.S.A. 42 D6 43 50N 83 16W
Piketberg, S. Africa 31 C2 32 55S 18 40 E
Pikeville, U.S.A. 42 G6 37 29N 82 31W
Pilcomayo →, Paraguay 47 E4 25 21S 57 42W
Pilibhit, India 23 E7 28 40N 79 50 E
Pilica →, Poland 11 C11 51 52N 21 17 E
Pinang, Malaysia 22 C2 5 25N 100 15 E
Pindus Mts., Greece 13 E9 40 0N 21 0 E
Pine Bluff, U.S.A. 41 D8 34 13N 92 1W
Pinetown, S. Africa 31 B5 29 48S 30 54 E
Pingxiang, China 20 D5 22 6N 106 46 E
Piotrków Trybunalski, Poland 11 C10 51 23N 19 43 E
Pipmuacan L., Canada 43 A12 49 45N 70 30W
Piraiévs, Greece 13 F10 37 57N 23 42 E
Pirmasens, Germany 10 D4 49 12N 7 36 E
Pisa, Italy 12 C4 43 43N 10 23 E
Pistóia, Italy 12 C4 43 55N 10 54 E
Pitcairn I., Pac. Oc. 37 K14 25 5S 130 5W
Piteå, Sweden 6 E12 65 20N 21 25 E
Piteşti, Romania 11 F13 44 52N 24 54 E
Pittsburgh, U.S.A. 42 E8 40 26N 80 1W
Pittsfield, U.S.A. 43 D11 42 27N 73 15W
Piura, Peru 46 C1 5 15S 80 38W
Plata, Río de la, S. Amer. 47 F4 34 45S 57 30W
Plattsburgh, U.S.A. 43 C11 44 42N 73 28W
Plauen, Germany 10 C7 50 30N 12 8 E
Plenty, B. of, N.Z. 35 H14 37 45S 177 0 E
Plessisville, Canada 43 B12 46 14N 71 47W
Pleven, Bulgaria 13 C11 43 26N 24 37 E
Płock, Poland 11 B10 52 32N 19 40 E
Ploieşti, Romania 11 F14 44 57N 26 5 E
Plovdiv, Bulgaria 13 C11 42 8N 24 44 E
Plymouth, U.K. 7 F4 50 22N 4 10W
Plymouth, Ind., U.S.A. 42 E4 41 21N 86 19W
Plymouth, Wis., U.S.A. 42 D4 43 45N 87 59W
Plzeň, Czech Rep. 10 D7 49 45N 13 22 E
Po →, Italy 12 B5 44 57N 12 4 E
Podgorica, Montenegro, Yug. 13 C8 42 30N 19 19 E
Podolsk, Russia 14 C6 55 25N 37 30 E
Pofadder, S. Africa 31 B2 29 10S 19 22 E
Point Pleasant, U.S.A. 42 F6 38 51N 82 8W
Pointe-à-Pitre, Guadeloupe 44 L20 16 10N 61 30W
Pointe Noire, Congo 32 E2 4 48S 11 53 E
Poitiers, France 8 C4 46 35N 0 20 E
Poitou, France 8 C3 46 40N 0 10W
Poland ■, Europe 11 C10 52 0N 20 0 E
Polillo Is., Phil. 22 B4 14 56N 122 0 E
Poltava, Ukraine 15 E5 49 35N 34 35 E
Polynesia, Pac. Oc. 37 H11 10 0S 162 0W
Ponce, Puerto Rico 45 D11 18 1N 66 37W
Pondicherry, India 25 D6 11 59N 79 50 E
Ponta Grossa, Brazil 47 E4 25 7S 50 10W
Pontarlier, France 8 C7 46 54N 6 20 E
Pontchartrain L., U.S.A. 41 D9 30 5N 90 5W
Pontevedra, Spain 9 A1 42 26N 8 40W
Pontiac, U.S.A. 42 D6 42 38N 83 18W
Pontianak, Indonesia 22 D2 0 3S 109 15 E
Pontine Mts., Turkey 15 F6 41 30N 35 0 E
Pontivy, France 8 B2 48 5N 2 58W
Poopó, L. de, Bolivia 46 D3 18 30S 67 35W
Popayán, Colombia 46 B2 2 27N 76 36W
Popocatépetl, Volcán, Mexico 44 D5 19 2N 98 38W
Porbandar, India 23 J2 21 44N 69 43 E
Pori, Finland 6 F12 61 29N 21 48 E
Porkkala, Finland 6 G12 59 59N 24 26 E
Port Alfred, S. Africa 31 C4 33 36S 26 55 E
Port Antonio, Jamaica 44 J17 18 10N 76 30W
Port Arthur, U.S.A. 41 E8 29 54N 93 56W
Port-au-Prince, Haiti 45 D10 18 40N 72 20W
Port Augusta, Australia 34 G6 32 30S 137 50 E
Port-Cartier, Canada 39 C13 50 2N 66 50W
Port Elgin, Canada 42 C7 44 25N 81 25W
Port Elizabeth, S. Africa 31 C4 33 58S 25 40 E
Port-Gentil, Gabon 32 E1 0 40S 8 50 E
Port Harcourt, Nigeria 30 D3 4 40N 7 10 E
Port Hedland, Australia 34 E2 20 25S 118 35 E
Port Huron, U.S.A. 42 D6 42 58N 82 26W
Port Kelang, Malaysia 22 C2 3 0N 101 23 E
Port Moresby, Papua N. G. 34 B8 9 24S 147 8 E
Port Nolloth, S. Africa 31 B2 29 17S 16 52 E
Port of Spain, Trin. & Tob. 44 S20 10 40N 61 31W
Port Pirie, Australia 34 G6 33 10S 138 1 E
Port Said, Egypt 29 B11 31 16N 32 18 E
Port St. Johns, S. Africa 31 C4 31 38S 29 33 E
Port Shepstone, S. Africa 31 C5 30 44S 30 28 E
Port Sudan, Sudan 29 E12 19 32N 37 9 E
Port Vila, Pac. Oc. 35 D12 17 45S 168 18 E
Port Washington, U.S.A. 42 D4 43 23N 87 53W
Portage La Prairie, Canada 38 D10 49 58N 98 18W
Portland, Maine, U.S.A. 43 D12 43 39N 70 16W
Portland, Oreg., U.S.A. 40 A2 45 32N 122 37W
Porto, Portugal 9 B1 41 8N 8 40W
Pôrto Alegre, Brazil 47 F4 30 5S 51 10W
Porto Novo, Benin 30 C2 6 23N 2 42 E
Porto-Vecchio, France 8 F8 41 35N 9 16 E
Portsmouth, U.K. 7 F6 50 48N 1 6W
Portsmouth, N.H., U.S.A. 43 D12 43 5N 70 45W
Portsmouth, Ohio, U.S.A. 42 F6 38 44N 82 57W
Porttipahta Res., Finland 6 E13 68 5N 26 40 E
Portugal ■, Europe 9 C1 40 0N 8 0W
Posadas, Argentina 47 E4 27 30S 55 50W
Postmasburg, S. Africa 31 B3 28 18S 23 5 E
Potchefstroom, S. Africa 31 B4 26 41S 27 7 E
Potenza, Italy 12 D6 40 38N 15 48 E
Potgietersrus, S. Africa 31 A4 24 10S 28 55 E
Potomac →, U.S.A. 42 F9 38 0N 76 23W
Potsdam, Germany 10 B7 52 25N 13 4 E
Potsdam, U.S.A. 43 C10 44 40N 74 59W
Pottstown, U.S.A. 43 E10 40 15N 75 39W
Pottsville, U.S.A. 43 E9 40 41N 76 12W
Poughkeepsie, U.S.A. 43 E11 41 42N 73 56W
Powell L., U.S.A. 40 C4 36 57N 111 29W
Powers, U.S.A. 42 C4 45 41N 87 32W
Poyang Hu, China 21 D6 29 5N 116 20 E
Poznań, Poland 11 B9 52 25N 16 55 E
Prague, Czech Rep. 10 C8 50 5N 14 22 E
Prairies, Canada 38 C9 52 0N 108 0W
Prato, Italy 12 C4 43 53N 11 6 E
Prescott, Canada 43 C10 44 45N 75 30W
Prespa, L., Macedonia 13 D9 40 55N 21 0 E
Presque Isle, U.S.A. 43 B13 46 41N 68 1W
Pretoria, S. Africa 31 B4 25 44S 28 12 E
Prieska, S. Africa 31 B3 29 40S 22 42 E
Prince Albert, Canada 38 C9 53 15N 105 50W
Prince Albert, S. Africa 31 C3 33 12S 22 2 E
Prince Edward I. □, Canada 43 B16 46 20N 63 20W
Prince George, Canada 38 C7 53 55N 122 50W
Prince of Wales I., Canada 38 A10 73 0N 99 0W
Prince Rupert, Canada 38 C6 54 20N 130 20W
Princeton, Ind., U.S.A. 42 F4 38 21N 87 34W
Princeton, Ky., U.S.A. 42 G4 37 7N 87 53W
Princeton, W. Va., U.S.A. 42 G7 37 22N 81 6W
Pripet →, Europe 11 C16 51 20N 30 15 E
Pripet Marshes, Europe 11 B15 52 10N 28 10 E
Priština, Serbia, Yug. 13 C9 42 40N 21 13 E
Privas, France 8 D6 44 45N 4 37 E
Prizren, Serbia, Yug. 13 C9 42 13N 20 45 E
Prokopyevsk, Russia 18 D10 54 0N 86 45 E
Prome, Burma 25 D8 18 49N 95 13 E
Provence, France 8 E6 43 40N 5 46 E
Providence, U.S.A. 43 E12 41 49N 71 24W
Provins, France 8 B5 48 33N 3 15 E
Prut →, Romania 11 F15 45 28N 28 10 E
Przemyśl, Poland 11 D12 49 50N 22 45 E
Puebla, Mexico 44 D5 19 3N 98 12W
Pueblo, U.S.A. 40 C6 38 16N 104 37W
Puerto Montt, Chile 47 G2 41 28S 73 0W
Puerto Rico ■, W. Indies 45 D11 18 15N 66 45W
Punakha, Bhutan 23 F12 27 42N 89 52 E
Pune, India 25 D6 18 29N 73 57 E
Punjab □, India 23 D5 31 0N 76 0 E
Punjab □, Pakistan 23 D4 32 0N 74 30 E
Punta Arenas, Chile 47 H2 53 10S 71 0W
Punxsatawney, U.S.A. 42 E8 40 57N 78 59W
Puralia, India 23 H11 23 17N 86 24 E
Puri, India 23 K10 19 50N 85 58 E
Purnia, India 23 G11 25 45N 87 31 E
Purus →, Brazil 46 C3 3 42S 61 28W
Pusan, S. Korea 21 C7 35 5N 129 0 E
Puttalam, Sri Lanka 25 E6 8 1N 79 55 E
Putumayo →, S. Amer. 46 C2 3 7S 67 58W
Puy-de-Dôme, France 8 D5 45 46N 2 57 E
P'yŏngyang, N. Korea 21 C7 39 0N 125 30 E
Pyrenees, Europe 9 A6 42 45N 0 18 E

Q

Qandahār, Afghan. 24 B5 31 32N 65 30 E
Qatar ■, Asia 24 C4 25 30N 51 15 E
Qattâra Depression, Egypt 29 C10 29 30N 27 30 E
Qazvin, Iran 24 B3 36 15N 50 0 E
Qena, Egypt 29 C11 26 10N 32 43 E
Qingdao, China 21 C7 36 5N 120 20 E
Qinghai □, China 20 C4 36 0N 98 0 E
Qinghai Hu, China 20 C5 36 40N 100 10 E
Qingjiang, China 21 C6 33 30N 119 2 E
Qiqihar, China 21 B7 47 26N 124 0 E
Qom, Iran 24 B4 34 40N 51 0 E
Québec, Canada 43 B12 46 52N 71 13W
Québec □, Canada 43 B10 48 0N 74 0W
Queen Charlotte Is., Canada 38 C6 53 20N 132 10W
Queen Maud G., Canada 38 B9 68 15N 102 30W
Queensland □, Australia 34 E7 22 0S 142 0 E

Place names on the yellow-coded large scale map section are to be found in the index at the end of that section

INDEX TO WORLD MAPS

Queenstown Saser

Queenstown, *S. Africa* **31 C4** 31 52S 26 52 E
Querétaro, *Mexico* **44 C4** 20 36N 100 23W
Quezon City, *Phil.* **22 B4** 14 38N 121 0 E
Qui Nhon, *Vietnam* **22 B2** 13 40N 109 13 E
Quimper, *France* **8 B1** 48 0N 4 9W
Quincy, *U.S.A.* **43 D12** 42 15N 71 0W
Quito, *Ecuador* **46 C2** 0 15S 78 35W

R

Raahe, *Finland* **6 F12** 64 40N 24 28 E
Raba, *Indonesia* **22 D3** 8 36S 118 55 E
Rabat, *Morocco* **28 B3** 34 2N 6 48W
Râbigh, *Si. Arabia* **24 C2** 22 50N 39 5 E
Racine, *U.S.A.* **42 D4** 42 41N 87 51W
Radford, *U.S.A.* **42 G7** 37 8N 80 34W
Radom, *Poland* **11 C11** 51 23N 21 12 E
Rae Bareli, *India* **23 F8** 26 18N 81 20 E
Ragusa, *Italy* **12 F6** 36 55N 14 44 E
Rahimyar Khan, *Pakistan* **23 E3** 28 30N 70 25 E
Raigarh, *India* **23 J9** 21 56N 83 25 E
Rainier, Mt., *U.S.A.* **40 A2** 46 52N 121 46W
Raipur, *India* **23 J8** 21 17N 81 45 E
Raj Nandgaon, *India* **23 J8** 21 5N 81 5 E
Rajahmundry, *India* **25 D7** 17 1N 81 48 E
Rajasthan □, *India* **23 F4** 26 45N 73 30 E
Rajasthan Canal, *India* **23 F3** 28 0N 72 0 E
Rajkot, *India* **23 H3** 22 15N 70 56 E
Rajshahi, *Bangla.* **23 G12** 24 22N 88 39 E
Rajshahi □, *Bangla.* **23 G12** 25 0N 89 0 E
Rakaposhi, *Pakistan* **23 A5** 36 10N 74 25 E
Rakops, *Botswana* **31 A3** 21 1S 24 28 E
Raleigh, *U.S.A.* **41 C11** 35 47N 78 39W
Ramgarh, *India* **23 H10** 23 40N 85 35 E
Ramotswa, *Botswana* **31 A4** 24 50S 25 52 E
Rampur, *India* **23 E7** 28 50N 79 5 E
Rancagua, *Chile* **47 F2** 34 10S 70 50W
Ranchi, *India* **23 H10** 23 19N 85 27 E
Randers, *Denmark* **6 G10** 56 29N 10 1 E
Rangoon, *Burma* **25 D8** 16 45N 96 20 E
Rangpur, *Bangla.* **23 G12** 25 42N 89 22 E
Rantoul, *U.S.A.* **42 E3** 40 19N 88 9W
Rasht, *Iran* **24 B3** 37 20N 49 40 E
Ratangarh, *India* **23 E5** 28 5N 74 35 E
Ratlam, *India* **23 H5** 23 20N 75 0 E
Raurkela, *India* **23 H10** 22 14N 84 50 E
Ravenna, *Italy* **12 B5** 44 25N 12 12 E
Ravi →, *Pakistan* **23 D3** 30 35N 71 49 E
Rawalpindi, *Pakistan* **23 C4** 33 38N 73 8 E
Raz, Pte. du, *France* **8 C1** 48 2N 4 47W
Ré, I. de, *France* **8 C3** 46 12N 1 30W
Reading, *U.K.* **7 F6** 51 27N 0 58W
Reading, *U.S.A.* **43 E10** 40 20N 75 56W
Recife, *Brazil* **46 C6** 8 0S 35 0W
Red →, *U.S.A.* **41 D8** 31 1N 91 45W
Red Deer, *Canada* **38 C8** 52 20N 113 50W
Red Sea, *Asia* **24 C2** 25 0N 36 0 E
Redon, *France* **8 C2** 47 40N 2 6W
Regensburg, *Germany* **10 D7** 49 1N 12 6 E
Réggio di Calábria, *Italy* **12 E6** 38 6N 15 39 E
Réggio nell'Emília, *Italy* **12 B4** 44 43N 10 36 E
Regina, *Canada* **38 C9** 50 27N 104 35W
Rehoboth, *Namibia* **31 A2** 23 15S 17 4 E
Reichenbach, *Germany* **10 C7** 50 37N 12 17 E
Reims, *France* **8 B6** 49 15N 4 1 E
Reindeer L., *Canada* **38 C9** 57 15N 102 15W
Reitz, *S. Africa* **31 B4** 27 48S 28 29 E
Renfrew, *Canada* **42 C9** 45 30N 76 40W
Rennes, *France* **8 B3** 48 7N 1 41W
Reno, *U.S.A.* **40 C3** 39 31N 119 48W
Resistencia, *Argentina* **47 E4** 27 30S 59 0W
Réthímnon, *Greece* **13 G11** 35 18N 24 30 E
Réunion ■, *Ind. Oc.* **27 J9** 21 0S 56 0 E
Revilla Gigedo, Is., *Pac. Oc.* **37 F16** 18 40N 112 0W
Rewa, *India* **23 G8** 24 33N 81 25 E
Rewari, *India* **23 E6** 28 15N 76 40 E
Reykjavík, *Iceland* **6 B3** 64 10N 21 57W
Reynosa, *Mexico* **44 B5** 26 5N 98 18W
Rheine, *Germany* **10 B4** 52 17N 7 26 E
Rheinland-Pfalz □, *Germany* **10 C4** 50 0N 7 0 E
Rhine →, *Europe* **10 C4** 51 52N 6 2 E
Rhode Island □, *U.S.A.* **43 E12** 41 40N 71 30W
Rhodes, *Greece* **13 F13** 36 15N 28 10 E
Rhodope Mts., *Bulgaria* **13 D11** 41 40N 24 20 E
Rhön, *Germany* **10 C5** 50 24N 9 58 E
Rhône →, *France* **8 E6** 43 28N 4 42 E
Riau Arch., *Indonesia* **22 C2** 0 30N 104 20 E
Ribeirão Prêto, *Brazil* **46 E5** 21 10S 47 50W
Richards Bay, *S. Africa* **31 B5** 28 48S 32 6 E
Richlands, *U.S.A.* **42 G7** 37 6N 81 48W
Richmond, *Ind., U.S.A.* **42 F5** 39 50N 84 53W
Richmond, *Ky., U.S.A.* **42 G5** 37 45N 84 18W
Richmond, *Va., U.S.A.* **42 G9** 37 33N 77 27W
Ridder, *Kazakstan* **18 D10** 50 20N 83 30 E
Ridgway, *U.S.A.* **42 E8** 41 25N 78 44W
Riet →, *S. Africa* **31 B3** 29 0S 23 54 E
Riga, *Latvia* **14 C3** 56 53N 24 8 E
Riga, G. of, *Latvia* **14 C3** 57 40N 23 45 E
Rijeka, *Croatia* **10 F8** 45 20N 14 21 E
Rímini, *Italy* **12 B5** 44 3N 12 33 E
Rîmnicu Vîlcea, *Romania* **11 F13** 45 9N 24 21 E
Rimouski, *Canada* **43 A13** 48 27N 68 30W
Rio de Janeiro, *Brazil* **47 E5** 23 0S 43 12W
Río Gallegos, *Argentina* **47 H3** 51 35S 69 15W
Rio Grande →, *U.S.A.* **41 E7** 25 57N 97 9W
Ripon, *U.S.A.* **42 D3** 43 51N 88 50W
Riverhead, *U.S.A.* **43 E11** 40 55N 72 40W
Riversdale, *S. Africa* **31 C3** 34 7S 21 15 E
Riverside, *U.S.A.* **40 D3** 33 59N 117 22W
Rivière-du-Loup, *Canada* **43 B13** 47 50N 69 30W
Riyadh, *Si. Arabia* **24 C3** 24 41N 46 42 E
Roanne, *France* **8 C6** 46 3N 4 4 E
Roanoke, *U.S.A.* **42 G8** 37 16N 79 56W
Roberval, *Canada* **43 A11** 48 32N 72 15W
Robson, Mt., *Canada* **38 C8** 53 10N 119 10W
Rochefort, *France* **8 D3** 45 56N 0 57W
Rochester, *Ind., U.S.A.* **42 E4** 41 4N 86 13W
Rochester, *Minn., U.S.A.* **41 B8** 44 1N 92 28W
Rochester, *N.H., U.S.A.* **43 D12** 43 18N 70 59W
Rochester, *N.Y., U.S.A.* **42 D9** 43 10N 77 37W
Rockford, *U.S.A.* **41 B9** 42 16N 89 6W
Rockhampton, *Australia* **34 E9** 23 22S 150 32 E
Rockland, *U.S.A.* **43 C13** 44 6N 69 7W
Rocky Mts., *N. Amer.* **38 C7** 55 0N 121 0W
Rodez, *France* **8 D5** 44 21N 2 33 E
Rogers City, *U.S.A.* **42 C6** 45 25N 83 49W
Rohtak, *India* **23 E6** 28 55N 76 43 E
Roma, *Australia* **34 F8** 26 32S 148 49 E
Romania ■, *Europe* **11 F12** 46 0N 25 0 E
Romans-sur-Isère, *France* **8 D6** 45 3N 5 3 E
Rome, *Italy* **12 D5** 41 54N 12 29 E
Rome, *U.S.A.* **43 D10** 43 13N 75 27W
Romney, *U.S.A.* **42 F8** 39 21N 78 45W
Romorantin-Lanthenay, *France* **8 C4** 47 21N 1 45 E
Rondônia □, *Brazil* **46 D3** 11 0S 63 0W
Ronne Ice Shelf, *Antarctica* **48 E4** 78 0S 60 0W
Roodepoort, *S. Africa* **31 B4** 26 11S 27 54 E
Roraima □, *Brazil* **46 B3** 2 0N 61 30W
Rosario, *Argentina* **47 F3** 33 0S 60 40W
Roscommon, *U.S.A.* **42 C5** 44 30N 84 35W
Roseau, *Domin.* **44 M20** 15 20N 61 24W
Rosenheim, *Germany* **10 E7** 47 51N 12 7 E
Ross Ice Shelf, *Antarctica* **48 F16** 80 0S 180 0 E
Ross Sea, *Antarctica* **48 E15** 74 0S 178 0 E
Rossignol Res., *Canada* **43 C15** 44 12N 65 10W
Rostock, *Germany* **10 A7** 54 5N 12 8 E
Rostov, *Russia* **15 E6** 47 15N 39 45 E
Rotorua, *N.Z.* **35 H14** 38 9S 176 16 E
Rotterdam, *Neths.* **10 C3** 51 55N 4 30 E
Roubaix, *France* **8 A5** 50 40N 3 10 E
Rouen, *France* **8 B4** 49 27N 1 4 E
Roussillon, *France* **8 E5** 42 30N 2 35 E
Rouxville, *S. Africa* **31 C4** 30 25S 26 50 E
Rouyn, *Canada* **42 A8** 48 20N 79 0W
Rovaniemi, *Finland* **6 E13** 66 29N 25 41 E
Rovno, *Ukraine* **11 C14** 50 40N 26 10 E
Royan, *France* **8 D3** 45 37N 1 2W
Rub' al Khali, *Si. Arabia* **24 D3** 18 0N 48 0 E
Rügen, *Germany* **10 A7** 54 22N 13 24 E
Ruhr →, *Germany* **10 C4** 51 27N 6 43 E
Rumania = Romania ■, *Europe* **11 F12** 46 0N 25 0 E
Rumford, *U.S.A.* **43 C12** 44 33N 70 33W
Rupat, *Indonesia* **22 C2** 1 45N 101 40 E
Ruse, *Bulgaria* **13 C12** 43 48N 25 59 E
Rushville, *U.S.A.* **42 F5** 39 37N 85 27W
Russia ■, *Eurasia* **18 C12** 62 0N 105 0 E
Rustenburg, *S. Africa* **31 B4** 25 41S 27 14 E
Ruteng, *Indonesia* **22 D4** 8 35S 120 30 E
Ruwenzori, *Africa* **32 D5** 0 30N 29 55 E
Rwanda ■, *Africa* **32 E5** 2 0S 30 0 E
Ryazan, *Russia* **14 D6** 54 40N 39 40 E
Rybinsk, *Russia* **14 C6** 58 5N 38 50 E
Rybinsk Res., *Russia* **14 C6** 58 30N 38 25 E
Ryūkyū Is., *Japan* **21 D7** 26 0N 126 0 E
Rzeszów, *Poland* **11 C11** 50 5N 21 58 E

S

Saale →, *Germany* **10 C6** 51 56N 11 54 E
Saar →, *Europe* **10 D4** 49 41N 6 32 E
Saarbrücken, *Germany* **10 D4** 49 14N 6 59 E
Saaremaa, *Estonia* **14 C3** 58 30N 22 30 E
Saba, *W. Indies* **44 K18** 17 42N 63 26W
Sabadell, *Spain* **9 B7** 41 28N 2 7 E
Sabah □, *Malaysia* **22 C3** 6 0N 117 0 E
Sabhah, *Libya* **29 C7** 27 9N 14 29 E
Sabie, *S. Africa* **31 B5** 25 10S 30 48 E
Sable, C., *Canada* **43 D15** 43 29N 65 38W
Sachsen □, *Germany* **10 C7** 50 55N 13 10 E
Sachsen-Anhalt □, *Germany* **10 C7** 52 0N 12 0 E
Saco, *U.S.A.* **43 D12** 43 30N 70 27W
Sacramento, *U.S.A.* **40 C2** 38 35N 121 29W
Safi, *Morocco* **28 B3** 32 18N 9 20W
Saginaw, *U.S.A.* **42 D6** 43 26N 83 56W
Saginaw B., *U.S.A.* **42 D6** 43 50N 83 40W
Saguenay →, *Canada* **43 A12** 48 22N 71 0W
Sahara, *Africa* **28 D5** 23 0N 5 0 E
Saharan Atlas, *Algeria* **28 B5** 33 30N 1 0 E
Saharanpur, *India* **23 E6** 29 58N 77 33 E
Sahiwal, *Pakistan* **23 D4** 30 45N 73 8 E
Saidabad, *Iran* **24 C4** 29 30N 55 45 E
Saidpur, *Bangla.* **23 G12** 25 48N 89 0 E
St. Albans, *Vt., U.S.A.* **43 C11** 44 49N 73 5W
St. Albans, *W. Va., U.S.A.* **42 F7** 38 23N 81 50W
St. Boniface, *Canada* **38 D10** 49 53N 97 5W
St.-Brieuc, *France* **8 B2** 48 30N 2 46W
St. Catharines, *Canada* **42 D8** 43 10N 79 15W
St. Christopher-Nevis = St. Kitts-Nevis ■, *W. Indies* **44 K19** 17 20N 62 40W
St. Clair, L., *Canada* **42 D6** 42 30N 82 45W
St.-Dizier, *France* **8 B6** 48 38N 4 56 E
St.-Étienne, *France* **8 D6** 45 27N 4 22 E
St-Félicien, *Canada* **43 A11** 48 40N 72 25W
St.-Flour, *France* **8 D5** 45 2N 3 6 E
St. Gallen, *Switz.* **10 E5** 47 26N 9 22 E
St.-Gaudens, *France* **8 E4** 43 6N 0 44 E
St-Georges, *Canada* **43 B12** 46 8N 70 40W
St. George's, *Grenada* **44 Q20** 12 5N 61 43W
St. Helena □, *Atl. Oc.* **26 H3** 15 55S 5 44W
St. Helena B., *S. Africa* **33 L3** 32 40S 18 10 E
St-Hyacinthe, *Canada* **43 C11** 45 40N 72 58W
St. Ignace, *U.S.A.* **42 C5** 45 52N 84 44W
St-Jean, *Canada* **43 C11** 45 20N 73 20W
St-Jean, L., *Canada* **43 A11** 48 40N 72 0W
St-Jérôme, *Canada* **43 C11** 45 47N 74 0W
St. John, *Canada* **43 C14** 45 20N 66 8W
St. John's, *Antigua* **44 K20** 17 6N 61 51W
St. John's, *Canada* **39 D14** 47 35N 52 40W
St. Johns, *U.S.A.* **42 D5** 43 0N 84 33W
St. Johnsbury, *U.S.A.* **43 C11** 44 25N 72 1W
St. Joseph, *Mich., U.S.A.* **42 D4** 42 6N 86 29W
St. Joseph, *Mo., U.S.A.* **41 C8** 39 46N 94 50W
St. Kitts-Nevis ■, *W. Indies* **44 K19** 17 20N 62 40W
St. Lawrence →, *Canada* **43 A13** 49 30N 66 0W
St. Lawrence, Gulf of, *Canada* **43 A16** 48 25N 62 0W
St.-Lô, *France* **8 B3** 49 7N 1 5W
St-Louis, *Senegal* **28 E1** 16 8N 16 27W
St. Louis, *U.S.A.* **41 C8** 38 37N 90 12W
St. Lucia ■, *W. Indies* **44 P21** 14 0N 60 50W
St. Lucia, L., *S. Africa* **31 B5** 28 5S 32 30 E
St.-Malo, *France* **8 B2** 48 39N 2 1W
St-Martin, *W. Indies* **44 J18** 18 0N 63 0W
St. Marys, *U.S.A.* **42 E8** 41 26N 78 34W
St.-Nazaire, *France* **8 C2** 47 17N 2 12W
St.-Omer, *France* **8 A5** 50 45N 2 15 E
St. Paul, *U.S.A.* **41 B8** 44 57N 93 6W
St. Petersburg, *Russia* **14 C5** 59 55N 30 20 E
St. Petersburg, *U.S.A.* **41 E10** 27 46N 82 39W
St.-Pierre et Miquelon □, *St- P. & M.* **39 D14** 46 55N 56 10W
St.-Quentin, *France* **8 B5** 49 50N 3 16 E
St. Stephen, *Canada* **43 C14** 45 16N 67 17W
St. Thomas, *Canada* **42 D7** 42 45N 81 10W
St.-Tropez, *France* **8 E7** 43 17N 6 38 E
St. Vincent & the Grenadines ■, *W. Indies* **44 Q20** 13 0N 61 10W
Ste-Marie de la Madeleine, *Canada* **43 B12** 46 26N 71 0W
Saintes, *France* **8 D3** 45 45N 0 37W
Saintonge, *France* **8 D3** 45 40N 0 50W
Sak →, *S. Africa* **31 C3** 30 52S 20 25 E
Sakai, *Japan* **19 B4** 34 30N 135 30 E
Sakhalin, *Russia* **18 D16** 51 0N 143 0 E
Sala, *Sweden* **6 G11** 59 58N 16 35 E
Salado →, *Argentina* **47 F3** 31 40S 60 41W
Salamanca, *Spain* **9 B3** 40 58N 5 39W
Salamanca, *U.S.A.* **42 D8** 42 10N 78 43W
Salayar, *Indonesia* **22 D4** 6 7S 120 30 E
Saldanha, *S. Africa* **31 C2** 33 0S 17 58 E
Salekhard, *Russia* **18 C8** 66 30N 66 35 E
Salem, *India* **25 D6** 11 40N 78 11 E
Salem, *Ind., U.S.A.* **42 F4** 38 36N 86 6W
Salem, *Mass., U.S.A.* **43 D12** 42 31N 70 53W
Salem, *Ohio, U.S.A.* **42 E7** 40 54N 80 52W
Salem, *Va., U.S.A.* **42 G7** 37 18N 80 3W
Salerno, *Italy* **12 D6** 40 41N 14 47 E
Salisbury, *U.S.A.* **43 F10** 38 22N 75 36W
Salon-de-Provence, *France* **8 E6** 43 39N 5 6 E
Salt Lake City, *U.S.A.* **40 B4** 40 45N 111 53W
Salta, *Argentina* **47 E3** 24 57S 65 25W
Saltillo, *Mexico* **44 B4** 25 25N 101 0W
Salto, *Uruguay* **47 F4** 31 27S 57 50W
Salvador, *Brazil* **46 D6** 13 0S 38 30W
Salween →, *Burma* **25 D8** 16 31N 97 37 E
Salyersville, *U.S.A.* **42 G6** 37 45N 83 4W
Salzburg, *Austria* **10 E7** 47 48N 13 2 E
Salzgitter, *Germany* **10 B6** 52 9N 10 19 E
Samar, *Phil.* **22 B4** 12 0N 125 0 E
Samara, *Russia* **14 D9** 53 8N 50 6 E
Samarkand, *Uzbekistan* **18 F8** 39 40N 66 55 E
Sambalpur, *India* **23 J10** 21 28N 84 4 E
Sambhal, *India* **23 E7** 28 35N 78 37 E
Sambhar, *India* **23 F5** 26 52N 75 6 E
Samoa ■, *Pac. Oc.* **35 C16** 14 0S 172 0W
Sámos, *Greece* **13 F12** 37 45N 26 50 E
Samsun, *Turkey* **15 F6** 41 15N 36 22 E
San →, *Poland* **11 C11** 50 45N 21 51 E
San Agustin, C., *Phil.* **22 C4** 6 20N 126 13 E
San Angelo, *U.S.A.* **40 D6** 31 28N 100 26W
San Antonio, *U.S.A.* **40 E7** 29 25N 98 30W
San Bernardino, *U.S.A.* **40 D3** 34 7N 117 19W
San Bernardino Str., *Phil.* **22 B4** 13 0N 125 0 E
San Diego, *U.S.A.* **40 D3** 32 43N 117 9W
San Francisco, *U.S.A.* **40 C2** 37 47N 122 25W
San Gottardo, P. del, *Switz.* **10 E5** 46 33N 8 33 E
San Jorge, G., *Argentina* **47 G3** 46 0S 66 0W
San José, *Costa Rica* **45 F8** 9 55N 84 2W
San Jose, *U.S.A.* **40 C2** 37 20N 121 53W
San Juan, *Argentina* **47 F3** 31 30S 68 30W
San Juan, *Puerto Rico* **45 D11** 18 28N 66 7W
San Lucas, C., *Mexico* **44 C2** 22 50N 110 0W
San Luis Potosí, *Mexico* **44 C4** 22 9N 100 59W
San Marino ■, *Europe* **12 C5** 43 56N 12 25 E
San Matías, G. of, *Argentina* **47 G3** 41 30S 64 0W
San Miguel de Tucumán, *Argentina* **47 E3** 26 50S 65 20W
San Pedro Sula, *Honduras* **44 D7** 15 30N 88 0W
San Remo, *Italy* **12 C2** 43 49N 7 46 E
San Salvador, *El Salv.* **44 E7** 13 40N 89 10W
San Salvador de Jujuy, *Argentina* **47 E3** 24 10S 64 48W
San Sebastián, *Spain* **9 A5** 43 17N 1 58W
Sana', *Yemen* **24 D3** 15 27N 44 12 E
Sancy, Puy de, *France* **8 D5** 45 32N 2 50 E
Sand →, *S. Africa* **31 A5** 22 25S 30 5 E
Sandakan, *Malaysia* **22 C3** 5 53N 118 4 E
Sandusky, *U.S.A.* **42 E6** 41 27N 82 42W
Sangli, *India* **25 D6** 16 55N 74 33 E
Sankt Moritz, *Switz.* **10 E5** 46 30N 9 50 E
Santa Ana, *U.S.A.* **40 D3** 33 46N 117 52W
Santa Clara, *Cuba* **45 C9** 22 20N 80 0W
Santa Cruz, *Bolivia* **46 D3** 17 43S 63 10W
Santa Cruz de Tenerife, *Canary Is.* **28 C1** 28 28N 16 15W
Santa Fe, *Argentina* **47 F3** 31 35S 60 41W
Santa Fe, *U.S.A.* **40 C5** 35 41N 105 57W
Santa Maria, *Brazil* **47 E4** 29 40S 53 48W
Santa Marta, *Colombia* **46 A2** 11 15N 74 13W
Santander, *Spain* **9 A4** 43 27N 3 51W
Santarém, *Brazil* **46 C4** 2 25S 54 42W
Santarém, *Portugal* **9 C1** 39 12N 8 42W
Santiago, *Chile* **47 F2** 33 24S 70 40W
Santiago de Compostela, *Spain* **9 A1** 42 52N 8 37W
Santiago de Cuba, *Cuba* **45 D9** 20 0N 75 49W
Santiago de los Caballeros, *Dom. Rep.* **45 D10** 19 30N 70 40W
Santo André, *Brazil* **47 E5** 23 39S 46 29W
Santo Domingo, *Dom. Rep.* **45 D11** 18 30N 69 59W
Santorini, *Greece* **13 F11** 36 23N 25 27 E
Santos, *Brazil* **47 E5** 24 0S 46 20W
São Francisco →, *Brazil* **46 D6** 10 30S 36 24W
São José do Rio Prêto, *Brazil* **46 E5** 20 50S 49 20W
São Luís, *Brazil* **46 C5** 2 39S 44 15W
São Paulo, *Brazil* **47 E5** 23 32S 46 37W
São Roque, C. de, *Brazil* **46 C6** 5 30S 35 16W
São Tomé & Principe ■, *Africa* **27 F4** 0 12N 6 39 E
Saône →, *France* **8 D6** 45 44N 4 50 E
Sapporo, *Japan* **19 F12** 43 0N 141 21 E
Sarajevo, *Bos.-H.* **13 C8** 43 52N 18 26 E
Saranac Lakes, *U.S.A.* **43 C10** 44 20N 74 8W
Sarangani B., *Phil.* **22 C4** 6 0N 125 13 E
Saransk, *Russia* **14 D8** 54 10N 45 10 E
Saratoga Springs, *U.S.A.* **43 D11** 43 5N 73 47W
Saratov, *Russia* **14 D8** 51 30N 46 2 E
Sarawak □, *Malaysia* **22 C3** 2 0N 113 0 E
Sarda →, *India* **23 F8** 27 21N 81 23 E
Sardinia □, *Italy* **12 D3** 40 0N 9 0 E
Sargodha, *Pakistan* **23 C4** 32 10N 72 40 E
Sarh, *Chad* **29 G8** 9 5N 18 23 E
Sarlat-la-Canéda, *France* **8 D4** 44 54N 1 13 E
Sarnia, *Canada* **42 D6** 42 58N 82 23W
Sarreguemines, *France* **8 B7** 49 5N 7 4 E
Sarthe →, *France* **8 C3** 47 33N 0 31W
Sasebo, *Japan* **19 C1** 33 10N 129 43 E
Saser, *India* **23 B6** 34 50N 77 50 E

Place names on the yellow-coded large scale map section are to be found in the index at the end of that section

INDEX TO WORLD MAPS

Place names on the yellow-coded large scale map section are to be found in the index at the end of that section.

Place names on the yellow-coded large scale map section are to be found in the index at the end of that section

INDEX TO WORLD MAPS

Vanino, Russia . . . . . 18 E16 48 50N 140 5 E
Vännäs, Sweden . . . . 6 F11 63 58N 19 48 E
Vannes, France 8 C2 47 40N   2 47W
Vanrhynsdorp,
  S. Africa . . . 31 C2 31 36S 18 44 E
Vanua Levu, Fiji . . 35 D14 16 33S 179 15 E
Vanuatu ■, Pac. Oc. 35 D12 15 0S 168 0 E
Varanasi, India . . 23 G9 25 22N 83 0 E
Varberg, Sweden . . 6 G10 57 6N 12 20 E
Varanger Fjord,
  Norway . . . . . 6 D13 70 3N 29 25 E
Varberg, Sweden . . 6 G10 57 6N 12 20 E
Varna, Bulgaria . . . 13 C12 43 13N 27 56 E
Västerås, Sweden . . 6 G11 59 37N 16 38 E
Västervik, Sweden . 6 G11 57 43N 16 33 E
Vatican City ■, Europe 12 D5 41 54N 12 27 E
Vatnajökull, Iceland . 6 B5 64 30N 16 48W
Vättern, Sweden . . 6 G10 58 25N 14 30 E
Vega, Norway . . . . 6 E10 65 40N 11 55 E
Vellore, India . . . 25 D6 12 57N 79 10 E
Vendée □, France . . 8 C3 46 50N   1 35W
Vendôme, France . . 8 C4 47 47N   1 3 E
Venezuela ■, S. Amer. 46 B3   8 0N 66 0W
Venice, Italy . . . . 12 B5 45 27N 12 21 E
Ventoux, Mt., France 8 D6 44 10N   5 17 E
Veracruz, Mexico . . 44 D5 19 10N 96 10W
Veraval, India . . . 23 J3 20 53N 70 27 E
Vercelli, Italy . . . 12 B3 45 19N   8 25 E
Verdun, France . . . 8 B6 49 9N   5 24 E
Vereeniging, S. Africa 31 B4 26 38S 27 57 E
Verkhoyansk, Russia 18 C15 67 35N 133 25 E
Verkhoyansk Ra.,
  Russia . . . . 18 C14 66 0N 129 0 E
Vermont □, U.S.A. . 43 D11 44 0N 73 0W
Verona, Italy . . . . 12 B4 45 27N 11 0 E
Versailles, France . . 8 B5 48 48N   2 8 E
Verviers, Belgium . . 10 C3 50 37N   5 52 E
Vesoul, France . . . 8 C7 47 40N   6 11 E
Vesterålen, Norway . 6 E10 68 45N 15 0 E
Vesuvio, Italy . . . 12 D6 40 49N 14 26 E
Veszprém, Hungary . 11 E9 47 8N 17 57 E
Vicenza, Italy . . . 12 B4 45 33N 11 33 E
Vichy, France . . . . 8 C5 46 9N   3 26 E
Victoria, Canada . . 38 D7 48 30N 123 25W
Victoria □, Australia 34 H7 37 0S 144 0 E
Victoria, L., Africa . 32 E6   1 0S 33 0 E
Victoria de Durango =
  Durango, Mexico . 44 C4 24 3N 104 39W
Victoria Falls,
  Zimbabwe . . . 33 H5 17 58S 25 52 E
Victoria I., Canada . 38 A8 71 0N 111 0W
Victoria West, S. Africa 31 C3 31 25S 23 4 E
Victoriaville, Canada 43 B12 46 4N 71 56W
Vienna, Austria . . . 10 D9 48 12N 16 22 E
Vienne, France . . . 8 D6 45 31N   4 53 E
Vienne →, France . . 8 C4 47 13N   0 5 E
Vientiane, Laos . . . 22 B2 17 58N 102 36 E
Vierzon, France . . . 8 C5 47 13N   2 5 E
Vietnam ■, Asia . . 22 B2 19 0N 106 0 E
Vigo, Spain 9 A1 42 12N   8 41W
Vijayawada, India . . 25 D7 16 31N 80 39 E
Vikna, Norway . . . 6 F10 64 55N 10 58 E
Vilaine →, France . . 8 C2 47 30N   2 27W
Vilhelmina, Sweden . 6 F11 64 35N 16 39 E
Villach, Austria . . . 10 E7 46 37N 13 51 E
Villahermosa, Mexico 44 D6 17 59N 92 55W
Ville-Marie, Canada . 42 B8 47 20N 79 30W
Villeneuve-sur-Lot,
  France . . . . 8 D4 44 24N   0 42 E
Vilnius, Lithuania . . 14 D4 54 38N 25 19 E
Vilyuy →, Russia . . 18 C14 64 24N 126 26 E
Vilyuysk, Russia . . 18 C14 63 40N 121 35 E
Viña del Mar, Chile . 47 F2 33 0S 71 30W
Vincennes, U.S.A. . . 42 F4 38 41N 87 32W
Vindhya Ra., India . 23 H6 22 50N 77 0 E
Vineland, U.S.A. . . 43 F10 39 29N 75 2W
Vinnitsa, Ukraine . . 11 D15 49 15N 28 30 E
Vire, France 8 B3 48 50N   0 53W
Virgin Is. (British) □,
  W. Indies . . . 45 D12 18 30N 64 30W
Virgin Is. (U.S.) □,
  W. Indies . . . 45 D12 18 20N 65 0W
Virginia, S. Africa . . 31 B4 28 8S 26 55 E
Virginia □, U.S.A. . . 42 G8 37 30N 78 45W
Visby, Sweden . . . 6 G11 57 37N 18 18 E
Vishakhapatnam, India 25 D7 17 45N 83 20 E
Vistula →, Poland . . 11 A10 54 22N 18 55 E
Viterbo, Italy . . . . 12 C5 42 25N 12 6 E
Viti Levu, Fiji . . . 35 D14 17 30S 177 30 E
Vitória, Brazil . . . 46 E5 20 20S 40 22W
Vitoria, Spain 9 A4 42 50N   2 41W
Vitsyebsk, Belarus . 14 C5 55 10N 30 15 E
Vladikavkaz, Russia . 15 F7 43 0N 44 35 E
Vladimir, Russia . . 14 C7 56 15N 40 30 E
Vladivostok, Russia . 18 E15 43 10N 131 53 E
Vlissingen, Neths. . . 10 C2 51 26N   3 34 E
Vlóra, Albania . . . 13 D8 40 32N 19 28 E
Vltava →,
  Czech Rep. . . 10 D8 50 21N 14 30 E
Vogelkop, Indonesia . 22 D5   1 25S 133 0 E
Vogelsberg, Germany 10 C5 50 31N   9 12 E
Vojvodina □,
  Serbia, Yug. . . 13 B9 45 20N 20 0 E
Volga →, Russia . . 15 E8 46 0N 48 30 E
Volga Hts., Russia . 15 D8 51 0N 46 0 E
Volgograd, Russia . . 15 E7 48 40N 44 25 E
Volksrust, S. Africa . 31 B4 27 24S 29 53 E
Vologda, Russia . . . 14 C6 59 10N 39 45 E
Vólos, Greece . . . 13 E10 39 24N 22 59 E
Volta →, Ghana . . 30 C2   5 46N   0 41 E

Volta, L., Ghana . . . . 30 C2   7 30N   0 15 E
Volzhskiy, Russia . . 15 E7 48 56N 44 46 E
Vorkuta, Russia . . . 14 A11 67 48N 64 20 E
Voronezh, Russia . . 14 D6 51 40N 39 10 E
Vosges, France . . . 8 B7 48 20N   7 10 E
Vrede, S. Africa . . . 31 B4 27 24S 29 6 E
Vredenburg, S. Africa 31 C2 32 56S 18 0 E
Vryburg, S. Africa . . 31 B3 26 55S 24 45 E
Vryheid, S. Africa . . 31 B5 27 45S 30 47 E
Vyatka →, Russia . . 14 C9 55 37N 51 28 E

W

Waal →, Neths. . . . 10 C3 51 37N   5 0 E
Wabash, U.S.A. . . . 42 E5 40 48N 85 49W
Wabash →, U.S.A. . 42 G3 37 48N 88 2W
Waco, U.S.A. 41 D7 31 33N 97 9W
Wâd Medanî, Sudan . 29 F11 14 28N 33 30 E
Waddington, Mt.,
  Canada 38 C7 51 23N 125 15W
Wagga Wagga,
  Australia . . . 34 H8 35 7S 147 24 E
Wah, Pakistan . . . 23 C4 33 45N 72 40 E
Waigeo, Indonesia . 22 D5   0 20S 130 40 E
Wainganga →, India 23 K7 18 50N 79 55 E
Waingapu, Indonesia 22 D4   9 35S 120 11 E
Wakayama, Japan . . 19 B4 34 15N 135 15 E
Wałbrzych, Poland . 10 C9 50 45N 16 18 E
Wales □, U.K. . . . 7 E5 52 19N   4 43W
Walgett, Australia . 34 F8 30 0S 148 5 E
Wallaceburg, Canada 42 D6 42 34N 82 23W
Wallachia = Valahia,
  Romania . . . 11 F13 44 35N 25 0 E
Wallis & Futuna, Is.,
  Pac. Oc. . . . 35 C15 13 18S 176 10W
Walvis Bay, Namibia 31 A1 23 0S 14 28 E
Wanganui, N.Z. . . . 35 H14 39 56S 175 3 E
Wapakoneta, U.S.A. 42 E5 40 34N 84 12W
Warangal, India . . . 25 D6 17 58N 79 35 E
Wardha →, India . . 23 K7 19 57N 79 11 E
Warmbad, S. Africa . 31 A4 24 51S 28 19 E
Warrego →, Australia 34 G8 30 24S 145 21 E
Warren, Mich., U.S.A. 42 D6 42 30N 83 0W
Warren, Ohio, U.S.A. 42 E7 41 14N 80 49W
Warren, Pa., U.S.A. . 42 E8 41 51N 79 9W
Warrenton, S. Africa 31 B3 28 9S 24 47 E
Warrnambool,
  Australia . . . 34 H7 38 25S 142 30 E
Warsaw, Poland . . . 11 B11 52 13N 21 0 E
Warsaw, U.S.A. . . . 42 E5 41 14N 85 51W
Warta →, Poland . . 10 B8 52 35N 14 39 E
Warwick, U.S.A. . . 43 E12 41 42N 71 28W
Wasatch Ra., U.S.A. 40 B4 40 30N 111 15W
Washington, D.C.,
  U.S.A. 42 F9 38 54N 77 2W
Washington, Ind.,
  U.S.A. 42 F4 38 40N 87 10W
Washington, Pa.,
  U.S.A. 42 E7 40 10N 80 15W
Washington □, U.S.A. 40 A2 47 30N 120 30W
Washington, Mt.,
  U.S.A. 43 C12 44 16N 71 18W
Washington I., U.S.A. 42 C4 45 23N 86 54W
Waterbury, U.S.A. . 43 E11 41 33N 73 3W
Waterford, Ireland . 7 E3 52 15N   7 8W
Waterloo, Canada . . 42 D7 43 30N 80 32W
Watertown, U.S.A. . 43 D10 43 59N 75 55W
Waterval-Boven,
  S. Africa . . . 31 B5 25 40S 30 18 E
Waterville, U.S.A. . 43 C13 44 33N 69 38W
Watseka, U.S.A. . . 42 E4 40 47N 87 44W
Watubela Is.,
  Indonesia . . . 22 D5   4 28S 131 35 E
Waukegan, U.S.A. . 42 D4 42 22N 87 50W
Waukesha, U.S.A. . 42 D3 43 1N 88 14W
Wauwatosa, U.S.A. . 42 D4 43 3N 88 0W
Wawa, Canada . . . 42 B5 47 59N 84 47W
Wayne, U.S.A. . . . 42 F6 42 16N 82 27W
Waynesboro, U.S.A. 42 F8 38 4N 78 53W
Waynesburg, U.S.A. 42 F7 39 54N 80 11W
Wazirabad, Pakistan 23 C5 32 30N 74 8 E
Webster Springs,
  U.S.A. 42 F7 38 29N 80 25W
Weddell Sea,
  Antarctica . . 48 E5 72 30S 40 0W
Weifang, China . . . 21 C6 36 44N 119 7 E
Welch, U.S.A. . . . 42 G7 37 26N 81 35W
Welkom, S. Africa . 31 B4 28 0S 26 46 E
Welland, Canada . . 42 D8 43 0N 79 15W
Wellesley Is., Australia 34 D6 16 42S 139 30 E
Wellington, N.Z. . . 35 J13 41 19S 174 46 E
Wellsboro, U.S.A. . 42 E9 41 45N 77 18W
Wellsville, U.S.A. . . 42 D9 42 7N 77 57W
Wels, Austria . . . 10 D8 48 9N 14 1 E
Wenzhou, China . . . 21 D7 28 0N 120 38 E
Wepener, S. Africa . 31 B4 29 42S 27 3 E
Weser →, Germany . 10 B5 53 36N   8 28 E
West Bend, U.S.A. . 42 D3 43 25N 88 11W
West Bengal □, India 23 H11 23 0N 88 0 E
West Beskids, Europe 11 D10 49 30N 19 0 E
West Fjord, Norway . 6 E10 67 55N 14 0 E
West Point, U.S.A. . 42 G9 37 32N 76 48W
West Pt., Canada . . 43 A15 49 52N 64 40W
West Virginia □,
  U.S.A. 42 F7 38 45N 80 30W
Westbrook, U.S.A. . 43 D12 43 41N 70 22W

Western Australia □,
  Australia . . . 34 F3 25 0S 118 0 E
Western Ghats, India 25 D6 14 0N 75 0 E
Western Sahara ■,
  Africa 28 D2 25 0N 13 0W
Western Samoa =
  Samoa ■, Pac. Oc. 35 C16 14 0S 172 0W
Westerwald, Germany 10 C4 50 38N   7 56 E
Westminster, U.S.A. 42 F9 39 34N 76 59W
Weston, U.S.A. . . . 42 F7 39 2N 80 28W
Wetar, Indonesia . . 22 D4   7 30S 126 30 E
Whangarei, N.Z. . . 35 H13 35 43S 174 21 E
Wheeling, U.S.A. . . 42 E7 40 4N 80 43W
White →, U.S.A. . . 42 F4 38 25N 87 45W
White Nile →, Sudan 29 E11 15 38N 32 31 E
White Sea, Russia . 14 A6 66 0N 38 0 E
Whitefish Point, U.S.A. 42 B5 46 45N 84 59W
Whitehorse, Canada 38 B6 60 43N 135 3W
Whitewater, U.S.A. 42 D3 42 50N 88 44W
Whitney, Mt., U.S.A. 40 C3 36 35N 118 18W
Whyalla, Australia . 34 G6 33 2S 137 30 E
Wiarton, Canada . . 42 C7 44 40N 81 10W
Wichita, U.S.A. . . . 41 C7 37 42N 97 20W
Wichita Falls, U.S.A. 40 D7 33 54N 98 30W
Wiener Neustadt,
  Austria . . . . 10 E9 47 49N 16 16 E
Wiesbaden, Germany 10 C5 50 4N   8 14 E
Wilge →, S. Africa . 31 B4 27 3S 28 20 E
Wilhelmshaven,
  Germany . . . 10 B5 53 31N   8 7 E
Wilkes-Barre, U.S.A. 43 E10 41 15N 75 53W
Willemstad, Neth. Ant. 45 E11 12 5N 69 0W
Williamsburg, U.S.A. 42 G9 37 17N 76 44W
Williamson, U.S.A. . 42 G6 37 41N 82 17W
Williamsport, U.S.A. 42 E9 41 15N 77 0W
Williston, S. Africa . 31 C3 31 20S 20 53 E
Willowmore, S. Africa 31 C3 33 15S 23 30 E
Wilmington, Del.,
  U.S.A. 42 F10 39 45N 75 33W
Wilmington, Ohio,
  U.S.A. 42 F6 39 27N 83 50W
Winchester, Ky.,
  U.S.A. 42 G6 38 0N 84 11W
Winchester, Va.,
  U.S.A. 42 F8 39 11N 78 10W
Windhoek, Namibia . 31 A2 22 35S 17 4 E
Windsor, Canada . . 42 D6 42 18N 83 0W
Windward Is.,
  W. Indies . . . 44 P20 13 0N 61 0W
Winnebago, L., U.S.A. 42 D3 44 0N 88 26W
Winnipeg, Canada . 38 D10 49 54N 97 9W
Winnipeg, L., Canada 38 C10 52 0N 97 0W
Winooski, U.S.A. . . 43 C11 44 29N 73 11W
Winston-Salem, U.S.A. 41 C10 36 6N 80 15W
Winterthur, Switz. . 10 E5 47 30N   8 44 E
Wisconsin □, U.S.A. 41 B9 44 45N 89 30W
Witbank, S. Africa . 31 B4 25 51S 29 14 E
Witdraai, S. Africa . 31 B3 26 58S 20 48 E
Wkra →, Poland . . 11 B11 52 27N 20 44 E
Włocławek, Poland . 11 B10 52 40N 19 3 E
Wokam, Indonesia . 22 D5   5 45S 134 28 E
Wolfsburg, Germany 10 B6 52 25N 10 48 E
Wollongong, Australia 34 G9 34 25S 150 54 E
Wolverhampton, U.K. 7 E5 52 35N   2 7W
Wŏnsan, N. Korea . 21 C7 39 11N 127 27 E
Woods, L. of the,
  Canada 38 D10 49 15N 94 45W
Woodstock, Canada 42 D7 43 10N 80 45W
Woonsocket, U.S.A. 43 E11 42 0N 71 31W
Worcester, S. Africa 31 C2 33 39S 19 27 E
Worcester, U.S.A. . 43 D12 42 16N 71 48W
Worms, Germany . . 10 D5 49 37N   8 21 E
Wrangel I., Russia . 18 B19 71 0N 180 0 E
Wrocław, Poland . . 11 C9 51 5N 17 5 E
Wuhan, China . . . 21 C6 30 31N 114 18 E
Wuhu, China . . . . 21 C6 31 22N 118 21 E
Wuppertal, Germany 10 C4 51 16N   7 12 E
Würzburg, Germany 10 D5 49 46N   9 55 E
Wutongqiao, China . 20 D5 29 22N 103 50 E
Wuxi, China . . . . 21 C7 31 33N 120 18 E
Wuzhou, China . . . 21 D6 23 30N 111 18 E
Wyndham, Australia 34 D4 15 33S 128 3 E
Wyoming □, U.S.A. . 40 B5 43 0N 107 30W

X

Xau, L., Botswana . 31 A3 21 15S 24 44 E
Xenia, U.S.A. . . . 42 F6 39 41N 83 56W
Xiaguan, China . . . 20 D5 25 32N 100 16 E
Xiamen, China . . . 21 D6 24 25N 118 4 E
Xi'an, China . . . . 21 C5 34 15N 109 0 E
Xiangfan, China . . 21 C6 32 2N 112 8 E
Xiangtan, China . . 21 D6 27 51N 112 54 E
Xingu →, Brazil . . 46 C4   1 30S 51 53W
Xining, China . . . 20 C5 36 34N 101 40 E
Xuzhou, China . . . 21 C6 34 18N 117 10 E

Y

Yablonovyy Ra.,
  Russia . . . . 18 D13 53 0N 114 0 E
Yakutsk, Russia . . 18 C14 62 5N 129 50 E
Yamagata, Japan . . 19 A7 38 15N 140 15 E
Yambol, Bulgaria . . 13 C12 42 30N 26 36 E

Yamdena, Indonesia 22 D5   7 45S 131 20 E
Yamethin, Burma . . 25 C8 20 29N 96 18 E
Yamuna →, India . 23 G8 25 30N 81 53 E
Yangtze Kiang →,
  China . . . . 21 C7 31 48N 121 10 E
Yanji, China . . . . 21 B7 42 59N 129 30 E
Yantai, China . . . 21 C7 37 34N 121 22 E
Yaoundé, Cameroon 30 D4   3 50N 11 35 E
Yapen, Indonesia . . 22 D5   1 50S 136 0 E
Yarkhun →, Pakistan 23 A4 36 17N 72 30 E
Yarmouth, Canada . 43 D14 43 50N 66 7W
Yaroslavl, Russia . . 14 C6 57 35N 39 55 E
Yatsushiro, Japan . 19 C2 32 30N 130 40 E
Yazd, Iran . . . . . 24 B4 31 55N 54 27 E
Yekaterinburg, Russia 14 C11 56 50N 60 30 E
Yellow Sea, China . 21 C7 35 0N 123 0 E
Yellowknife, Canada 38 B8 62 27N 114 29W
Yellowstone →,
  U.S.A. 40 A6 47 59N 103 59W
Yellowstone National
  Park, U.S.A. . . 40 B5 44 40N 110 30W
Yemen ■, Asia . . . 24 D3 15 0N 44 0 E
Yenbo, Si. Arabia . 24 C2 24 0N 38 5 E
Yenisey →, Russia . 18 B10 71 50N 82 40 E
Yeniseysk, Russia . 18 D11 58 27N 92 13 E
Yeola, India . . . . 23 J5 20 2N 74 30 E
Yerevan, Armenia . 15 F7 40 10N 44 31 E
Yeu, I. d', France . 8 C2 46 42N   2 20W
Yibin, China . . . . 20 D5 28 45N 104 32 E
Yichang, China . . . 21 C6 30 40N 111 20 E
Yining, China . . . 20 B3 43 58N 81 10 E
Yogyakarta, Indonesia 22 D3   7 49S 110 22 E
Yokkaichi, Japan . . 19 B5 34 55N 136 38 E
Yokohama, Japan . . 19 B6 35 27N 139 28 E
Yokosuka, Japan . . 19 B6 35 20N 139 40 E
Yonkers, U.S.A. . . 43 E11 40 56N 73 54W
Yonne →, France . . 8 B5 48 23N   2 58 E
York, U.K. 7 E6 53 58N   1 6W
York, U.S.A. 42 F9 39 58N 76 44W
Yosemite National
  Park, U.S.A. . . 40 C3 37 45N 119 40W
Yoshkar Ola, Russia 14 C8 56 38N 47 55 E
Youngstown, U.S.A. 42 E7 41 6N 80 39W
Yuan Jiang →, China 21 D6 28 55N 111 50 E
Yucatán, Mexico . . 44 D7 19 30N 89 0W
Yucatan Str.,
  Caribbean . . . 44 C7 22 0N 86 30W
Yugoslavia ■, Europe 13 B9 44 0N 20 0 E
Yukon →, U.S.A. . . 38 B3 62 32N 163 54W
Yukon Territory □,
  Canada 38 B6 63 0N 135 0W
Yunnan □, China . . 20 D5 25 0N 102 0 E
Yuzhno-Sakhalinsk,
  Russia . . . . 18 E16 46 58N 142 45 E
Yvetot, France . . . 8 B4 49 37N   0 44 E

Z

Zabrze, Poland . . . 11 C10 50 18N 18 50 E
Zagreb, Croatia . . 10 F9 45 50N 16 0 E
Zagros Mts., Iran . 24 B3 33 45N 48 5 E
Zahedan, Iran . . . 24 C5 29 30N 60 50 E
Zaïre = Congo →,
  Africa . . . . 32 F2   6 4S 12 24 E
Zaïre = Congo, Dem.
  Rep. of the ■, Africa 32 E4   3 0S 23 0 E
Zákinthos, Greece . 13 F9 37 47N 20 57 E
Zambezi →, Africa . 33 H7 18 35S 36 20 E
Zambia ■, Africa . . 33 G5 15 0S 28 0 E
Zamboanga, Phil. . . 22 C4   6 59N 122 3 E
Zamora, Spain . . . 9 B3 41 30N   5 45W
Zamość, Poland . . 11 C12 50 43N 23 15 E
Zanesville, U.S.A. . 42 F6 39 56N 82 1W
Zanjan, Iran . . . . 24 B3 36 40N 48 35 E
Zanzibar, Tanzania . 32 F7   6 12S 39 12 E
Zaporozhye, Ukraine 15 E6 47 50N 35 10 E
Zaragoza, Spain . . 9 B5 41 39N   0 53W
Zaria, Nigeria . . . 30 B3 11 0N   7 40 E
Zaskar Mts., India . 23 C6 33 15N 77 30 E
Zeebrugge, Belgium 10 C2 51 19N   3 12 E
Zeerust, S. Africa . 31 B4 25 31S   2 4 E
Zenica, Bos.-H. . . 13 B7 44 10N 17 57 E
Zhangjiakou, China 21 B6 40 48N 114 55 E
Zhangzhou, China . 21 D6 24 30N 117 35 E
Zhanjiang, China . . 21 D6 21 15N 110 20 E
Zhejiang □, China . 21 D7 29 0N 120 0 E
Zhengzhou, China . 21 C6 34 45N 113 34 E
Zhigansk, Russia . . 18 C14 66 48N 123 27 E
Zhitomir, Ukraine . 11 C15 50 20N 28 40 E
Zibo, China . . . . 21 C6 36 47N 118 3 E
Zielona Góra, Poland 10 C8 51 57N 15 31 E
Zigong, China . . . 20 D5 29 15N 104 48 E
Ziguinchor, Senegal 28 F1 12 35N 16 20W
Žilina, Slovak Rep. . 11 D10 49 12N 18 42 E
Zimbabwe ■, Africa 33 H5 19 0S 30 0 E
Zion National Park,
  U.S.A. 40 C4 37 15N 113 5W
Zlatoust, Russia . . 14 C10 55 10N 59 40 E
Zlin, Czech Rep. . . 11 D9 49 14N 17 40 E
Zonguldak, Turkey . 15 F5 41 28N 31 50 E
Zrenjanin, Serbia, Yug. 13 B9 45 22N 20 23 E
Zug, Switz. . . . . 10 E5 47 10N   8 31 E
Zunyi, China . . . . 20 D5 27 42N 106 53 E
Zürich, Switz. . . . 10 E5 47 22N   8 32 E
Zwickau, Germany . 10 C7 50 44N 12 30 E
Zwolle, Neths. . . . 10 B4 52 31N   6 6 E

Place names on the yellow-coded large scale map section are to be found in the index at the end of that section